The Myths
of Japanese Quality

Ray and Cindelyn Eberts

For book and bookstore information

http://www.prenhall.com
gopher to gopher.prenhall.com

Prentice Hall P T R
Upper Saddle River, New Jersey 07458

Library of Congress Catalog Number: 9513290

ISBN 0-13-180803-6

90000

9 780131 808034

Acquisitions editor: Bernard Goodwin
Editorial assistant: Diane Spina
Cover design: Anthony Gemmellaro
Cover design director: Jerry Votta
Copyeditor: Lynne Lackenbach
Proofreader: Roger M. Stern
Interior design: Gail Cocker-Bogusz
Production coordinator (Buyer): Alexis R. Heydt
Production editor and formatter: John Morgan

©1995 Prentice Hall PTR
Prentice-Hall, Inc.
A Simon & Schuster Company
Upper Saddle River, New Jersey 07458

The publisher offers discounts on this book when ordered in bulk quantities. For more information, contact: Corporate Sales Department, PTR Prentice Hall, One Lake Street, Upper Saddle River, NJ 07458   Phone: 800-382-3419   Fax: 201-236-7141   E-mail (Internet): corpsales@prenhall.com

Excerpt from "American Letter", *New Found Land*, in COLLECTED POEMS 1917–1982 by Archibald MacLeish. Copyright © 1985 by The Estate of Archibald MacLeish. Reprinted by permission of Houghton Mifflin Co. All rights reserved.

Quotation from "This Land is Your Land", words and music by Woodie Guthrie. TRO © Copyright 1956 (Renewed), 1958 (Renewed) and 1970 Ludlow Music, Inc., New York, NY. Used by Permission.

Quotation from "If I Had a Hammer" (The Hammer Song), words and music by Lee Hays and Pete Seeger. TRO © Copyright 1958 (Renewed), 1962 (Renewed) and 1970 Ludlow Music, Inc., New York, NY. Used by Permission.

Printed in the United States of America

10 9 8 7 6 5 4 3 2 1

ISBN 0-13-180803-6

Prentice-Hall International (UK) Limited, *London*
Prentice-Hall of Australia Pty. Limited, *Sydney*
Prentice-Hall Canada Inc., *Toronto*
Prentice-Hall Hispanoamericana, S.A., *Mexico*
Prentice-Hall of India Private Limited, *New Delhi*
Prentice-Hall of Japan, Inc., *Tokyo*
Simon & Schuster Asia Pte. Ltd., *Singapore*
Editora Prentice-Hall do Brasil, Ltda., *Rio de Janeiro*

Contents

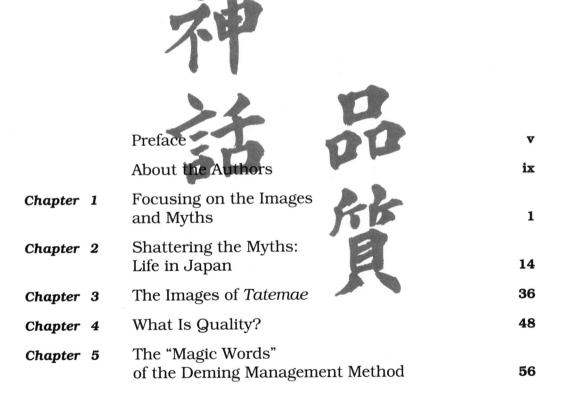

Preface

In Japan, quality cannot be separated from culture. To comprehend the Japanese quality techniques, therefore, one must understand the society and the culture. This important premise has two implications which we explored. First, Japanese culture places a primary emphasis on image instead of reality. Consequently, the perceived image of Japanese quality techniques is usually different from the reality. The image is critical in maintaining a favorable consumer perception of the superior quality of Japanese products even though those products may not be better than other products. Good overall images can be maintained through positive media exposure to Japanese culture and business practices. Positive images of products are also maintained by emphasizing outside appearances of the product through packaging and finishing, either of which may have little to do with the intrinsic quality of the product. The second implication of the inseparability of Japanese culture and quality is that transferring the management methods for manufacturing products or delivering services from Japanese businesses to American businesses may not work. Many Japanese management or business practices rely on discipline and conformity of the group and cannot be exported to other countries because they will not work in the absence of the underlying supporting culture.

Previous books about Japan have explored the culture or how to manage people to produce quality products, but rarely both. The books exploring the culture, often written by American English teachers brought over by the Japanese government to teach English in the schools, address those authors' experiences while living in Japan. The close correspondence of these books to our own experiences in Japan is eerie, and made us realize that most foreigners in Japan are exposed to the same attitudes and behaviors. These books are perceptive and well written. Since the role of these visitors is to teach English, though, these books do not explore technical matters. Books about Japanese business quality techniques have been written under different circumstances. Usually they are written by management or business professors or consultants. Many of these people have not lived in Japan nor do they have the training or the perception to understand and analyze culture. Their purpose is to sell themselves and their technical expertise. If they can pass themselves off as experts on Japanese business practices, if those practices will increase the quality of products, and if those practices can be exported easily, then their services will be in demand by American businesses. These books make the mistake of not considering the culture while analyzing Japanese business practices. This serves the authors' purpose, though, because if culture is so critical, as we propose, then their expertise is not so valuable. Thus the myths of Japanese quality are propagated.

Different perspectives are needed to explore the cultural and technical sides of Japanese business quality techniques. We found that our different backgrounds, on the technical and cultural perspectives, were invaluable when researching and writing the book. On the technical side, Ray is an Industrial Engineering professor at Purdue University in Indiana who teaches, researches, and writes about aspects of quality. On the cultural side, the observations of Cindelyn, having been trained as a psychologist and anthropologist in graduate school and college, provided a different perspective on how the approach to quality of Japanese businesses is a unique reflection of Japanese culture which may not be transferable to other places. The chapters dealing with the culture and living in Japan (Chapters 2, 9, 10, and 13) were written primarily from Cindelyn's perspective. The remaining chapters were written from Ray's perspective. Ray was invited to be a visiting professor at one of Japan's elite research institutions. Very few researchers from the U.S. get the chance to work in a research institute and to live in Japan simply because technologically advanced Japanese companies think they have little to learn from prolonged stays by foreign researchers but a lot to lose if perceptive outsiders see how things actually work. Our family's unique situation allowed us to experience a side of Japan outsiders are rarely allowed to see. A role as a visiting researcher, talking to Japanese colleagues about how they performed research or how their company practiced quality, was not enough to understand the quality culture in Japan. One also has to be a housewife, salaryman (the Japanese expression for a man who works at a large company), mother, father, friend, consumer, and shopper. The collaboration in writing this book provides background on a broad spectrum of technical and cultural practices needed to understand the quality techniques of Japan. The book is filled with personal experiences about traveling in Japan, the interactions of Cindelyn with the other company wives, parenting our children as they played with the Japanese children, and playing the role of Japanese consumer in buying and using typical Japanese products. Ray's role as colleague to the Japanese researchers and as an American engineering professor is presented in the book through discussions with high-level Japanese businessmen and the technical descriptions of quality and Japanese management methods in the book.

This book contains both personal anecdotes and well-documented facts. It is meant to entertain, while at the same time providing valuable information and lessons about how to apply, or misapply, Japanese quality techniques to American business practices. Consequently, the book should be read by business people who want to learn more about quality practices from Japan and who don't mind being entertained in the process. It could also be used as a supplementary textbook for management and engineering classes on quality techniques.

The first three chapters of the book include anecdotes about living in Japan while exploring the culture and the importance of image over reality in Japanese life. The next four chapters provide a technical description of quality and the techniques used to achieve quality products. In the last part of the book, ten myths of Japanese quality are examined. The first four myths address product quality and the last six myths address the management techniques used to produce and manufacture quality products. In the 16th century book Gargantua, Rabelais contrasts Gargantua's education provided by the sophists to his education under the tutelage of Ponocrates. With the traditional education under the sophists, Gargantua's first attempt at education was a long boring process of reading, memorization, and recitation of irrelevant material. At the end of the drudgery, *Gargantua* had not learned a thing because when he wanted to speak, the best he could do was to "bellow like a cow." In contrast, the less traditional education under the philosopher Ponocrates was based on the idea that work should be mixed with play and that learning should be a process of varied personal observation, experience, and experimentation. Under Ponocrates a casual conversation would turn into an opportune time to learn relevant passages from the classics. We follow the spirit of Rabelais and Ponocrates with this book. A casual conversation of our experiences in Japan becomes an opportune time to teach others about important concepts in manufacturing quality products and delivering quality services.

Acknowledgments   We have many people to thank. First, we made many good friends in Japan. Some of these friends told us that the only way Japan could change was through criticism and pressure from the outside. Realizing that privacy and acceptance within the group is very important to these friends in Japan, we have not used their real names when telling their stories. Marilyn March and Dianna Chalk helped us with the comparison of the education systems. We would also like to thank all our friends who patiently listened to our stories of Japan and encouraged us to write this book: Harry and Jane Hake, Charlie Caldwell, Shidan Habibi, June Johnson, Myra Leap, Shawna Lockhart, Bob Kneibel, Sam Lock, Jay Rho, Yuehwern Yih, and Jim Longuski. Several family members provided valuable suggestions on earlier drafts of the chapters: Harry Eberts, Dorothy Eberts, Randy Eberts, Iris Gray, and Philip Gray. Special thanks go to Holly Longuski who provided support and keen insights on how to tell our story. The staff at Prentice Hall—Mike Hayes, Bernard Goodwin, Diane Spina, and John Morgan—provided the editorial support needed to produce this book.

Cindelyn's parents, Philip and Iris Gray, provided a place to set our computer in the midst of the Rocky Mountains in Montana as we did the bulk of the writing. Our two sons, Wescott and Russell, although very young at the time of the trip to Japan, provided surprisingly perceptive comments and opinions on their playmates and the consumer products of interest to them.

Ray and Cindelyn Eberts
Lafayette, Indiana

About the Authors

RAY EBERTS has been an industrial engineering professor for eleven years teaching at Purdue University and at the University of Southern California as a visiting associate professor. He has written or edited three previous books and has published about 100 research articles and book chapters in the areas of human factors, design of computer software and commercial products, and statistics. His course on the design of experiments is one of the most popular satellite courses out of Purdue and is taken by students at most of the large corporations throughout the Midwest. He has worked for and consulted for various corporations including Digital Equipment Corporation and Honeywell. He helped to design and analyze work environments and equipment used by the U.S. Post Office for fast and highly productive processing of mail. He was the first in his field of human factors to be awarded the Presidential Young Investigator Award from the National Science Foundation.

Cindelyn Eberts received a Bachelor of Science degree from Montana State University and masters and Ph.D. degrees in experimental psychology from the University of Illinois at Urbana-Champaign. Since graduating, she has taught industrial engineering statistics courses at the University of Southern California and Purdue University where she won the Pritsker Outstanding Undergraduate Teaching Award. She has done consulting in human factors for A T & T's Bell Labs and Consumer Products Group in Indianapolis. She is particularly proud of her current work with the Lafayette School Corporation and Family Services of Lafayette on a project which provides a sense of community and belonging to parents of school-children who have traditionally been outside the parent network due to poverty, being new to the community, or some other reason. Both Ray and Cindelyn spend much of their free time with volunteer groups within Lafayette. Ray is board chair for the Lafayette Urban Ministry which is a nonprofit organization of churches for aiding the homeless, unemployed, and disenfranchised in Lafayette. Cindelyn works with art groups and environmental groups in Lafayette. In the summers, Ray and Cindelyn like to spend as much time as possible on their property in the shadow of Montana's Tobacco Root Mountains.

CHAPTER ONE

Focusing on the Images and Myths

First impressions are important in Japan. They're probably important everywhere, but in Japan, impressions involve a whole language, which must be spoken with skill and fluency. You don't have to say a word to communicate strong first impressions in Japan: The clothes you wear (preferably a dark blue or black suit), the car you drive (white or light gray), your position in your company (prominently displayed on your business card), the way you give someone a business card (with two hands and a short bow), and how deeply you bow (deeper bows to those with more status); all are noted and form lasting impressions. My Japanese colleagues in the lecture hall may well remember me not by the wisdom of my words, but by how the overhead projector I was using suddenly became an incendiary source of focused power inflaming (almost) everything in its path. Before turning to this story, however, some background is in order.

GOING TO JAPAN   I agreed to go to Japan on a sabbatical from the Industrial Engineering School at Purdue University in Indiana to satisfy my curiosity. I was curious about the Japanese economic miracle, about Japanese quality management techniques, about Theory Z. I was curious about workaholic salary-men, the Japanese education system, the mothers devoted to educating their children. I knew about W. Edwards Deming, the guru of quality. I knew how his ideas had been rejected in his own country, how he had come to Japan after World War II, and how he had been credited by the Japanese with changing the "Made in Japan" label from a joke to a symbol of quality recognized throughout the world. I wanted to know why the Japanese could make quality products while Americans supposedly could not.

I had quite literally bought into the Japanese quality concept, because all my big purchases—automobiles and electronic products—were from Japan. I wasn't sure how I had formed such positive opinions about Japanese products. Maybe these opinions had been formed by reading articles or watching television shows. Certainly they had been formed at least in part by reading publications such as *Consumer Reports,* which in the late 1980s always seemed to reserve solid red circles for Japanese cars, and blank, striped, or solid black circles for American cars. (In the *Consumer Reports* rating system, solid red circles mean high quality and solid black circles mean unacceptable quality.)

FROM ZEROS FORWARD   My area of expertise is human factors engineering. Human factors engineers study how to make machines, especially complicated machines, easier to use. In Europe and the United States, human factors engineering has a strong research tradition. Much of the impetus in the United States for this area of research occurred during World War II, when the military, particularly the U.S. Air Force, realized that even though they could build technologically advanced airplanes, pilots could not fly them to their full effectiveness unless the planes were designed, or human factored, for the pilots. In Europe, because of the strength of labor unions, large emphasis has always been placed on the safety and comfort of the worker. Thus, research began in the European countries to try to understand the human factor in the work situation, so that comfort and safety could be increased, thereby satisfying the demands of the unions and their workers.

Japan had a different tradition, which did not provide reasons to perform research on human factors or the usability of machines. Japan also had advanced military machinery during World War II, but the Japanese military relied on long hours of training and devotion to the service of the country—the Japanese spirit which was supposed to overcome all obstacles—to ensure that the machines could be operated. Military personnel were expected to adapt themselves to the machines;

the machines were not deliberately designed for people. As an example of this type of thinking, the Mitsubishi-manufactured Zero, distinguished in the Pacific War by its long range, maneuverability, and speed, could outperform Allied planes. These performance advantages were not achieved entirely through technological advances, but rather by reducing the weight of the plane.[1] The weight reductions were a trade-off against pilot safety: The protective armor for the pilots and self-sealing gas tanks were eliminated, so any hit on a Zero, however minor, was likely to be fatal to the pilot. The agility of the Zeros was supposed to allow them to maneuver out of dangerous situations. Allied planes, on the other hand, were designed with pilot safety in mind; protective armor and self-sealing gas tanks were designed into the planes. Japan's heavy losses of trained and experienced pilots was a decisive factor in the Pacific War. Japan started with only 3500 pilots, and training new pilots was expensive and difficult (in one class, of 1500 applicants, only 25—less than 2%—graduated from the program).

After the war, the necessity of rapidly rebuilding Japanese industries precluded the development of strong unions. Once again relying on devotion and service, to the company in this case, workers were expected to endure; the safety and comfort of the worker were not considered important. Unions were not allowed to develop independently of the company. In fact, one of the stepping stones on the path to top management was to be a negotiator for the company union against (or for) management. Needless to say, job performance was measured not by how well the person negotiated for the union but by how well he (this person was almost always male) did for management.

Since there was no pressure to design machines to fit the person or to design the workplace to be comfortable and safe, Japan had no training ground for human factors engineers or usability engineering. In recent years, Japanese company officials have realized that designing products that are not usable will hurt sales, especially as the products become more complicated. As has been the case throughout Japan's history, if the expertise does not exist locally, then foreign experts are brought in and local expertise is developed. I was one of the foreigners brought in for this purpose.

PRECONCEPTIONS OF JAPANESE QUALITY   Usability is

my main area of research and expertise and, as will be seen in Chapter 4, it is an important component of how consumers perceive the quality of products. Overall, I have a professional interest in quality and, consequently, a high regard for the con-

---

[1]Richard B. Frank, *Guadalcanal* (New York: Random House, 1990). Discusses the Zeros, machinery, and training program on pp. 65–67.

tributions Japan has made in this area. One of the courses I teach, which is often broadcast over a satellite television system to engineers in the largest corporations in the Midwest, deals directly with quality control.

During my visit to Japan, I was anxious to see Japanese quality for myself. At the company-owned apartment where my family and I were to live, what was the quality of the television, the kitchen appliances, and the furniture? At my company-assigned office, what kind of computer system was I given, what was the quality of the desk, or the quality of the chair? For my first lecture, what was the quality of the equipment in the lecture room?

Although I came to Japan with preconceptions of the high quality of Japanese products, I felt uneasy about the human factors components that went into these products, because I knew that this was not important in the Japanese design process. The Japanese products with which I was familiar were appealing in many ways, but they were often difficult to use. Japanese cars were good but, like the Zeros, they sacrificed safety by reducing weight to increase gas mileage and handling. Japanese products were good because everybody said they were good, yet many products my wife and I encountered initially in Japan (see Chapter 2) were not so good. How could these contradictions be resolved? How could these products be both good and bad? I found the answer in the overhead projector, so now it is time to return to that story.

THE OVERHEAD PROJECTOR   My job duties included giving weekly lectures and consulting with Japanese researchers on research projects. Before beginning my first lecture, I noticed activity around the overhead projector, followed by a team huddle of the senior men in the room. When a test viewgraph was placed on the machine, I saw the reason for the quick consultation. The image of the viewgraph would not focus on the screen because the arm was bent; it could not be placed in the correct orientation. I could turn the knob to focus the top part of the image, but then the bottom part was unfocused. If I adjusted the knob to focus the bottom part of the image, then the top was out of focus.

The projector appeared to be fairly new, but the problem occurred because the arm was bent at an angle. This could have resulted from misuse or overuse, or perhaps the overhead projector was manufactured poorly and had never worked properly. Either reason indicated a poor-quality product, something I had not expected to find in Japan. For my lectures back home at the university, and for talks at conferences or companies, I had used many types of overhead projectors and had never had a focusing problem.

I glanced quickly at the product name on the overhead projector and saw that it had been manufactured by a Japanese company. Most people in the audience was aware of the focusing problem, but no attempt was made to find another machine. I decided to make do by focusing on the middle of the viewgraph. The periphery would have to remain slightly out of focus.

As I began my lecture, I looked around the room. As is usual in Japan, my audience was seated according to their place in the company hierarchy. The Japanese place great importance on status and job level, as I was well aware, since my company-supplied host, Mr. Uchimura, had helped me distribute gifts to all my new colleagues according to their positions in the company. Most people sat in groups of four to seven people, and these groups were situated at various places in the room. The senior groups sat toward the front of the room and the less senior in the back. The most senior people were in the second row.

One person was different. From my understanding of his rank, he belonged in about the middle of the room. I also remembered that he had been a member of the team huddle a few minutes previously, but he had the lowest status of that senior group. This man positioned himself in the middle of the room, all by himself, directly in front of the overhead projector. When I placed my first viewgraph on the screen, I saw why he was out of position. The solution to the nonfocusing projector, produced in the team huddle, was to loop a string around the arm of the projector. The man in the middle, by pulling back on the string from his strategic position, could straighten the arm so that the viewgraph image would be in focus as long as the string was taut. Because this action required some strength, the string was not pulled back constantly. When I glanced back to the screen, the string was pulled tight. When I gazed toward the audience, the string was released. Glance back, the string was tight and the image I saw was in focus. This was all done very discreetly, and I did not dwell on it or draw attention to the string, because after my first week in Japan I had learned it is not polite to draw attention to problems. A problem is not a problem if it is ignored.

Unfortunately, this solution only worked for about two minutes. The first indication of trouble was a slight smell of something burning. Then, out of the corner of my eye, I saw smoke coming from the vicinity of the projector. Scarcely missing a word in the lecture—maybe this was some weird initiation ritual for visiting professors—I noticed that the string, jury-rigged to hold the arm of the projector, was burning from the middle toward both ends, like a fuse on a firecracker.

Just as a magnifying glass can be used to focus sunlight onto and burn a piece of paper, the light of the projector was focusing on and burning the string. Nobody in the audience said anything, although I knew everybody could see the burning string. The audience were acting as if this was a perfectly normal event: You turn on the projector, place your viewgraph on the machine, pull the string to focus the image, the string burns up.

To be polite, I tried not to notice. The burning string quickly ran its course, there being no more incendiary objects in its path. Nobody ever said anything, and the same malfunctioning, slightly out-of-focus overhead projector remained in the lecture room for the next three months and all my succeeding lectures. It may still be there.

THE OVERHEAD PROJECTOR AS METAPHOR   The nonfocusing overhead projector, the string solution, and the consequences of this solution provide powerful metaphors for the myths and realities of the quality of Japanese products and techniques.

To be effective, an overhead projector must project a clear image on a screen. An image, of course, is not real; it is only a mental representation of something that is real. The Japanese word for image is *tatemae* (TAH-teh-mah-eh). *Tatemae* is a very important concept in Japan, and especially in Japanese companies. To these companies, a good image is more important than the reality. The Japanese company Canon, makers of photographic equipment and photocopiers, summarizes this thinking in their slogan, "Image is everything." The photographic image is important, but the image projected by the company may be more important.

In Japan, the image is separate from the reality. Japanese people understand this, but Westerners have some trouble with this dichotomy. My hosts were not worried about the quality of the overhead projector image for the Japanese audience. They were worried about my perception of the image projected on the screen. Consequently, the string was pulled to focus the image only when I looked at the screen, because it was important that I, as a Westerner, see the image as being the same as the reality. The string was not pulled taut for the Japanese audience, because they could accept the difference between the image and the reality. Both could exist on their separate terms.

The image of Japan and its products that we see in the United States is a transformed image, one that has been filtered through space and through cultural differences. The strings are pulled to create a better image of Japan and its products. We see only the image, not the reality. Only by observing the real Japan, not the tourist attractions reserved for foreigners, and critically evaluating the unfiltered reality, can the images be interpreted.

My wife and I tried to focus the image of Japan; we tried to remove the filters. The defective overhead projector could not provide a fully focused image of the transparency on the screen. Analogously, we looked more closely at the images we had of Japanese quality. We found that individual images did not hold together under close scrutiny. We would think we understood one part of the image, but upon closer examination we would find that the whole image did not quite focus.

In the lecture hall, the solution to a bad image was to have someone pull a string to fix it. Analogously, somebody or some organization always seems to be pulling a string to create a better image of Japanese products. What organizations in Japan pull the strings so that we receive positive images of Japan and Japanese products? How are these strings pulled? What happens when the strings go up in smoke, can no longer be pulled, and the images can no longer be manipulated?

The reality of Japanese quality and efficiency was different from my perception of them before arriving in Japan. This scene played out again and again.

THE QUALITY BATTLEGROUND   The economic battle of the next decade will be won or lost on the quality of the products that a country can produce. The perception of Americans seems to be that the United States is losing that battle to Japan. We have been told in business schools, college courses, and the popular press about the techniques Japanese companies use to produce high-quality products: Theory Z, total quality management, Deming management methods, continuous improvement, quality function deployment, quality circles, Taguchi methods, zero defects. We assume that all Japanese companies practice the methods. How can we possibly win this quality battle without an arsenal of quality methods of our own?

Our feelings about low-quality American products seem to be epitomized by the high-mileage but low-quality American small cars that were rushed out of plants in response to the first oil crisis of the 1970s. Those were sorry products. We had the exploding Ford Pinto and cars that seemed to roll off the assembly line pre-rusted and predinged. These products, and similar products from other American industries, created a low-quality legacy that has been difficult to shed.

There is no question that many of the Japanese products we see in the United States are manufactured well. The purpose of this book is not to argue that all Japanese products are of low quality. Rather, the purpose is to take a critical look at the reasons for the perceptions of Japanese high quality and American low quality. Many of the objective differences in the quality of the products from the two countries have changed in the last few years. Our subjective feelings of differences in quality will take longer to change. Those American industries that have improved quality should not be penalized because of the legacy of past low-quality products, any more than the Japanese industries should be dismissed for the junk produced in the 1940s and 1950s.

MYTHS   There is another side to the story, however. The Japanese put as much effort into manufacturing the *myth* of Japanese quality as they put into manufacturing the product. The myth of Japanese quality relies on manipulating public opinion; this book addresses how the myths are perpetuated. Upon close inspection, the myth exceeds the reality in many cases.

A myth is a story used to support a set of beliefs. Myths are fiction, but many are based on actual events. Finding the source of a myth, and how it has been changed since the original event, is difficult. In addition, people tend to hang onto myths even when they are no longer relevant. The myths of Japanese quality, as discussed in this book, follow the same paths as classical myths. They once had some basis in reality, but they are becoming less and less relevant. The explanations and stories in support of the myths often approximate fiction more than they do reality. A good company, though, with an eye to good public relations, will try to generate myths that cast a positive aura over the company's products.

Consider the evolution of a real situation into a story and then into a myth. General Motors at one time had a bad image, which sometimes was well deserved. They sought to cure that image by creating a new company, Saturn, which did not carry all the excess baggage of the parent company. Advertisements for Saturn immediately started to build stories from the reality. There was the advertisement about the Saturn engineer who traveled to Alaska to replace a seat that the customer thought was defective (it turns out that the seat was not defective). This event actually happened, it was turned into a story, and it may eventually become one of the myths about the company. Even though it is true, it is a myth because not all complaints would get the same kind of service.

In another effective Saturn advertisement, a customer ordered a new car and sent a letter to the plant along with a picture; the picture was placed on the car so the workers would know whom the car was being built for. This event actually happened, and the advertisement turned it into a story. More important, it evolved into a myth that each Saturn will be made individually for you.

Saturn has a very good reputation, which it deserves, for building high-quality products. Part of the perception of high quality, though, has to do with the stories the company has crafted about the product. As the stories become myths, the source, and the reality, will no longer be important. American companies are learning, or perhaps regaining, some of their expertise from the past; Japanese companies are masters at the creation of myths.

Consider another example. Japanese companies have a reputation for imitating rather than innovating, a reputation that parallels the low-quality-product reputation of Japanese companies in the 1950s and early 1960s. A book published recently, *Created in Japan: From Imitators to World-Class Innovators*, written by S. M. Tatsuno, tries to change this perception of Japanese companies. The first part of the book explains how Japanese creativity is different from Western creativity. The second part explains the formalized methods supposedly used by Japanese companies when innovating products: the KJ method, creativity circles, the Mitsubishi brainstorming method (MBS), the NHK brainstorming method, the lotus blossom technique, and the feed-forward method. The third part of the book examines some of the innovations made by Japanese companies: making computers smaller, increasing the speed of supercomputers, high-definition television (HDTV) based on analog circuits, and superconductors. The problem with these examples is they were all achieved by tweaking Western technology. The main source of evidence for innovation throughout the chapters seems to be quotations from Western observers about how Japanese companies are now actually performing basic research.

This book illustrates myth making in its early stages. Japanese companies have an image problem with regard to innovativeness. An American consultant with ties to Japan sees an opportunity to capitalize on the success of Japanese companies and the thirst of American businesspeople to find out about that success. He relates the formal management techniques used to create innovative products; these methods provide the stories for the myth. The problem is that these methods are not used by Japanese companies, nor do they result in innovative products. Evidence for innovation comes by quoting "experts" from the West. The myth, although based on the stories, is different from the reality. The hype is more important than the reality.

This book examines the reality, the stories, and the myths.

LET'S ENJOY OUR WORLD CONVERSATION "Let's
enjoy. Comic talk! Things friends all over world will be on your side. English. Oh! Wonderful to join in world conversation! If you lesson English every day, you know. Comic magic bag."

The above pseudo-English phrases appear on a popular pencil bag for Japanese school children. They are exhorted to "lesson" their English every day, so that friends all over the world will be on their side. The message implies, though, that we can either be on their side, or on the other side. On the bottom of the bag, in case we did not already know, the following is written: "We have personally inspected this manufacture to be sure it meets with our high quality standards."

So, when reading this book, let's enjoy. We will join in world conversation, but we will try not to take sides. If we are critical of some Japanese practices, this does not mean that all Japanese practices are bad.

In examining some of the myths, we are not "Japan-bashing," although one way to stop the world conversation—and critical examination of the myths—would be to accuse us of Japan-bashing. Other critical examinations of Japanese attitudes or of Japanese government policies have been dismissed as bashing by Japanese officials. We are merely reporting our own observations, and we have tried to be objective throughout this book.

A critical examination of the myths is not necessarily bad for Japan. Japanese government officials and company representatives would be the first to tell you that the inroads made by Japanese companies into American markets were especially good for American consumers, because Americans now have good-quality products at low prices from sources all over the world. If the competition was eliminated, by closing the markets or a massive buy-American boycott of foreign products, then choices would be limited, prices would be higher, and American companies would not be motivated by market forces to compete on quality. Japanese business practices are open to criticism, much as American business practices are open to criticism. The criticisms in this book should not be interpreted as bashing but rather as critical examinations of current practices which can only make Japanese companies stronger and better.

Japanese consumers do not have the same kinds of choices as American consumers have, and they are at a disadvantage as a consequence of the policies of the Japanese government. In the following chapters, we shall chronicle some of the poor-quality products we saw while in Japan, products that can only be foisted upon consumers because of the lack of competition. In Japan we saw Japanese products selling for much higher prices than the same products in the United States. Selling products for export at lower prices than in the country of origin—known as dumping—is illegal under international trading laws. Japanese consumers are paying the price for this policy. Is it Japan-bashing to expose this practice? Changing the policy will only help the Japanese consumer, just as American consumers have benefited from Japanese product competition. Japanese criticism of American product quality led to improvements in the American products offered to American consumers. If American criticism of Japanese policies leads to more American companies entering Japanese markets, then that competition will be good for Japanese companies and for Japanese consumers.

Criticizing practices that are illegal or unacceptable in American society is not Japan-bashing; it is constructive criticism that can be used to modify Japanese business practices so they can be exported to the United States and elsewhere. For instance, lifetime employment may be good in some ways, but Japanese companies often use it as a means of eliminating job choices or pressuring employees to accept lower pay, slower promotions, and unwanted job assignments. Japanese companies expect employees to work long hours, making normal family life difficult. Japanese companies often hire women, not on ability, but with the goal of providing potential marriage partners to male employees, whose long hours leave little time to seek wives.[2] The low status of women, and blindness to the problem, results in sexual harassment in the Japanese workplace.

As another example, the homogeneity of the Japanese workforce may lead to unacceptable policies when Japanese companies are transplanted into heterogeneous societies. At Mazda's Flat Rock, Michigan, plant, the Japanese management did not tell employees they would have to work overtime until an hour before closing, even though union rules required 24 hours' notice.[3] This was a hardship especially for single mothers who had children to take care of after work. Because there are so few married women working the lines in Japan, Mazda's management was insensitive to the needs of its American employees.

Thoughtful Japanese citizens often told us that demands for change from the outside are the only mechanisms for improvement to Japanese society. Even Shintaro Ishihara, the Japanese politician famous for writing the America-bashing book, *The Japan That Can Say No,* said in his book that Japan can change only if pressured from outside. The Japanese culture has been designed to maintain the status quo and has few societal mechanisms for change. Until very recently, the same political party had been in power for almost 40 years; only one layer of bureaucrats, who are more powerful than the politicians, changes with a change in administration, as opposed to three layers in the United States. The Chrysanthemum Throne of the emperor has ruled for over 2500 years (since 600 B.C.). Japanese market share levels are protected at home because the companies are afraid of changes in the status quo. For example, Japanese life insurance companies have maintained about the same market share, by law or by coercion, since World War II. One Japanese friend told us that he was glad for Carla Hills, the U.S. trade representative at the time, because the policies she advocated in the name of the U.S. government were good for the Japanese consumer. In his opinion, forcing change on the Japanese government from the outside was the only way to effect change.

If they are to survive over the long term, Japanese companies must change their policies and techniques. As long as the Japanese market is closed, through either official or unofficial policies, these companies can continue to design and manufac-

---

[2]Jared Taylor, *Shadows of the Rising Sun* (New York: Morrow, 1983), pp. 64-6:: "When a major corporation hires a woman, it is not hiring a worker. It is hiring a potential wife. The company expects to squeeze a lot of quality work from its brides-to-be, but beauty and culture are important hiring criteria. Many companies are quite open about the qualities they are looking for. Some, for example, will not hire a woman unless she lives at home with her parents. There is no telling what manner of mischief an unsupervised woman might be up to, and a woman with a past does not make a fit wife for a future executive."

[3]Joseph Fucini and Suzy Fucini, *Working for the Japanese* (New York: The Free Press, 1990), p. 153. "According to its contract with the UAW, Mazda was required to give workers advance notification of mandatory overtime—one day's notice of daily overtime....These requirements were routinely ignored. The company usually told workers that they were being required to work daily overtime less than an hour before a shift was scheduled to end."

ture low-quality products and sell them domestically at high prices. There is no incentive to design better products or to manufacture them more efficiently. Japanese consumers lose, and Japanese companies will lose in the long run.

Japan's interests, and America's interests, are not served by presenting only the positive aspects of Japanese business practices. Japanese quality techniques have such a positive image that they cannot always live up to the high expectations. In sports, a smart coach—even one with a very good team—will work at the beginning of the season to lower expectations for the performance of the team so that, if the team does well, it will look even better, and if it does only a mediocre job, then it will still meet expectations. A dumb coach will publicize the team's best attributes, thus raising expectations to a level that may not be achieved. By extolling the virtues of the team, the dumb coach provides motivation and a game plan for the competition.

MYTH CREATION   Japan has been very successful in bringing its economy and industry out of the ashes of World War II. Americans have always been quick to seek out success, to analyze every little nuance that might be related to that success, and to try to use the subsequent analyses as models for change in their own companies. This is a good mechanism for change. We have a tendency to attribute characteristics, reasons, and absurdly complicated explanations to simple phenomena. We write books and articles about Japanese management practices that can lead our companies to success. Many respected management professors (e.g., Lester Thurow and William Ouchi, in particular) have played amateur anthropologist searching for complicated reasons for Japanese successes. The journals are filled with learned analyses of Japanese manufacturing and management techniques. Popular magazines such as *Fortune* send their writers to Japan to speak to Japanese officials and see the vaunted techniques for themselves. The Japanese officials are all very glad to accommodate these visitors and thus add to the *tatemae* of Japanese quality practices.

While we are engaged in these activities, what are the Japanese doing? For one thing, they are probably spending their time trying to make a better VCR or adding ten more buttons to that copy machine. While we are overanalyzing Japanese techniques, how are they accounting for and ensuring their business success? They are building shrines to Tiari, the foxlike Shinto god who is responsible for business success. While we are spending grant or corporate money on the analysis of Japanese business practices, they are spending their money to build better shrines to Inari— The New Miyaki Hotel in Kyoto spent $25,000 to build a rooftop Inari shrine.[4] Why bother with complicated explanations when simple or mystical ones are better?

In building shrines to Inari, perhaps the Japanese are just trying to cover all possibilities. Maybe we are trying to cover all our bases when we overanalyze every nuance of Japanese business practice so that we can be on good terms with our business gods of Profit or maybe even Quality. We should not indulge our tendencies to analytic excesses by formulating complicated explanations when simple ones will do. The explanation for Japanese quality, and subsequent business successes, can be quite simple. This book attempts to reevaluate the myths that are used to support these complicated analyses.

If we want to emulate the Japanese, we have to separate the myths from the reality. We should not try to emulate practices that are not good or that would not transfer to other cultures. When Americans look to Japan for the answers to building quality products, we are busy digging holes; the holes can be used either as foundations or as waste dumps. When we dig, we must find the sources of the myths so that the foundations will be solid.

To set the stage, a good place to start is with our personal experiences in Japan. We did not stay at a hotel for foreigners, where Westernized and sanitized products were on display. We lived in a company apartment, like our Japanese colleagues. We did not just go to the tourist attractions; we tried to find the Japan of the Japanese. We lived in our apartment, and we used typical Japanese products that would not be found outside Japan. I interacted with my business colleagues, my wife had tea with the wives in the company apartment complex, and our children played baseball with the Japanese children. We lived the Japanese experience. But, being outsiders, or *gaijin*, we could critically examine the myths of Japanese quality.

---

[4]Jared Taylor, *Shadows of the Rising Sun* (New York: Morrow, 1983), p. 158.: "A recent fad has been the revival of an old business technique that went out of fashion during the heady days of double-digit GNP growth. More and more Japanese managers are turning for help to Inari, the Shinto fox god that is in charge of business prosperity. As times get tougher, Japanese companies try to outfox the competition by building private Inari shrines on corporate property."

Shattering the Myths: Life in Japan

*B*efore going to Japan, we really wanted to believe that there was a business utopia out there across the Pacific, where companies manufacture quality products, the workforce was efficient and productive, the workers worked harmoniously in teams, and the people were polite and well mannered. Glowing reports from newspapers and magazines had reinforced this image. Books written by academics, usually based on brief visits, described high-technology manufacturing plants, researchers engaged in world-class work, and egalitarian treatment of workers by a benevolent and omniscient ruling class of managers. The managers were the philosopher-kings of Plato's vision of utopia in *The Republic,* they were the planners and managers from Skinner's utopian *Walden Two,* or they had the spirituality of the ruling lamas of Shangri-La, the utopian valley in James Hilton's *Lost Horizon.* We had been so programmed by myths that we were not prepared for the reality of poor-quality Japanese products or the attitudes of Japanese people toward foreigners. In this chapter we relate some experiences about life in Japan that caused us to reformulate our images of the quality of Japanese products and how that quality is achieved at large Japanese corporations.

We realized that this trip would provide us with a lifetime experience. It was an unusual opportunity for us to live among our counterparts in Japan. Our neighbors in the company apartment complex were similar to us in education level, age, number of children, and age of the children (Wescott was six and Russell was four at the time). As social scientists, we viewed our sojourn as an anthropological field trip of sorts. For a brief three months we experienced daily life in Japan. We would shop in the same stores and ride the same commuter trains. Our apartment was the same size as the others. When our children ran across the floor, our neighbor below could hear their footsteps just as we could hear the footsteps of those above us. Our neighbors became part of our lives. Our landlady, who had three boys, gave birth to her dream—a baby girl—the day we arrived. We were witnesses to the tragic aftermath of the death of a neighbor's husband from overwork. From a personal perspective, we were anxious to learn about the customs, crafts, and culture to satisfy our lifelong curiosity about Japan. From a professional perspective, knowledge of these cultural aspects was crucial to comprehending the management of Japanese companies and their attitudes toward product development.

A SUITCASE FULL OF GIFTS   A colleague at Purdue told us about the importance of gift exchange in Japan, so the seven months prior to leaving were spent hunting for appropriate gifts. The souvenirs from Purdue University—key chains, sweatshirts, T-shirts, pens, and tie pins—were fairly easy to find. A business trip to Washington, D.C. afforded an opportunity to find more expensive gifts for the senior management at the company. A clerk in the American handicraft store in Washington's Union Station had experience with Japanese tourists and knew what they liked to buy. So I asked her to show me the items the Japanese preferred. Fused glass dishes and inlaid wooden pieces seemed to be particular favorites. With great care and deliberation, I selected a walnut kaleidoscope for the director of the labs, two inlaid oval mirrors for the next-level managers, (presents are often for wives or other family members) numerous little octoscopes and small boxes, and a glass dish for our host.

When we arrived in Japan, our host, Mr. Uchimura, was very pleased with our thoughtfulness. He spent all afternoon sitting on the floor of our apartment dividing up the gifts for all the people at work and for the neighbors. He was very careful to choose the gifts so that they reflected the social hierarchy of the research laboratory or the neighborhood. When we had everything arranged with everyone's names spelled correctly on a list, Mr. Uchimura left so I could wrap the presents. I had read once that the Japanese take special delight in the presentation of a gift and that sometimes the wrapping was more important than the contents. With that in mind, I had brought special gift wrap and tape from the United States.

After the gifts for the neighbors were all wrapped, Mr. Uchimura took us around to the neighbors' apartments and introduced us. We had lived in several apartment complexes and a couple of different houses in the United States during our married life. The sad part of this typical American experience was that we could live in a place for a year and never see our neighbors, much less socialize with them. A special thing about Japan for us was the sense of community. We had proper introductions to everyone in the apartment building, and were invited into their homes frequently. During the three months we lived there I envied my neighbors their community.

One afternoon Mrs. Matsuoka and I were standing outside the apartment while the children played baseball in the driveway. I was describing how lonesome I had been when my husband and I first moved to West Lafayette. I told her how I had been working on my Ph.D. with a new baby at home and how I didn't know anyone in town. I tried to explain the depression, the desperation, the sense of isolation.

She looked at me sympathetically and said gently, "We don't have that problem. We Japanese, we have each other. So here, we are never lonely."

Even though I knew I didn't belong there, I felt a security due to the community provided by my neighbors. I still miss it. In that small space of time, I came to understand Archibald MacLeish's poem, "American Letter," with an intensity I never experienced when I first read it in college:

> America is neither a land nor a people,
> A word's shape it is, a wind's sweep—
> America is alone: many together,
> Many of one mouth, of one breath,
> Dressed as one—and none brothers among them:
> Only the taught speech and the aped tongue.
> America is alone and the gulls calling.
> It is a strange thing to be an American.
>
> It is strange to sleep in the bare stars and to die
> On an open land where few bury before us:
> (From the new earth the dead return no more.)
> It is strange to be born of no race and no people.
> In the old lands they are many together. They keep
> The wise part and the words spoken in common.
> They remember the dead with their hands, their mouths dumb.

They answer each other with two words in their meeting.
They live together in the small things. They eat
The same dish, their drink is the same and their proverbs.
Their youth is like. They are like in their ways of love.
They are many men. There are always others beside them.
Here it is one man and another and wide
On the darkening hills the faint smoke of the houses.
Here it is one man and the wind in the boughs.

AMERICANS HAVE FAT FINGERS   My mother came to visit us in Japan, and Mrs. Matsuoka invited us to tea at her house. She was a very gracious hostess, serving us tea, coffee, and her specialty dessert using her best china. Mrs. Tanaka, our company-appointed cultural liaison, had already told me that Mrs. Matsuoka made marvelous Bavarian cake and that it was quite an honor to be invited to her house. During our conversation, we asked her about the beautiful object sitting on her buffet. She brought it over and told us proudly that it was origami she had made herself. It was composed of 60 folded petals all carefully glued together to form a sphere. The special two-sided origami paper with different colors on each side gave it a particular richness of color. She carefully cut a piece of origami paper into a square no bigger than her thumbnail. With a needle, she proceeded to fold an origami crane which was only 1/4 inch long when it was finished.

"Americans can't do origami," she said gravely to me as she handed me the perfect tiny crane, "because they have fat fingers."

Later that evening, mulling over the remark, I decided to take it as a challenge. Like Tom Sawyer's nemesis, Mrs. Matsuoka had drawn a line in the sand and double-dared me to cross it. Despite the realization that my fingers are kind of fat, I was determined to learn how to make an origami ball like Mrs. Matsuoka's. The origami books I had brought from home turned out to be useless: I couldn't make any sense of them. The directions were obscure and the patterns horribly difficult. I had seen Mrs. Matsuoka's son fold little paper frogs, which led me to believe that there must be books for children on origami. I asked Mrs. Tanaka, and she lent me her daughter's book. I started at the beginning with the simplest patterns and worked my way through the book until I could do every pattern. For several weeks I studied every night for two or three hours after the children went to bed. I became fascinated with the different kinds of paper and the patterns. I perused bookstores looking for origami books with new patterns and paper shops looking for new types of paper.

I folded and folded and folded, until I felt confident enough to ask Mrs. Matsuoka to teach me to do the ball. She was flattered and surprised that I had studied so hard. She made half of the 60 necessary petals and I made the other half. She gave me her petals, showed me how to glue them together, and left me to finish the ball. The finished joint product was stunning. My other neighbors coveted it, but I brought it home with me in my suitcase. Four years later, our ball is sitting in a place of honor on my coffee table, and I still have fat fingers.

TRICK OR TREAT?   We took our role in the cultural exchange seriously. Just as we wanted to discover as much as possible about our Japanese neighbors, we wanted to reciprocate by telling them about our lifestyle, customs, and culture. With this in mind, I brought cookie cutters along with my mother-in-law's famous recipes for cookies and pies. I thought it would be great fun to celebrate the American holidays in Japan so I packed cardboard decorations for Halloween, Thanksgiving, and Christmas.

After consulting with my neighbor, Mrs. Tanaka, about an invitation list, I planned a big Halloween party for my neighbors' children. Because twenty children were to be invited, we decided to have two parties that Saturday. Mrs. Tanaka thought it best to invite the girls to the first one because, as she put it, girls don't make such a big mess as boys. She also figured out which neighbors knew each other so that this could be taken into consideration in planning the guest list.

My newly-found origami skills were used to fold large orange samurai hats as invitations. I printed carefully the time and date of the party on each one and requested that the children come in costume. Then I hand delivered all the invitations. Several days later, a rather worried Mrs. Tanaka came to my door and asked very apologetically what was meant by "dressing up in costume." I explained, and only afterwards discovered how my neighbors had worried over their children's costumes.

For the party, one boy came as a praying mantis with paper legs dangling down from his belt, and another boy came as a fish. One boy was either Abraham Lincoln or Count Dracula—we were not quite sure which one. One of the girls came as Little Red Riding Hood and another was the Easter Bunny. My mother-in-law, who opportunely visited us in late October, had brought American corn and pumpkin candy as well as prizes for the games. We baked sugar-cookie pumpkins, witches, moons, and cats. The candy for each child was placed in an origami basket folded from special origami paper. We ate too many cookies, drank too much American Kool-aid, and had too much fun playing games like pin-the-tail on the Halloween cat.

STICKY VOICES   Soon after I arrived, my neighbor across the hall asked me to give her English lessons. Every Friday afternoon for almost three months we sat in our kitchens, ate great desserts, drank coffee, and tried to converse in English. I hadn't anticipated teaching English, so the only materials I had on hand were children's books and various paperbacks my husband and I had brought to read. The adult literature was too difficult for Mrs. Kimura. The children's books seemed like a better place to start. I couldn't use the obvious choice of McGuffey's Readers because my oldest son needed them for his lessons.

We weren't using A.A. Milne's *Winnie-the-Pooh,* so I assigned the first chapter to Mrs. Kimura. I remembered my mother reading *Winnie-the-Pooh* in Latin when I was small so I thought it would be okay. I was wrong. I had totally forgotten that in the first chapter the author switches narrators back and forth as he introduces the character of Pooh to his son, who is also a character in the stories. Very confusing. We tried Chapter 2, which I assured her was going to be easier. However, after spending half an hour the next Friday afternoon trying to explain the use of the term "sticky voice" I decided we needed another "textbook." For the next lesson I bought a copy of Laura Ingalls Wilder's *Little House in the Big Woods* at a Japanese department store. Mrs. Kimura had seen the *Little House on the Prairie* series on Japanese television, and she was relieved not to have to endure any more Poohisms. Lessons went better after that, with only an occasional hurdle. One tense moment occurred when I tried to explain what headcheese is. Fortunately, between my *Joy of Cooking* cookbook and the Webster's dictionary, I was able to explain what the Ingalls were doing with those animal brains.

GO FISH   I was also asked to teach the neighborhood girls' English lesson. Their usual English teacher, who came from the American naval base to instruct the six elementary-age girls, was entertaining company from the States and wouldn't be able to teach for three weeks. Mrs. Tanaka informed me I was needed and I couldn't figure out how to get out of it. As it turned out, I had a wonderful time, and I was sorry when my three weeks were done. Mrs. Tanaka came along to help interpret for me since, unlike the regular teacher, I knew no Japanese. The first day the girls practiced saying the alphabet and getting the letter sounds correct. As I expected, L and R were the tough ones. They also spent some time writing the English letters. I noticed that they were having a hard time with the proportions of the letters. Their paper wasn't traditional penmanship paper, which has dotted lines to indicate the lowercase letter heights. I resolved to bring some of the paper my youngest son used in his lessons for the next class. I also decided to liven the class up a little.

The girls had a very limited vocabulary consisting mostly of color names and the numbers under ten. I had a brainstorm. The next lesson started with the usual pronunciation practice and writing of the alphabet. The new paper helped a lot, and I gave each girl some extra sheets for homework practice. Then the fun began. I brought out my pack of "Fish" playing cards and had Mrs. Tanaka translate the rules for me. We instructed the girls to say the following necessary phrases: "Give me red, please;" "Go fish;" and "Thank you." They had a terrific time. When I left Japan, I made sure that each of my pupils had her own Mickey Mouse English penmanship tablet and a set of "Fish" cards. As a farewell present, the mothers of the girls presented me with a beautiful set of blue-and-white, hand-painted ceramic Japanese plates.

CURIOUSER AND CURIOUSER   Many interesting mom-and-pop shops as well as big department stores were located in or near the train stations. I was particularly interested in the merchandise sold in the girls' stores. These were shops that catered strictly to young schoolgirls, and they were full of items for toiletry and school. Everything you could possibly need came in various product lines, so, for instance, you could stock your entire school bag with "Peter Rabbit" or "Alice in Wonderland" items. It was at such a shop that I began to wonder if the highly touted Japanese school system was everything I had been led to believe by the American media.

The notebooks intended for practicing English, were especially interesting. Unlike the books for practicing Japanese, which were ruled vertically, the English notebooks were ruled horizontally, and some even said "English notebook" on them. The first school notebook that caught my eye was "Alice in Wonder World." The price was 200 yen, which at the time was $3.00 American. The cover, which had gold writing, had a beautiful embossed beige surface that looked like leather. There were various silhouettes of Alice and the other popular characters. The pictures were based on the John Tenniel illustrations for the original American 1865 edition of Lewis Carroll's classic.

The curious thing about the Japanese notebook, other than the substitution of the word "World" for "Land," was the selection of quotations from *Alice's Adventures in Wonderland*: "That's none of your business." "'Two!' said Seven." "The Cat only grinned when it saw Alice." "'Consider your verdict,' the King said to the jury." "'Anything you like,' said the Footman and began whistling." "She went on: 'What's your name, child?'"

Initially, I was impressed. The Japanese appeared to be reading Lewis Carroll's classic, and it seemed particularly noteworthy that school children were familiar with the book. *Alice's Adventures in Wonderland* is a biting satire, not easy reading for a non-English speaker. I was mystified, however, by the particular selections that had been used. Nowhere to be found were the famous lines: "What is the use of a book . . . without pictures or conversations?" "I can't explain myself, I'm afraid, sir . . . because I'm not myself, you see." "Off with her head." "Will you, won't you, will you, won't you, will you join the dance?" "Twinkle, twinkle, little bat!" The more I thought about it, the more convinced I became that the quotations on the notebook had been taken at random from the book. Perhaps the most famous line from the book was appropriate in this case: "Curiouser and curiouser."

Another English notebook that I purchased was bright red with a picture of Jerry, the mouse in the American "Tom and Jerry" cartoon on the cover. The cover also bore the following inscription:

"Jerry was born in back of refrigerator under the roof, as the youngest brother among of ten brothers. He has 155 of intelligence quotient, the greatest stage of his life in the outdoor will be extended to him. He was scouted by a scout man as taking a chocolate-soda at tearoom. He is destined to be a movie star. His most favorites sport is taking a nap. Besides, he is also talented musician." This description of Jerry did not fit my recollection of the childhood cartoon classic.

By this time I was really beginning to wonder what was going on. Why were interpretations of English literary classics so hopelessly muddled? I remembered my own high school French teachers in both Canada and the United States. They were so concerned about getting the language right, they would never have tolerated French written as poorly as the English on the "Tom and Jerry" notebooks. Wouldn't an English teacher in Japan be upset at getting lessons from students on paper decorated with such bad grammar and spelling? What of the renowned Japanese school system? Shouldn't the most literate country in the world be concerned about accuracy and coherent prose? The American press is constantly comparing the English-speaking Japanese to Americans who can't or won't learn foreign languages. My image of a literate and quality-driven culture was rapidly being distorted by the experiences I was having and by the observations I was making. My curiosity deepened and I began asking questions of my neighbors and my husband's colleagues. The strings of *tatemae* focusing my positive image of Japan's educational system were beginning to singe.

I asked Mr. Uchimura about *Alice in Wonderland*. I told him I was impressed that Japanese children would be familiar with the story, because it is considered to be a complex satire. A reader must know that the story's underlying structure is a card game in order to interpret the actions of characters such as the King and Queen of Hearts. He looked at me with great amusement and laughed. "No, no," he said. "We haven't read the book, we've seen the cartoon."

SEE DICK SPOUT   We often spent our afternoons exploring the shops in our neighborhood. As time passed we expanded our range of exploration to include the station stops up and down the train line. I observed that people on trains in Japan read two types of things: newspapers and comics. It was rare to see someone reading a real book or a news magazine.

Manga is the Japanese word for "comics," which translates as "not serious pictures." Adults make up 35% of the readership of *manga*; 80% of those adults are male. With 256 publications and sales of over $5 billion, *manga* has a market share of 25% of the entire publishing market in Japan. Of the 13 magazines with the highest circulation, 12 are *manga*.[1] These action-oriented comics are becoming popular in the United States and now account for 2% of the American comic book market.[2] *Manga* are often very pornographic, and it was disconcerting to see the salarymen of the world's most literate nation getting off the trains in their natty dark suits, with briefcases and comic books tucked under their arms. I sometimes tried to imagine the equivalent scene in America—Amtrak riders on the East Coast in Armani suits reading *Penthouse* and *X-Men* comics in full view of the other passengers.

Claims have been made that Japanese *manga* are more than just comic books. Tomofusa Kure, of the Tokyo Science University, said, "Japanese *manga* have reached the level of literature. It shows all the complex emotions and dramas of human beings. It should be dealt with in the same way we deal with novels."[3] If *manga* is to be taken seriously as literature, we wanted to find out more about it.

After returning to Indiana, I went down to the local comic book store and inquired about Japanese *manga*. I was directed to the section of Japanese comics and told which were the biggest sellers. I bought two: *Maison Ikkoku* and *Caravan Kidd*. Both are written and drawn by Japanese and then translated with the creators' permission for the American market. They are not written for export; they are written for a Japanese audience. I also purchased a copy of the latest *X-Men* adventures, the most popular American comic book, for comparison.

One way to measure the difficulty of reading material is to perform a "readability test" on the material. This is often done for things like instruction manuals to determine if they are readable by the general public. I decided to do this for the Japanese comic books and compare them to the American comic book. The Japanese comic books had a Flesch-Kincaid reading level of grade 1 versus the American comic book's reading level of grade 3.This means that a first grader would have the

---

[1]Merrill Goozner, "Manga Mania Headed for the US," *Chicago Tribune*, May 23, 1994, Section 2, p. 1.
[2]Luke Cyphers, "Japanese Comics are Poised to Grab More Fans at Home," *Wall Street Journal*, October 25, 1991, p. 96.
[3]Goozner, "Manga Mania ...", Section 2, p. 1.

vocabulary to read the Japanese *manga* but not the *X-Men*. A third-grade vocabulary was needed for *X-Men*.[4] This measure of readability indicates the American comic book to be about two grade levels more difficult to read than comparable Japanese comic books. If the Japanese professor is correct about *manga* being like a novel to Japanese readers, I started wondering about Japanese literature written at a first-grade level. Comic-book novels and a large adult population reading them did not fit an image of the most literate society in the world. I tried to imagine what a great American novel such as *Moby Dick* would read like if it were written at a first-grade level ("See Dick spout").

UNCLE JAM AND LADIES COMIC YOU   We were introduced to the world of Japanese cartoons and comics by Mr. Uchimura, who gave our children a present of five glasses in a box. Each bore a different character from the children's cartoon series, *Ampan Man.* Ampan Man is a character with a biscuit head full of bean jam. His friend Uncle Jam, a baker, occasionally fashions a new head for Ampan. His superhero friends are made of other types of food. Tempura Man has a head consisting of a pot with a lid; Kuri Pan man blows curry spice at the bad guys, such as the evil Baikin Man. Baikin Man is black, with a permanent scowl on his face, and is often accompanied by a little red devil girl, Dokin Chan, who has a crush on Ampan Man. My neighbor told me that Baikin Man was a virus. He is always eating Tempura man's tempura and spoiling Ampan's biscuit head. Whenever there is trouble, Ampan's good friend Uncle Jam and his helper make more necessary food and repair the superheros.

I accidentally discovered the darker side of Japanese comics as I idly leafed through a Japanese woman's magazine called *Lady's Comic YOU* while returning by train from a sightseeing trip to Kamakura. Someone had left the *manga* magazine on the train and I was tired of doing origami which is how I usually amused myself on trains. The magazine was all comics and advertising. I was about to give it to my four-year-old son Russell, who was getting bored, when I realized that a story in the middle of the magazine had depictions of a school girl being raped. The story went on to show scenes of bondage and of a ménage à trois. Russell didn't get to read that particular comic.

In keeping with Japanese taboos, the drawings in *Lady's Comic YOU* showed no genitalia. In their vicinity, the drawing gets fuzzy or there are big blank spaces, but it is never hard to tell what is happening. On TV and in videos in Japan, genitalia are

---

[4]In calculating the index, all place names and character's names are eliminated, since they tend to have more syllables than the rest of the text. The Flesch-Kincaid Index looks at the number of syllables in words to calculate readability.

covered up by little black squares. These black squares are seen in imported videos as well. Spoofs of this censorship often appear on Japanese TV. In comedy skits the characters may be dressed in flesh-colored body suits with big black squares pasted on strategic areas. At the Narita airport point-of-entry, the customs officers were interested in only one thing: "Do you have any pornography?"

Even American magazines like *Playboy* and *Penthouse* are censored in Japan. Instead of airbrushing over offending areas, the printing ink is removed by hand with a razor blade. Such censorship struck me as odd given the proliferation of bondage, torture, and prepubescent girls in Japanese comics and pornography magazines. I didn't have to go out of my way to see these things, either. They were everywhere. Unlike American shops, where pornography is wrapped up, displayed on high shelves with blinders, or in an adults-only section, Japanese pornography is sold in full view of children. In fact, in one shop, the pornography section was right next to the children's comics. I kept busy trying to cover them up with business magazines before my too-curious youngest son saw all the naked ladies with chains and black squares.

THE MOTHER BEAR SYNDROME   We were visiting Kamakura on the coast of Japan, which is famous for its large Buddha and its temples. After a day of visiting temples, tourist shops, and climbing through the Buddha, the children were tired. Kamakura has a sandy beach close to the temples so we thought this would be a good place for the boys to play before heading back on the train to our apartment.

The boys were soon busily building a sand castle and placing little sticks on it. Nearby on the beach, a Japanese group was having a big barbecue. Our castle was a good distance from them. As the children finished their work, I noticed that one of the members of the Japanese party had come over near the boys and was scowling at them. When Russell went to get some more sticks, the stranger stuck out his foot and tripped him. Like a mother bear with small cubs, I decided that he was a threat and it was time to go. As we left, I looked back over my shoulder and saw the man destroying the sand castle with his foot. I hoped the children hadn't noticed.

Back at the apartment complex, there was a small sandbox opposite our kitchen window. This was one of the few play areas for children. My boys liked to build forts and hideouts for their Ninja turtle action figures. Japanese action figures and monsters were soon added to this group. I was happy to get them out of the house, but one afternoon they came in early looking rather upset. Russell had a scratch on his face, so I asked what was the matter.

"The boys won't let us play."

"Where did you get that scratch?" I demanded.

"They threw sticks and rocks at us, Mom," replied Wescott after some encouragement from me. He was reluctant to rat on his peers.

"Is this the first time this has happened?" I asked.

"No, Mom."

I had been in Japan long enough to know that if there was a problem in the group, the mothers got together and solved it. I decided to use the Japanese system to get some protection for my boys. I consulted with Mrs. Tanaka and very firmly reminded her that we were guests of her husband's company. I wouldn't tolerate such behavior in my country, and I wasn't about to allow Japanese boys to throw sticks and stones at my boys. I laid on the guilt a bit, reminding her that such behavior made her company and the neighbors look bad. She said very little but told me she would speak with the other mothers. Every day for about a week, a different mother with sullen boys in tow would greet me and apologize. Some of these women I had never met before. I've often wished I had a comparable network to call upon in the states when my boys have scraps during soccer games at school.

Mrs. Tanaka also told me the problem was that my boys were not communicating with the other children. They were not playing like Japanese. So she wrote me out some brief Japanese phrases for the boys to learn and she practiced with them. She told me that the Japanese children were used to playing in each others' apartments and that my boys should feel free to ring doorbells and play wherever they could gain entrance. She then specifically invited them to play at her house. I also told my boys to play in the sandbox when the Japanese children were at school. After three o'clock, all castle building had to stop and group games must commence. We didn't have any real problems after that, although I noticed that my youngest son, who is very strong willed and loud, yelled *"Yamate"* at his playmates frequently but to no avail. *Yamate*, as he had been taught by Mrs. Tanaka, is Japanese for "Stop it."

We realized that as long as we were considered part of a group, we were treated as guests. As soon as we ventured out on our own, however, away from the community provided by the research lab, we were no longer guests but were *gaijin*. This is the Japanese word, used in a derogatory manner, for foreigner or outsider. People regularly called us this behind our backs at tourist attractions not caring whether we knew what it meant.

We also started to see the downside to the vaunted Japanese economic miracle. If manufacturing quality products conforming to rigid standards requires a disciplined workforce, then individuality suffers in the process. If teamwork is required in manufacturing, then peer bullying of young children who play differently or by themselves is accepted. The consequences, reduced creativity and individual expression of freedom of thought and action, are worth the price of the continued strength and harmony of the group. If a spirited and motivated workforce is required, then emotions also turn xenophobic, with a rejection of anything foreign or different. We discovered things about the quality of Japanese products in people's homes. If an economy based on exports is needed for growth, then the high-quality products are exported and low-quality products remain at home.

AGITATING OVER THE WASHING MACHINE   On the outside, the washing machine in my apartment looked similar to an American washing machine. It had an enameled exterior but was smaller than our washing machine at home. It was a top loader with an arsenal of knobs and dials for the soak, spin, and rinse cycles. Inside, however, the washing machine was different. It was just a giant bucket with no agitator. Initially, I was so relieved to find washing facilities in the apartment, that I didn't give much thought to the missing agitator. I had nightmares of doing laundry by hand or in a laundromat, so the machine in my bathroom was a blessing. That blessing soon turned into a curse.

Think about what an agitator does. It has a spiral action that, in a soak or rinse cycle, moves the clothes around. In the soak cycle, this distributes the soap so it is dispersed evenly throughout the clothes. In the rinse cycle, the agitation removes the soap from the clothes. Without an agitator, the clothes clump together in a tangled mass. If soap has penetrated the folds of the clothes and managed to migrate into a tangle where no water is able to reach, then the soap eventually solidifies, leaving big white spots when the clothing dries.

Japanese washing machines do one thing better than any others I've ever used: They spin fast and long. During the two spin cycles following the soak and rinse cycles, the clothes are thrown violently to the side of the machine, intensifying the tangles and clumps. Various parts are stretched out of proportion. Loose threads become wrapped around other clothing. At the end of the washing, unloading the clothes involves untangling a massive wet chaotic blob. After only five washings, our clothes were starting to show the results of this abuse: frayed cuffs and collars along with washcloths that were unravelling.

When my husband's new shirt collars and cuffs began to fray, I panicked. He is too big to buy clothes for in Japan, and my mother-in-law wasn't due to visit for six more weeks. By then his clothes would be in shreds, and I worried about the kind of impression this would make at the office.

Because the machine mangled the clothes, I concluded that it was broken, probably because it stayed in the spin cycle too long. Mrs. Tanaka agreed to call the repairman. He came, she translated, he took the machine apart, and said there was nothing wrong with it. I asked if the cycles could be shortened.

"No, can't do that," said the repairman.

I showed Mrs. Tanaka the ruined washcloths, the T-shirts with holes in them, and my husband's frayed collars. She explained that the machine was not broken. The problem was that I did not understand how to wash clothes the Japanese way. She explained that I needed to stop the machine by hand before the spin cycle finished and remove the clothes. Some things would need to be washed by hand and not washed "automatically" in the machine. Also, the clothes had to be scrubbed before being placed in the washing machine. I had just assumed that a Japanese automatic washing machine was as automatic as an American automatic washing machine. Mrs. Tanaka seemed quite accepting of the machine the way it was. I could not accept something that would not work. In the 1930s, my grandfather used to redesign the dashboards of his cars by replacing the knobs and switches. Acceptance of poor design does not come easily in my family.

To make the best of a bad situation, my sons and I made a game of washing clothes. Our Japanese neighbors must have wondered what was happening when they heard yells of "Spin!" coming from our apartment and the sounds of running feet as we raced to be the first to turn off the machine. I solved the problem of the lack of the agitator with the futon beater. The futon beater was lightweight plastic, so it wasn't much good for beating futons. I put it into service as a washing machine stirrer. Soap would not dissolve in the ice cold water, so I would fill up the machine, put in the soap, stir it up with the futon beater, and then add the clothes. (The futon beater was also good for stirring up the bathtub water so the kids wouldn't get burned.) My neighbors didn't know what I was doing with my futon beater, but then they didn't know I was taking off my shoes before answering the front door.

If the washing machine was evaluated on its separate features, it would seem to be of high quality. It was durable, it performed the soak and rinse cycles reliably. If washing machines were evaluated in terms of rpm's on the spin cycle, none could touch the Japanese machines. They spin longer and faster than American models. Putting the various features together, however, the machine did not wash clothes very well. Quality cannot necessarily be measured by separate parts or features. Products must be evaluated as a whole.

In 1977, Matsushita was the first Japanese company to achieve zero defects in the manufacture of washing machines over a seven-month period.[5] Quality is often measured in terms of the number of defects per product. However, the critical determinant of quality should be performance. Definitions of quality will be considered in Chapter 4.

---

[5]Dean M. Schroeder and Alan G. Robinson, "America's most successful export to Japan: Continuous improvement programs." *Sloan Management Review*, Spring, 1991, p. 80.

THE CLOTHES DRYER   We were one of the few families in the apartment complex with a clothes dryer. Since most Japanese apartments do not have clothes dryers, there was no room for the dryer next to the washing machine in the bathroom. Instead, our dryer was in the kitchen. Once again, the dryer looked like an American clothes dryer, but it did not perform like one.

An important feature that was missing from the Japanese clothes dryer was a vent to allow the hot, moist air to escape to the outside. With no outside vent, the air accumulates in the dryer and in the apartment.

In dry weather, I hung my clothes on the balcony line, saving the dryer for touching up heavier items that weren't completely dry by late afternoon. On damp days, however, I had to use the dryer because I couldn't dry the clothes outside. Because of the lack of a vent I had to stop the machine every twenty minutes, take out the clothes and shake them, wipe the inside of the dryer, put the clothes back for another twenty minutes, and then start the process again.

I asked Mrs. Tanaka how she dried clothes during wet spells. She told me that she would hang the wet clothes in the living room, turn on the air conditioner at maximum power, and then go shopping because the apartment would become too cold to remain there. By the time her children came home from school, the clothes would be dry enough that she could turn off the air conditioner. I used the dryer and coped.

HIS HOUSE IS SO CONVENIENCE. IT CALLED CORA.   A popular brand of products for school girls is called "The Tortoise Club." Children buy Tortoise Club pencil boxes, notebooks, and book bags. The logo is a turtle with all body parts labeled. His mustache is his charm point. The shell is called his house or, for some reason we could never determine, it is called Cora. The "convenience" of the house refers to the convenience of the tortoise carrying his own house on his back. Convenience could also be used to describe the toilet in our apartment.

We were lucky that our apartment complex had Western-style toilets instead of the usual ceramic holes in the floor. In public places, perhaps because nobody ever had to touch them, toilets appeared never to be cleaned. We quickly realized that hand towels were not provided in public bathrooms. I watched the other women in the restroom and discovered that they carried tiny towels in their handbags. I purchased some in Tokyo, and we used "Alice in Wonderland" and "Winnie-the-Pooh" towels for the rest of our stay. My youngest son was always in a hurry and wouldn't wait to use the towel. He still uses his pants to wipe his hands; some convenient habits are difficult to break.

The toilet in our apartment was unusual. Following the Japanese design practice of combining several functions into one product, the toilet was a combination toilet, sink, and drinking fountain. Instead of a shelf on top of the tank, our toilet had a little basin. When the toilet flushed, an arc of water spouted from the faucet on top of the tank—similar to a water fountain—went into the basin, and then down into the tank of the toilet to facilitate the flushing cycle. Our Western taboos proved too strong. We couldn't bring ourselves to use toilet water to wash our hands.

THE TOASTER OVEN   Most Japanese cooking is done on a two-burner portable gas stove and with specialized appliances such as rice cookers, bread makers, pressure cookers, toaster ovens, and microwaves. Very few traditional Japanese dishes require an oven, so ovens are not considered essential in Japanese kitchens. We had one, but we were warned not to use it.

There were many potential dangers in our kitchen. All the gas stoves in our apartment complex were located next to the sliding glass doors to the balcony. The doors had heavy pleated draperies, so any wind gust from outside might cause the curtains to go up in flames if the gas burner was on. There were no windows in the kitchen, so most people kept their doors open in good weather. I was always very careful to push my curtains to the side away from the door, although to do so I had to unhook the curtain hooks from the pull tabs in the center.

The kitchens in our complex suffered from a shortage of electrical outlets and counter space. Many of my neighbors ran electrical cords across or over doorways to solve the problem. We didn't have many electrical appliances besides our toaster. I was one of the few women in the area who cooked rice in a pan. Mr. Uchimura was quite impressed that I knew how to wash, soak, and cook rice correctly, since everyone in his generation had been reared with rice cookers which did all that automatically. It was true that cooking Japanese rice was time consuming, but all I had to do was follow the recipe in the cookbook.

With all these minor safety problems, we were given a stern warning when we moved into the apartment: Don't use the oil heaters or the oven. With no central heating, our sole source of heat was two floor oil heaters. We were told that they were very difficult to use and very easy to tip over and, worst of all, incredibly stinky. They were also a severe fire hazard. We never touched them, and were lucky enough to leave Japan in early December before it got really cold. During our last few weeks in Japan, the children and I spent a lot of time in stores just to stay warm. Our apartment was very damp and cold.

The oven was on top of a filing cabinet, and we were told to leave it alone because everything, including the filing cabinet, would become extremely hot if we turned it on. Forget about touching the oven itself: It was not insulated.

After a few weeks, we began to miss basic American foods such as biscuits and cookies, so we decided to purchase a toaster oven. We paid $75.00 for a toaster oven from one of the largest consumer products firms in Japan, known in America for making high-quality products.

Once again, outside appearances were deceiving. The toaster oven looked like the one we had in Indiana, with the usual door and metal racks inside. When I brought it home, my husband asked me how to set the oven temperature. I had never thought to look for a thermostat. You could set the power level for 75 watts, 150 watts, and 300 watts, but I soon discovered that the oven burnt everything regardless of which setting I used. You don't need to be a physicist to understand that a toaster oven operating at a constant wattage in a small enclosed space will become hotter and hotter the longer it is on.

To bake anything, therefore, we had to adjust the temperature manually. We would put something in the oven, pick a wattage button, and then watched the food cook through the door. When we judged that the oven was getting too hot, we would open up the door. When it looked cool enough, we would close the door and continue watching. The food we baked this way tasted especially good because of the amount of effort that went into the cooking.

The toaster oven had another feature that was quite annoying. The rack in the toaster oven had little hooks sticking up on both sides so that it was attached to the door. When the door was opened, the rack moved out and down. Of course, your wrist would usually be in the path of the hot rack or the hot food. After a while, we learned to open the door about halfway, reach in with a hot pad holder (trying not to touch the hot door or oven), and hold the pan in place as the door was opened the rest of the way.

I expressed an interest in making cookies and pies to my neighbor, Mrs. Tanaka. She loaned us her very expensive oven, which was slightly bigger than the toaster oven and had a thermostat. She said she didn't use it very often, so we tried to keep her and her family well supplied with pastries. As with the other ovens, however, the lack of insulation caused the outside of the oven to become very hot.

OTHER PRODUCTS   Many other everyday products had similar quality problems. Toys were made of a type of plastic that we seldom see in the United States because it is too brittle. Our youngest son bought action-figure monster toys of *Ultraman*, a popular children's television show. Little pieces often broke off. These figures would probably be illegal in the United States because of the danger of small children swallowing the tiny pieces.

The vacuum cleaner was a source of continuous problems. Unlike most canister vacuums we were familiar with, this one did not have a dust bag. Instead, it had a plastic compartment that was supposed to collect the dirt and dust. To empty it you had to turn the vacuum cleaner upside down and hope your aim was good. I would take it outside and empty it directly into the garbage sack. The vacuum also had such low horsepower that it collected hardly any dirt. The suction was not strong enough to pick up anything that had any weight to it. Our floors were a combination of linoleum, *tatami* mat, and indoor-outdoor carpet. The only way to vacuum the carpet was to take off the attachment, get down on my hands and knees, go over the rug inch by inch with the nozzle end, and pull the fuzz and hair out of the carpet by hand as I went along.

We had several unhappy encounters with our metal mailbox. When the mailbox was manufactured and the metal was cut, the edges were not finished off, so the corners inside the door were very sharp. The sharp edges were right next to the part one grasped to open the door. We had to think about that when opening the door to prevent cutting our hands.

The front door had a similar trap. It had a very heavy spring that closed the door automatically. I worried about my children being caught by it, so I would hold it open for them. When I opened the door for myself, I almost always had something in my hands, so I would stand in front of the door. It would close onto my legs, and the package compartment built into the door would slam into my calf. The slot had a sharp handle on it which caused bruises on my legs. I decided to fix it instead of enduring. I used some foam and tape to cover the handle. Duct tape would have been better, but the stores did not carry this American fix-all item.

Even the quality of the food was poor. Heads of lettuce came complete with dead crickets. Cartons of eggs averaged about one bad egg per dozen. Eggs were not refrigerated at the stores but sold at room temperature. Once we bought a package of salmon and were looking forward to this delicacy. In the store, we noticed some white rings on top, but paid no further attention to them. After preparing the salmon and placing it in the toaster oven, I noticed that the white rings were starting to move around as they thawed out. We rode the train to the nearest McDonald's that night for supper.

The construction of the apartment was very poor and would probably not satisfy building codes in most U.S. communities. There was no weather stripping, the ventilation was poor, and sound seemed to travel easily from one apartment to the next. No hot water was available directly in the kitchen. If hot water was needed, one had to go into the bathroom, turn on the heater, and wait for the flow into the kitchen. We were told not to leave the hot water heater on when we left the house. The heater was just a gas flame on the water pipe; there was no holding tank. The washing machine did not have a hot water supply, and the water drained directly onto the floor instead of into a pipe. To wash a load of white laundry, I had to haul buckets of hot water from the bathtub to the washing machine. I looked everywhere, but I could not find a big bucket in Japan, so filling the washing machine took a long time. A bit of hose and duct tape would have solved that problem.

There was no landscaping around the apartment buildings. Concrete blocks, probably from when the apartments were constructed about twenty years ago, were still strewn along the grounds. The neighborhood children were always falling over them and hitting their heads and knees. I said something about this to my neighbors, but they told me the stairs worried them more because the concrete was slippery after rains and snowfalls. Several children had gone to the hospital with injuries suffered on the stairs. They told me to be very careful.

THE OFFICE   The outside of the my husband's research laboratories looked like any American office building, probably because it was copied from its American counterpart in New Jersey. The exterior may have been the same, but the interior was very different.

The inside of the building was partitioned into four large rooms per floor. Each of these large rooms served about 200 researchers. Movable partitions divided the researchers into groups of about 15, which included the senior managers, the junior researchers, and the secretaries. The desk area was a series of tables, and often the tables were shared.

The purpose of this kind of environment is to promote teamwork. The close proximity of people means that communication will occur and ideas can be shared. It also means that the square footage required for each worker is much less than in a typical American office building, so costs are lower.

My husband had his desk area, a chair, and three drawers in a movable desk section. Ray was fortunate to be given an Apple Macintosh computer for his own use; most of the researchers shared a personal computer.

Sharing resources was the norm. Although Ray was working for a large company, there were very few telephones in the office area—about four phones for the 15 workers. Personal calls were frowned upon. In three months, he received perhaps four personal calls from me. Once I called in tears after a particularly fearsome bout with the washing machine. The reception on the phone was so poor it sounded like I was talking through water, and when I tearfully explained I was having trouble with the washing machine, the gurgling sounds over the telephone became a concern to him. After deciphering the words, Ray concluded that the apartment was not flooded, but I had lost another shirt to the clothes-eating washing machine. All other phone calls had the same poor gurgling-water reception.

As a human factors engineer, Ray is always very picky about chair design. The chair should be the right height so as not to put too much pressure on the lower thighs, the back should have lower lumbar support, and the chair should support the right kind of sitting posture. His office chair had all the wrong features. The chair had two positions: tilted forward so that he felt like he was falling into the computer or tilted back so that his feet were off the floor. No lower back support was provided.

After two-and-a-half months of sitting in the chair, with Ray's back slowly acquiring a constant pain, he decided to see if there were any adjustments he could make. While he was down on the floor unsuccessfully trying to adjust the chair, his colleagues inquired about what he was doing. Ray told them about the back pain he had been enduring. One of his fellow workers graciously offered his chair as a replacement. My husband tried to refuse, especially after he told Ray of the difficulty he had experienced finding this special, ergonomically designed chair. Once a gift is offered, however, refusals are not accepted. This chair, unique in Ray's office area and maybe throughout the building, was a much better design, which helped alleviate the back problems. My husband accepted it with some embarrassment.

QUALITY IN SERVICE   Quality should apply not only to products but also to services. Americans take the quality of many services for granted. We don't think about the convenience of being able to pay bills by checks sent through the mail. We expected the same level of convenience in Japan, but most Japanese banks do not offer checking accounts.

Think about the implications of no checking accounts. With credit cards still not widely accepted, people generally pay for everything with cash. When my in-laws were visiting, we all went to a mountain resort town to sample life in the Japanese Alps. We stayed in a traditional Japanese inn. We had one large room with a bathroom and a small enclosed porch. When dinner was served, the table was brought to the middle of the room, and we enjoyed a multicourse meal. When dinner was finished, the table was moved to the side and the futons were rolled out. Since my youngest son was too young to be charged, he did not get his own futon. With five futons on the floor, there was very little room to walk. Russell fell asleep on one of the adult futons, so rather than awaken him I took the chair cushions and slept on the porch with coats as blankets. I have never slept so poorly in such expensive surroundings.

The next morning it was time to settle our account: $150 per adult and $75 for the older child. This amounted to $675 for one night in a cramped room, small mats on the floor as beds, dinner included. At Takahara, you'd better bring cash, because they don't take American Express. Ray had anticipated this, of course, so he had traveled like a Japanese tourist with a wallet stuffed with cash.

The lack of checking accounts also makes paying bills very difficult. Don't expect to send your utility bill payment through the mail. To pay my bills I had to go to the bank with my kids and pay all my bills every two weeks and wait while they did the paper work. Their records were not computerized and not accurate. We had to sort out several mistakes during the three months we were there.

Further, both the banks and the post office are open only from 10:00 to 4:00 on weekdays. A wife cannot join the workforce because then who would pay the bills?

Another alternative, which I never used, was to go to the post office and send cash through the mail. I had enough trouble at the post office without trying to send cash. I mailed a lot of letters and postcards back to friends and family in America. The letters cost varying amounts, which didn't bother me because of the different weights involved, but I thought the postcards should always be the same price, especially when they were going to the same destination. I never knew, however, how much the clerk would charge and without a mastery of the Japanese language I could not ask why the price fluctuated so.

We asked several of our Japanese neighbors, first, why did they not have checking accounts, and, second, didn't they think it would be more convenient to have them? Everybody we asked gave the same answer: Checking accounts are bad because you never know exactly how much money you have in your account. The Japanese way is better because you can't spend money you don't have.

Eight of the ten largest banks in the world are Japanese; they did not achieve this status because of the quality of their service to Japanese customers. Even though Ray opened his savings account in a branch at the company site where he was working, he could not close the account there. He had to travel by train to the main office in Tokyo, about a two-hour trip, in order to close his account. Ray later learned that Japanese banks as a rule are not as computerized as American banks. Therefore, one cannot close an account at a branch office because there is no computer link between the branches and the main office.

When Ray was visiting a plant with a former student of his, the student pointed with pride to the automatic teller machine (ATM) that was located in the plant. He said that it was very convenient to have this machine so close to his job. Ray was already familiar with Japanese ATMs and asked him why, when the ATM was only open banking hours: 10:00 to 4:00 on weekdays, closed on holidays. His former student had no good answer to this question and had obviously never thought about it.

A SHIFTING PERCEPTION OF JAPANESE QUALITY

That people would buy poor-quality products or pay for poor-quality services without complaint or comment was very surprising to us, because we had bought into the myth of Japanese quality, and we thought this myth applied to all Japanese products and services. Why would anybody buy a washing machine, pay more money for it than for a top-of-the-line American machine, and end up with a machine that is not automatic and that destroys clothes? One of the myths about Japanese products is that the designers listen to customers, yet it seemed no designer had bothered to discover how the machine really worked or how the women were using it.

All of these products had similar characteristics: They looked like products we were familiar with, but they were missing key parts. They were analogous to the image from the projector. We could focus on an image of the product, but only part of the image. When we tried to focus on other essential parts, the whole image was no longer in focus. Appearances were maintained, but the whole product did not work as it should work. One can conjure up an image of a washing machine by looking at the outside. The image becomes blurred when it is opened and nothing is inside. We wondered if Japanese quality was just an image.

We probably would not be complaining if we had been living in an Eastern European or some Third World country. The "hardships" we endured would be inconsequential in underdeveloped countries, where the people do not have the money to pay for conveniences we take for granted. But Japan in 1990 was being hailed as the number-one economic power in the world: It was not an underdeveloped country. Our neighbors were elite researchers in a company-owned apartment complex. Japanese consumers were supposed to be the most discerning in the world—they would not buy low-quality American products. We were under the impression that they demanded high-quality products from their companies and were willing to pay extra money for them. It was hard to believe, living there and using their products, that this country was beating us economically in so many markets.

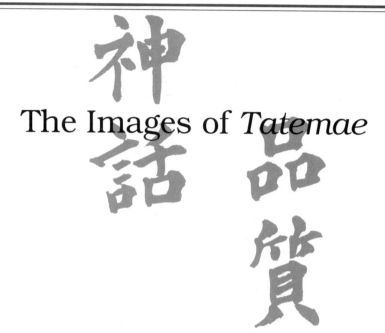

CHAPTER THREE

The Images of *Tatemae*

The last chapter showed how our image of Japanese products changed for the worse once we got to Japan and saw the quality of those domestic products for ourselves. Our image of Japanese products had been better than the reality. We started examining other aspects of Japanese life and discovered that the image, or *tatemae,* is very important in all aspects of Japanese life. *Tatemae,* roughly translated, means the image or the perception of the situation. Product quality depends, at least in part, on the perception of quality, and *tatemae* is a way to change that perception.

Japanese companies have created a perception that they design and manufacture high-quality products. The components of this perception include the Japanese education system, high worker productivity, management practices, consumer attitudes, and lifestyles. These components are used to reinforce the image of high-quality Japanese products. For instance, the Japanese education system is often portrayed as the best in the world. Why is this important? Because there is a widespread belief that only a well-educated workforce can produce high-quality products. The Japanese feel that if the perception of these key components is altered, then consumers worldwide may begin to question the quality of their products. Maintaining the integrity of the image becomes an economic and policy issue. *Tatemae* is so important in all aspects of Japanese life that setting policy to create the image of high-quality products is a natural extension of Japanese culture.

In Japanese culture, it is more important that the image be correct than that the reality match the image. Our experiences indicated that more effort in Japan is devoted to enhancing the image than to improving the reality. *Tatemae* usually involves stories that try to change the perception of reality in Japan or alter how the rest of the world views events happening in Japan.

THE PRICE OF LAND   Land in Japan is very expensive. Some of the Japanese people we talked to were happy to note that the land in the Tokyo area is worth more than all the land in the United States.[1] In 1987 Japan's Economic Planning Agency reported the market value of all the land in Japan was 4.1 times that of all the land in the United States. At the height of the market, a square meter of prime real estate on the Ginza in Tokyo was worth $300,000.[2] Michael Lewis, in his book, *Pacific Rift*, relates a discussion with an employee of Mitsui Real Estate who was responsible for buying New York real estate for Japanese investors.[3] One investor from Japan owned a parking lot in Osaka worth $600,000,000. Lewis went with the Japanese real estate agent to visit this lot and was surprised to see a relatively small piece of land with a small tin building on it. The owner was using this land as collateral at a Japanese bank so he could buy a skyscraper in New York City.

Japanese land is high-priced for several reasons. Foremost, Japan is a mountainous island country with just a few plains inhabited by large numbers of people. Any chunk of land in these plains is a scarce commodity and thus is very valuable. Government and business policies, however, are also responsible for the high prices. First, the government has coddled the remaining rice farmers even though these enterprises are inefficient and produce rice that is seven to ten times more expensive than rice produced anywhere else in the world. Because so much of the habitable land is occupied by rice farmers, who pay little in taxes, not enough land is available for other uses. Second, Japanese businesses own much of the rest of the habitable land. Their policy has been to hold onto the land, thus driving up prices. They then use these high prices as collateral to secure loans for plant and equipment purchases. Government and business have made a decision to support these special interests, at the expense of affordable housing prices for most of the people.

---

[1]Karel van Wolferen, *The Enigma of Japanese Power* (New York: Vantage Books, 1989), p. 401.
[2]"Japan's Reversal of Fortune," *US News & World Report*, January 11, 1993, p. 38.
[3]Michael Lewis, *Pacific Rift* (New York: W. W. Norton, 1991), pp. 81–84.

If people think land in Japan is too expensive, how can that belief be changed? A Westerner might think that the solution would be to review and change policies that encourage high land prices. In Japan, though, high land prices are considered an image problem. Japan's National Land Agency decided that the problem was really one of image—high land prices are a myth that could be debunked.[4] Their solution was a campaign utilizing bumper stickers that said: "Bring down the land price myth," and "In this new age, utilization of land comes before ownership rights." The stickers were posted on government vehicles and taxicabs, and in Tokyo subway stations. If people believe that land prices are not too high, then a problem no longer exists. Maybe it worked. Recently, both land prices and stock prices have fallen, resulting in an estimated $1.1 trillion dollar loss.[5]

HAPPY-FACE PLUTONIUM

HAPPY-FACE PLUTONIUM   In 1993, Japan shipped highly toxic plutonium from France to Japan over the oceans. This shipment led to international protests and concern from those who realized that Japan currently has no nuclear power plants that can use this type of plutonium, and the countries that do have plants that can use it are abandoning them in favor of safer ones. Without nuclear power plants, the only use for this material is to make nuclear weapons. Why was the plutonium shipped at this time?

The environmental concerns of shipping plutonium halfway around the world across three oceans were serious. Any accident in which the plutonium escaped the containers would cause severe ecological damage.

Japanese officials were surprised by the international uproar over the shipment. They could have responded by confronting the problem. They could have indicated why they needed the plutonium. They could have explained how they were handling the safety concerns. Instead, they turned to the standard practice of *tatemae*: The problem must be merely an image problem. The solution: They printed a pamphlet, to be distributed to the Japanese public, which portrayed the plutonium containers as having happy faces, so that even if the ship sank, the containers would still be happy and the citizens would have no reason for concern.

COWS, BEER, AND MASSEUSES

COWS, BEER, AND MASSEUSES   Kobe beef, produced in a southern area of Japan, is reputed to be the highest quality beef in the world. If it is not the highest quality, it is certainly the most expensive. A pound of Kobe beef can run around $60. Kobe beef is characterized by the heavily marbled texture of the fat running through the meat. Fat is very important to the appearance of beef in Japan.

---

[4]"Agency Campaign Will Seek to Dispel Land Cost 'Myth,'" *Japan Times*, November 17, 1990, p. 2.
[5]"Japan's Reversal of Fortune," p.39.

Kobe beef can be appreciated only if the customer buys into the image of this kind of beef. The producers of the beef claim that its high quality is a result of the effort put into producing it. According to this image, a Kobe cow actually leads a blissful life before being slaughtered. This life includes having beer and sake mixed with its feed and being massaged by the farmer, and all this contributes to the high quality and the high price. If we want to sell more beef in Japan, we need to provide more beer to our cattle on the range and bring in masseuses to replace the cowboys.

As it turns out, the image of beer and massages is just that, an image and not the reality. A reporter familiar with the situation says that the beer runs and the massages occur only when reporters are present. "Hand-feeding, rubdowns and barnyard beer fests are staged by clever Kobe cattle farmers strictly for the benefit of reporters and photographers," says the columnist in the *Japan Times*.[6] The rest of the time the cows live a normal cow life. The Japanese consumer does not necessarily buy the beef based on how it tastes—the reality—but will pay high prices for the beef based on the *tatemae*. If the *tatemae* is not the reality, this does not matter because the image is the important thing.

WILL THE TWAIN EVER MEET   Often the long working hours the Japanese are famous for are due to *tatemae* rather than necessity. The *Japan Times* has an interesting column about business etiquette for foreign workers entitled "The Twain Meet."[7] It is sort of a "Dear Abby" for the salaryman or office lady. (In Japan, an employee on a career track—nearly always a man—is called a salaryman; an office lady, or OL, is not on a career track.) The unusual feature is that there are two responses to each question: one from a Japanese woman expert on office etiquette and one from an American woman who has worked in Japan for a number of years.

An American woman working in a Japanese office wrote that the Japanese OLs complained about her leaving for home after finishing her work after a normal eight-hour day. The OLs stayed at their desks, even if they had nothing to do except read the paper or talk to other workers. They would not leave until their bosses left. The American worker would leave when she had finished her work for the day.

The responses from the two columnists were very different, reflecting the important differences between *tatemae* and reality. The Japanese columnist explained that it was important to the image of the office team for everybody to stay at work even if they had nothing to do. Damage the image of the team, and the office atmosphere would be damaged. The American columnist thought that leaving after the workday, as long as all the work was finished, was all right. To the Japanese

---

[6]Clint Hall, "An Occasion for Kobe Beef," *Japan Times,* October 4, 1990, p. 20.
[7]Fumiyo Miytake and Joy Norton, "Difficulty Managing the Gaijin Employee," October 4, 1990, p. 18.

workers the image of working long hours is more important than the reality of the work done, or the productivity achieved.

MOB-ENFORCED HARMONY   Japan has a stock market at which shares in companies are bought and sold. Japanese companies, like others around the world, hold annual shareholder meetings where company officials respond to questions from shareholders. Unlike investors in the American stock market, however, Japanese shareholders very seldom receive a stock dividend. The payoff comes in the form of rising stock prices, so that shares bought in previous years can be sold for a profit at a later date. This strategy presupposes a stock market and an economy that are continually expanding, a model that held for many years. In recent years, however, stock prices have fallen, and shareholders might be expected to be unhappy.

In Japan, though, shareholders are supposed to be happy. They are expected to invest in the company for the long run, and to be patient with some quarterly losses. In turn, the shareholders expect the company to be run efficiently, to have a plan for growth, and to be a vehicle for wise investment. The happy shareholders and the happy company officials are supposed to reinforce this harmonious relationship at the annual shareholders' meeting.

To have a disharmonious annual meeting would damage the image of happiness. If a bad image results from tough shareholder questions, then the image may become the reality. Japanese companies sometimes try to ensure that this does not happen. A profitable extortion business has been built by the Japanese Mafia, called the *Yakusa,* and other organized crime members to help Japanese corporations reinforce the harmonious shareholder meeting image.

Van Wolferen, in his book, *The Enigma of Japanese Power,* explains how the extortion business got started and how it works.[8] Shareholder meetings in Japan are an illusion; Japanese corporations do not really respond to questions or explain what they are doing, and Japanese shareholders are not really part of the corporate process. In a long and protracted court case after industrial poisoning allegedly caused deaths and birth defects, the victims decided that the court system was not allowing them access to company officials to answer questions about business practices. The Japanese court system is notoriously slow to respond when industrial concerns are involved; one case has been in the courts for over 30 years. Since the people who bring a case are required to foot all the legal bills while the case is in progress, very few victories can be expected when going against well-heeled companies.

---

[8]van Wolferen, *The Enigma of Japanese Power,* pp. 105-107.

The victims in the industrial poisoning case decided that one way they could get some answers would be to buy shares in the company, go to the annual shareholders' meeting, and ask tough questions. The result was a very un-Japanese meeting.

Members of the *Yakuza* were sent to beat up the victims of the industrial poisoning and enforce harmonious meetings. The *Yakuza*, and other crime figures, were quick to see the profit potential in this development.

Van Wolferen states that the extortion is very well organized, and almost genteel in the way it is carried out. The extortionists set up "research institutes" that publish economic reports on the company. The company pays to support the "research institute" and retain the "consultants." If the companies do not pay enough, company officials are grilled for hours at shareholder meetings. Van Wolferen reports that there were 6300 of these extortion businesses in 1982.

THE QUESTION OF OPEN MARKETS   The U.S. trade imbalance with Japan surpassed $60 billion in 1994. Such a massive imbalance is difficult to comprehend, and Japanese officials are very concerned about keeping American markets open. At the same time, they maintain that Japanese markets are also open to American products. If Japanese markets were really open, however, the imbalance would not be so high.

Before our trip to Japan, we bought the official line that Japan has open markets and American products do not sell in Japan because they are of inferior quality. Noboru Hatakeyama, Japan's vice minister for trade and industry listed the following reasons for America's poor import record in Japan:[9]

1. Japanese consumers will not buy low-quality American products.
2. American companies are not committed to staying in the Japanese market for the long haul.
3. Foreign companies are not punctual.
4. American companies have difficulty establishing long-term relationships because of their lack of knowledge of the Japanese culture, inability to speak the language, etc.

After living in Japan, and interacting daily with high-priced, low-quality Japanese products, we were less willing to accept the official reasons for the trade imbalance and were more likely to believe that there are severe impediments to trade.

Trade impediments do exist. For years, any foreign car brought into Japan to be sold had to be inspected individually by a Japanese inspector. The inspection and

---

[9]Prodigy interactive personal service news report, December 20, 1992.

the paperwork delayed each car by two months. There are no such restrictions for Japanese cars sold in the United States.

The Japanese retailing system is archaic, set up to support little mom-and-pop stores that would not be profitable if they had to operate in a more competitive environment. Among other restrictions, Japanese law limits the square footage allowed for retail outlets. Thus, products go through several middlemen, each of whom adds to the price, and getting products into this pipeline is extremely difficult for outsiders. It would be much simpler to sell foreign products in Japan if they could be sold through large chain stores, as in the United States, but the mom-and-pop store law limits this possibility.

If the laws do not ensure limited access for foreign products, then the matter can be turned over to the *Yakuza*. Michael Lewis reports in *Pacific Rift* that an American company decided to combat the problem of high-priced beef by flying over American cows, raising them in Japan, and then processing the beef there. There were no laws to cover this scenario, so the company's Japanese competitors brought in the *Yakuza* to convince the Americans that their scheme was not a good idea. The Japanese employees of the American companies were told that it might be detrimental to their health to continue working there. As a result, the cow-raising scheme was quickly put to pasture, so to speak.[10]

The reality is that trade impediments do exist. The reality does not always have to correspond to the image, however. Noboru Hatakeyama, the vice minister mentioned previously, was worried about the new Clinton administration's approach to the trade imbalance between the two countries. After talking to officials in Washington, Hatakeyama said, "We can't find the right measures to cure the situation [trade friction] if the US doesn't change its perception that Japan is closed."[11] It is interesting to note that he did not say Japan's markets were open; he merely said that the image, or perception, of a closed market must be changed. As long as the image corresponds to official policy, then everything will work fine.

After talking to American business representatives about the advantages of leaving the economy to "market mechanisms," Kiyohiko Nanao, Japan's top economic representative to the United States, let his guard down while talking to an American reporter. The ability of this high-level Japanese minister to separate the rhetoric of the image of an open market in Japan from the reality was revealed briefly. The reporter asked him if Japan would voluntarily open, its markets out of self-interest. The reply was quick: With a shake of his head, Nanao said that opening the markets by removing the structural barriers of rules and restrictions on foreign goods would be difficult politically, because too many Japanese workers would lose

---

[10]Lewis, *Pacific Rift*, pp. 25–28.
[11]Prodigy interactive personal service news report, December 10, 1992.

their jobs.[12] The implication was that many Japanese industries are not competitive and would lose out under foreign competition. The image conveyed officially to the rest of the world—the image of an open market in Japan—does not correspond to the reality even in the minds of the Japanese officials projecting the image.

LIKE A MADONNA   Japanese officials are certainly cognizant of the image Japan presents to the rest of the world. Tsuyoshi Nakai, the director for international trade policy planning at the powerful Ministry of International Trade and Industry, wrote an article entitled "Wanted: A New Image."[13] In it he states that "Americans have some difficulty in conjuring up a well-balanced vision of Japan, with images swinging between a Japan of traditional beauty and a Japan of highly competitive industries and technologies." He goes on to state that the positive image of America, which "emphasizes its virtues of human rights and fairness," has been achieved internationally because foreigners flock to see American movies where people can "discover the 'human face' of ordinary American society."

Nakai wonders "how many Japanese movies I would have been able to see in Paris" and "why can't movies depicting the dramas of young contemporary Japanese be daily fare for theaters in European cities?" He complains that one of the only movies on Japan seen by wide audiences was *The Last Emperor*, which presented a poor image of Japan because it showed the "cruelty of the Japanese military."

This last comment is reflective of the differences between the image and the reality. It does not really matter that the movie was based on actual events. The Japanese military *was* cruel during the occupation of China before World War II. In Japan, past reality, if unpleasant, can be dismissed as an image problem. In fact, many Asian countries, remembering the cruelty imposed upon them by the Japanese military occupations of the 1930s, are very worried about evidence indicating that Japan is ignoring and revising this sordid past. They are worried that, as Japan becomes more powerful, the same kinds of things could happen again. South Korea's foreign minister, Choi Ho Joong, responding to the possibility that Japan would start sending troops abroad in response to the Gulf War, stated: "We who suffered from Japanese militarism in the past cannot help but take a deep interest and concern, along with other Asian nations who experienced similar suffering."[14]

---

[12]John McCarron, "The Trade Medicine Japan Is Afraid to Take," *Chicago Tribune,* November 6, 1994, Section 7, p. 2.
[13]Tsuyoshi Nakai, "Wanted: A New Image: The 'Human Face' of Today's Japan Is Hidden Behind Images of Samurai and Ukiyo-e Paintings," *Japan Times,* October 22, 1990, p. 9.
[14]"Fear of Militarism Spreads: Japan's Neighbors Wary of Changes in SDF Role," *Japan Times,* October 26, 1990, p. 3.

Like most people, the Japanese try to see their military forces in the best possible light. They looked on with envy as American movie studios produced films such as *Top Gun*, in which the best Navy pilots are sent to an elite combat school. When these symbols of American *machismo* arrive at the school, they are surprised to find that a top instructor is a woman. After initial disbelief that a woman could teach them anything, the pilots come to respect her and learn all about the important things such as love, life, and death.

In reaction to this positive image of American militarism, Japan's Self-Defense Forces (SDF) decided that they needed some good image enhancement, and two movies were produced: *Best Guy* and *A La Maniere de Madonna ("Like a Madonna")*. Although the essence of *Top Gun* was copied in these two films, they had to be changed to make them more believable to Japanese audiences. Whereas in *Top Gun* the woman character was a strong person who could live and teach in the world of tough Navy pilots, in *Like a Madonna* the woman lead was an older Japanese businesswoman whom the two elite SDF personnel, as described by a film reviewer, "end up 'sharing'. . . in a single house."[15]

Japan can keep on serving its purposes well if Japanese movies are *not* seen by the rest of the world. Too often, Japan's insularity and misunderstanding of the rest of the world is manifested in its popular culture, and especially its movies. The rest of the world is generally ignorant of Japanese attitudes toward foreigners. If Japanese movies were shown worldwide, their attitudes toward foreigners would become obvious.

DOUBLE PANIC '90   The images presented on television and in movies have a powerful influence on perceptions of other societies and cultures. The export of American action films, for instance, reinforces the Japanese belief that America is an amoral, violent society on the verge of collapse. Some of the images we saw in Japan are difficult for us to ignore. There was, for instance, the Japanese prime-time comedy show in which a Japanese actor, made up in blackface, portrays a black jazz musician in New York City. The high comic point comes when he walks in on his prostitute mother right when she is finishing with a Japanese customer. On the basis of the canned laughter on the laugh track, this was supposed to be a very funny part of the show.

Japanese stereotypes of foreigners and Americans in particular were exemplified in a movie shown on Japanese TV during our visit to Japan. This movie, called *Double Panic '90 Los Keisatsu Dai-sosasen*, must have been produced with an American audience in mind because the actors, both Americans and Japanese, spoke

---

[15]Akiko Kusaoi, "Silver Screen Seen as Key to Improved SDF Image," *Japan Times*, November 25, 1990, p. 2.

English throughout the movie. The plot centered around a third-generation Japanese-American working in the Asian special investigation unit of the Los Angeles Police Department. Shortly after having a quarrel with his wife over his job, his daughter and a neighbor's daughter are kidnapped for ransom.

The abduction occurs in a Japanese bank in downtown Los Angeles and the American villains randomly gun down innocent bystanders. Being bad but inept, the bank robbers botch the robbery after being foiled by a high-tech security system, and decide instead to kidnap the two Japanese-American children for ransom.

After chasing around the Los Angeles area, including scenes of all the graffiti, desolation, and destruction in the poorest LA neighborhoods, the bad guys retire to their isolated mountain cabin to demand the ransom. Somehow, one of the children outsmarts the kidnappers so she can communicate their location.

In one of the weirdest rescue scenes ever filmed, the police detective decides that a Japanese tourist bus, carrying dozens of Japanese-American policemen, his wife, and other interested onlookers, will provide a good cover for sneaking up on the kidnappers. The detective fakes a breakdown of the tourist bus (probably American-made) at the cabin so he can ask to make a phone call to get a replacement for the bus. With a Japanese tourist bus parked in front of the cabin in the middle of nowhere, even the doltish kidnappers perceive that something is not quite right.

A standoff ensues when the kidnappers threaten to kill the children if they are not allowed to escape from their mountain cabin. The kidnappers retreat to an inner room and the pregnant girl friend of one of the kidnappers is left in the kitchen with the wife of the police detective. This provides the opportunity for the wife to gain the confidence of this American woman.

Wife: "Why did you kidnap the children?"

Girl friend: "I am pregnant, and we do not have any money to support the child. We decided to rob the Japanese bank because the Japanese have all the money, and we have none. We have to do something for the child."

The wife then tries to gain the confidence of the woman by talking about her pregnancy.

Wife: "You know you have to take care of the baby before it is born, don't you? Do you know about prenatal care?"

Girl friend (getting very worried): "What is that ten-dollar word, prenatal care? What does it mean?"

Then the wife explains to the ignorant American about how the baby should be cared for before it is born. The American is fascinated by this bit of knowledge and trust develops between the two women. The wife also offers to help the woman with the care of the unborn child. As a result, the girl friend finally persuades her boy friend to give up the kidnapped children.

The movie portrays Americans as being randomly violent, poor, and unbelievably ignorant. The Americans are too lazy to try to work for the money to support the unborn child, and so they rely on violence against the hard-working Japanese to achieve their goals. Americans are portrayed as being jealous of the wealth the Japanese have achieved, and willing to do anything to get the money away from them. The underlying message is that if Americans would just listen to the motherly advice from Japan, then all our problems could be solved. We really don't need to be violent; we will be taken care of. This movie, if typical, is illuminating of the perceptions the Japanese have of Americans.

"HIT THE DECK"   We watched American movies that appeared on Japanese TV, which usually were broadcast with English dialogue provided on the SAP (Second Audio Program). The selection of American movies on Japanese television stations seemed to be chosen to emphasize the negative aspects of American society. *Robocop,* one of the more violent movies ever produced, was a particular favorite on Japanese television.

Another American movie was *Death Wish,* which helped pioneer excessive violence in American cinema. In *Death Wish,* Charles Bronson's daughter is raped and his wife killed by archetypal American crazies. Because of the breakdown of society, especially the judicial system which provides undue rights to criminals, Bronson has to take matters into his own hands by hunting down and killing the villains. The week before the movie was aired, advertisements appeared promoting it during the hours preceding dinner time. Several promotional ads appeared during *Wonder Woman,* a show that our two sons usually watched. The advertisement showed perhaps the most violent scene in the movie, the rape and killing of the women. In order to watch *Wonder Woman,* our children had to agree to close their eyes and put their heads down whenever the theme music for the movie previews started or whenever we yelled "Hit the deck!" (One advantage of a small apartment is that you can keep an ear on whatever shows your children are watching.) Japanese children probably don't have such rules and learn at an early age the negative stereotypes of Americans selected to be shown on Japanese TV.

Another American movie on Japanese TV during our visit was *No Way Out,* the Kevin Costner/Sean Young movie in which Costner is a Soviet spy who has turned against his own country. Once again, the movie was heavily promoted during showings of *Wonder Woman.* The scene used in the promotion was the one where Sean Young is thrown off a balcony and comes crashing down on a glass coffee table. "Hit the deck!"

STEREOTYPES   Images in American movies are created by Hollywood about Americans. Most adult Americans accept these images as fiction and are able to separate the images from the reality. Children have a difficult time with this concept, though. Our problem with these violent American movies was not that they were shown on Japanese television, but that they were shown unedited and in prime time. Also, choosing the most violent scenes to promote during children's viewing times provided Japanese children with powerful images about foreigners which will shape their opinions and attitudes as they grow up.

One of the surprising things about talking to people in Japan was the widespread belief that life in the United States must be worse than our experiences indicated. We could not understand how the perceptions of the United States held by the people we talked with could be so much worse than the reality. The adults apparently came to think of these violent movies as being closer to documentaries than fiction.

We began to understand the power that Hollywood movies have on Japanese perceptions of foreigners. In Japan, everyone knows the difference between the *tatemae* (the image) and the *honne* (the reality). In the United States, the opposite is true. We tend to emphasize the negative, for whatever reasons. Television news shows always seem to feature the most violent crimes, we will search for any kind of corruption that may occur in government, and we are fascinated by the possible evil-doings of big business. Sometimes the smallest problem gets the biggest scrutiny. In the United States, the image is usually worse than the reality.

To the Japanese, the image is often better than the reality. The reverse is true in America. Japanese TV shows seem to emphasize the negatives about life in the United States. To the Japanese, if the image is bad, the reality must be even worse. This characterized the beliefs of the Japanese we talked to during our stay. The image of foreigners as portrayed in films is one of violence. The image of foreigners presented by Japanese politicians is often one of laziness and lack of discipline. These images affect how Japanese consumers view American and other foreign products. Images can have a powerful effect on the perception of reality.

CHAPTER FOUR

What Is Quality?

How does a country remain prosperous? How does a group of people stay prosperous? Some people will say it is because those people work hard, or because they have a manufacturing base upon which to build. Recently, many prophets of quality have been saying that prosperity is based on a people's or a country's ability to produce high-quality products. What is the secret of high-quality products and, consequently, the secret of prosperity?

Quality prophets often gain a following by reciting the magic words: quality function deployment, continuous improvement, Taguchi methods, total quality management. How does one separate the true prophets from the false prophets, the substantive methods from the superstitious practices? How readily superstitious behavior can be resorted to is illustrated by the story of the Cargo Cult.

THE CARGO CULT In World War I and again in World War II, the natives of New Guinea were discovered by the outside world because of the strategic location of their islands. The natives were amazed by the exotic possessions of the foreigners and were naturally curious about the source of the cargo which was unloaded first from ships and then from planes. They determined that the cargo probably had been made by gods in some far-off location. They wanted to learn the secret of the cargo and, thus, the secret of the prosperity of the foreigners.

Through the years, many groups came to the New Guineans promising prosperity, salvation, or some equivalent. The natives had difficulty understanding these abstract concepts, so the foreigners tried to tie them to something the natives knew about: cargo.

Christian missionaries were among the first foreigners to visit New Guinea. The successful missionaries soon realized that abstract Christian dogma would not make converts of the natives: They had to promise something more concrete in exchange for the natives' devotion. They promised cargo. The natives soon understood Bible verses when they were put in more meaningful words. The anthropologist Marvin Harris, in the book *Cows, Pigs, Wars and Witches*,[1] reports that the natives took the Bible phrase "and God blessed Noah," to mean "and God gave Noah cargo." The natives translated the famous verse from Matthew, "Seek ye first the kingdom of God, and his righteousness; and all these things shall be added unto you," as "Good Christians will be rewarded with cargo."

The natives attended to their Christian duties by singing hymns, by reciting what to them were the magic words, and by giving up their extra wives. By the 1930s, however, the natives were becoming agitated because they realized that even with all their hard work, the cargo was still going to the foreigners.

In the early 1940s, the Japanese landed and they claimed they held the secrets of the cargo. They told the natives that if they helped the Japanese win the Pacific War, the secret of the cargo would be revealed to them and they would be part of Japan's Greater East Asia Co-Prosperity Sphere.

Imperial Japan had a vision in the 1920s and 1930s that Japan would lead Asia out of Western influence and into a new Asian world dominated by Japan. The invasion and subsequent occupation of China, so Japan could obtain China's natural resources, was justified on the basis of the Co-Prosperity Sphere as the first step that would lead China to greater riches under Japan's leadership. Japan's invasion of Indonesia in the first stages of the Pacific War, although ostensibly to allow Japan control over the crucial oil fields, was justified as eventually leading Indonesia to greater prosperity.

In 1942, Japanese soldiers landed in New Guinea with the promise that, although they did not come bearing cargo for the natives, shiploads of cargo would be delivered once New Guinea became a part of the Greater East Asia Co-Prosperity

---

[1]Marvin Harris, *Cows, Pigs, Wars and Witches*. (New York: Vintage Books, 1974), p. 139.

Sphere after the war. But as the Allies cut their supply lines, the Japanese were left without any cargo at all. Harris describes the situation: "The [Japanese] began to strip the native gardens, coconut groves, and banana and sugar-cane plantations. They stole every last chicken and pig. When they were all gone, they fell upon the dogs and ate them. And when the dogs were gone, they hunted down the natives and ate them, too."[2]

The Americans and Australians also promised the New Guineans cargo if they assisted in the war effort. The natives were especially intrigued by the airstrips that were built on the island, the communication systems to summon the planes, and the planes themselves—loaded with cargo. After the war, the soldiers eventually left, along with their cargo. The natives, though, thought they had the secret of the cargo. They erected airstrips in the middle of the jungle. Primitive thatched-roof huts were built close to the airstrips. Tin-can phones were placed inside the huts to communicate with the cargo planes. They said the magic words into the tin cans: "Over and out," "Roger," "Ten-four," and so forth. None of this worked. Some planes flew overhead, the natives went through their incantations, but the magic words from the foreigners off the island always managed to summon the planes elsewhere.

In subsequent years, several local prophets emerged, based on their perceived ability to summon the cargo. One prophet and his followers decided that an obscure G.I. by the name of John Frum was the king of America. Frum had apparently been on the island and had promised the natives cargo. It appears that Frum was a sergeant and a medic, because the natives decided that wearing a sergeant's field uniform would bring the cargo. Being a medic, it is possible that Frum was responsible for burying dead soldiers in graves surrounded by fences and topped by crosses. Observing this behavior, the natives placed crosses surrounded by fences all across the island to lure John Frum back. In 1970, the natives were still waiting for the second coming of John Frum with his promise of cargo.

Another prophet and his followers decided that the President of the United States, Lyndon Johnson at the time, must hold the secret of the cargo. They managed to save $75,000 to pay Johnson to become their king as long as Johnson told them the secret of the cargo. There is no word whether or not Johnson accepted the offer and the money.

Some Western leaders were concerned about the existence of the Cargo Cult and how the superstitions were misleading the natives. The Australians brought one of the better-known prophets to Australia to explain the secrets of the cargo. They showed him the manufacturing facilities. They showed him the breweries. He was especially impressed by the zoo. He visited the museum and was amazed to see native New Guinean artifacts carefully preserved behind glass cases; Austra-

---

[2]Ibid., p. 142.

lians came to this great museum building to reverently worship his culture's items—the same items the missionaries had scorned as being unworthy of worship by the natives.

The prophet was told that Australians worked hard for these items, and that the secret of the cargo was the presence of the manufacturing facilities. The prophet was somewhat skeptical, because he observed some people with a lot of cargo who apparently never worked in the factories or the breweries. He could not see the relationships between what these people did and the availability of the cargo.

THE QUALITY CULT   Is the cargo cult much different from the quality cult? The New Guineans tried to understand complex issues by translating them into their own experiences, religious beliefs, and superstitious practices. They could not comprehend the manufacturing process, so they believed that their ancestors came back as gods in far-off places and were therefore responsible for the exotic cargo.

They observed behavior such as planes landing at airstrips after GIs summoned them by radio. They tried to mimic this behavior without really understanding the technology involved or the underlying purpose of the behavior. The natives learned to recite the magic words, but the magic words did not work very well.

Prophets arose among the people. The fate and credibility of the prophets ebbed and flowed with the accuracy of their predictions and prophecies.

The natives developed myths about the cargo. When the ancestor-gods did not bring the cargo to the islands, they developed myths and stories about how the ancestor gods had been kidnapped but would soon be free to come with the cargo.

We have a quality cult which engages in some of the practices of the New Guinea cargo cult. Like the New Guineans, we want the cargo deliveries to continue. The prophets have told us that the secret of the cargo is in manufacturing high-quality products. We learn the magic words from the quality cult. We make up stories and myths about how products are manufactured in far-off places. We try to understand these things by translating them into our own experiences.

In our ignorance, we misunderstand the stories or the reasons behind the myths. To understand quality, we must disconnect the myths from the reality. A good starting place is a definition of quality.

DIMENSIONS OF QUALITY   Probably few people know exactly what is meant by quality. Quality actually has several different dimensions, which are all considered by consumers purchasing products. An article in the *Sloan Man-*

agement Review listed the five properties of quality as follows: manufacturing-based, user-based, product-based, value-based, and transcendent.[3]

The dimension that is most often associated with quality is the manufacturing-based one. Quality is defined as conformance to set requirements and is associated with the reliability of the product. An automobile that operates with high reliability would by this definition be judged as high quality. *Consumer Reports* analyzes this aspect by receiving feedback from readers on any problems they have had with products in the past. Japanese products often score high on this quality dimension.

Consumers may have different needs and wants, and if the product satisfies them, then it is high in user-based quality. This aspect can be associated with the number of features available on the product. A copy machine, as an example, may be perceived as high quality if it includes a collating function. In some cases, however, the needs and wants of the customer may be to reduce the number of features so that use of the product is simplified. Japanese manufacturers have recognized this recently by including fuzzy logic intelligence in washing machines, for example, which analyzes the dirtiness of the laundry and automatically sets the controls so that the user needs to push only one button to start it. Designers need to know the desires of the customers or users.

In the product-based approach, quality reflects the presence or absence of a chosen measurable product attribute. An automobile may be evaluated by the amount of trunk space or cabin space. A microchip for computer processes may be evaluated by the speed with which the chip can perform calculations. These attributes can be quantified and measured. In many cases, however, trade-offs with other measurable attributes are necessary. As an example, horsepower can be easily measured for automobiles, but increased horsepower leads to lower gas mileage. The size of the car, and thus the trunk space and cabin space, must also be traded off with gas mileage. Many trade-offs are involved with price. One microchip may be faster than others, but it will also cost more. The kinds of trade-offs consumers are willing to make is a subjective decision.

The fourth approach to quality is value-based in terms of cost and price. If a product can be manufactured at a low cost and still maintain quality on the other dimensions, then this is perceived as a high-quality product. Quality is, therefore, a reflection of the efficiency of manufacturing the product. If a company can turn out a product in a short amount of time, manufacturing costs will be lower and, thus, the price will be lower. If the workers are motivated, well trained, and educated, then the products should be high quality because they can be produced at a lower cost. This does not always hold true, however, because sometimes consumers believe that higher quality can only be achieved at a higher price. Given a choice between two

---

[3]David A. Garvin, "What Does 'Product Quality' Really Mean?," *Sloan Management Review,* Fall 1984, pp. 25-43.

products, with quality the main consideration instead of price, the consumer would likely choose the higher-priced product.

Although we as consumers may not know precisely what we mean by quality, we all recognize quality when we see it. This is the premise behind the transcendent approach, which defines quality as something that is accepted universally and that has an unanalyzable property recognized by experience.

MEASURING THE UNMEASURABLE   The perception of transcendent quality can be based on many things. An experiment run by an American car company illustrates the transcendent nature of quality. The company decided that the perception of quality depended partly on the way the car door or the trunk sounded when it was closed. They ran an experiment to try to confirm this by asking people to provide a rating for quality based on audio recordings of the sounds of various car doors closing. They found that the perception of quality did, indeed, change with different sounds and different cars. As expected, even though people in the experiment did not know which sounds were associated with which cars, Japanese cars scored higher on the sound of quality than American cars. The sound that a car door makes when closing can be manipulated during car design without changing the reliability of the door or any other objective factor of quality. Car designers should take into account this transcendent quality dimension. Quantifying the sound of a quality car is almost impossible, but everybody in the experiment seemed to agree on certain kinds of sounds as representing high quality. The Japanese car makers are very good at paying attention to these little things which affect the perception of quality; American manufacturers have not paid as much attention to these details. They should.

THE SUBJECTIVE COMPONENTS OF QUALITY

In analyzing the five approaches to quality, it becomes apparent that quality is largely subjective. Two of the approaches are based almost totally on subjective perceptions, two of them are based partially on these subjective perceptions, and the last is more objective but still has a subjective aspect.

The transcendent and user-based approaches are totally subjective when a product choice is being made. In the transcendent approach, the consumer feels that the product is high quality, but he or she cannot quantify this subjective feeling. The user-based approach is subjective because different consumers may have different needs. The manufacturer must conform to the subjective wishes of the consumer.

The value-based approach can be objective because price is quantifiable, but the consumer must decide if the price is lower because the quality is lower or because the product is being produced more efficiently. There is no simple way to determine this objectively. The product-based approach is somewhat objective because the attributes being considered are all quantifiable and measurable but, as indicated earlier, the trade-offs that must be made across these attributes are subjective on the part of the consumer.

Finally, reliability should be objective because data can be obtained on product problems. But even objective measures can have subjective components. As indicated earlier, *Consumer Reports* relies on self-reports from readers on reliability problems with products. Other questionnaires, such as the J. D. Power report on automobiles, also rely on self-reports from consumers. Sometimes these self-reports can be biased because of prior perceptions. If *Consumer Reports* indicates that a certain car has low reliability, then a consumer may be more likely to notice problems or consider something to be a problem when it actually is not.

Consider the following personal example to illustrate this point. We have a Ford Explorer which we took four-wheel driving in the Montana mountains. We were in a situation where we needed the low-range four-wheel drive. When the button was pushed to put the vehicle into this gear, nothing happened. Our first reaction was that this problem was because we were driving a poor-quality American car. We had owned this vehicle less than a year and were disappointed that it was already breaking down. We took it back to the dealer and told the mechanic the problem. He drove it and said nothing was wrong. However, when he saw how we had tried to get into low gear, he told us we were doing it incorrectly. The vehicle has to be in neutral before low gear will engage. We thought that depressing the clutch was the same as putting the car in neutral. It was not. Low gear turned out to work correctly. When we checked the owner's manual, there was no indication that the car has to be in neutral in order to engage low gear. Because of our perception of the quality of American products, our first reaction was that a reliability problem had occurred when it had not. The owner's manual was actually the source of the problem.

The perception of reliability can go in the other direction too. Previous to owning the Explorer, we owned a Toyota Celica. After 50,000 miles, which is the average lifespan of a car in Japan, we started having problems with the car. The electronic fuel injection system did not work correctly. The Toyota dealer said that the fuel injection rod was bent. Also, the throttle stuck every once in a while. Finally, the brakes squeaked whenever they were applied and the whole car shimmied; the dealer told us the drum brake was pitted. We had taken good care of this car, always servicing it at the intervals suggested by Toyota. After all these problems developed, we took the car in to get the problems fixed, and the Toyota mechanic told us the engine was shot. We decided to trade in the car, and bought a Toyota Supra. We still believed in Toyota quality.

This illustrates how people perceive quality, even something as supposedly objective as the reliability of the product. In the one case we were quick to attribute the problem to mechanical breakdown when it actually was not, and in the other case we ignored serious reliability problems and purchased another car from the same manufacturer despite numerous problems with the first. We had been so conditioned on the subjective aspects of quality that it was difficult for us to evaluate it objectively.

If we had to do a self-report on reliability problems with the two cars, we might have reported any minor thing that occurred on the Ford. We might have dismissed, however, the problems with the Toyota as being anomalies not worth reporting. After all, our problems seemed to be unique. From reading *Consumer Reports* and similar publications, other people did not seem to have the same kinds of problems. If our problems with the Toyota were not unique, then maybe, somehow, they were our fault. We had ourselves to blame for not driving the car correctly, not changing the oil often enough, or committing some other kind of perceived car ownership sin.

If the Toyota Celica had been an American product, we probably would have referred derogatorily to the poor American quality and vowed never again to buy a product from that American company. We had bought into the myth of Japanese quality.

COGNITIVE DISSONANCE   Our personal experience with ignoring reliability problems in Japanese products but overplaying perceived reliability problems in American products may or may not be typical. Whatever the case, there is a term in psychology to explain this kind of phenomenon: cognitive dissonance. According to this concept, we build up certain expectations, and when our expectations are not met, we experience cognitive dissonance and blame ourselves instead of changing our expectations. With Japanese products, we have developed high expectations of quality and reliability. When these expectations are not met, we blame ourselves for not using the product properly. In other words, we "sinned" by not using the product correctly, and we had to "atone" by buying another product from the same company and then using it correctly.

The issue is really how the high expectations developed in the first place. That is what the rest of this book is about. How have the myths of Japanese quality products been created and perpetuated? Additionally, how have the perceptions of Japanese consumers been molded so that they will not buy non-Japanese products because they expect foreign products to be inferior to their own?

Just as the cargo cult people developed their own magic words to explain difficult concepts, the prophets of the quality cult have developed magic words. The next two chapters examine the magic words of quality.

The "Magic Words" of the Deming Management Method

Most people in business have heard the "magic words" of quality, but not everyone knows what they mean. The following terms should, however, be familiar to anyone planning to compete in world markets: the Deming management method; statistical quality control; Taguchi methods; continuous improvement; just-in-time manufacturing; and quality function deployment. The contributions of each of these will be examined in this and the following chapter. First, consider the Deming management method.

DEMING'S WILD WEST SHOW W. Edwards Deming has become almost a mythical character, a prophet of considerable stature among the followers of the quality cult. Deming was an early adherent of statistical quality control (SQC), a method for controlling manufacturing processes by determining when products are out of statistical control and, thus, when they are no longer being manufactured within specifications (see Chapter 6). When a product deviates from specification—that is, it is out of statistical control—quality decreases. Although these statistical methods were developed in the United States, mainly at AT&T, the story and the emerging myth is that American companies paid very little attention to Deming's message and to quality in general following World War II.

Deming accompanied the occupational forces to Japan after World War II. Starting in the late 1940s and continuing through the 1950s, Deming held long, patient meetings with Japanese business leaders in which he indicated that Japanese business could be rebuilt if statistical quality techniques were implemented. Although they were skeptical at first, Deming finally found a following among the top management of several Japanese businesses.

Thus, Japanese business was reborn. The quality of Japanese products increased to the point where they were hailed as world leaders in quality. The Japanese businesses credited Deming as being one of the main components in their successful effort to manufacture quality products. The Deming award, created by the Japanese government in recognition of his contributions to Japanese industry, is awarded annually to the company that exhibits the best techniques in manufacturing quality products. Deming spent his later years carrying the same message to American companies; this time they listened. Many American companies, including Ford, IBM, and Xerox, have made the commitment to Deming management methods, with tangible improvements in quality.

Since this book deals with myths, it is interesting to note that when Deming was growing up in Cody, Wyoming, he knew the most famous resident of the town, Buffalo Bill Cody. Deming speaks fondly of the time he went to see Buffalo Bill's Wild West Show in Los Angeles and Buffalo Bill himself recognized Deming in the audience. Buffalo Bill was the premier myth maker at the turn of the century. In many ways, W. Edwards Deming inherited this myth maker mantle.

Buffalo Bill Cody and W. Edwards Deming have much in common. They apparently knew each other. They had the same first name, although Deming preferred to use his middle name. Buffalo Bill's Wild West Show included a pageant called the Pages of Passing History. Deming's Wild West Show demonstrated that history had passed by American industry.

Most important, the two Williams put on good shows. Both shows traveled the world entertaining audiences by creating and perpetuating myths about the Wild West. The faceless American workers in Deming's show—similar to the parade of cowboys, Indians, mountain men, and Rough Riders at the end of Buffalo Bill's show—are paraded across world stages as uneducated and violent people living in a fantasy world of American industrial supremacy that may have existed at one time but no longer does. In Deming's show, American managers are similar to the cowboys or Rough Riders in the Wild West Show: They would rather shoot from the hip, accomplishing short-term solutions while the ramifications of their decisions are lost in the void of short attention spans.

Buffalo Bill was very colorful and put on a good show. His depiction of the Wild West was not supposed to be accurate; it was supposed to be entertaining. The myths were much more entertaining than the reality. Nobody would come to see Buffalo Bill's Tame West Show. Deming's Wild West Show was also entertaining. The anecdotes and myths in Deming's show were much more entertaining than the reality.

A QUALITY TEST   To be entertaining and popular, a story line must be simple and easy to follow. One of the desirable attributes of the Deming method is its simplicity. He relates his management technique in terms of a small set of points which must be adhered to (the "Fourteen Points") and those which must be avoided (the "Seven Deadly Diseases"). Quality commitment requires a dedication to the cause from top management down. Before talking about the Fourteen Points and the Seven Deadly Diseases, a test designed by the authors in terms of 12 scenarios has been prepared to determine how well you would adhere to the Deming management method.

To take the test, read the following 12 scenarios, and then consider the two actions, a and b. For each of the actions, place a number in the space provided depending on whether you agree or disagree with the action. Use the following rating system:

4	I agree completely with the action.
3	I agree somewhat with the action.
2	I have no opinion on this action.
1	I disagree somewhat with the action.
0	I disagree completely with the action.

Scenario 1 A company is positioned in an aging market and hasn't made a profit for seven quarters. Instead of repositioning the company in another market, which may mean job losses, the company has decided not to shed any jobs. To their credit, they have retained their market share, but the overall market may be in decline. Indicate what you would do.

___(a)   Continue with the present policy and forgo profits.

___(b)   Reposition the company within another market and accept some job losses.

Scenario 2 *You, as a consumer, have read that Product A has been rated as being of higher quality than Product B. The consumer magazines agree on this, although they do not state exactly how they have determined this. Both products have the same kinds of features, although Product B costs 20% less than product A.*

___(a)   Buy Product A.

___(b)   Buy Product B.

Scenario 3 *In striving to keep down costs, a company decides to switch from a long-time supplier to a new supplier because the new supplier has offered to produce the product at a lower price. The company receives pressure from the bank which has been lending money to the supplier to retain the status quo.*

___(a)   Retain the old supplier.

___(b)   Switch to the lower-cost supplier.

Scenario 4 *A company has decided that the best way to improve efficiency and pro-ductivity is to make only small process improvements. Management predicts that if this company continues to make the same kinds of products on the same kind of produc-tion line, in ten years they will be able to achieve a 5% improvement in productivity due to these small changes. This will result in less disruption to the workers. Outsiders argue that in the ten-year period, new technology advances will become available and the company can make a "great leap" forward by implementing this advanced technol-ogy. What would you do in this situation?*

___(a)   Maintain the policy of making small changes.

___(b)   Make the "great leap" forward by implementing advanced technology.

Scenario 5 *The educational system is considered by insiders to be boring, irrelevant to the real world, with a concentration on menial and tedious tasks. Those students who excel in this system have distinguished themselves precisely because they have become adept at performing these irrelevant tasks. Students who show initiative or curi-osity are not rewarded and are often punished. Once the students get to college or university, most of their time is spent drinking, partying, and cutting classes. When these people are hired, the company has to spend much time and effort training them.*

___(a)   The company should hire only workers who have distinguished themselves in this kind of educational system.

___(b)   The company should place pressure on the educational system to produce a different kind of student so training costs can be reduced.

Scenario 6 A supervisor has decided that employees will no longer be evaluated using a standard system of performance assessment. Instead, the supervisor claims that she has a subjective evaluation for each employee in her head. She does not want to verbalize the evaluation method or commit it to paper so that the employees can see how the others were evaluated.

___(a)　　　Each person should be evaluated individually, and this evaluation should remain subjective.

___(b)　　　Some employees feel that the system is arbitrary and capricious, because each person is evaluated under different unspecified criteria. They argue that they are not getting any feedback on how to perform better.

Scenario 7 The company says that Janice has promise and has performed her duties well. The company has refused to give her a promotion, however, because people with more seniority, but without her ability, are above her in rank and pay. If you were in Janice's position, what would you do?

___(a)　　　Wait, do your job, and hope that a promotion will come eventually as the people with lesser ability move on to other positions.

___(b)　　　Write a resume and look for a job which will compensate you for your ability.

Scenario 8 A company has a large cafeteria in which everybody from all the departments eats together in the same room. Social pressure forces team members from the same department to eat together at the same table at the same time everyday. Anybody who decides to eat with another group or at another time is ostracized because he or she is hurting team cohesion.

___(a)　　　Team cohesion is more important than any benefits that may accrue when people from different departments and teams mingle with each other.

___(b)　　　Management should concentrate on eliminating the social pressure to eat with the team so that ideas can be exchanged freely between departments.

Scenario 9 *A large company has decided that all employees in the company, including secretaries and receptionists, should take a course on statistical quality control. The course would teach people how to recognize when a manufacturing process is out of control and is producing lower quality products.*

___(a)   Everybody in the company, regardless of his or her job duties, should know about these statistical concepts.

___(b)   Giving this training to everybody would be a waste of time, especially if the employee is never going to be on the production line.

Scenario 10 *In the last two quarters, the company has been losing profits because, some believe, it refuses to be flexible and deviate from the goals and purposes it set for itself several years ago.*

___(a)   The company should stay on the same plan and course that was set several years ago.

___(b)   The company should revise its goals and purposes based on its present performance.

Scenario 11 *A highly successful management team is hired by a company to turn it around. This management team has been credited with turning around five other companies in the last ten years. Outside directors felt that fresh ideas and a fresh perspective are needed.*

___(a)   This is a mistake, because this team has no stake in the company.

___(b)   The past successes of this management team should result in successes in the current situation.

Scenario 12 *Scenario 12. A company is considering the possibility of bringing in an outside expert to try to design a safer product in response to several lawsuits filed by lawyers working on contingency fees.*

___(a)   The money would be poorly spent, because there will always be lawyers complaining about products.

___(b)   The company should spend the money to bring in the outside expert to increase the safety of its products.

Now, go back and put negative signs in front of all the scores for action b; action a scores should remain positive. Add together all 24 scores (actions a and b for the 12 scenarios). Evaluate your scores as follows:

25 to 48 points   According to the Deming management method, you are committed to producing high-quality products.

1 to 24 points   According to the Deming management method, you are leaning in the right direction but are probably not willing to make the all-out effort to transform your company into one which produces high-quality products.

-24 to 0 points   According to the Deming management method, you are leaning in the wrong direction, but there still may be hope.

-48 to -25 points   According to the Deming management method, you have little hope of producing high-quality products in your company.

Everyone who has taken the test has scored in the negative numbers, which suggests that people find Deming's methods nonintuitive. We chose the scenarios, anecdotes, and stories to support a position counter to the Deming management method which can be quite radical and nonintuitive. Is this fair? Our choice of anecdotes could certainly be criticized because we do not offer a balanced view of the situation. Our evaluation of the Deming management method should not be based solely on an anecdotal test, because an anecdote can always be found to support an opposite position. Choosing anecdotes, stories, and scenarios to support a certain position is easy. We chose scenarios and anecdotes to show how radical the Deming management method can be. Deming chose other anecdotes to show how reasonable his method was when compared to others.

Just as our "quality test" can be termed unfair because of the scenarios and anecdotes that we chose to make our points, Deming's practice of supporting his Fourteen Points and Seven Deadly Diseases can also be termed unfair. When we went back to Deming's original writings to determine how he supported his methods, we found that support was provided only through anecdotes and stories. The purpose of our test is to show how anecdotes can be found to support any position and other anecdotes can be found to counter that same position. A war of anecdotes cannot produce a clear winner.

FOURTEEN POINTS   As the Fourteen Points and the Seven Deadly Diseases are discussed, the scenarios will be discussed in relation to relevant points. The Fourteen Points are:

1. *Create constancy of purpose for improvement of product and service.* Deming insists that the most important business of business is not necessarily to make money, but to create jobs and stay in business. An overreliance on making money often means that important job-creating functions such as training, research, and constant improvement are neglected. In scenario 1, the company would be unwilling to do anything to lose jobs, so Deming would agree with part a and not part b. This policy works as long as the market is expanding.

2. *Adopt the new philosophy.* Deming claims that Americans are too tolerant of poor workmanship. In one sense, this may be a reflection of the standards of American consumers, who shop based on price as much as quality. Scenario 2 describes a buying decision. A Japanese consumer would buy solely on the reputation of the product; an American consumer would consider price. Since price is not a consideration in Japan, Japanese products are very high priced.

3. *Cease dependence on mass inspection.* Mass inspection is needed if the process produces poor-quality products, and some products must be scrapped or reworked. If the process can be improved, and if the workers in the process have the power to shut down the line when a problem occurs, then scrap and reworks are not produced, thus saving money.

4. *End the practice of awarding business on price tag alone.* Most manufacturing companies depend on suppliers for products. Often the supplier is chosen on price alone, without regard to quality. Western companies think that encouraging competitive bidding provides incentives to keep prices low. In the Deming management method, quality is more important than price because poor quality will result in more scrap and more rework in the company being supplied. Manufacturing companies must develop good relationships with suppliers, and both must work to maintain quality. Japanese companies have developed tightly knit cartels, called *keiretsu,* which work together to produce high-quality products. Each *keiretsu* is usually controlled by a single bank, and the *keiretsu* cannot be pulled apart by price alone. This is one of the reasons that American companies have failed to become suppliers to Japanese transplant companies in the United States—

they cannot become part of the *keiretsu* by offering lower prices or, in some cases, even superior quality products. In scenario 3, the bank would dictate that the *keiretsu,* and thus the old supplier, be maintained whatever the cost.

5. *Improve constantly and forever the system of production and service.* One of the great successes of Japanese companies is continuous improvement in the manufacturing process. Whereas American companies have relied on the "great leap" to improve process efficiency, Japanese companies rely on small improvements which, taken together over a long period of time, amount to significant change. Japanese manufacturing plants are often less automated than their American counterparts. For continuous improvement, though, a manufacturing plant must turn out a large number of items over a long period of time. American plants, through loss of market share in high-quantity items, are turning to more specialized products which do not afford the kinds of quantity needed for the institutionalization of continuous improvement. In scenario 4, a company managed under the Deming management method would maintain the policy of making small changes.

6. *Institute training.* American workers often rely for training on poorly trained coworkers. Japanese companies place great emphasis on training their own workers, and less emphasis on the kind of training that workers receive in a university. Japanese workers' educational training prior to getting a job rewards those people who are highly trainable, as evidenced by their willingness to spend long hours learning irrelevant material. Scenario 5 describes the Japanese educational and university system (see Chapter 13), which produces the highly trainable but uncreative workers described in part (a).

7. *Institute leadership.* Leadership is not necessarily used to provide incentives or punishment to workers. Leaders should try to understand each worker individually, and decide what is needed to make each person perform to his or her level at the correct job. Scenario 6 describes such a subjective system of performance assessment. This provides the manager with much control over employees because the assessment does not have to be standardized or justified.

8. *Drive out fear.* One of the biggest fears is loss of one's job. This often pits the American worker against management. Japanese workers, with the promise of lifetime employment—at least within the large companies—do not fear the loss of their jobs. If a worker fears that his or her job will be lost, there is little motivation to perform the job to high standards. Scenario 7 describes a

person caught in this kind of system. If Janice leaves the company she may have trouble finding another job, because other companies will doubt her willingness to stay with a company and share in its company spirit.

9. *Break down barriers between staff areas.* Workers must operate as a team. In many cases, the team is from the same department. The problem comes when teamwork must be achieved with people from different perspectives and different departments. Conflicting goals from different departments must be resolved and must not hurt the company. Scenario 8 describes an effort to break down the barriers. In Japan, though, the small teams are so important that team members spend all their time together. Anyone who tries to break away from the team, even by eating lunch with someone else, is ostracized. It is difficult to break down the barriers between teams while at the same time the teams are trying to develop their cohesion and team spirit.

10. *Eliminate slogans, exhortations, and targets for the workforce.* Slogans such as zero defects or increasing productivity do not really attack the problem about how to achieve these goals.

11. *Eliminate numerical quotas.* Quotas can be achieved at the expense of quality. This point runs counter to the business practice of management by objective, where quotas and goals are set at each level of the organization. Leadership should be substituted for quotas.

12. *Remove barriers to pride of workmanship.* Deming claims that workers want to feel proud of their jobs. No matter how trivial the job, the Japanese worker is made to feel proud of his or her work. American workers often downplay the significance of their jobs, and rationalize poor performance.

13. *Institute a vigorous program of education and retraining.* The Deming maagement method must be taught to all workers. They should understand teamwork and statistical quality control. Scenario 9 describes this situation.

14. *Take action to accomplish the transformation.* Both management and lower-level workers must take action to implement these methods. Lower-level workers cannot do it on their own; top management cannot do it on their own either, but they can provide the important direction.

SEVEN DEADLY DISEASES The seven deadly diseases are:

1. *Lack of constancy of purpose.* A company must have a long-range plan, constantly pursued, for staying in business. Much has been made of the fact that some Japanese companies have a 200-year plan. Long-range plans are good, but scenario 10 describes a situation where a company must be flexible instead of locked into an unworkable plan. Sometimes long-range plans are written in such general terms that they become meaningless.

2. *Emphasis on short-term profits.* This is just the opposite of constancy of purpose. If the plan is pursued, profit may be eliminated in some quarters, but that must be accepted. Scenario 10 also describes a situation where a company has not made a profit but it causes no concern.

3. *Evaluation by performance, merit rating, or annual review of performance.* Ratings of performance can destroy teamwork and encourage unhealthy competition among the workers. Leadership should be used to provide feedback and training to the workers, and to provide individual help when needed.

4. *Mobility of management.* Constancy of purpose, for achieving quality and productivity, will not occur if management moves around too much. Under the Deming management method, an outside management team (described in scenario 11), even though successful in similar areas, would be suspect. Japanese companies have difficulty finding fresh ideas inside a company.

5. *Running a company on visible figures alone.* Some effects, such as customer satisfaction, are not so easy to measure but could be important to the performance of the company.

6. *Excessive medical costs.* These costs hurt American companies especially, because they cannot be added to the quality of the product. When Japanese transplant companies build plants in the United States, they are careful to hire young, healthy workers to reduce health care costs. Competing American companies do not have this benefit because they are locked into their older workers.

7. *Excessive costs of warranty, fueled by lawyers who work on contingency fees.* The litigious nature of American society hurts American products. Scenario 12, though, describes a situation in which lawsuits could actually help to make products safer. Before going to Japan, we also believed that lawyers were hurting American companies. After seeing unsafe Japanese products, we started to believe that a healthy dose of litigiousness would increase the safety of their products. Japanese companies now have no incentive to build safety into their products at home.

DEMING AT WORK   Do these management techniques work? As we stated earlier, Deming's proof for these management methods is entirely in the form of anecdotes and stories. Mary Walton, in *The Deming Management Method*,[1] illustrates how good the method is by providing examples of its use in several American businesses: Ford; Honeywell Information Systems; Malden Mills of Lawrence, Massachusetts; the AT&T Merrimack Valley Works in Andover, Massachusetts; Janbridge, Inc., in Philadelphia; Microcircuit Engineering Corporation in Mt. Holly, New Jersey; and the Campbell Soup Company. The examples provided are quite compelling as evidence for these techniques.

Where are these companies now, ten years after the Walton book was published? We still eat Campbell's soup. In recent years, Ford has been a dramatic success story, incorporating all kinds of quality techniques to manufacture quality cars with short development times. Malden Mills continues to be a leader in the textile industry, utilizing many imaginative techniques to improve its processes and services to customers. Two of the other companies are fairly small and are not heard from very often.

Honeywell Information Systems is another story, though. The Walton book, published in 1986, extolled the efforts made by Honeywell Information Systems to implement the Deming management method. In 1987, the division was bought out by Groupe Bull, the government-owned French computer company, and NEC Corporation, the giant Japanese electronics company. Since NEC is a Japanese company pursuing quality products, and Honeywell Information Systems practiced the Deming management method, good things should have emerged from this alliance. But one of the first things the new management did was to lay off 1600 workers and close several U.S. plants in 1987. Honeywell had most of its business in U.S. government contracts, but this business soon dried up as the agencies changed to other computer manufacturers. A search of a business database on Honeywell Bull, as it is now called, turned up only six entries between 1990 and 1994, and most of these articles dealt with how companies were moving away from Honeywell computers to the products of other companies. Being unresponsive to changing customer needs, Honeywell completely missed out on the move from mainframes to smaller networked computer systems and workstations. Practicing the Deming management method is not enough to ensure success. Likewise, being owned by a Japanese company does not guarantee success either.

The Deming management method will be critiqued further in later chapters (refer to Chapters 12 and 16. The test earlier in this chapter shows that, for certain scenarios and anecdotes, many of Deming's ideas are radical. His writings are also very inconsistent and difficult to follow. *Out of the Crisis*, the main source for Dem-

---

[1]Mary Walton, *The Deming Management Method* (New York: Dodd, Mead, 1986),

ing's management method, is not an example of quality prose. Two things should be taken from his teachings, though. First, top management must be involved in advocating quality. Second, statistical quality control should be used on the production line. As will be shown in later chapters, it is unclear whether successful companies, in Japan or the United States, follow his management method.

CHAPTER · SIX

More "Magic Words" of Quality

Other "magic words" of quality have been invoked to keep the cargo coming. These include statistical quality control, Taguchi techniques, constant improvement, just-in-time manufacturing, and quality function deployment.

STATISTICAL QUALITY CONTROL Two products manufactured on the same manufacturing line approximately at the same time will be different from each other. Sometimes this can be accepted, other times it cannot. Unacceptable variability occurs when something in the process can be changed to reduce the variability. The temperature in a chemical process may be set wrong, the operator of a machine may do something slightly different, the dials on a machine may be set wrong, the tool for drilling a hole in metal may become dull, or the orifice of a paint gun may become clogged. When these things happen, statistical quality control (SQC) techniques are used to determine if the process is statistically out of control.

Variability which cannot be assigned to a particular cause is called random variability. W. Edwards Deming used a paddle-and-bead demonstration to illustrate random variability. In this demonstration, 800 red and 3200 white beads are mixed up inside a bag. Deming explained that the company manufactured white beads, although sometimes red beads get into the process. The company's customers will not accept any red beads. The paddle, which has 50 holes large enough to accommodate the beads, is inserted into the bag, mixed around, and removed so that beads reside in all the holes. With 50 holes in the paddle and 20% red beads, approximately ten of the beads which are removed from the bag in the paddle will be red. As can be expected, sometimes a person will get more or fewer red beads than ten. The differences are due to random variability. Over time, though, the number of beads removed will average out to around ten if there are no physical differences such as weight or size between the red and white beads in the bag.

The whole purpose of statistical quality control is to determine, statistically, when the variability, which is always present in a manufacturing process, is due to random variability and when it is due to controllable variability. If it is due to controllable variability, then something can be changed to produce higher-quality products. If it is due to random variability, such as would occur when removing red beads from a bag, then nothing can be done to reduce the variability, except to find the source of the red beads. If the variability is controllable, then the paint gun can be unclogged, the correct dial settings entered, or the worn tool replaced. If variability is random, nothing should be done because random variability cannot be eliminated.

Responding to random variability by making changes in the process can be just as harmful as not reacting when the variability can be controlled. If a tool is changed when it is not worn, then the production line was stopped unnecessarily, resulting in a loss of productivity, and the tool might be adjusted improperly, resulting in a loss of quality.

If a worker is chastised for performing poorly, when in fact the differences in products are the result of random variability, then the worker will soon learn to pay no attention to the directives from management which purport to maintain the quality of products. Deming's reluctance to use employee assessment techniques (see the Third Deadly Disease) is due partially to the possibility of assessing employees on aspects of the job which are not under their control. If the worker is assessed on random variability, then the assessment itself will be random, misleading, and worthless. It will also decrease the morale and motivation of the workers.

Statistics are used to separate controllable variability from random variability. Statistical quality control uses graphs, called control charts, to plot measurements of attributes of a product to determine when a manufacturing process is in control and when it is out of control. If it is in control, no intervention is needed; if it is out of control, intervention is needed to improve the quality of the product.

A control chart is constructed in the following way. First, the target values for different aspects of quality in the product are determined. The specification for a drilled hole in a piece of metal may be 1.5 inches. The required oven temperature for baking the paint onto the product may be 80 degrees Celsius. Of course, due to random variability, the temperature setting may be slightly different or the hole may vary slightly in size.

Second, the amount of random variability which can be expected in the target values is determined and calculated when the process is in control and producing quality products. Variability in a sample of products can be conveniently summarized using a statistical term called the standard deviation which, in essence, provides a measure of the differences between the individual values and the overall average value. If, in the drilled hole example, the average or target value is 1.5 inches, then the standard deviation is determined by examining the differences between this average and all the values for the manufactured samples. For values of 1.48, 1.55, 1.60, 1.40, 1.45, and 1.52 inches, the average is 1.50 inches and the standard deviation is found from the formula

$$\text{s.d.} = \sqrt{\frac{\sum_{i=1}^{n}\left(X_i - \overline{X}\right)^2}{n-1}}$$

Filling in the numbers from the example, the standard deviation is .072.

$$\text{s.d.} = \sqrt{\frac{(1.52-1.50)^2 + (1.48-1.50)^2 + (1.55-1.50)^2 + (1.60-1.50)^2 + (1.40-1.50)^2 + (1.45-1.50)^2}{6-1}}$$

Of course, a quality engineer would take many more than six samples with the process in control to establish a good and valid standard deviation.

Third, a control chart is constructed so that the quality of the product can be tracked. A control chart contains the target value along with upper and lower control limits. If the attribute of a product is outside the upper or lower control limits, then the process is defined as out of control. As a rule of thumb, statisticians set the upper and lower control limits as three standard deviations on either side of the target value. For the example, the upper control limit is 1.50 + 3(0.072) or 1.716 inches; the lower control limit is 1.284 inches.

Fourth, samples are tested to determine if the process is in control or out of control. The average value from s statistical sample of is taken periodically and is plotted on the control chart. If the sample average is within the control limits, then the process is in control and nothing is done. If the sample average is outside the control limits, then the process is statistically out of control and steps must be taken to determine the cause of the problem. An example of a control chart and values for a process that is out of control are shown in Figure 6-1.

Statistical quality control cannot be called a Japanese quality technique, because it was developed by Walter Shewhart and others at AT&T in the 1920s. It was used extensively during World War II by American defense contractors to assure quality, and its use grew rapidly during the 1950s and 1960s. Although he was trained in physics, Deming studied with Shewhart to learn these techniques.

SQC is fairly simple in concept and easy to implement, so there is little reason for it not to be used. The standard deviation is straightforward to calculate and the control chart, with its upper and lower limits, utilizes an easy, albeit a theoretical, rule of thumb for when intervention is required. No special training is needed to understand or implement this technique, because the process is not based on complex mathematics or abstract theory. Most statistics textbooks have a chapter on SQC. Almost any junior college, college, or university will offer courses which cover SQC, but because it is so simple, this technique will constitute only a small part of the course.

In more recent years, SQC has been modified and enhanced as a method to predict problems before they occur. With enough data, the time at which a tool, such as a drill, will wear out can be predicted and, consequently, the tool can be replaced before the wear results in a loss of quality to the product.

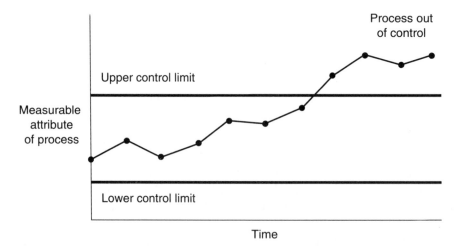

Figure 6-1 *An example of a control chart and values for a process that is out of control.*

TAGUCHI TECHNIQUES   SQC can identify when a process is statistically out of control. But once this is determined, somebody has to investigate and identify the underlying cause for the system being out of control. The premise behind Taguchi techniques is to design the process or the environment so that the sources of variability are understood. If they are understood, then the variances can be reduced by monitoring and controlling the environment or the process. The only way to understand the sources of variability is to run experiments to see which variables do and which do not have an effect on the quality of the product.

The problem with running experiments, and the reason for the existence of Taguchi techniques, is that experimentation is costly, time consuming, and sometimes not feasible if many possible causes for the variability exist. Consider a car door that does not fit well and the desire of the car company to improve the fit and thus the quality of the door. Numerous possibilities may be causing the poor fit: The latch on the car door may not be aligned correctly; the catch on the car body may not be aligned properly; the hinges on the door may not fit right; the front fender may be misaligned; the door may be too heavy for the hinges; the spring in the door may be the wrong type; or the panel where the front door closes may fit poorly because of misalignment with the back door.

For this small example, we have hypothesized seven possible variables for the causes of the poor-fitting door; other possibilities would also exist. To improve the fit, let's say that the company wants to try other possibilities for these seven variables to determine experimentally if the fit can be improved. With seven possibilities, the company would certainly want to compare, as a minimum, one new possibility with the old. For example, the company might want to investigate a new latch in comparison to the old latch. With seven variables to be tested, and two possibilities for each of the seven variables (at a minimum), the experiment would have to include all combinations of the two possibilities for each of the seven variables, resulting in 2^7 conditions or 128 possible configurations for the car door. Each configuration would have to be tested at least twice to obtain a measure for randomness in the experiment. At a minimum, then, 256 measurements would have to be made to run the experiment. All possible combinations are needed because there is the possibility that one variable may interact with another variable. For example, changing the size of the front fender, which would move the door farther to the front, might require a change in the size of the panel at the rear of the door. Interactions like these can only be tested by including all possible combinations.

Constructing all possible configurations for the car door would be time consuming and costly. Doing tests to obtain measures of the fit for all possible combinations would also be expensive. If the experimenter wanted to do more complex experiments, by testing three possibilities for each variable, the experiment would have 3^7 experimental conditions exploding to 2×3^7 or 4374 measurements.

Taguchi techniques reduce the number of configurations which have to be included in the experiment by making several assumptions about the data before it is collected. One of the main assumptions, and one of the most controversial, is that interactions are unimportant. In the example about moving the fender, in a typical Taguchi design the assumption would be that this displacement of the fender would not interact with any other variable in the fit of the door. This assumption will not be valid under many conditions. Another assumption is that the average (or mean) of the data will not be independent of the variance (the standard deviation squared) of the data. Taguchi techniques assume that the higher the average, the higher the variance of the data. Every other statistical test taught in a statistics course always assumes that the average and the variance are independent of each other.

Taguchi techniques employ a cookbook approach to the design and analysis of these experiments so that they can be used by people who know very little statistics or even very little about the product design or the manufacturing process being investigated. In the "recipe," the following steps are taken:

1. The possible variables which affect the design or process are identified. In our example, seven variables were identified.
2. Values are chosen for the variables. Usually, new values are compared to the old values. Typically, two or three values are chosen for each variable.
3. An appropriate matrix of experiments is selected. Taguchi has constructed several matrices of experiments. The choice of the appropriate matrix depends on the number of variables in the experiment and the number of values for each of the variables. Table 6-1 shows a matrix for an $L_8(2^7)$ experiment. This designation means that eight conditions or experiments will be run, each variable has two levels (new and old), and there are seven variables. The matrix identifies which conditions or configurations must be run in the experiment. The number of conditions is reduced by a large factor to reduce the cost of running the experiment. As an example, the 2^7 experiment, which requires 256 conditions in a normal experimental design, requires only eight conditions using Taguchi techniques. Eliminating some of the conditions comes with a cost, however.
4. Data is collected to measure the effect. In our example, the measure would be the fit of the car door.

Table 6.1 An example of an $L_8(2^7)$ Taguchi design to test the fit of the car door. The columns show the seven variables being tested. Each variable has two levels: the new design and the old design. The conditions refer to the number of prototypes which must be built and then tested in this experimental design. Condition 1 is the old car door design for all the variables. In the other conditions, new and old designs for the variables are combined.

Condition	Latch	Catch	Hinges	Fender	Front Weight	Door Springs	Panel
1	old	old	old	old	old	old	old
2	old	old	old	new	new	new	new
3	old	new	new	old	old	new	new
4	old	new	new	new	new	old	old
5	new	old	new	old	new	old	new
6	new	old	new	new	old	new	old
7	new	new	old	old	new	new	old
8	new	new	old	new	old	old	new

5. The data is summarized through the use of a signal-to-noise (S/N) ratio. Taguchi has specified three possible S/N ratios depending on whether a nominal, or target, value is desired, whether the smaller the value the better, or whether the larger the value the better. The S/N ratio combines values for the average (mean) and range (standard deviation).

6. The S/N ratios are interpreted. Each of the values for each of the factors has a S/N ratio associated with it (for the above example, 2 x 7 or 14 ratios are calculated). The experimenter then goes down the list of variables, comparing the ratios, to determine which value for the variable should be used in the final configuration. In other words, for the nominal S/N ratio, the experimenter goes down the list of seven variables, comparing the ratios for the two values, and chooses as a configuration the value which has the highest S/N ratio. As an example, for the latches variable, the new latch might have a S/N ratio of -204 and the old latch might have a ratio of -481. The experimenter would choose the new latch for the final door design because -204 is larger than -481. This process is continued for the other six variables.

7. A door design is chosen based on the optimal configuration as determined by the S/N ratios.

Does the Taguchi technique work? The main evidence for its effectiveness can be traced to a newspaper article which appeared in Japan, comparing television sets produced by Sony of Japan and sets produced by Sony of America.[1] The article stated that customers preferred the quality of the color on the Japanese sets even though they were the same design and manufactured in a similar manner. The difference in the production of the sets was due to the use of Taguchi techniques in Japan as opposed to SQC in the United States.

A graph that is often reprinted from this newspaper article and is similar to the one shown in Figure 6-2 compares the color density of the two kinds of sets. Most televisions sent from the Japanese plant clustered around the color densities which were perceived by customers to be of the highest quality. The sets produced at the American plants did not cluster around an ideal level for color quality. Instead, the televisions exhibited the whole range of acceptable color quality according to the control charts. The American plants did not send out any televisions at the two extremes of the range, which would represent very bad quality. The Japanese plants sent out some of these televisions at the far ranges, past the control limits which indicated low-quality color.

With the Japanese-manufactured sets, a consumer had a higher possibility of getting one which had a color density close to the target value. With the U.S.-made sets, a customer had about an equal chance of getting a television which was close to the target value or one which was close to the upper and lower control limits for color quality. Because sets outside the control limits were not shipped to customers from the U.S. plant, sets of very poor quality were not a problem. Control limits were not set at the Japanese plant, however, and so some of the sets sent to customers were of lower quality than those produced at the U.S. plant.

The graph provides compelling evidence of differences in Japanese and American quality due to Taguchi methods. If Taguchi methods are used, then most products sent by a plant will cluster around a quality target value, with the possibility of some very low-quality products escaping from the plant. If control limits and SQC are used, then no extremely low-quality products will be shipped. The trade-off is that the products may not cluster around an ideal target value for quality.

Taguchi techniques are not the best statistical methodology, but they are an improvement over some other methods currently in use. Some companies often employ a best-guess approach or test-one-variable-at-a-time approach. In a best-

---

[1] *The Asahi Shimbun* (Japanese language newspaper), April 15, 1979. Reported by Genichi Taguchi during lectures at AT&T Bell Laboratories in 1980.

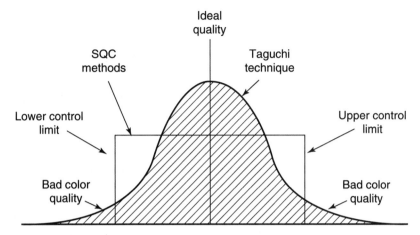

Figure 6–2 *The frequencies for sending out products when using SQC and Taguchi techniques. When using Taguchi techniques, more products will cluster around the ideal values for quality, but some will be shipped of very poor quality. When using SQC, no very poor quality products will be shipped but the products will not cluster around the ideal quality value.*

guess approach, a person guesses which design is the best. As an example, a person may simply guess that the new latch design is better than the old, without considering any data. In the test-one-variable-at-a-time approach, a person would run one experiment to test the latch designs and then another experiment to test the catch designs. Separate experiments would be conducted for each of the seven variables. This technique, unlike the best-guess approach, relies on data, but the interactions between the variables tested in the separate experiments are not considered. Interactions between the variables could have an important influence on the quality of the car door.

Taguchi methods are better than the nonstatistical best-guess approach or the statistically faulty test-one-variable-at-a-time approach. Researchers have conducted many experiments to show this. Other methods for the design of experiments, which also limit the number of conditions tested and the cost of the experiment, are also possible. These possibilities include fractional replication designs and response-surface methodologies. Both of these methods are based on solid assumptions and good statistical techniques. They accomplish the same goals as Taguchi techniques.

When compared to these other possibilities and when exposed to careful scrutiny, Taguchi techniques do not hold up very well. A statistical test is only as good as its assumptions. The aforementioned assumption that the average and variance of the data both increase can have serious implications for the interpretation of the results if this does not actually happen. If the data does not adhere to this assumption—for example, the average may increase while the variance decreases—then the interpretation may be exactly opposite from how it should be interpreted if the assumptions were upheld. In this case, the company would choose all the wrong values for the variables, which would actually *decrease* the quality of the design or the process.

Another questionable assumption is that the interactions among the variables are unimportant. Interactions, although not typically considered in Taguchi designs, can be tested. If an experimenter wanted to test for an interaction, one of the columns in Table 6-1 would have to be changed from a single variable to an interaction between two or more variables. As an example, the third column could be changed from testing the hinges variable to testing the interaction between the latch and the catch variables. If this was done, then the number of variables tested, to remain with eight configurations in the $L_8(2^7)$ design, would have to be reduced from seven to six. In addition, the experimenter would have to determine which interaction to test. With seven variables, there are 56 possible interactions. All of these interactions cannot be tested when only eight configurations are tested experimentally. Instead of going through the long process of considering which interactions may be important, the easiest thing to do is ignore all interactions. If an interaction does exert an influence on the quality of the product in this case, and it is ignored in the experimental design, the interpretation of the results will be wrong and decisions could be made which could result in a decrease in the quality of the product or process.

Some researchers have run simulation studies to test the robustness of Taguchi techniques, and those results show that the technique is not very robust. Results using Taguchi methods are especially influenced by data points which are outliers, ones that were aberrations rather than reflections of the true state of the world.[2] Good statistical tests are not sensitive to these aberrations.

If Taguchi techniques have all these problems, why are U.S. companies so interested in applying them? For one thing, the techniques are very easy to apply by following the cookbook approach. One does not have to be an expert on the design or the process in order to use Taguchi techniques. Fractional replication techniques and response-surface methodologies require more knowledge about the product design or the manufacturing process in order to make the correct choices in applying the techniques to a real problem. The Taguchi techniques fit with the practice of Japanese companies of hiring and then training people who do not have specialized

---

[2]S.R. Schmidt and J.R. Boudot (1989). "A Monte Carlo Simulation Study Comparing Effectiveness of Signal-to-Noise Ratios and Other Methods for Identifying Dispersion Effects." Talk presented at the *Rocky Mountain Quality Control Conference*, 1989.

skills, such as training in statistics or expertise in design. Since these people possess only general skills, Japanese companies provide them with simple techniques which can be applied even with little understanding of the design or process.

Another reason for the current popularity of Taguchi techniques is the tendency to adopt any quality technique that is Japanese, without really understanding its validity. Taguchi has achieved quite a reputation in Japan, having twice received the Deming award for individuals. This is all the more ironic because Deming states in his book, *Out of the Crisis*, that experiments are a waste of time and should never be utilized.[3] If you adhere to the teachings of Deming, then you would never think of using Taguchi techniques.

The conclusion is that Taguchi techniques are probably better than nothing. If you are already using experimental design statistical techniques, such as fractional replications, Taguchi techniques would be a step backward because of the many problems with the techniques and assumptions. If you are not using any experimental design techniques, however, Taguchi techniques can improve the quality of your products, but other statistical techniques based on better assumptions and better methods are superior.

CONSTANT IMPROVEMENT   The Japanese practice of constant improvement, or *kaizen*, is a policy of continually making changes, even if they are small, to constantly improve the product, process, or service. Emphasis is on improving the manufacturing process to eliminate defects. Increases in the efficiency of the process result in productivity improvements. Overall, the idea is that even if changes are small, they add up to a large improvement over time. Japanese companies are less likely than American companies to opt for a "great leap forward," with large changes. Large changes mean uncertainty, which is anathema to Japanese companies, but small changes can be handled with less disruption.

Kaizen did not start in Japan, although Japanese companies have formalized the methods very well. Frederick Taylor, along with others, developed the concept of "scientific management" in the United States in the late 1800s, which applied the scientific method to work. The goal was to find the one best way to perform a job to increase efficiency and then to standardize the job. An unfortunate by product of this was that it often de-skilled the job and removed the worker from any decisions about how to improve the job. The burden to find the one best way was placed on management, with little input from the workers.

Others realized that this burden should be placed on the worker because it would help to make the de-skilled jobs more interesting. In 1871, a Scottish ship-

---

[3]W. Edwards Deming, *Out of the Crisis* (Cambridge, MA: MIT Press, 1982), pp. 131-133, 350-351.

builder, Denny of Dumbarton, instituted an awards scheme to elicit suggestions from workers for improving the building of ships. Employees could submit a suggestion to a committee to receive a cash award. Five suggestions resulted in an additional cash bonus.

In the United States, the National Cash Register Company (NCR) of Dayton, Ohio, was one of the earliest to implement a cash incentive program for improvement suggestions. The founder of the company, John H. Patterson, set up a program to solicit written suggestions from employees in 1894 because he realized that many ideas could be found if everyone, not just management, was involved in the improvement process. The best ideas were rewarded $30, and this prize amount was increased to $500 three years later. By 1946, NCR was receiving 3000 suggestions per year.

Lincoln Electric Company in the United States changed their compensation package based on these earlier models. In 1929, Lincoln instituted a system that remunerated employees half of the money saved during the first year after the suggestion. Lincoln had implemented many other innovative employee relation programs which increased the trust between worker and management.

In some ways, Japan can trace its constant improvement suggestion system back to 1721 and the eighth shogun, Yoshimuni Tokugawa, who had a suggestion box placed at the entrance to his castle with the following notice: "Make your idea known. Rewards are given for ideas that are accepted." It should be noted, though, that this was the only avenue open for subjects to make suggestions, because "any policy suggestions directly to the shogun remained punishable by decapitation."[4]

There is no indication that the shogun's practice was implemented by Japanese companies. The first evidence of Japanese companies implementing constant improvement or suggestion boxes was in response to practices of the American companies. Kanebuchi Boseki, a Japanese textile firm, incorporated a box for employee suggestions in 1905 after a management team had observed the one at NCR.[5] Eiji Toyoda, the CEO of Toyota for many years, explained that he implemented constant improvement at Toyota in 1950 after visiting Ford Motor Company and seeing how even minor changes resulted in significant improvements.

The Japanese innovation in the constant improvement program came in the form of quality circles. Japanese companies that imported suggestion boxes from the United States quickly discovered that Japanese employees did not like to submit

---

[4]Dean M. Schroeder and Alan G. Robinson, "America's Most Successful Export to Japan: Continuous Improvement Programs," *Sloan Management Review*, Spring 1991, p. 71.
[5]Ibid., p. 71.

individual suggestions in writing. Instead, with a quality circle program, employees can meet in a group and submit ideas directly to management.

This brief history shows that implementing a constant improvement process requires little more expenditure than a suggestion box on the wall and a cash prize which is more than offset by the monetary benefits accruing from the suggestion. With little cost, the payoff can be high. With a cost of $2.2 million during a ten-year period starting from 1973, Canon achieved a savings of $200 million from suggestions.[6] Almost all of the cost (96%) of the program was due to cash prizes, so one can see how the prize expenditure can realize a large payoff.

For constant improvement to work, however, the cultural environment within a company must change. First, everybody in the company must become accustomed to and comfortable with making suggestions for small improvements. Just by implementing such a process, adherents claim, employees are made to feel more actively involved with their jobs.

Second, management must accept the suggestions from the employees. This often means that management acknowledge that the person who knows the most about a job is the person who actually performs it. Management must accept a loss of some of its authority.

Third, a constant improvement program requires quick feedback on suggestions. Workers must be told that their suggestions are important by having a committee quickly review suggestions. Even if the suggestion is not accepted, the committee must provide feedback about why it was not accepted and training so that the next suggestion can more directly affect the work process or the quality of the product.

Finally, employees must be assured that the suggestions will not eliminate their jobs. Constant improvements may lead to elimination of certain jobs.

When these four changes in company culture have been implemented, the greatest benefit may not be due to employee suggestions but may be due to workers' perceptions that they have more control over their jobs. NUMMI, the joint auto manufacturing venture between GM and Toyota in California, implemented several changes from its previous incarnation as a heavily unionized GM plant. One of the changes was to implement a constant improvement process which turned out to be wildly successful in eliciting suggestions from the employees. Even though a majority of the workers came from the earlier GM plant, problems such as absenteeism and grievances against management were reduced.

Not many people will argue with the basic principle of constant improvement. Improvements to the product, process, or service are, by definition, good. The cost to implement such a program is very low, and the payoff can be extremely high. Con-

---

[6]Ibid., p. 71.

stant improvement works best, though, on a manufacturing process where the same product is produced day in and day out. The workers in such a process spend long hours learning their jobs, which are often boring, and the mental challenge of finding ways to improve the job can make it less tedious. Constant improvement works less well in a situation where products are manufactured in small batches with many product changes. One could argue, however, that this situation is also ripe for constant improvement in the process for changing the line over to a new product.

If it is not implemented in a well-meaning manner, though, the constant improvement process can turn into an utter disaster in the eyes of the workers. Mazda's Flat Rock, Michigan, manufacturing facility, with its Japanese management team, implemented a constant improvement program. The workers complained, however, when they found that suggestions for improving job safety were ignored, but suggestions for improving work efficiency were implemented quickly.

The workers at Mazda also discovered that *kaizen* suggestions greatly increased their workload. One worker complained that *"kaizen* creates more pressure. You might figure out a way to get your job down from a minute to 30 seconds, but then they find you something else to do [for] 30 seconds."[7] Another worker complained, "Honest to God, some of these people [already] don't have the time to put a stick of chewing gum in their mouth."[8]

The *kaizen* process at the Mazda plant managed to keep all workers occupied almost all of the time. Mazda workers were actively engaged in work for 57 seconds out of a minute, so there was hardly any slack time. This can be compared to the 45 seconds out of a minute for a worker at a Big Three plant.[9] In essence, Mazda workers have a 29% longer workday, with no extra pay, as compared to a Big Three worker. This is equivalent to working an extra 11-and-a-half-hour day each week. The workers at the Mazda plant experienced weight loss, fatigue, carpal tunnel syndrome, and other health problems. Often, these workers were accused by management of sandbagging or slacking when they complained of these health problems.

Workers at Mazda came to resent other workers who made *kaizen* suggestions. A suggestion for improving efficiency by 5 seconds at one location meant that the assembly operation would get to the next location 5 seconds faster. This would mean that the workers at the next location would have to improve their efficiency by 5 seconds by discovering some more efficient technique, or they would just have to work harder. The stress produced by such a system worked itself down the whole line.

---

[7]Joseph J. Fucini and Suzy Fucini, *Working for the Japanese. Inside Mazda's American Auto Plant* (New York: The Free Press, 1990), p. 161.
[8]Ibid.
[9]Ibid., p. 147.

Constant improvement can increase the quality of the product by decreasing the number of defects. The system can be abused, however, if constant improvement is used only to increase the time that workers spend actively engaged in work. A tired worker is more likely to make mistakes, so speeding up the line can actually result in reduced quality, which is the opposite of the desired effect.

JUST-IN-TIME MANUFACTURING   The purpose of just-in-time (JIT) manufacturing, called *kanban* in Japan, is to reduce the number of parts which are inventoried and stored at the plant. Instead of storing parts, the parts are delivered to the plant by outside vendors as they are needed. Once they are inside the plant, the parts are not put at the point of assembly until required. The whole purpose is to reduce costs by eliminating the warehouse space at the plant which is used for storing parts. *Kanban* can save money if plant space and land are at a premium, as they often are in Japan. JIT also reduces waste. Waste occurs when a product is changed and previous parts become obsolete. If JIT is not being practiced, the leftasseover stored parts become waste once a product change is made.

JIT switches much of the burden for storing parts to the suppliers. The supplier is allowed to ship only what is needed instead of what has been produced. Thus, shipping costs are increased. A large shipment of parts may only require one truck and one driver for a couple hours a day if the supplier plant is close to the assembly plant. The driver is then free to ship to other plants. Under JIT as practiced in Japan, some suppliers deliver parts up to ten times a day. Sometimes JIT is more accurately abbreviated as WITS for "wait in the street."[10] The result is that transportation costs are increased because deliveries are often made with partial truckloads of materials rather than full truckloads. Personnel costs are also increased with added deliveries, and more fuel is needed for the trucks. Reduction of waste from obsolete parts may be offset by increased fuel waste by the trucks and increased environmental pollution.

Companies in Japan keep down costs by placing the burden of JIT on the suppliers. The people working for suppliers do not have the lifetime employment and high wages found at the larger companies. To protect the high wages and job status of their employees, the larger companies often pass the cost of the improvement processes down to the lower-cost suppliers. Inventory costs at the suppliers are traded off with labor costs at the assemblers.

This kind of strategy for reducing costs for the large-company assemblers can work only if the large company has unquestioned authority over the supplier. In a *keiretsu* system, where one supplier is tied to an assembler, both financially and tra-

---

[10]Jeremiah T. Sullivan, *Invasion of the Salarymen. The Japanese Business Presence in America* (Westport, CT: Praeger, 1992), p. 214.

ditionally through the cartel, imposition of costs onto the supplier will be accepted. The supplier has no choice because it cannot supply parts to companies outside the *keiretsu*. In the United States, where the cartel like behavior of the *keiretsu* is illegal, Japanese companies have had less success in implementing JIT.

With increased automation in the warehouses, JIT is slowly being eliminated even in Japan.[11] The inventor of JIT, Taiichi Ohno of Toyota, died in 1990, and Toyota's commitment to *kanban* has been decreasing. Other companies in Japan follow Toyota's lead.

With the difference in land prices between the United States and Japan, and with the decreasing practice of JIT in Japan, why do some Japanese transplant companies still adhere to it? Probably the most important reason is that JIT can work hand in hand with the constant improvement process to expose problems in the manufacturing process. During training at Mazda's Flat Rock plant, the Japanese management team showed the trainees a picture of a boat in water with rocks at the bottom of the river.[12] The deep water kept the rocks from causing problems for the boat. They then showed the employees another picture of the boat in shallow water, with the rocks now exposed and threatening the boat. The deep water represented a large inventory; the shallow water represented the situation when JIT was implemented. With JIT, the employees had to find ways to eliminate the problems, represented by the rocks, by improving the process. In deep water, the problems are hidden. The instructors claimed that Mazda kept the waters low on purpose to expose any problems so they could not be ignored.

QUALITY FUNCTION DEPLOYMENT   As shown in the definition of quality in Chapter 4, an important part of quality, user-based quality, is to translate the needs of the user or consumer into design features of the product. We often hear phrases such as "The customer is always right" or "Always listen to the customer." These slogans or phrases are fine in theory, but user-based quality is difficult to deliver in practice. One of the main problems with listening to the customer is that the customer tends to make suggestions in general terms and these generalities must then be transformed into engineering design specifications. The engineering design specifications must, in turn, be translated into a product which can be manufactured economically.

The process of taking a customer suggestion and turning it into a manufactured product can be very difficult because it involves several diverse team members who

---

[11]Sullivan, *Invasion of the Salarymen*, p. 214.
[12]Ibid.

must be able to communicate on common grounds. A multidisciplinary team for this design process, often called concurrent design, must as a minimum cover four very diverse areas: expertise in the design and engineering of the product; manufacturing and production engineering; quality control; and marketing and sales. The customer is usually represented by marketing and sales people and is seldom brought into the actual design process.

Japanese companies have formalized the design process and the integration of these diverse team members into the process called quality function deployment (QFD). The process utilizes a series of matrices in which team members perform a series of exercises beginning with customer suggestions and ending with engineering terms which can be used for actual design and production.

QFD is often organized around the concept of a "house of quality," which is a simplifying logical and visual rendition of QFD. In QFD, the goal of the multidisciplinary team is to map customer requirements into design requirements. Customer requirements are determined by marketing and sales people along with support from data sources such as questionnaires and surveys. Throughout the process, the diverse team members interact so that the new product satisfies the design, customer, and engineering requirements. With the participation of the manufacturing engineers, the manufacturability of the design is considered. At the end of the QFD process, a technical competitive benchmark summarizes how the new design compares with the competition.

Using QFD has been credited with reducing the time needed to bring a product to market by reducing the number of engineering changes that are needed.[13] In addition, QFD enhances teamwork by providing a structure in which diverse team members can discuss and contribute.[14] Perhaps most important of all, it ensures that customer needs will be mapped into manufacturable specific design features.

In our discussions with industry people who use QFD, almost all seem to agree on the importance of QFD in the design process, but they are often limited by the practical concerns of controlling the paperwork involved in the process, questions about knowing how to perform the process, and the problem of getting all team members together at a common site where these practices can occur.

FROM CUSTOMER TO PRODUCT TO CUSTOMER   Japanese

companies have concentrated on increasing the efficiency of the design and manufacturing process. QFD is used in the whole design process by taking customer

---

[13]L. P. Sullivan, "Quality Function Deployment," *Quality Progress,* June 1986, pp. 39-50.
[14]J. R. Hauser and D. Clausing, "The House of Quality," *Harvard Business Review,* May-June, 1988, pp. 63-73.

requirements, turning these requirements into a product, and then continuing the process with customer reactions to the new process. Taguchi techniques can be used to determine design features for quality products experimentally.

When a product is manufactured, SQC, JIT, and Taguchi techniques can be used to increase the efficiency of the product and ensure the quality of the product. SQC is used to determine when a process is out of control and thus is having an adverse effect on product quality. JIT can be used to increase the efficiency of the process because problems cannot be hidden if inventories on the line are kept low. The process can be improved through the use of Taguchi techniques, which determines robust manufacturing conditions experimentally.

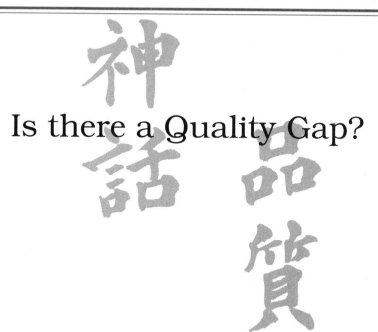

Is there a Quality Gap?

All the ingredients of a dynamite news story were present: passion, vice, and danger. The passion was golf. Japanese men and women will pay huge amounts of money to indulge their 18-hole passion. Salarymen, usually so reserved in public, can often be seen pantomiming golf shots, in full business uniform, while waiting at a station for a train.

The vice was cigarettes. Cigarette smoking fits the frenetic lifestyle of Japanese men. One of the many paradoxes of Japan is how it can have one of the healthiest and most long-lived populations on earth when smoking is both acceptable and widespread. Over 60% of Japanese men smoke.[1]

The danger was the possibility that the golf course might blow up. The golfers knew that the next eagle, bogie, or birdie might be their last. To a committed Japanese golfer, however, there might be no better way to go than after a perfect putt while sharing the moment with your business buddies and puffing away on a cigarette surrounded by the expansive green of the golf course.

---

[1]Merrill Goozner, "In Land of Smokers, Hotel Tries to Clear Air," *Chicago Tribune,* May 12, 1992. pp. 3-1, 3-2.

Passion, vice, and danger. The newscaster on the 11 p.m. newscast—our favorite television program because we never knew what to expect—explained that a new golf course had just opened. Because of the scarcity of land in Japan, golf courses are sometimes located in creative places. In this instance, the course was on top of a landfill which was still emitting highly explosive methane gas. The picture on the television showed the beautiful golf course, and a lot of ugly pipes sprouting where there should have been trees. The newscaster explained that the pipes were vents for the methane gas and explained further that smoking was prohibited on this course because the spark from a single cigarette could cause a methane gas explosion.

The newscast confirmed our belief that Americans have the highest-quality golf courses in the world. Ours have never exploded, or even been in danger of exploding. This might explain why Japanese companies have paid huge amounts of money for American golf courses, such as Pebble Beach in California. When it wants high-quality golf courses, the world comes to the United States. But what about other American products? How do products from other countries compare in quality to Japanese products? We hear so much about the quality of Japanese products; what are the facts?

SMOKESCREEN OR SMOKESTACK?   The analysis of product quality is important to public policy. If there is a difference between the quality of Japanese products and the quality of American products, then the problem American companies have in competing with Japan must be solved by developing and manufacturing higher-quality products. For this scenario, the playing field is assumed to be level and American companies are losing the quality game. It is not the fault of the Japanese government or the Japanese companies that American companies cannot compete. Japanese companies are merely manufacturing products that Americans want to buy because of their superior quality. If American companies want to beat Japanese companies, then they have to start competing on quality. Under this scenario, American companies are represented by smokestack industries which are outmoded, outdated, out of touch with the American consumer, and outmatched in quality. We will call this the smokestack scenario.

Consider the other possibility, which we will call the smokescreen scenario. If there is no difference or if American products are actually better than Japanese products, then the consequences are different. One can question why Japanese consumers are not buying American products of comparable or higher quality at lower cost than competing Japanese products. Of prime importance is the American trade deficit with Japan, of which more than half is due to imported automobiles. Is the trade deficit due to superior-quality products, or is it due to dumping—selling cars in America at lower prices than in Japan? As an example, at one time Japanese firms were found to be selling computer chips at $2 when it cost them $3 to make.[2] The American semiconductor industry almost failed as a consequence, losing $4 billion and 25,000 jobs between 1983 and 1989. There was nothing wrong with the quality of the American products; they were losing market share because of price undercutting. The Japanese were flooding the market with products priced below the cost of manufacturing them. In this case the playing field was not level, so even with comparable or higher-quality products, the products weren't moving in the marketplace. According to this scenario, the quality of Japanese products is just a smokescreen to hide the real reasons for the large trade deficit with the United States and the dearth of foreign products in Japan.

Many Americans who have not been to Japan support the smokestack scenario. We have read numerous articles in newspapers and magazines in which the writer talks about the trade impediments to foreign products which have been erected in Japan. Although these impediments are real, the author will often end the article by saying that the real fault may lie with American companies and their inability to compete with Japanese products.[3]

Japan would like us to believe in the smokestack scenario instead of concentrating on the real reasons for the trade deficit. Robert McCurry, executive vice president of Toyota Motor Sales, U.S.A., is pushing the smokestack scenario. "You can't force Americans to buy cars they don't want, at prices they can't afford," said McCurry. "Most of America's trade and economic problems originate at home—a budget deficit, an education deficit, an investment deficit, a quality and productivity deficit,"[4] he continues. Later in this book we show that Japan is running a productivity deficit with the United States, never having surpassed the United States in overall productivity.

Even Akio Morita, chairman of Sony Corporation, states that Japan's competitive advantage may not be due to the quality of the products or the productivity of the workers. "Japanese companies pay their employees less for longer hours worked, take slimmer profit margins and pay stockholders smaller dividends. This allows them to compete viciously on price."[5]

JAPAN'S RALPH NADER   Fumio Matsuda calls his office a bunker, giving it the connotation of being constantly under attack. He has been harassed. He

---

[2]James Coates, "U.S. Regains Lead in Chipmaking from Japanese," *The Chicago Tribune*, February 15, 1993, pp. 4-1, 4-4.

[3]James Healey, "Does Familiarity Breed Content?," *USA Today*, March 23, 1993, p. 6B.

[4]Jim Mateja, "Toyota Says U.S. Carmakers Have Only Selves to Blame," *Chicago Tribune*, January 10, 1992. pp. 3-1, 3-2.

[5]Associated Press, "More Japanese Firms See Need to Change Ways," *Los Angeles Times*, April 20, 1992, pp. D1, D9.

has been threatened repeatedly. His office has been broken into and burglarized. He guards with zealous secrecy the people he talks to. What is his offense? He has tried to protect the Japanese consumer by making Japanese cars safer. He could be called Japan's Ralph Nader. Although most Americans have heard of Nader, hardly anyone has ever heard of Fumio Matsuda.

Matsuda is a former quality control engineer at Nissan, who quit his job when his advice on safety was not heeded. "My criticism was not so easily accepted by my boss, making it very difficult for me to demonstrate what was needed to be done to maintain and improve the quality of the cars," Matsuda says. "They told me these changes would cost money. I felt very ignored by the people around me in the company. I saw that it was better to be outside the company rather than inside."[6] Since 1969 he has been running the Japan Automobile Consumer Union. Knowing quality himself, he has maintained secret contact with engineers and others within the Japanese automobile industry. He backs up his claims with actual blueprints from the companies and internal company documents. He uses his engineering expertise to interpret the problems for others.

"It's generally said that Japanese cars are of superior quality but this is totally incorrect," says Matsuda. "Each car has its potential defects. And what is wrong with Japanese manufacturers is that they are trying to hide this inherent weakness. When accidents happen due to mechanical failure, they try to hide it from the public."[7] Matsuda also states categorically that "American cars are superior from a safety standpoint."[8]

His documented list of unsafe practices of Japanese carmakers is extensive. Defective parts are installed to cut costs. Manufacturers act in collusion with the government so that the cars and trucks which are mass produced are different from those that undergo government crash tests. The carmakers install thinner floor pan sheets on their cars than regulations permit. Spot-welding points on the body structure of the car are farther apart than they should be, weakening the vehicle's structure. The car companies engage in secret recalls to conceal defects from customers. In a secret recall, dealers change parts when owners bring in their cars for regular service. The customers are billed for the service and parts, but they are not told that the parts have been changed to prevent recalls. Matsuda's informants have given him lists of defects provided by car companies to dealers who make the secret repairs. Secret recalls are illegal in the United States.

The secret recalls were made public in Japan in 1990. A Japanese newspaper, *Asahi Shimbun,* learned that Mazda had been replacing defective parts when owners brought their cars in for routine repairs.[9] Defective switches in the cars were causing

---

[6]Marcia Stepanek, "Letter from Tokyo," *Far Eastern Economic Review,* October 6, 1988, p. 92.
[7]Ibid.
[8]Dennis Pidge, "Consumer Advocate Challenges Superiority of Japanese Cars," *Japan Times,* October 10, 1990.

the brake lights to fail or, more seriously, causing the cruise control to fail to turn off immediately when the brakes were touched. After the government investigated, Mazda officials apologized and top executives took 10% pay cuts for six months.

Matsuda has been especially critical of the Suzuki Samurai. He says the Samurai was especially dangerous for American drivers because the ones they sold in the United States had a larger engine than those sold in Japan. The vehicle was not designed for an engine that large. Combining its thin tires and its high center of gravity with a more powerful engine made the car more dangerous for American consumers than for Japanese drivers. Even *Consumer Reports*, which often seems biased toward Japanese products, found the Samurai unacceptable because it repeatedly tilted on two wheels and would have rolled over except for the special safety apparatus *Consumer Reports* uses when testing cars on its crash avoidance test course.[10]

Nissan had a similar problem adapting a vehicle made for the Japanese market to sell in the American market. A Nissan van marketed in the United States in 1987, 1988, and 1990 was originally designed as an urban delivery vehicle for Japan. To take advantage of the expanding American market for minivans, Nissan increased the engine size from 2.0 to 2.4 liters and added an automatic transmission with overdrive, front and rear air conditioning, power windows and power locks, cruise control, and a rear window wiper and defroster. The engine was not designed to handle these luxury add-ons. The vehicle has been plagued by engine fires because the engine compartment is too small to accommodate the larger engine, claims consumer advocate Sean Kane.[11] Nissan has issued three recalls on 33,000 vans, but the recalls were always to fix symptoms caused by the small engine compartment, such as failed fan couplings, instead of fixing the problem. Nissan has refused to buy back the vans.

Anybody who is familiar with the was the Japanese legal system works will understand why Japanese companies have little incentive to design or manufacture safe products. From 1975 to 1990, only 130 product liability suits were filed in Japan. In the United States, 13,595 suits were filed in 1986 alone. There are several reasons for the low number of lawsuits in Japan. There the consumer must prove that the defect resulted from intent or overt negligence by the manufacturer. To prove this requires company or government documents. "Japanese companies can easily avoid providing information concerning the product in question merely by saying it is a corporate secret. And the government can also refuse to reveal the relevant information it holds,"[12] says Kiyomitsu Yoshimi, a law professor at Hitotsubashi University.

---

[9]Stephen Franklin, "Mazda Execs Take Pay Cuts for Hushing up Defect, *Chicago Tribune,* December 27, 1990, pp. 3-1, 3-4.

[10]*"How Safe Is the Ford Bronco II?," Consumer Reports,* June 1989, p. 393.

[11]Helen Kahn, "33,000 Nissan Vans Called Fire Risk; Buyback Urged," *Automotive News,* February 8, 1993, p. 96.

[12]Kyodo News Service, "Demands Grow for a New Law on Product Liability," *Japan Times,* October 19, 1990, p. 3.

Lawyers are reluctant to take on cases because there is so little chance that they will be successful. Matsuda has been able to file lawsuits against car companies because his informants inside the companies have provided him with the incriminating company documents.

Are Japanese cars better in quality than American cars? Matsuda, the former Nissan quality control engineer, says they are not. Are Japanese cars safer than American cars? They are usually smaller, which gives them a distinct disadvantage. Japan's legal system has never provided consumers with the power to force the automobile industry to improve the safety of their cars. Matsuda claims that company profits are more important to Japanese automakers than safety. "If Japanese manufacturers would invest their technology and profits in improving safety in their cars, they could save many lives,"[13] Matsuda says.

PRODUCT QUALITY SURVEYS
Total Research, in Princeton, New Jersey, conducted a survey called EquiTrend on a randomly selected sample of 2000 consumers. They asked consumers to rate the perceived quality of different products and published the top 100 products.[14] This survey is interesting because it includes things as varied as credit cards and amusement parks on the same scale. The scores run from 0 to 100.

American products dominate the list, holding down 82 of the top 100 spots. Japanese companies made the list with 7 products, while European companies had 11 in the top 100. Two of the Japanese products, Universal Studios in Florida and Universal Studios in Hollywood, were actually purchased by a Japanese company only recently, and they still have American management. Only five of the Japanese products—Lexus, Sony, Sega Genesis, Infiniti, and Acura—were actually developed and manufactured in Japan. The top ten products (Disney World, Disneyland, Kodak film, Hallmark greeting cards, Mercedes-Benz, Fisher-Price toys, Reynolds Wrap aluminum foil, AT&T long-distance telephone service, Levi's jeans, and Ziploc bags) are all American with the exception of Mercedes cars.

Not surprisingly, when the products are placed into categories, American products dominate throughout. All the computer companies, for example, are American (IBM personal computers, 16th; Compaq, 63rd; Apple, 64th; and Intel microprocessors, 66th). In Japan, personal computers are priced at least twice as high as comparable machines in the United States. The high prices have kept computers out of the hands of consumers. In 1991, Japanese consumers bought only 2 million personal computers, which is 20% of U.S. annual sales. Based on the size of their economy, one would expect sales three times as high.[15] The high prices and low quality of Jap-

---

[13]Dennis Pidge, "Consumer Advocate Challenges Superiority of Japanese Cars".
[14]"Measuring Quality Perception of America's Top Brands," *Brandweek*, April 4, 1994, pp. 24–26.
[15]Merrill Goozner, "In Japan, Compaq PC Prices User-Friendly," *Chicago Tribune*, November 20, 1992 ,. pp. 3-1,3-3.

anese computers have kept Japanese offices from becoming computerized and prevented typical Japanese citizens from becoming computer-literate. However, American companies, even though they offer a higher-quality product at lower prices, have a meager 15% share of the Japanese personal computer market. If you count IBM-Japan as a Japanese company, as Japanese consumers do, then that share drops to 8%.

American companies also dominate in home appliances. All the appliance companies in the top 100 are American: GE is 36th, Kenmore is 40th, KitchenAid is 48th, Cuisinart is 81st, and Mr.Coffee is 88th. Our experience in Japan was that the appliances were low quality yet very high priced. We have already discussed our problems with washing machines, dryers, and ovens in Chapter 2. We personally never saw a foreign brand of home appliance in any store. Foreign competition in Japan would help the Japanese consumer immensely by improving the quality of their domestically produced appliances and by lowering the prices.

American products also dominate household products, food, and drugs. Ten household products, such as Rubbermaid in 21st place and Tupperware in 24th place, made the list, and all ten were American. In Japan we found houseware products to be low quality and expensive. The Rubbermaid and Tupperware products with which we were familiar were much better than anything we found in Japan. Rubbermaid was not available in any stores we visited in Japan. Fourteen food and drug products made the list, and all but one, the Nestle Crunch Bar from the Swiss company, are American products.

The four retail stores on the list are all American (Wal-Mart, 35th; Sam's Club, 52nd; Nordstrom's, 93rd; and J. C. Penney, 96th). The five hotels on the list (Marriott, 35th; Hilton, 42nd; Hyatt, 43rd; Sheraton, 75th; and Holiday Inns, 92nd) all started as American companies, although Hilton and Holiday Inns are now owned by British companies. Michelin, a French company, is the highest-rated tire company at 20th; Goodyear, at 33rd, is the only other tire company on the list. Kodak (3rd) and Polaroid (77th), both American companies, are the only film companies rated highly.

Also high on the quality list are American telephone and communication companies. AT&T long-distance service was ranked 8th overall, Bell local telephone was ranked 31st, AT&T Personalink Information Services was 46th, AT&T cellular phone service was 70th, and AT&T video phone calling was 76th. Japanese companies often complain about the quality of the phone service. At the Japan Travel Bureau in Tokyo, the phone lines go dead up to 100 times a day, causing serious problems for the firm's reservations system.[16] Engineers from NTT, Japan's monopolistic phone company, have tried to solve the problem without success. The travel bureau has changed telephones and lines three times, at great cost, but to no avail. Even Shintaro Ishihara, perhaps one of the most nationalistic of Japanese politicians, has

---

[16]"Special Team Investigating Travel-Agent Phone Mystery," *Japan Times,* December 4, 1990. p. 3.

longed for American quality in the phone service. "I myself use an NTT-made car phone in Tokyo and the quality is very poor,"[17] says Ishihara. "Lines are often crossed and the system is very susceptible to being tapped." Through a long-negotiated agreement, Motorola, usually considered to have the highest-quality cellular phone products, was allowed to sell cellular products everywhere in Japan, except in the high-demand market of Tokyo.

Foreign companies also dominate the list of consumer electronics products. Sony televisions are rated highest, at 25th, followed by RCA (47th) and Magnavox (60th) televisions. Sony, of course, is a Japanese company, RCA is owned by the French, and Magnavox is a Dutch company. Both RCA and Magnavox originated as American companies. Sega Genesis video games also make the list, at 67th. Japanese companies account for 35% of the televisions sold in the United States. Although foreign companies dominate consumer electronics, there is some reason to believe that American consumers may not be pleased with the quality of the products. Consumer electronics have sales of $40 billion in the United States, but the Electronic Industries Association estimates that 5-25% of the products are returned each year because the customers find the products defective or too difficult to use.[18]

VEHICLE QUALITY   The most-watched battle on quality has been over automobiles and light trucks. The American public generally gauges the quality of Japanese products in terms of cars and trucks. At one point a few years ago, one-third of the cars sold in the United States were made by Japanese companies. Half the U.S. trade deficit with Japan has come from vehicle imports. The general perception was that Japanese companies made better-quality cars and that people bought these cars because of that superior quality. The public's poor regard for the quality of American cars had an effect on the perception of the quality of other American products.

It is generally accepted that American car companies have made great strides in improving the quality of American cars. At the same time, the perception is that the quality of Japanese cars is not remaining constant. The competition with Japan has been good for increasing the quality of American cars while keeping prices down. Previously, Detroit auto companies had become complacent.

With the increase in the quality of American cars, what is the status of the quality gap between American and Japanese cars? Are Japanese cars still better than American cars? As indicated in Chapter 4, quality is a multifaceted concept. Often, with cars in mind, we equate quality with reliability. A few publications, such as *Consumer Reports,* provide readers with data on the reliability of cars. Another com-

---

[17]"Playboy Interview: Shintaro Ishihara," *Playboy* October 1990, pp. 66.
[18]Coates, James. "It's high noon in showdown over electronics simplicity." *Chicago Tribune.* January 24, 1993, pp. 4-1, 4-5.

pany, J. D. Power and Associates, selects vehicle registrations for all car owners of various makes and sends questionnaires to these people. The results are not available to the general public but are partially reported in magazines and newspapers. One of Power's main questions is about the number of defects per car. In this case, quality is associated with defects.

Other analyses of car quality have also been conducted. In one survey, auto mechanics were questioned on car quality. Because they saw the cars which had problems, they were in a unique position to assess the quality of the different makes. Florida's attorney general has also assessed the quality of cars through the enactment of Florida's "lemon law," which requires car companies to repair defective cars until the customer is satisfied. By looking through the records, the attorney general's staff was able to determine which car companies made the fewest "lemons."

Perhaps the ultimate determinant of quality is whether or not customers will buy the product. Quality can also be determined by examining which company produces the most popular vehicles.

The analysis in Chapter 4 showed that quality has an additional subjective nature which is not assessed through the number of defects or the reliability of the car. Consumers may consider a car to be of high quality if it is designed well, if it has the right kinds of features, or if it handles well. Many other things could be considered in an analysis of quality. Perhaps consumers should just be asked about the perceived quality of a car, without equating quality to any one part. At least one study has looked at this kind of quality also. In reviewing the material on the perceived quality of cars from different sources, the findings are surprising. The different surveys varied remarkably in their results. *Consumer Reports* stood out because it had different results from the other surveys regarding vehicle reliability and quality. The following discussion will attempt to clarify and explain the differing views on quality.

J. D. POWER INITIAL QUALITY   J. D. Power is the company
which does the most comprehensive analysis of car quality, equating quality with the number of defects. The company uses several measures to assess quality. The primary measure is the number of defects. "Defects" can mean many things. A car can have a defect in the paint job, or a plastic stripe might be broken. A defect could also be more serious, such as one in the brakes or in the engine. J. D. Power does not consider the severity of the defect. Also, a car could have a design defect, such as an unprotected gas tank which might explode in a crash, which would not necessarily be counted in the number of defects. Equating defects with the quality of the car provides only a very narrow definition of quality, but it provides one of the most objective analyses, since defects can be counted.

Defects are measured by J. D. Power as the number of reported defects per 100 cars. The third column of Table 7.1a summarizes the ordering of the Japanese and

American car makes in the J. D. Power report for 1994. The 1993 data is shown in the fourth column.

For the 1994 data, the average for the Japanese makes was better than the average for the American makes, 102 defects to 115. This means that each Japanese car could be expected to come with 1.02 defects and each American car could be expected to come with 1.15 defects. Of course, a fraction of a defect makes no sense for a single car. To put this in the proper perspective, if you take 12 cars, half of them Japanese and half American, then all six Japanese cars can be expected to be delivered with one defect. Five of the six American cars would match this with one defect, but one of the six American cars would have two defects.

The picture gets fuzzier when you consider that some of the American brands, Eagle and Geo, may be more Japanese than American. At the time of this study, the only Eagle manufactured in the United States, the Talon, was produced at Mitsubishi's Diamond Star plant in Normal, Illinois, and it was classified as an imported car. The Geos are manufactured by Suzuki in Japan and also in partnership with Toyota. The only Geo made in the United States, the Prizm, is the same car as the Toyota Corolla, which was designed and developed in Japan. If Geo and Eagle are counted as Japanese makes instead of American makes, then Japanese cars average 109 defects per 100 cars and American cars average 112.1 defects, accounting for less than a 3% difference in defects between cars manufactured in the two countries. This means that if you took 100 Japanese cars and 100 American cars, only three of the 100 American cars would have more defects than the Japanese cars.

Are Japanese cars better than American cars? It depends on your perspective. Japanese makes pulled down the top three spots, but a Japanese company, Mitsubishi, was next to last. American makes pulled down the fourth through seventh spots and six of the top 12 spots, but an American make, Eagle, had the most defects. Eagle, however, has half of a percent of the market share for cars sold in the United States and, as discussed previously, is not produced at American-owned plants.

If this question of superior quality between Japanese and American cars on number of defects had to be settled scientifically, then a statistical test could be run to determine if the rankings of the car makes are statistically significant. A statistical test called a Mann-Whitney U test could be used to settle the issue that Japanese cars are ranked higher than American cars. By the use of statistics, the researcher tries to establish whether the differences in the rankings are due to actual differences or whether they are due to random effects. In this situation, it is possible that random effects may enter into the data just by the cars which were sampled, what respondents called a defect, the randomness of the respondents trying to remember all the defects which occurred, and so on. In science, differences between the groups tested are considered to be significant and not due to random variation if it can be established that the differences occurred with less than a 5% chance or, in some cases, less than a 10% chance. If the probabilities for occurring randomly are that low, then the differences in the rankings can be attributed with a great deal of certainty to specific causes.

When the statistical test was performed on the rankings for the Japanese and American makes, the differences between the rankings were not significant statistically. (For those who know statistics, the U statistic was calculated as 49 with sample sizes of 10 and 14, which is far from being significant.) This means that a researcher could not make the claim that Japanese cars were ranked higher in initial quality than American cars in terms of the number of initial defects based on the J.D. Power study.

The picture that seemed so clear—Japanese cars are superior in initial quality— loses its clarity when we focus on the total picture. A Japanese car make was the best, but some Japanese car makes had more defects than most American makes. When the data is subjected to a scientific test, the Japanese cars do not have significantly fewer defects than American cars.

J. D. POWER DURABILITY   Another method of measuring quality used by J. D. Power and Associates is to examine the durability of cars over a period of time. Perhaps this provides a better picture of reliability, because a reliable car should be one which does not break down often during its lifetime. Recently, Power surveyed 22,000 owners of 1989 cars to determine the incidence and severity of owner-reported problems over a five-year period.[19]

The fifth column of Table 7.1a shows the ordering of the Japanese and American car makes according to this J. D. Power report on durability. When just comparing Japanese to American cars, the American makes held down the first two spots, with Cadillac first and Buick second. Acura and Honda were third and fourth, followed by Oldsmobile. So, in the first five positions, American makes occupied three of the spots, with two American makes first and second.   Overall, American makes averaged 450 problems per 100 vehicles in the fifth year of ownership as compared to 428 problems per 100 vehicles for the Japanese makes. This is a 5% difference. When the 1989 vehicles were rated on initial quality, there was a 34% difference between the averages. American cars had more initial defects, but over the period of ownership the American and Japanese cars became more equal in terms of problems. In other words, over time, American and Japanese cars converge in terms of quality.

That Japanese cars would not perform as well on durability measures as they do in initial quality is not surprising for those familiar with car ownership practices in Japan. In Japan, all cars have to pass a stringent certification process after four years, so most cars are sold after three or four years and less than 50,000 odometer

---

[19]Arlena Sawyers, "Cadillac Earns Top Marks for Dependability," *Automotive News*, March 28, 1994, pp. 8, 54.

Table 7.1 a Comparison of survey results for American and Japanese cars.

Position	Equi-Trend	1994 Power	1993 Power	Power Durability	Power Customer Satisfaction	Will Buy Same Make
1	Lexus	Lexus	Lexus	Cadillac	Lexus	Cadillac
2	Cadillac	Toyota	Toyota	Buick	Infiniti	Lincoln
3	Chevy trucks	Infiniti	Infiniti	Acura	Saturn	Ford
4	GMC trucks	Lincoln	Lincoln	Honda	Acura	Saturn
5	Ford trucks	Saturn	Acura	Oldsmobile	Toyota	Toyota
6	Chevrolet	Mercury	Honda	Toyota	Honda	Chrysler
7	Infiniti	Buick	Buick	Lincoln	Lincoln	Buick
8	Jeep	Honda	Nissan	Mercury	Cadillac	Dodge
9	Acura	Nissan	Saturn	Nissan	Buick	Chevrolet
10	Buick	Acura	Oldsmobile	Mazda	Subaru	Pontiac
11	Ford	Cadillac	Mercury		Oldsmobile	Subaru
12	Saturn	Oldsmobile	Geo		Mercury	Mercury
13		Ford	Ford		Plymouth	Mazda
14		Mazda	Cadillac		Chevrolet	Acura
15		Plymouth	Suzuki		Chrysler	Plymouth
16		Suzuki	Chevrolet		Nissan	Honda
17		Geo	Chrysler		Pontiac	Nissan
18		Subaru	Pontiac		Dodge	Mitsubishi
19		Chevrolet	Plymouth		Mitsubishi	
20		Pontiac	Eagle		Ford	
21		Dodge	Subaru		Mazda	
22		Chrysler	Mitsubishi		Geo	
23		Mitsubishi	Dodge		Eagle	
24		Eagle	Mazda		Suzuki	
25						
26						
27						

miles. In Japan's domestic market, this encourages people to buy new cars, which gives the car companies more money than they might earn without this artificial economic stimulant. Because of this policy, Japanese automakers have never had to worry about making vehicles which lasted much longer than 50,000 miles and do not get feedback from dealerships or customers on durability after four years of use. Without this experience, continuous improvement is not possible.

Table 7.1 b   Comparison of survey results for American and Japanese cars.

Position	Chronic Defects-1	Chonic Defects-2	Chronic Defects Improved	Master Mechanics	Design Engineers	Consumer Reports
1	Lexus	Olds	Saturn	Dodge	Ford	Acura
2	Buick	Buick	Olds	Chevrolet	Dodge	Infiniti
3	Toyota	Toyota	Mercury	Ford	Chevy	Lexus
4	Honda	Lexus	Infiniti	Lincoln	Honda	Saturn
5	Cadillac	Cadillac	Pontiac	Cadillac	Buick	Honda
6	Subaru	Lincoln	Jeep	Oldsmobile	Jeep/ Eagle	Toyota
7	Oldsmobile	Honda	Eagle	Buick	Toyota	Nissan
8	Lincoln	Infiniti	Lincoln	Lexus	Pontiac	Mazda
9	Mitsubishi	Saturn	Suzuki	Toyota	Cadillac	Mitsubishi
10	Acura	Nissan	GMC	Acura	Chrysler	Suzuki
11	Nissan	Mitsubishi	Nissan	Pontiac		Lincoln
12	Plymouth	Subaru	Chevy	GMC		Geo
13	Dodge	Acura	Mitsubishi	Chrysler		Cadillac
14	Chevrolet	Chevy	Chrsyler	Plymouth		Subaru
15	Ford	Mercury	Plymouth	Jeep		Eagle
16	Isuzu	Plymouth	Acura	Infiniti		Oldsmobile
17	Chrysler	Chrysler	Cadillac	Honda		Chrysler
18	Infiniti	Pontiac	Toyota	Mazda		Mercury
19	Mazda	Ford	Daihatsu	Mitsubishi		Pontiac
20	Mercury	Dodge	Buick	Mercury		Plymouth
21	Pointiac	GMC	Ford	Nissan		Dodge
22	Saturn	Isuzu	Dodge	Saturn		Buick
23	Daihatsu	Daihatsu	Honda	Suzuki		Isuzu
24	GMC	Suzuki	Subaru	Subaru		Ford
25	Jeep	Jeep	Isuzu	Isuzu		Jeep
26		Mazda	Lexus			Chevrolet
27		Eagle	Mazda			GMC

J. D. POWER CUSTOMER SATISFACTION INDEX   J. D.

Power and Associates also tabulate a customer satisfaction index which measures car quality and dealer service. In the survey, 35,000 buyers who had owned their cars for 12 or 13 months and had been to the dealer two or three times were questioned on their satisfaction with their cars. Unlike the other Power surveys, which only considered defects, this survey also considered dealer service, which may have little to do with the actual reliability of the car but much to do with the perceived quality of the car. The sixth column of Table 7.1a shows this ordering of the Japanese and American car makes according to the J. D. Power report on customer satisfaction. Four of the top five makes were Japanese, with Lexus and Infiniti in the top two spots, followed by Saturn as number three. Acura, Toyota, and Honda were in the next three spots. Following this top tier were mostly American makes: Cadillac, Buick, and Oldsmobile, with Subaru between Buick and Oldsmobile. For the above-average makes, five were Japanese and five were American. Three Japanese makes were below average, along with seven American makes.

Although the top tier was dominated by Japanese makes, it is interesting to see that Saturn was right at the top with Lexus, Infiniti, and Acura. This is surprising because these Japanese makes sell for three to four times the price of a typical Saturn. Overall, the Customer Satisfaction Index was similar to the results from the other J. D. Power quality surveys.

In looking at the results, J. D. Power was quick to criticize some of the Japanese makes. He said that "second-tier Asian makes, including Suzuki, Mitsubishi, Hundai and Mazda," did not have dealers who treated their customers well. He characterized the Japanese brands and dealers as having "cruised on high-quality products and good value for 20 years," but now they are "slow to adjust as domestic and European competitors have improved quality and undercut Japanese prices."[20]

Another, slightly different way to look at customer satisfaction is to ask how many current owners of cars would buy a car of the same make. *Automotive News* commissioned J. D. Power to ask this question of 6,156 car owners of cars registered between May 1991 and October 1992.[21] As seen from the seventh column of Table 7.1a, nine of the top ten car makes were American. Six of the eight bottom spots were Japanese makes. The owners of American cars were more satisfied and more likely to buy the same make again than were the owners of Japanese cars.

CHRONIC DEFECTS   In 1989, the state of Florida enacted a "lemon law" which required vehicle manufacturers to include a booklet in each vehicle outlining the rights of the owner. If an owner has a chronic problem which is not repaired, the owner can appeal to the state to arbitrate with the manufacturer. In the period from 1989 to 1994, Florida's attorney general's office tracked the chronic problems for each car make, producing two reports, one on 1989-1991 cars[22] and another on 1992-1994 cars.[23] The Chronic Defect Index, constructed by the state, is a prediction of the number of complaints and the severity of the complaints. This

---

[20]James R. Healey, "Japan Carmakers Lose Edge," *USA Today*, July 6, 1994, p. 2B.
[21]William R. Diem, "Bond Stronger with Age," *Automotive News*, March 28, 1994, p. S-6.
[22]Robert A. Butterworth, *New Motor Vehicle Make, Model and Manufacturer Study, 1989-1991* (Tallahassee: State of Florida Office of the Attorney General Lemon Law Arbitration Program, no date).

measure is different from the initial quality measure taken by J. D. Power because it measures the severity of the defect and also considers dealer service in fixing the defect.

Using the Chronic Defect Index, American makes perform well compared to Japanese makes (see the second and third columns of Table 7.1b). We will first consider the 1989-1991 cars. The car model scoring highest overall was the Cadillac Seville, which beat such quality stars as the Lexus LS400 and the Acura Legend. Examining the sixteen car makes that performed above average, eight were American and eight were Japanese. The vehicles were also divided into eight categories: subcompact cars, compacts, mid-size, full-size, sports cars, utility, vans, and light trucks. Four models from General Motors led the categories: Buick Skylark in compact cars; Buick Electra/Park Avenue in full-size cars; Cadillac Seville in mid-sized cars, and Oldsmobile Silhouette in vans. In compact cars, the Buick Skylark and the Chevrolet Corsica both beat the Toyota Camry. In addition, besides the Buick and the Chevy, the Dodge Spirit also beat the Honda Accord. Japanese manufacturers scored best in the remaining four categories: Toyota FourRunner/Landcruiser in utility vehicles; Toyota pickup in light trucks; Mitsubishi Mirage in subcompact, and Mazda MX6 in sports cars.

For the 1992-1994 cars, American cars did even better. Of the top ten car makes, eight were American models. Only two Japanese models, the Lexus SC300/400 in first place and the Misubishi Mirage in fifth place, managed to break into the top ten. Whereas in the previous study eight of the top sixteen car makes were American, in this case twelve of the top sixteen were American. American models were tops in five of the eight car and truck categories, or only four categories if Geo Prizm from Chevrolet is counted as a Japanese car. The Prizm is the same as the Toyota Corolla, which is designed in Japan but built in the United States. American makes led in the four categories of mid-size cars (Oldsmobile Cutlass Ciera), full-size cars (Cadillac DeVille), utility vehicles (Oldsmobile Bravada), and vans (Oldsmobile Silhouette). Japanese makes led in compact cars (Lexus SC300/400), sports cars (Toyota Paseo), and light trucks (Toyota pickup).

An interesting analysis performed in the 1994 study was to compare the chronic defects of the earlier cars (1989-1991) and the later cars (1992-1994) to determine if car quality had gone up or down between those two time periods. The fourth column of Table 7.1b shows the ordering of the cars from most improved to least improved. Actually, car makes in places seventeen to twenty-seven got worse in quality. American makes dominate the top of the list. Seven of the eight and eight of the ten top spots were American makes. Of all the makes, eleven American makes

---

[23]Robert A. Butterworth, *New Motor Vehicle Make, Model and Manufacturer Study, 1992-1994* (Tallahassee: State of Florida Office of the Attorney General Lemon Law Arbitration Program, no date).

improved and only four got worse. Only five Japanese makes improved, and the remaining seven became worse. American makes had an average improvement of 19% compared to Japanese makes which, on average, were 18% worse than the makes three years earlier.

QUALITY ACCORDING TO THE EXPERTS

Who is better able to judge the quality and technology of cars than the mechanics who have to fix them or the design engineers who can judge the quality of cars from an engineering and design perspective? Surveys have been conducted by people in both these groups of experts. The National Institute for Automotive Excellence surveyed 200 institute-certified master automobile technicians.[24] Of 600,000 auto mechanics in the United States, only 70,000 have obtained this certification. And a random survey of design engineers was conducted by Design News, which is a professional magazine for design engineers.[25] Both sets of experts were asked several questions about the quality of American and imported cars.

When they were asked the question, "Have American cars improved in quality in the last five years?," 88% of the master mechanics answered yes; only 4% said American cars had become worse. In the previous year's survey, the mechanics had been asked if imported cars had improved in quality over the last five years, and most said that they had not improved.[26] This result was similar to the chronic defect index from Florida, which found a large improvement for American makes. When asked what make of car they would choose for themselves, 84% of the mechanics indicated that they would prefer to have an American model car, with the Dodge Viper and the Chevrolet Corvette being the most desired. Only 10% indicated that they would like to own a Japanese model car. When the scores were combined according to car make, American companies held down the first seven spots: Dodge, Chevrolet, Ford, Lincoln, Cadillac, Oldsmobile, and Buick. Lexus, Toyota, and Acura placed eighth through tenth with 3%, 2%, and 2% of the responses, respectively. This is summarized in the fifth column of Table 7.1b.

The master mechanics were asked which car makes they considered to be the most innovative or technologically advanced. American companies held down the top five spots: Ford (15%), Chrysler (13%), Chevrolet (12%), Cadillac (10%), and Buick (7%). Only Toyota (tied for fifth) and Honda (ninth position) were able to crack the top ten models. Several Japanese models (Infiniti, Mitsubishi, Suzuki, Subaru, and Isuzu) received no votes.

---

[24]*The Second Annual Poll of the American Mechanic* (Herndon, VA: National Institute for Automotive Service Excellence, 1994).
[25]Robert N. Boggs, "1994 Design News Auto Survey," *Design News,* October 10, 1994, pp. 104-108.
[26]Cox News Service, "Mechanics Say U.S. Car Quality Rises," *Chicago Tribune,* May 12, 1993, p. 3-4.

The results from the design engineers were very similar. They were asked which car model they would buy, and the results were summarized by car make. Eight of the top ten were American makes, with Honda in fourth position and Toyota tied for sixth (see the sixth column of Table 7.1b). In terms of improvement over the years, American car makers were the only ones to boost their scores on the perceived quality of cars every year for the 15 years of the survey.

RECALLS   Manufacturers' recalls of vehicles to fix unsafe components is always embarrassing to the automobile company. When the U.S. National Highway Traffic Safety Administration finds a problem with a vehicle which could result in a safety problem, the vehicle manufacturer is told to issue a recall on the affected vehicles and fix the identified problem. The manufacturer then makes a public announcement, sends letters to all the known owners, and fixes the defect. The public announcements of recalls are often reported in the papers; prospective buyers should take notice of these announcements.

Note that problems resulting in recalls may be different from the defects considered by the J. D. Power surveys. A defect is usually due to a manufacturing problem, resulting in something in the car not working correctly. A recall is usually due to an engineering design problem, not a manufacturing one. A part which is poorly designed can cause safety problems. Thus, defects are usually the result of problems with the manufacturing process, whereas a recall often results from a problem in the engineering design.

American car makes are often hammered in the media on recall data. Newspaper readers are told of a recall involving 200,000 vehicles by GM versus a recall of 30,000 vehicles by Nissan, as an example. The readers might assume that GM has a bigger quality problem than Nissan. The error in this reasoning is that GM has a market share of over 30%, while Nissan has a market share of less than 7%. Therefore, to examine the data in a more logical way, the percentages of cars which are being recalled by the different companies must be used to evaluate the quality differences between American cars and the imports.

The recall data examined in this way yields interesting results versus our prior assumption that American makes would fare worse than Japanese makes in terms of recalls. To gather data on recalls, recalls announced during the first six months of 1994 in the weekly *Automotive News* were tabulated. *Automotive News* is the chief source of information on vehicle manufacturing and sales and is widely read by manufacturers and dealers. The number of recalls for each of the car companies is shown in the second column of Table 7.2.

By merely looking at the raw numbers, one would think that the American car companies were not doing very well because of the large number of recalls. As mentioned previously, though, the American car companies hold a larger market share than the Japanese companies. To be fair, one must also take into account market share. In the third column of the table, the market shares for the car companies are given according to the sales of 1993 vehicles as listed in *Automotive News.* Market share in 1993 provides only a rough estimate of overall market share, because it does not take into account the older vehicles on the road. In recalls for any particular year, old vehicles are recalled along with newer vehicles. Since market share for the American companies has been going down in the last 10 years, the estimate for market share of the American companies based on 1993 sales may be a little low when considering all vehicles on the road.

To find an equitable way of comparing the car companies on recalls, taking into account market share, we decided to use GM as a baseline comparison score because it has the largest market share. The formula is shown below, where GM_{share} is the market share of GM cars, x_{share} is the market share of the car company being compared to GM, $x_{recalls}$ is the number of recalls by the car company being compared, and $GM_{recalls}$ is the number of recalls from GM.

$$\frac{GM_{share}}{x_{share}} \times \frac{x_{recalls}}{GM_{recalls}}$$

Table 7.2 Vehicles recalled in the first half of 1994 taking into account market share. The likelihood represents the probability of a car being recalled in relation to General Motors (GM) vehicles (a lower score is better). As an example, a Honda is 12.9 times more likely to be recalled than a GM vehicle.

Company	Vehicles Recalled	Market Share	Likelihood of Vehicle Being Recalled
Chrysler	119,100	14.7%	0.4
Ford	552,500	25.6%	1.0
General Motors	727,604	33.5%	1.0
Nissan	251,000	6.7%	1.7
Subaru	31,295	0.7%	2.1
Mazda	252,621	2.5%	4.7
Suzuki	48,500	0.2%	11.2
Honda	1,800,000	6.4%	12.9

The important thing to know about this formula is that GM recalls will have a baseline score of 1.0 and the other car companies will be compared to GM. As an example, if Ford has a score of 5.0, this means that, based on Ford's market share, Ford could be expected to recall five times as many cars as GM.

The recall scores using the above formula are shown in the fourth column of Table 7.2. To consider a few examples, almost twice as many vehicles were recalled by Nissan as were recalled by Ford. Honda had a very high score of 12.9, meaning that, based on market share, a Honda vehicle had almost 13 times the chance to be recalled as a GM vehicle. Chrysler had the lowest score, 0.4, which means that less than half as many Chrysler cars were recalled as GM cars. The Big Three held down the top three spots, while Japanese companies held down the last five spots. In the period examined, Toyota had no announced recalls, so no data on that company was available.

The Honda recall is especially interesting. In January 1992, Honda recalled 25,055 cars made and sold in Japan because of poorly made oil switches which could destroy the vehicles' engines. In the United States, Honda did not recall the same vehicles, with the same switches. "It wouldn't cause a dangerous situation, so the U.S. administration and we decided it would not have to be recalled," said Shin Tanaka, a spokesman for Honda.[27] After having been aware of the problem for two years, Honda eventually announced a recall in February 1994 of the 1.8 million 1988-1991 Civics and Accords that had been sold in the United States.

The high scores of the Japanese companies, especially Honda, may be an aberration due to the time period tested. Honda could just as easily have announced this recall in January 1992, as it did in Japan. The negative publicity in the United States may have hurt vehicle sales, however, as they were on their way to beating out the American companies by having their car make, the Accord, with the most sales in 1992. The recall data may be different for other time periods. Looking at 1990 data for the whole year, however, the numbers are similar. Ford and Chrysler again had low recall scores of 0.10 and 0.25, respectively. Nissan had a similar score of 1.6 and Subaru had a score of 6.8. This would support the conclusion that the 1994 scores are not out of line.

The recall data collected was surprising. It ran counter to our expectations because we hadn't seen the recalls reported in *Automotive News,* just the ones reported by the general newspapers, which don't cover all recalls. Apparently, the Japanese realize the impact that recalls have on consumer consciousness. Auto expert George Hoffer, of Virginia Commonwealth University, followed the recalls over a 14-month period.[28] Ford and General Motors, which combined have 59.1% of

[27]Merrill Goozner, "Recalls: Japan's Little Known Quality," *Chicago Tribune,* January 31, 1992, pp. 3-1, 3-2.
[28]James R. Healey, "Does Familiarity Breed Content?," *USA Today,* March 23, 1993, p. 6B.

the domestic American car market, announced publicly 62% of their recalls. The Japanese brands, with 24.3% of the American market, announced only 11% of theirs. Only Chrysler, with 14.7% of the market, was similar to the Japanese companies in announcing only 8% of its recalls. This carefully controlled image was effective in diverting consumer attention away from the recall problems of Japanese vehicles.

PERCEPTION OF QUALITY   Except for the survey of the master mechanics, the previous measures of car quality came from car owners, who are familiar with their car makes and have a vested interest in their cars. Few people want to admit that they spent thousands of dollars and made lousy decisions. Another way to look at quality is to ask people their perceptions of quality of various products even if they do not own the product. As an example, many people may want to own a Lexus but cannot afford one.

Of vehicles in the EquiTrend survey, fourteen makes made the list of top 100 products (see the second column of Table 7.1a). Of those fourteen, three were Japanese makes (Lexus, Infiniti, and Acura) and two were German (Mercedes and BMW). The nine remaining makes were American. The following is the ordering of the vehicle makes with the rank and the quality score, on a scale of 1 to 100, in parentheses: Mercedes (5th, 80.3); Lexus (19th, 76.7); Cadillac (32nd, 74.1); BMW (44th, 73.0); Chevy trucks (55th, 71.3); GMC trucks (65th, 70.7); Ford trucks (68th, 70.4); Chevrolet automobiles (78th, 69.5); Infiniti (80th, 69.4); Jeep (86th, 68.3); Acura (87th, 68.3); Buick (89th, 68.0); Ford (91st, 67.8), and Saturn (97th, 67.5).

Lexus had a very good score, with only one car make, Mercedes-Benz, perceived to be of higher quality. The other Japanese makes did not fare as well. Infiniti had eight vehicle makes ahead of it, including five American makes, two German makes, and one other Japanese make. Acura had ten makes ahead of it, including six American makes, two German makes, and two Japanese makes. The other Japanese car makes were not among the top 100.

Some surveys have asked people the simple question about which country, Japan or the United States, produces higher-quality cars. In a 1994 poll by Market Opinion Research of 1103 Americans, 40% said that American cars were better built than Japanese cars, 43% said that Japanese cars were better built, and 17% said that the quality was about the same.[29] This result is interesting because 10 months earlier, only 31% said that American cars were better and 52% said that Japanese cars were better. In a *Time* magazine poll in late 1993, 50% of the 500 adults surveyed said that the United States makes the best cars, 28% said Japan did, and 15% said Germany did.[30] The fact that the percentages in the *Time* poll are different than those in

---

[29]Tressa Crosby, "Big 3 Gain Ground with U.S. Buyers," *Automotive News,* February 21, 1994, p. 4.

the Market Opinion Research poll could be due to the different wordings in the two polls. In the *Time* poll people were asked to rate which country makes the best cars, and in the Market Opinion Research poll they were asked to rate who builds better cars. Making better cars includes factors such as features and how the cars operate. Building better cars considers only initial defects. The *Time* poll also asked whether the quality of cars built by U.S. companies had improved or declined in the past five years. Eighty percent agreed that it had improved, and only 14% said that it had declined. These numbers were similar, but not quite as high as those reported by the master mechanics. The perceptions of quality of American cars are changing fast.

VEHICLE SALES AS AN INDICATION OF QUALITY   In
the final analysis, the true gauge of quality, including reliability, durability, price, product features, and usability, is vehicle sales. If a company can manufacture a reliable vehicle with the features desired by customers and sell it at a reasonable price, then the definition of quality has been satisfied. Which companies make the products that customers want to buy?

Using the latest sales data available for 1993 models,[31] American makes dominate the lists. Nineteen of the top twenty-five car models are American. Among light trucks, minivans, and sport utility vehicles, American companies perform even better, holding down twenty-one of the top twenty-five positions. The first nine spots in the list are all American makes. Combining these two categories to consider all vehicles, American makes hold nineteen of the top twenty-five spots, with the first four being American models. The only Japanese models to make the list are the Honda Accord at number 5, the Toyota Camry at number 7, the Honda Civic at number 11, the Toyota Corolla at number 18, the Toyota compact pickup at number 21, and the Nissan Sentra at number 24.

When the vehicles are broken down into nine categories, American makes head the list in eight of them. The Honda Accord leads in compacts, and the Ford Escort is the leader in subcompacts. The Ford Taurus, the overall leader, is first in midsize cars. In full-size cars, the Ford Thunderbird is the sales leader. The Ford Mustang leads in sports cars. The Ford F-series leads in light trucks, and the Ford Ranger leads in compact trucks. The Ford Explorer leads in utility trucks. Among minivans, the Dodge Caravan is the sales leader.

Another way to look at quality is to consider how many people say they would buy the same make of car again. J. D. Power and *Automotive News* did a random survey of 6,156 registered car owners and asked this question. American makes were all

---

[30]William McWhirter, "Back on the Fast Track," *Time,* December 13, 1993, p. 64.
[31]*Automotive News 1994 Market Data Book,* May 25,1994, p. 29.

clustered at the top of the list. Seven American makes were all above average, led by Cadillac, for which 41.5% of the respondents reported they would buy the same make again. Lincoln was close behind, with 41.0% responding that they would buy the same make again. The only Japanese make to rate above average was Toyota in the number 5 spot, with 30.3% responding that they would buy the same make again. Five American makes scored below average, while six Japanese makes did.

There are some indications from Japan that even Japanese consumers are moving away from Japanese vehicles. In 1993, sales of imported vehicles in Japan rose by 9.1%. This is especially interesting because overall vehicle sales in Japan had declined 7.5% in 1992. Ford has tripled its sales in Japan.

CONSUMER REPORTS   *Consumer Reports* is one of the primary sources for American consumers to get information about products. The staff at *Consumer Reports* test the products and report on the products' appearance, performance, usability, and general perceptions of quality. These comments are largely subjective. The staff also performs extensive tests, such as on the safety of the product, and reports these objective results. One of the main sources of information about products comes from the readers of the magazine. For cars and trucks, *Consumer Reports* solicits responses about reliability problems. The rankings on reliability depend on readers sending in questionnaires.

Consumer Reports lists reliability problems in one of five categories: solid black circle is worst; half-black circle is bad; open circle is average; half-red circle is good; and solid red circle is best. If one looks through the magazine at the car rankings, the American models usually receive average to worst ratings and the Japanese makes usually receive good or best ratings. To provide a ranking of the car makes from *Consumer Reports* similar to the ones listed in Table 7.1a and b, the five-point rankings were averaged for all models within a make. The orderings are shown in the seventh column of Table 7.1b.

Their final conclusions about quality are different from those published by J. D. Power. As an example, consider the J. D. Power rankings for the durability of cars after five years of ownership. J. D. Power does not break down the published data in terms of car models; it gives only averages for the car makes. However, of the car makes they ranked above average, five were American (Cadillac, Buick, Oldsmobile, Lincoln, and Mercury) and five were Japanese (Acura, Honda, Toyota, Nissan, and Mazda).

To examine how well the data from J. D. Power corresponds to the data from *Consumer Reports*, we looked at the *Consumer Reports 1994 Buying Guide*. In that guide is a section on which used cars are recommended and which should be avoided. The 1989 cars evaluated in *Consumer Reports* can be compared to the 1989

Table 7.3 The J. D. Power report for durability of 1989 cars listed five American makes and five Japanese makes as being above average. Of those makes rated above average, *Consumer Reports* listed 36 American models and 53 Japanese models in its annual issue. The three rows show the recommended models, the models to avoid, and those for which *Consumer Reports* offered no opinion. If the J. D. Power durability study corresponded to the *Consumer Reports* suggestions, the percentages in each column should be about the same.

Consumer Reports	**American models above average in durability**	**Japanese models above average in durability**
Recommended 1989 models	6 (17%)	37 (73%)
1989 models to avoid	6 (17%)	1 (2%)
1989 models with no opinion	24 (69%)	15 (29%)
Totals	36	53

car makes which are above average in the 1994 J. D. Power five-year durability study. The five American makes with above-average ratings included thirty-five models rated by *Consumer Reports* in 1989 (see Table 7.3). Of these thirty-five models, *Consumer Reports* recommended six, told their readers to avoid six, and had no opinion on twenty-four. The results were different for the Japanese models rated above average by J. D. Power. *Consumer Reports* recommended thirty-seven of them, told their readers to avoid only one model, and had no opinion on fifteen.

As an example of the different findings of the J. D. Power survey and the *Consumer Reports* questionnaire, Oldsmobile was ranked fifth by J. D. Power on durability. Ten Oldsmobile models were considered by *Consumer Reports*, and none of those was recommended. On the other hand, Mazda was ranked tenth by J. D. Power, but eight of eleven Mazda models were recommended by *Consumer Reports*. Even though Cadillac had the highest durability score according to J. D. Power, the latest issue of *Consumer Reports* did not recommend them. "The reason why they [Cadillac] weren't recommended, although they tested rather well, was because of the reliability figures," said Rana Arons, a *Consumer Reports* spokesperson. "They were not as reliable as we would have liked for a recommended car."[32]

DEWEY WAS NOT THE 33RD PRESIDENT   The headline
of the Chicago paper in 1948 read that Dewey had defeated Truman to become the 33rd president of the United States. This is remembered as one of the most embarrassing moments in newspaper journalism. The Chicago paper used a telephone poll performed to project the winner instead of waiting for the results. Dewey, running as a Republican, out-polled the Democrat Truman by a substantial margin.

---

[32]Jennifer Heil, ". . . But Consumer Reports Says: Avoid Cadillacs," *Automotive News,* March 28, 1994, pp. 8.

What had happened? Republicans, as might be expected, preferred Dewey. Republicans were, on a whole, richer than those who voted Democrat. In 1948, not everybody had telephones; wealthy people owned more telephones than the general populace. When the pollsters phoned people to determine their Presidential choice, they phoned more Republicans than Democrats simply because more Republicans had phones. The sample was not representative of the population of voters, but was probably representative of the population of voters who had phones, hence the embarrassing headline.

Consumer Reports magazine falls into a similar hole. The results published in *Consumer Reports* come only from people who read *Consumer Reports;* they are not necessarily representative of all people who own vehicles. This makes the results from the survey different from all the other polls mentioned in this chapter. For the J. D. Power reports, all registered owners of the particular car model are potential candidates in the survey. The EquiTrend survey is based on a representative sample of consumers. The survey on the master mechanics is based on a random sample of these master mechanics. The results from the Florida attorney general's office on chronic defects are based on the whole population of Floridians who had complaints about cars. The recall data is based on problems people had with vehicles through-out the country. Only in *Consumer Reports* are the surveys based on a narrow segment of the population, in this case, those people who read the magazine.

When the quality of cars from all these surveys is collected in a single table, it becomes apparent that *Consumer Reports* is obtaining different results from the others. Table 7.4 compares the vehicle makes which were rated above average or recommended by the various quality surveys. Of all the polls, only *Consumer Reports*, by a large margin, recommended more Japanese makes than American makes. All the others recommended more American makes or rated Japanese and American makes the same. The numbers at the bottom of the table are the column sums. Taking into account all the studies, the margin between above-average and below-average models is greater for American makes than it is for Japanese makes. (The numbers do not average out to 50% because of the missing data in one row and because European cars, which usually score below average in quality, were not included in the table.) If the *Consumer Reports* data is removed from the table, American makes are more likely to be ranked higher than average, while Japanese makes are just average.

Consumer Reports and its editorial board are not necessarily biased for Japanese makes and against American makes, but a pretty good case could be made that their readers are biased in this direction. To test this conclusion, two statistical methods were used to determine if the readers of *Consumer Reports* are biased in favor of Japanese vehicles. In the first test, vehicles were examined which were manufactured at the same plant, usually at the same time, but which bore either a Japanese name-

Table 7.4 Summary of American and Japanese makes above and below average in the different suveys.

Survey	American Makes		Japanese Makes	
	Above	**Below**	**Above**	**Below**
J. D. Power 1994	6	6	6	4
J. D. Power 1993	6	6	6	4
J. D. Power 5-Year Durability	5	5	5	3
J. D. Power Customer Satisfaction	5	4	6	7
Customers Who Will Buy the Same Make	7	5	1	6
Master Mechanics—Make They Would Buy	10	4	3	8
Master Mechanics—Technologically Advanced	10	4	3	8
Design Engineers—Make They Would Buy	8	no data	2	no data
EquiTrend	9	no data	3	no data
Chronic Defect Index (1989-1991)	8	6	8	3
Chronic Defect Index (1992-1994)	10	5	8	4
Chronic Defect Index Improvement	11	4	5	7
Consumer Reports	3	11	9	2
Totals	88 (59%)	60 (41%)	65 (54%)	56 (46%)
Totals without Consumer Reports	85 (63%)	49 (37%)	56 (51%)	54 (49%)

plate or an American nameplate. The Ford Explorer and the Mazda Navajo are examples. Both are manufactured by Ford at the same plants, but one usually carries a Japanese company name and one an American company name. Another example is the Eagle Talon and the Mitsubishi Eclipse. Both are manufactured at Mitsubishi's Diamond Star plant in Normal, Illinois, with the main difference being the name on the vehicle.

If readers of *Consumer Reports* are unbiased, then they should report about the same number of problems with the American nameplate as with the Japanese nameplate, because the vehicle is the same. We looked at *Consumer Reports* from 1990 to 1994 and compared the ratings of these vehicles. Of 16 comparisons, the vehicle with the Japanese nameplate was rated better than the American nameplate seven times, the opposite was true only once, and the rest were ties. The seven-to-one ratio indicates a possible bias. To test the bias statistically, a sign test was performed on the data. The sign test showed that this kind of result could happen by chance with only a 3.5% probability; anything under 5% is usually taken as very good evidence that the result was not due to chance. The conclusion from this statistical test is that the readership of *Consumer Reports* is biased against American makes.

The second statistical test used to look at bias has to do with model fitting. A researcher will often try to find a simple model to fit complex data. The fit of the data to the model is determined statistically by correlating the data to the model and then squaring the correlation coefficient. In technical terms this is called the percent variance accountedf for. We will refer to it as the model fit. The model fit can range from 0%, which means that the model did not fit the data, to 100%, which means a perfect fit. Usually, if the fit is above 50%, the model is considered to be a very good fit for the data.

A simple model can be tested against the *Consumer Reports* data for 1994. This model can be called the "Japan as No. 1" model. For the test, the number 1 is assigned to all Japanese makes and the number 2 is assigned to all American makes. These two numbers were correlated with the *Consumer Reports* data and then a model fit percentage was calculated. The fit for the "Japan as Number 1" model was a very high 51.4%. When the same model was fitted to the J. D. Power 1994 reliability ratings, the model fit was only 3.4%, which means that it did not fit the data. For the Chronic Defect Index, the model fit was similarly low, 4.5%. The "Japan as Number 1" model fits only the *Consumer Reports* data, not the J. D. Power or Chronic Defects Index data.

The good fit to the data of the "Japan as Number 1" model indicates that a potential car customer does not have to go to the newsstand and buy *Consumer Reports*. The customer can be fairly certain that if he or she buys a Japanese car, then this will correspond to the recommendations in *Consumer Reports*. If one modification to the "Japan as Number 1" model is made by adding that all Japanese cars plus Saturn cars are good cars, then the model is almost perfect in its predictions of the *Consumer Reports* ratings.

Basing survey results and reliability ratings on the readership of a magazine is not a very good sampling technique. Among professionals, this kind of sampling went out of favor in 1948. If you sampled readers of other magazines, the results would probably be different. If the readers of *American Rifleman* were polled, for example, the results would probably be very different. We would not try to claim that the readership of *American Rifleman* is representative of the population of car owners as a whole and, in a similar way, *Consumer Reports* readers cannot be considered to be representative of all car owners.

CONSUMER REPORTS AND VEHICLE SAFETY *Consumer Reports* has a problem when it comes to safety, because it usually recommends Japanese cars. Japanese cars are typically smaller than American cars, and small cars are involved in more serious accidents than larger cars. Statistics of actual highway accidents show that small cars are involved in three times more accidents that result in injury than larger cars. With the accident statistics pointing to the differences in safety between small and large cars, how can small cars continue to be recommended so highly by *Consumer Reports*?

Discounting the higher accident rates of smaller cars, in 1992 *Consumer Reports* said that "all other things being equal, safety-conscious design can fully protect the small car's occupants...." The Insurance Institute for Highway Safety criticized that conclusion: "If readers purchase small cars based on such misinformation, they'll be increasing their risk of death or serious injury in the event of a crash," said Brian O'Neill, the president of the Institute.[33]

The Institute criticizes the crash testing used by the Department of Transportation and reported by *Consumer Reports*. Crash testing is done head on, and then the results on the electronically monitored dummies are put into a complicated formula to determine the likelihood of injury to human passengers. The institute argues that head-on crashes are unrealistic and that cars are more likely to crash at a slight angle. In *Consumer Reports*, the small Geo Storm has an index similar to the much larger Buick Park Avenue for a head-on crash. For a crash at an angle, the Geo Storm sustains much more damage than the Buick and provides more chance of injury to the occupants.

In its ratings, *Consumer Reports* does not compare vehicles between size categories. Trunk space is called large if it is larger than the trunk space of other cars within

---

[33]Ralph Vartabedian, "Magazine's Safety Advice Assailed," *Los Angeles Times*, April 8, 1992, p E5.

the same category. Both a small car and a large car could have the same rating for trunk space even though the large car may have a trunk space twice as large as the small car.

The same philosophy applies to vehicle safety. A high safety rating is meaningful only within the category. Unless readers take the time to examine the fine print, they may not understand the safety results for small cars. As an example, if both a small car and a large car have the highest safety rating, the reader may not understand that this rating applies only within the category and not when comparing the small car to the large car. *Consumer Reports* states that "the most meaningful comparison [for safety] is within size categories."[34] This kind of comparison is meaningful only when cars of the same size run into each other. If a large car runs into a small car, the size differences between the cars becomes very meaningful to the occupants of the small car.

Prevention magazine considered on-road safety records and government crash tests for 1990-1992 vehicles to calculate the safest vehicles. The vehicles given the award and recommended by the magazine were all American makes: Plymouth Voyager/Dodge Caravan, Buick LeSabre, Ford Taurus/Mercury Sable, and Plymouth Sundance/Dodge Shadow.[35] Did *Consumer Reports* recommend these vehicles? To determine this we went to the 1994 *Consumer Reports Buying Guide* book and looked under the category of "Good & bad bets in used cars," which considered models from 1987 to 1991. *Consumer Reports* listed 136 models from 1990 and 1991 which were good bets in used cars; 111 models were Japanese or manufactured at Japanese plants, 18 were European, and only 7 were American. Out of all these possibilities, only the Buick LeSabre in 1990 and 1991 managed to make the "good bets" list. In fact, the Voyager and Caravan, along with one model of the Taurus, were placed on the list of cars to avoid.

Another disturbing aspect of *Consumer Reports* is that it recommends Japanese vehicle models even when its own evidence indicates that the car may be unsafe. In 1992, *Consumer Reports* compared sport utility vehicles by examining the Jeep Grand Cherokee, the Ford Explorer, the Isuzu Trooper, and the Mitsubishi Montero. These vehicles were made for four-wheel driving, and a prime safety consideration should be that they will not lean and roll over. When reviewing the Trooper, *Consumer Reports* stated, "The Isuzu handled very sloppily and leaned a lot through our avoidance course."[36] The Mitsubishi was worse: "In normal handling, the Mitsubishi feels tippy and cumbersome, with vague, slow steering," said *Consumer Reports*. "In our emergency-avoidance course, it responded slowly and leaned sharply, and

---

[34]Ibid.

[35]"Prevention Magazine Honors Safety Efforts", *Automotive News*, May 2, 1994., p. 23.

[36]"Road Test," *Consumer Reports*, November, 1992, p. 732.

the tail swung out too easily.... Sometimes a rear wheel lifted off the ground."[37] Yet in the recommendations for the vehicles later in the same article,[38] *Consumer Reports* stated that the Isuzu Trooper "feels substantial and refined" and the Mitsubishi offers a "sophisticated" four-wheel-drive system. Although the Explorer did not lean or lift its wheels off the road, *Consumer Reports* said that it had "clumsy handling." It generally liked the Jeep but ended its recommendation by stating: "[O]ne big caution: Past Jeep models have been very unreliable." A bigger caution should have been the safety of the Isuzu and Mitsubishi as tested objectively on the avoidance course. The final recommendations, which readers are most likely to read, did not mention the objective results from the safety tests. More emphasis was placed on subjective perceptions of sophistication. Do you want to go four-wheel driving or drive on ice and snow in a "tippy" vehicle that is sophisticated and refined or in one that keeps all four wheels firmly planted on the road?

IS THERE A QUALITY GAP?   In the original proposal for this
book, the title of this chapter was listed as "Closing the Quality Gap." We had been led to believe that there was a quality gap between Japanese products and American products. We expected to find that Japanese products were of higher quality than American products. We had been told this repeatedly. "[The United States] must learn to produce good products again," says Shintaro Ishihara, the Japanese politician and author of *The Japan That Can Say No*.[39] After looking through the evidence, though, the title of this chapter had to be changed. The surveys indicate that there is no quality gap; looking at all products, the quality gap may actually be in the opposite direction.

We had perhaps missed out on a recent trend in public perceptions of quality. In 1993 a marketing group surveyed 1000 American consumers and 1000 American executives from the largest manufacturing companies.[40] For the first time since this survey had been taken, more Americans thought that American companies produce higher-quality products than Japanese companies. A majority of the executives, though, still agreed that Japanese companies produce higher-quality products, echoing what had been the trend of the consumers prior to the 1993 survey.

There are some very good Japanese companies. In most surveys, Toyota has products which are consistently at or near the top of the list. Consumers perceive Sony consumer electronics to be of consistently high quality. After these two companies, however, the perceived quality of products from Japanese companies falls off.

[37]Ibid., p. 733.
[38]Ibid., p. 734.
[39]"Playboy Interview: Shintaro Ishihara," *Playboy*, October, 1990, p. 66.
[40]Ronald E. Yates, "Japan's Image Fading Fast," *Chicago Tribune*, November 29, 1993, pp. 4-1, 4-4.

Honda has had a good reputation, but the car recall data and the other surveys place Honda lower on the lists. There are many other companies in Japan that make low-quality products, and Americans have been buying them only because of price. Health officials in Philadelphia decided to buy 625,000 condoms for public distribution from Okamoto Industries of Tokyo because they could save half a cent a unit. Users said they were too tight and too easily torn.[41] Defective items like this, purchased solely on price, could have serious health consequences.

We were a little surprised at the high quality ratings for American vehicles. We had been led to believe that Japanese automobile companies were consistently better than American companies. However, it appears that American companies are making the kinds of vehicles that customers want to buy, with a clear dominance in pickup trucks, minivans, and sport utility vehicles. Although American makes perform well on reliability ratings by J. D. Power and the Chronic Defect Index, quality means more than reliability. Quality also means building vehicles which are safe and affordable. The vehicles must have the features and characteristics desired by consumers. The dominance of American models among the twenty-five best-selling vehicles shows that American companies are building quality into their vehicles.

Dale Dauten writes a column called the "Corporate Curmudgeon" for King Features Syndicate, which is printed in many high-circulation newspapers such as the *Chicago Tribune*. Like us, he grew up in an age when we just assumed that Japanese products were high quality. However, Dauten recently started to question that assumption when his own experiences indicated otherwise.[42] "[A]s I lugged my 2-year-old Japanese TV back to the repair shop for the second time, I recollected a year of lousy experiences with Japanese products: the cellular phone that never worked right, the CD player "not worth fixing," the buttons that fell off my son's new personal stereo, the eyeglass frames that snapped apart, the tire on my wife's car that self-destructed, and the car itself—it would take too long to go into," says Dauten. Then he asked his readers to do an exercise: Walk through your house and note which products you have a special affection for. When he did this, only one was made by a Japanese company. He was surprised to find that most of the others were made by American companies such as Apple, Hewlett-Packard, Cannondale, Motorola, AT&T, GE, and Sears. We urge you to do this exercise on your own. Your reaction may be similar to Dauten's and to ours after finishing this chapter. "Am I crazy, or are American products once again the best in the world?" asks Dauten at the end of his column.

---

[41]UPI-Kyodo, "Tokyo-Made Prophylactices Cause Controversy in Philly," *Japan Times*, October 26, 1990, p. 2.
[42]Dale Dauten, "The Corporate Curmudgeon: New Sense to 'Made in Japan,'" *Chicago Tribune*, November 1, 1993, p. 3-5.

Myth 1:
Japanese Companies Are More
Advanced Technologically

It has been claimed that Americans are losing their technological edge to Japan. This loss has implications for national security. During the Cold War between the United States and the Soviet Union, Shintaro Ishihara, the Japanese politician who wrote *The Japan That Can Say No*, stated that if Japan decided to stop selling semiconductors to the United States, the United States would not be able to produce weapons and the Soviet Union would gain the advantage. Is Japan becoming more technologically advanced? Are Japanese products superior in quality to American products? If so, how has this superiority been achieved? What is myth, and what is reality?

SUPPORTING TECHNOLOGY One curious Japanese research trend is in the technology of bras. We are talking about big bras, gold bras, and bras that play music. Japanese companies are leading the world in bra technology. American researchers, cups in hand, should clamor for a government-sponsored research program to lift up American technology in bras. We are being beaten back by Japanese researchers in bras.

117

Triumph International in Japan, for some reason, developed the world's largest bra and displayed it on the roof of a high-rise building in Tokyo. The bra had an underbust measurement of 24 meters and a bust measurement of 28 meters. Why were these measurements chosen? Americans will be glad to know that the size was not chosen to fit a Japanese woman, but to fit a well-known American lady of French origin. Christian Thoma, the marketing director of Triumph International, explained that the size was his idea. "I was thinking," he said, "of the Statue of Liberty. If you put a bra on her, what size would it be?"[1]

Determining the bust size of the Statue of Liberty required high technology. An electronics firm was hired to write the software for a computer modeling of Miss Liberty's bra. The company claims that the dimensions are correct down to the centimeter. It takes a hefty woman, though, to wear a 35-kilogram (77-pound) bra.

Triumph International has also achieved other technological successes with bras. A few years ago, the company had a promotional campaign in which it gave free panties to women who submitted two old bras. What do you do with 300,000 old bras? They used them to make a pyramid-shaped form near Tokyo Tower (the one Godzilla is always knocking down) and then used dry ice to create the illusion of smoke being emitted from the tip of a volcano.

If you have the money, you can purchase the ultimate in bra technology. One Japanese manufacturer has created the world's first pure gold bra. For women thinking about purchasing this item, it has a AA cup size and a value of $280,000.[2]

How do you commemorate the 200th anniversary of Mozart's death? One Japanese lingerie company decided to develop a musical bra. The bra played Mozart for 20 seconds.

BUT DOES IT HAVE AN AGITATOR?   Kenji Kawakami is a Japanese inventor who has come up with all kinds of ideas. Sashimi is a raw fish dish considered by Japanese consumers to be a prime delicacy. It must be handled carefully, however, to reduce the chances of parasites and other contaminants tainting the fish. Although we were not too excited about raw fish, we tried the delicacy when invited by our Japanese hosts to fancy restaurants. One of the problems with eating sashimi is that you must look into the eyes of the fish—just recently deceased—while munching on it. Kawakami has just the thing for sensitive Americans: fish masks that can be placed on the sashimi so you do not have to look your dinner in the eye.

---

[1]David Lazarus, "Firm Is Uplifted by World's Biggest Bra?," *Japan Times,* October 14, 1990, p. 18.
[2]"Golden Opportunity," *Chicago Tribune,* November 6, 1992, p. 1-4.

Riding the trains in Japan can be difficult if one does not know how to read Japanese characters. Americans traveling in Europe can match the alphabetic characters and arrive at the right destination even if their pronunciation is atrocious. In Japan, all bets were off. Identifying a destination or a type of train (local or express) is a painstakingly difficult visual process of comparing the lines and marks of a character to some target character. Whizzing by a station in a train car, or having a train pass by while standing on the platform, does not provide enough time to identify the complex characters.

Many times we would just hop on a train, not knowing if it was a local train or an express train, not knowing if the train was going to continue in the same direction, or if it was going to turn around. We did manage to pick up some cues. If everybody got off the train, then we knew that we should get off the train.

One time we were on a train heading back from Kamakura to our home station, or so we thought. It was a Sunday night around dinner time, so the train was empty of the usual crush of school children and commuters. At the first stop, everybody got off the train except one person who was asleep. We figured that even though he was asleep, he must know where he was going, so we stayed on the train. The train started up in the opposite direction, returning us to Kamakura. When we got back to Kamakura we stayed on the train, but this time when everyone got off at the second stop we took our cue and disembarked as well. We followed the other people and switched trains. After that, we held our breath, never quite sure whether our trains would run backward or forward. As for the sleeping gentleman, we never knew if he got anywhere.

Japanese workers work long hours and use whatever opportunities they can to sleep. This is a widespread problem in Japan for which Kawakami has devised a solution. He invented "sleep well" signs which can be attached to a person's face. The signs serve two functions: They block out the light for sounder sleep and they also provide a place to affix another sign indicating at which station the person should disembark. The cooperation of fellow passengers is essential.

Kawakami seems to be one of the few Japanese inventors or product developers who are really concerned with reducing the workload of housewives. Have a cat in the family home? Put the pet to work by buying "pussi-mops." These are padded booties to be placed on all four legs so that when little Muffy walks through the house, or on the tables and furniture, "pussi-mops" dust the furniture.

Finally, Kawakami has developed a miniature washing machine that can be strapped to a person's calf so that the housewife can go to the store or even a movie while doing the laundry. Based on our experience, mobility may be an important reason for inventing a miniature washing machine, but equally important may be that the housewife does not have to run into the bathroom to change the setting whenever the washing machine enters the spin cycle (see Chapter 2). It's right there on your leg. Talk about being hobbled by your housework. Kawakami did not indicate whether or not the washing machine had an agitator.

Japanese researchers and inventors have obviously had fun developing these products. Outside Japan, we often think of the stereotypical Japanese researcher calculating which design to concentrate on so as to maximize the return to the company. These examples provide a refreshing look at applying technology in order to have fun.

"WE DO NOT THINK LOGICALLY"   The research institute I was working at was the first of its kind in Japan and has been the training ground and model for other corporations' research institutes. In the United States, most researchers are trained in the university system. Americans tend to believe that people follow their talents, thus researchers have different personality characteristics than elementary teachers or lawyers. In fact, our counselors give undecided students personality tests to help them choose their careers. The Japanese believe that hard work will make anyone successful at anything. Universities reflect the theoretical differences in career choice between the two countries. For the most part, American university professors, especially at the graduate level, serve as mentors to their students. Doctoral candidates work alongside their professors, benefitting from their experience and guidance. An ideal doctoral candidate is very independent and creative, which are not personality characteristics encouraged in Japan.

Research requires creativity, curiosity, and independence of thought; and none of these personality attributes is valued or nurtured in Japan. A famous Japanese saying is "The nail that sticks up is pounded back in." The Japanese educational system discourages characteristics which would make students stand out. They are pounded back in to be like everybody else. The emphasis in Japanese schools on rote learning suppresses any curiosity that students may have about the subject matter. School is for learning facts, not for learning how to think.

When I met my colleagues at the research institute, they did not fit the idea of researchers I had come to know in the United States and other countries. Most did not have advanced degrees. An advanced degree itself may not be important, but the degree does mean that a person has been trained in research methods. In the sciences and engineering, an advanced degree also means that students have done one or more projects by themselves, demonstrating initiative and competence as researchers. My colleagues did not have this kind of training. They had bachelors' degrees earned in an educational system which does not demand much from its college students. Most had transferred from nonresearch jobs in other divisions of the company. Not only did they lack training in research methods, they did not have rigorous training in the basic subject matter being investigated. For example, a human factors researcher for AT&T Bell Labs would have a Ph.D. in industrial engineering or psychology. He or she would be capable of collecting and analyzing experimental data and understanding the psychological theories behind human factors design guidelines. Without this training and expertise, they will make mistakes and waste the company's valuable time. Hiring people with the right training is efficient. But my Japanese colleagues had no background or practical experience in the areas they were supposed to be investigating. This was not an efficient way to conduct research into new technologies.

My colleagues did not have the independence of thought that I expected in researchers. Most of the research projects they had undertaken were initiated because of contacts with foreign researchers. One project was being done because a Dutch researcher had visited; they were continuing some of the research he had done in Holland. A university researcher from California had come, and projects were promptly started following his line of research. A research idea was good because somebody else was doing it; the researchers in my group seemed to have no way of independently evaluating which research directions would be fruitful or which new ideas should be initiated.

Most surprising of all was that my fellow researchers did not know how to think logically, and were proud of it. They told me this themselves. It sounds racist to say that a group of people do not think logically, because it implies that they do not have the capacity to do so. But we are not being insulting when we say that Japanese people do not think logically because they see the lack of logical thinking as one of their assets.

In the West, logical thinking is the basis of scientific reasoning and the underpinning of technology. The scientific method is a way to evaluate information in the framework of scientific theories. When testing hypotheses, a researcher considers alternative hypotheses and eliminates as many as possible. Data is collected from experiments. Statistical analyses are performed to determine if the differences between hypotheses are due to chance or due to actual differences. Researchers have to be trained in the logic of the scientific method.

In Japan, I was visited by a man who used to work in the research lab where I was working. We were talking about research in general, and he was talking about the differences between American and Japanese researchers. He said, "You know, Japanese researchers are different because we do not think logically." I was astounded that someone who was the director of a research institute would admit something like this. I later found out that it was not an admission of weakness, but a statement of what the Japanese had identified as one of their main strengths. Most Japanese are proud to say that they think emotionally, thus avoiding the shackles of logic.

The popular press in Japan is full of examples of authors who are writing from the heart instead of from the head. In these writings, logical arguments are often reduced to emotional responses. Whereas in the United States we would criticize an author for being irrational and nonobjective, the Japanese culture has a different standard of critique.

A particularly emotional issue is the banning of imported rice from Japan. This results in rice prices which are seven to ten times higher in Japan than they would be in a free market. Outside Japan, most people do not realize that opening up the Japanese rice market would kill all of Japan's birds. In an award-winning essay, Michio Matsuda stated that opening Japan to imports of rice would drive out the rice farmers, fields would no longer be flooded for rice farming, the lack of flooded fields would change the weather patterns, it would no longer rain in Japan, Japan would turn into a desert, and all the birds would die.[3]

In addition, the Japanese have a special fondness for moistness ("The Japanese people like moisture"), which Americans do not understand because we eat dry cookies ("Western cookies are dry") whereas Japanese eat moist cookies ("Japanese cakes are gently moist and peculiar to Japan"). We are trying to destroy their moistness ("It is the United States that is pressing Japan to open its doors to rice imports . . ."), which would destroy their identity ("The heart of the Japanese will change if the paddies disappear and aridity spreads"). This essay breaks down as a logical argument; it can only be understood on an emotional level.

The traditional lack of conflict in Japanese society results in "simple" literature,[4] and a lack of philosophical writings using formal deductive systems.[5] In an interesting book on the origins of philosophy and religions in Japan, Hajime Nakamura, a professor of philosophy at the prestigious Tokyo University, explains the reasons for the lack of logical thinking. "[T]he natural sciences have almost never been established on the foundation of traditional Japanese thinking,"[6] nor has there been any development of mathematical physics.[7] In addition, the Japanese before 1868 had no standard system of grammar and no tradition of linguistic study.[8] What all of these fields—natural sciences, mathematical physics, the study of literature and linguistics—have in common is a dependence on the development and usage of logic systems and critical discourse.

Dogen (1200-1253), one of the most influential thinkers of the Japanese Zen sect, asserted that enlightenment was attained not through the function of the mind

---

[3]Michio Matsuda, "Will the Sparrows Vanish?," *Japan Times*, November 20, 1990, p. 24.
[4]Hajime Nakamura, *Ways of Thinking of Eastern Peoples: India-China-Tibet-Japan,* (Honolulu: East-West Center Press, 1964), p. 402.
[5]Ibid., p. 550.
[6]Ibid., p. 574.
[7]Ibid., p. 576.
[8]Ibid., p. 576.

but through the body. "Only when one lets go of the mind and ceases to seek an intellectual apprehension of the Truth is liberation attainable. . . . To do away with mental deliberation and cognition, and simply to go on sitting, is the method by which the Way is made an intimate part of our lives. That is why I put exclusive emphasis upon sitting."[9] Thinking emotionally through the heart is part of attaining enlightenment through the body. Truth for the Japanese philosopher is not found through the laws of reason, but can change depending on the vicissitudes of heart-felt emotions.

CREATED IN JAPAN   *Created in Japan* is a book written by Sheridan Tatsuno[10] to dispel the myths that Japanese companies do not create their own products but merely copy the technology of others. He discusses methods used in Japan to innovate products, successes in product design, and the challenge posed to the United States to maintain technological superiority. The book contains some interesting passages on Japanese technical prowess, trying to create a myth of Japanese innovativeness to replace the myth of master copiers.

The best examples of Japanese achievements are ones where companies have refined ideas created outside Japan. According to Tatsuno, refinements have occurred through the four processes of miniaturization, simplification, completion, and transformation. Without a doubt, the technological success of Japanese products can be found in these techniques.

The Japanese have a long tradition of miniaturization. The bonsai gardens were developed for miniature trees. Automobiles have been miniaturized, which saves parking space in Japan and allows them to fit on the narrow Japanese roads, but is not always a desirable feature for selling cars in the United States. Japanese companies, especially Sony, have built whole industries on miniaturization. Many products can be used as examples: transistor radios, Walkman radios, notebook computers, small calculators, Watchman televisions, and minicopiers. The Japanese companies have had unparalleled success in this area.

Tatsuno also claims that Japanese companies have excelled at making products simpler. This point is debatable. Consumers who own Japanese-made VCRs that are always flashing 12s, because setting the clock is too difficult, would argue with this assessment. As the example of simplicity, Tatsuno discusses Fuji Photo's disposable camera. Because the film is already loaded when it is purchased, the complicated procedure of loading the film is eliminated. The picture taker has only to point and

---

[9]Ibid., p. 367.
[10]Sheridan Tatsuno, *Created in Japan: From Imitators to World Class Innovators* (New York: Harper and Row, 1990).

shoot; then the still-loaded camera is sent to the film developer for processing. Many Japanese products, however, are unnecessarily complicated. For instance, my Japanese-designed stereo tuner requires 43 cognitive steps to turn on if you follow the instructions provided. One Japanese-designed and -manufactured VCR requires 257 cognitive steps to set the clock; another is slightly simpler, requiring 207 cognitive steps. To program the VCR to record a program, one VCR requires 221 cognitive steps and the other requires 216 cognitive steps. These are the most complicated common consumer products, not counting personal computers, that I have ever analyzed for usability.

By completion, Tatsuno means that a Japanese manufacturer will think that any product can be improved. This corresponds to the philosophy of constant improvement which was discussed in Chapter 6. Constant improvement also applies to product design and incorporating technology into the product. As an example, Tatsuno uses the camera industry when Japanese camera companies improved cameras by incorporating auto-focus capabilities. This may have been an unfortunate choice for an example, because Tatsuno fails to mention that the Japanese camera companies were forced to compensate Honeywell over $300 million for infringements on its auto-focus patent and technology.[11] Minolta, like the other Japanese camera companies, had failed to obtain a licensing agreement to use Honeywell's technology. A headline in *Business Week* magazine declared: "From the Mind of Minolta—Oops, Make That Honeywell."[12]

Product designs incorporating transformation, which means rearranging the parts into something else, have been important in Japan but have had few commercial successes elsewhere where space is not at a premium. The space limitations in Japan require that rooms in houses perform multiple functions, and so the rooms and furnishings are designed to be transformed. Nissan sold a car in the United States which could be changed by removing and placing panels, to be a sporty car or a station wagon. The model was not, however, a commercial success in this country. Because American houses are not as small as Japanese houses, transformable room and furniture design has not been exported to the United States. One notable exception to these failures is the transformer toys in which superhero figures can be changed to cars or trucks.

Besides the practice of miniaturization, refinements, or repackaged designs, have had mixed success. However, Tatsuno claims that Japanese companies are now advancing beyond refinements and achieving creative breakthroughs. Once again,

[11]"Business Brief—Honeywell Inc.: Three More Japanese Firms Settle in Camera Patent Case," *Wall Street Journal,* December 29, 1992, p. A3.

[12]Brian Bremner, "From the Mind of Minolta—Oops, Make That 'Honeywell,'" *Business Week,* February 24, 1992, p. 34.

his examples may be unfortunate choices: high-definition televisions (HDTV), computers, and superconductors.

Japanese companies, with the cooperation of the government, were the first to develop HDTV, a television system which increases the resolution of televisions and changes the dimensions of screens to be closer to those in movie theaters. Unfortunately for the companies that invested $10 billion in this technology, it was predicated on several wrong decisions. The technology was based on analog signals; American companies have cooperated to decide on a digital standard which provides more flexibility, control, better compatibility with computer equipment, and higher-quality pictures and sound. The Japanese also chose a signal system which is incompatible with existing signals, so that different signals must be sent for HDTV and regular television. American companies cooperated to make the two systems compatible.

Recently, a Japanese government official, Akimasa Egawa of the Ministry of Posts and Telecommunications, proclaimed that the Japanese analog HDTV system was obsolete and investments should be made in the digital system adopted by the United States. The reaction from Japanese companies was quick. Unwilling to admit that they had made a mistake on their flagship research project, Egawa was forced to retract his decision and statement. Although continuing to produce obsolete products may be a waste of money, some people think Japan can use it to their advantage. By having a standard in Japan which is obsolete, only Japanese companies will make these products, and they will have the home market to themselves. They can still use the American digital standards to produce HDTV products for the rest of the world. The only people who will be hurt are the Japanese consumers, because they will be forced to pay high prices for lower-quality products, if they choose to buy HDTV sets at all.

FIFTH-GENERATION FAILURES?   In computers, Japanese companies have also made technological mistakes. For many years, Japanese companies, with the cooperation of the government, have committed large amounts of research money to what they called fifth-generation computer systems. These systems were supposed to utilize artificial intelligence (AI) techniques to leapfrog American computer technology by making their computer products more intelligent. It never happened, and even with the large outlay of research money, no viable products have been produced. The companies have quietly abandoned this ambitious technological research program, and we do not hear about fifth-generation computers anymore.

Japanese computer companies have also missed the three most important recent trends in computer systems. These trends change rapidly, so only agile companies can compete. The Japanese missed the trend toward computer workstations favored by most scientists, researchers, and advanced companies. They have not been able to develop the fast computer processors which form the heart of PC-based computers. They missed the trend toward user-friendliness developed by the Xerox Star, popularized by the Apple Macintosh, and replicated, in some ways, through the Microsoft Windows software for PCs. They have stayed with the large mainframes and slow PCs, with little software support. All of these decisions, in the unprotected and competitive American market, would have sunk American companies.

Tatsuno also trumpeted superconductor research in Japan. Superconductors experienced many rapid advances in past years, but the hype has died down recently. It is still too early to comment on possible products which may result from this technology.

The inside jacket of Tatsuno's book states that the book "puts to rest once and for all the repackagers-only myth. The new rallying point for Japanese industry is innovation and creation." Upon close inspection, however, the examples provided by Tatsuno do not support the hype. Japanese companies have made technological mistakes just like other companies. They are hanging on to outdated technologies even though this policy will result in lower-quality products.

Shintaro Ishihara, in *The Japan That Can Say No*, is also part of the hype but with very little substance to back it up. "[W]e have a long, distinguished history of creativity," asserts Ishihara. "You see it everywhere among people from all walks of life."[13] These are very broad statements unburdened by evidence. The two pieces of evidence he does provide are not very convincing. First, as evidence of creativity he cites the increasing influence of Japanese literature in the Western world by asserting that "French engineers . . . read modern Japanese novels and find them fascinating." The second example of creativity is from Sony. He describes how Sony took the transistor, which was researched and developed at AT&T's Bell Labs, and manufactured the transistor radio. Bell Labs, in its policy of openness, generously gave Sony a license to use the technology, and Sony became a major consumer electronics company because of it. Without the transistor, the transistor radio would be impossible. The transistor radio, of course, is a repackaging of two components—radio and transistor—both of which were invented in America.

The best examples provided by people trying to dispel the myth that Japanese companies are imitators instead of creators are not very convincing. The products that Tatsuno and Ishihara tout are HDTV, auto-focusing cameras, transistor radios, fifth-generation computer systems, and superconductors. Two of them, HDTV and fifth-generation computer systems, have been the result of government-sponsored and -directed research and have been large failures resulting in no commercially via-

---

[13]Shintaro Ishihara, *The Japan That Can Say No* (New York: Simon & Schuster, 1991), p. 37.

ble or competitive products. The auto-focusing lenses were actually stolen from Honeywell. Sony did obtain a license to use transistors in the transistor radio, but obtaining a license could hardly be called a creative breakthrough. The breakthrough in superconductivity was made by IBM researchers in Europe. Japanese researchers have not come up with any commercially viable products in this area.

HARVESTING THE TECHNOLOGICAL GARDEN   One day toward the end of my stay at the research labs, the company set up a mysterious meeting about which I was given few details. At the time of the meeting, I was brought to a room on the lower floor and a gentleman introduced himself as being from the Japan Futures Society. He said he was writing a report on trends in human-computer interaction or how to make consumer computer systems more user-friendly. This is one of my research areas and is an area in which Japanese companies find themselves lagging behind their American and European competitors.

Before I was willing to share my research ideas with him, I asked him a few questions. "Will I be able to see the final report once you write it?"

"No, you will not be able to see the final report," was the reply.

"Will the report be written in English or just in Japanese?"

"The report will be in Japanese," said the gentleman. "You will not be able to see it, so it does not matter much anyway."

"What kind of agency are you working for? Is it a government agency or is it supported by Japanese companies?"

"I work for a government agency," was the reply.

"Where does the funding come from for the project? Does the funding come from Japanese companies?"

"The funding for our agency comes from Japanese companies," he replied.

"Why should I cooperate with you? Has anybody else cooperated with you?"

"I traveled to Apple and IBM in the U.S., but they were reluctant to cooperate with me," he said.

"Why should I cooperate with you? What do I get out of it? I don't even get to see the final report."

"I could possibly give you some other reports we have written in Japanese for other projects."

"Have you ever given these reports to Americans in the past if they asked for them?"

"No, we have not," he replied.

I figured it was time to end the interview. "My government has paid a lot of money to educate me," I said. "They have paid a lot of money to support my research. Now, you want me to give you my best ideas for future research and I don't get to see the final report. In the U.S. we talk about reciprocal relationships where I give something to you and you give me something back. But this is a one-way street. You are just taking. I don't want to continue with this interview."

"I could possibly give you $200."

I was insulted and refused. Considering the amount of money the U.S. government spent on my education, he certainly would have had a bargain.

In the United States, we believe that the only way for research and science to advance is to publish the results in open archives so that other researchers can make use of the best ideas. One party may make a discovery and another party may find that this discovery can be applied in a new way to solve a different research problem. This system works in a university setting and in some corporate laboratories because knowledge is public; it is not hoarded as private secrets. You trust other researchers will publish their results so that you can utilize some of their ideas if they utilize yours. It is a reciprocal relationship. Everyone benefits. Science advances and technology follows.

In Japan, though, the important research is carried out in corporate laboratories, limiting the spread of knowledge and thus the progress of science and technology. The company benefits in the short term because it can make money on its "secrets," but it is not a good long-term strategy for the whole scientific and engineering community. Obviously, breakthroughs that are shared with other Japanese companies are not going to be available to other countries. Japanese researchers have been good at harvesting the technological garden in the United States, which provides them with some of their best ideas with no financial outlay. They are unwilling to provide their fellow gardeners with any of their technological seeds.

Before leaving Japan, I asked the director of the research labs if his organization would be willing to support more of the basic research done in the United States—the research on which his organization had so effectively capitalized. His response was straightforward and practical. He said that the relationship had worked well in the past, and he saw no reason for change. He elaborated. The Americans pay for and perform the basic research. The Japanese companies take that research, turn it into products, and capitalize on it. We should not upset the harmony.

Japanese companies have been successful at some kinds of refinements such as miniaturization. These companies have not been good at performing the research to develop new products. This is not a distasteful stereotype, it is fact. As Westerners, we might feel guilty for taking and never giving, but we make a mistake when we assume that the Japanese think as we do. On the contrary, the Japanese businessmen I talked to did not feel shame. They thought they were being practical and smart. They are right. Why pay for something you can get for free? They did not deny that they were repackaging ideas harvested from others. They claimed that was their strength. This relationship had worked in the past. Why should they tamper with a relationship which has been bountiful for them?

FACTS AND FIGURES   Measuring the technology of companies is difficult. One way is to look at royalties and licensing fees for high-tech ideas paid by Japanese companies to American companies and vice versa. This is what happened when Bell Labs gave Sony a license to use the transistor in radios. American companies have enjoyed a lopsided advantage in this area, and the differences are expanding. In 1982 Japanese companies paid American companies less than $1 billion in licensing and royalty fees; this increased to over $2.58 billion in 1990. On the other side of the coin, American companies paid Japanese companies less than $100 million in licensing and royalty fees in 1982, and this increased to less than $500 million in 1989.[14] Japanese companies are using American ideas and high technology in their products more than American companies are using Japanese ideas and high technology in their products.

Americans consumers are purchasing Japanese products based upon American technology which was licensed to Japan. In 1980 the U.S. imported around $6 billion of high-tech products from Japan and in 1988 this had expanded to over $32 billion, an almost six-fold increase. On the other side, the U.S. exported less than $5 billion of high-tech products to Japan in 1980 and this doubled by 1988 to over $10 billion of exports.[15] Japanese companies have harvested our technological garden quite effectively.

The technology of products can also be measured in terms of the varieties of high-tech products that companies can produce. In 1992 then-Senator Lloyd Bentsen ordered the U.S. General Accounting Office (GAO) to perform a study analyzing the U.S. lead in eleven leading high-tech industries: pharmaceuticals, civilian aircraft, telecommunications equipment, fiber optics, semiconductors, semiconductor equipment, robotics, flexible manufacturing systems, supercomputers, advanced materials, and consumer electronics. The headlines from the report were frightening for American companies: "GAO: US Falls Behind in Advanced Industries."[16] Of the eleven industries, the only one with a clear technical advantage was pharmaceuticals.

Americans are guilty of fostering myths to make a point. Upon closer analysis, the headlines were hype, intended to make a political point. Bentsen wanted to wake up American companies and highlight the failures of the outgoing Bush

---

[14]Susan Moffat, "Picking Japan's Research Brains," *Fortune*, March 25, 1991, p. 88.
[15]Ibid., p. 88.
[16]"GAO: US Falls Behind in Advanced Industries," Prodigy interactive personal service, November 17, 1992.

administration. The incoming Clinton administration intended to place an emphasis on technology and to provide more cooperation with companies to produce high-tech products. The fine print in the report actually stated that the United States had in recent years gained ground in six of the eleven categories. In addition, the eleven industries were chosen because they were ones in which there were questions about who was leading: The selection wasn't random. Key industries in the lead, such as software, in which U.S. industry is clearly the worldwide leader, were not included in the study.[17]

American companies lead the world in computers, software, aerospace, communications, chemicals, and pharmaceuticals. The United States recently regained its leading market share in the manufacture of semiconductors and threatens to overtake Japan in HDTV because the new digital standard relies on American strengths in sophisticated computer chips, software, and networking. Motorola leads in cellular phones and pagers. AT&T leads in cordless phones. Hewlett-Packard is the world leader in computer printers. American companies dominate in computer software, microprocessors, and peripherals such as disk drives.

The *Wall Street Journal* claims that even these numbers for American leadership in high technology do not tell the whole story, because they do not distinguish between cutting-edge technology and easier-to-master technology. The United States clearly leads in custom semiconductors and biotechnology, while Japan has taken the lead in easier-to-master technologies. For the low-end technology products, Japan is feeling the heat from South Korea and other Asian countries.[18] In fact, the large Japanese consumer electronics companies are staggering because they are "weakened by some bad bets (on digital-audio tape, for instance), too much capacity and too few hit products," according to the *Wall Street Journal*.[19] The article states that American companies could soon take the lead in some areas of consumer electronics because of their investment in computing, software, and wireless communications essential for a new class of "information appliances."

The U.S. Commerce Department tracks international trade in leading-edge products, those products that are the most high-tech. The United States has continually run a trade surplus in this area, and it has been expanding. After hitting a low of $15.6 billion in 1986, the surplus rose to around $36 billion by 1992.

In some other measures of high-tech competence, such as new patents, the numbers are somewhat mixed when comparing American and Japanese companies. Each year when the numbers of patents granted are released, the newspapers usu-

---

[17]G. Pascal Zachary, "Coming Back: U.S. High-Tech Firms Have Begun Staging Little-Noticed Revival," *Wall Street Journal*, December 14, 1992. p. A1.
[18]Ibid.
[19]Ibid.

ally break down the figures according to the number of patents awarded to individual companies ignoring the overall numbers. By individual company, Japanese companies dominate the top ten, an analysis which the news media use to complain about the downfall of high technology in American companies. Breaking down patent awards like this, however, ignores the fact that in the United States, unlike Japan, many of the innovations come from small companies and individuals. An accurate assessment of technology can be made only by looking at the total number of patents, and then the picture is not nearly as bleak for the United States. In 1992, the U.S. Patent Office issued 59,760 patents (54.5% of the total) to U.S. residents and companies while issuing 23,481 patents (21.4% of the total) to Japanese individuals and companies.[20] Looking at the patents awarded worldwide, in 1990 American companies had 30.1% of the international patent registrations, Japan had 24.2%, and Germany had 16.5%.[21]

Some Japanese companies place much emphasis on tackling the patent process rather than looking for the great advancements. One journal article states that "Aggressive patent management is vital for the Japanese whose inventions are more innovation than breakthrough."[22] Toshiba Corp., often the leader in the number of patents awarded, employs 400 engineers in its intellectual property department.[23] Instead of sending these employees to law school, as most companies do, Toshiba employees attend the training course for patent examiners run by the U.S. government.

Sometimes the number of patents issued to Japanese companies may be inflated because some Japanese companies will patent-flood a technology in order to gain concessions from the company originating the technology. In a famous case, an American company called Fusion System Corp. developed a technology for manufacturing high-intensity ultraviolet lamps. Mitsubishi coveted this technology and filed nearly 300 patent applications that looked like Fusion's patented microwave technology.[24] This patent-flooding tactic was an attempt to extract a cross-licensing agreement with Fusion for selling products in Japan.

American companies are not always savvy to the differences in patent applications between Japan and the United States. A Japanese company is awarded a patent in Japan, on average, about two years after an application. A foreign-owned company is awarded a patent in Japan, on average, seven years after the application.

[20]Richard Seltzer, "Americans Earn Rising Share of U.S. Patents," *Chemical & Engineering News*, February 22, 1993, pp. 16–17.
[21]Richard C. Morais, "Patently Absurd," *Forbes*, January 18, 1993. p. 46.
[22]Richard Meyer, "Patent Management: Toshiba," *Financial World*, September 26, 1992, p. 56.
[23]Ibid., p. 56.
[24]Donald M. Sperio, "Patent Protection or Piracy—A CEO Views Japan," *Harvard Business Review*, September-October 1990, pp. 58-67.

In Japan, companies are awarded patents on the basis of the first to file. In the United States, patents are awarded according to the first to invent. Therefore, Japanese companies can hold Japanese patents even though the technology was invented in the United States.

American companies hold a good lead over Japanese companies in the production of high-tech products and especially leading-edge products. Americans are awarded more patents in the United States and worldwide as compared to their Japanese competitors. Japanese companies have made some serious mistakes in consumer electronics and computer products which may increase the gap between the two countries. Some individual stories support the myth of Japanese advantages in high-tech industries, but it is not supported by the overall figures.

Is this myth of superior technology by Japanese companies supported at all anymore? The bellwether industry for comparison has always been the automotive industry. A poll carried out by Market Opinion Research asked 1103 Americans which automakers are more technologically advanced.[25] American automakers were said to be more technologically advanced by 42% of the respondents; 40% said that Japanese automakers were better technologically. When this poll was compared with a similar one made ten months earlier, the numbers had been higher for Japanese automakers by about 10 percentage points. One could argue that car customers are not trained to recognize differences in technology under the hood. Maybe master mechanics would be better qualified. A survey asked master mechanics, the ones who are probably the most familiar with the technology of American and Japanese car companies, to rate which car models were the most technologically advanced and innovative. Eighty-two percent of them cited American car makes as the leaders. People's perceptions of the technological prowess of Japanese companies are changing rapidly.

---

[25]Tressa Crosby, "Big 3 Gain Ground with U.S. Buyers," *Automotive News,* February 21, 1994, p. 4.

Myth 2:
Foreign Products Don't Sell in Japan Because of their Poor Quality

A common refrain from Japanese officials, often repeated by Americans, states that American products don't sell well in Japan because of their poor quality. Many different Japanese people told my husband and me that when they come to America, the only thing worth buying and giving as presents to family and friends back home is maple syrup. Akio Morita, the head of Sony, justified the Japan-U.S. trade imbalance when he wrote, "There are few things in the U.S. that Japanese want to buy, but there are a lot of things in Japan that Americans want to buy. It could never be the case that we are selling too much; it is not because we are exporting, the imbalance arises as a result of commercial transactions based on preferences. Therefore, the only thing that Americans or Europeans can do to correct this imbalance is reassess themselves and make an effort to produce products which are attractive to Japanese consumers".[1] These sentiments are *tatemae*, not the

---

[1]Akio Morita and Shintaro Ishihara, *The Japan That Can Say No,* unofficial translation entered into the *Congressional Record,* November, 1989, pp. 29-30.

133

reality. Reality is more complicated. Foreign products don't sell well in Japan for three fundamental reasons.

The first is the strong nationalistic tradition in Japan and the feeling of the Japanese people that they are unique. They believe that the Japanese people are hardworking, disciplined, and have a deep sense of beauty. They think they understand quality products. Foreign products are inferior, substandard, and lower in quality than Japanese products. Foreigners do not work very hard to produce good products.

The second reason is the mismatch of cultures. The Japanese have systematic ways of doing most things, and products from other cultures, which function differently, will not find acceptance in Japan. Upon arriving in Japan, I was informed by my neighbor, with great seriousness, that the teapot I was using was for green tea only. My serving Lipton's black tea in a Japanese green tea teapot was a violation of sensibilities. As a stubborn and very naive *gaijin*, my response was that as long as I only had one teapot and one kind of tea, this particular teapot had a new identity—it was going to be a teapot for Lipton's tea. Americans have trouble understanding this Japanese tradition, since we have a different one. In our culture, someone's cleverness is illustrated by creative use of tools and implements for multiple purposes.

The final and most important reason that the Japanese don't buy foreign products is lack of availability. The Japanese government systematically excludes foreign products which would provide competition for domestic products. Obviously, you can't buy what isn't in the stores.

PEACH BOY AND THE GOLDEN APPLES   Folk tales and

myths provide fascinating windows into different cultures. A brief comparison of Japanese and Western classic stories will illustrate the nationalistic spirit of Japan versus the individualistic spirit of the West. Momotaro, or Peach Boy, is a favorite Japanese story.

Peach Boy springs from the pit of a peach to be the child of an elderly couple who had given up hope of becoming parents. Like Moses, he is found in a stream and grows to deliver his chosen people from the oppression of a foreign culture. In this case, the foreigners are ogres (some versions of this story refer to the foreigners as devils), who live on an island and pillage and terrorize the Japanese whenever they have the urge. Interestingly, neither Peach Boy nor his adoptive parents have had any experience with these ogres. His adoptive parents are not even aware of the ogres' existence; Peach Boy knows because of his omniscient, divine origin.

On the way to the seaside, Peach Boy joins forces with a pheasant, a monkey, and a dog. When he reaches the coast, the boy builds a boat for himself and the animals. Arriving at the ogres' island fortress, Peach Boy delivers an ultimatum via his friend the pheasant. The ogres laugh at the pheasant's speech, so the pheasant attacks and kills one of the ogres. The monkey and the dog join the attack and take care of all but the chief ogre. After the defeat of the ogres, Peach Boy helps himself to their riches, including a coat and a hat which make the wearer invisible, a mallet which produces gold at every strike, and various amounts of pearls, coral, and other treasure. Peach Boy takes his loot back to Japan, where he lives happily ever after. Unlike most Western stories, however, there is a down side to this happy ending. Although Peach Boy enjoys vast power and wealth, he is responsible for "ever-increasing dependents and retainers."[2]

This traditional Japanese story bears an odd resemblance to the old English folk tale, Jack the Giant Killer.[3] Jack becomes the owner of the Cap of Knowledge, the Coat of Invisibility, and the Shoes of Swiftness. Unlike Peach Boy, Jack acquires these items from the three-headed giant after Jack performs a good deed and saves the giant's life. He later uses these items to save maidens, kill Lucifer, and dispose of three more giants. Jack's reward for his good work is the hand of the Duke's beautiful daughter and the accompanying status. No mention is made of increasing numbers of dependents. Note that Peach Boy's mallet parallels the goose that laid the golden egg for another English giant-and-Jack tale, Jack and the Beanstalk.

In classic Western folk tales, the young man who journeys to a strange land in search of treasure and monsters always has a motive which is higher than his own self-serving greed. "Chylde Roland and the Goblin King,"[4] tells the adventures of Roland. The Elfland goblin has stolen away Roland's sister because she went widershins around the village church. If you make the mistake of going counterclockwise around a church, widershins, the goblins will get you. Roland's task is increased when his two elder brothers are captured trying to save their sister. He succeeds in his rescue because he is brave, obedient, and resistant to temptations of the flesh.

Young Jack, in "How Jack Sought the Golden Apples,"[5] must submit to various tortuous experiences in order to obtain the golden apples which will save his elderly father's life. Like Roland, Jack is triumphant because of his own virtue and ability to follow instructions. His undoing comes at the hands of his own evil brothers, who steal the apples away from him. Justice is served in the end when Jack's faithfulness to his father is revealed and Jack marries the beautiful princess who is responsible for his deliverance.

The Greek hero Jason is more nationalistic in his goals, as he must retrieve the golden fleece to regain his father's kingdom and save his people from the rule of his

[2]Iwaya Sazanami, Japanese Fairy Tales (Tokyo: Hokuseido Press, 1938), p. 40.
[3]Olive Miller, "Jack the Giant-Killer," in My Book House, vol. 6, Through Fairy Halls (Chicago: The Book House for Children, 1954), pp. 140-159.
[4]Miller, "Chylde Roland and the Goblin King," in My Book House, vol. 6, pp. 11-18.
[5]Olive Miller, "How Jack Sought the Golden Apples," in My Book House, vol. 5, Over the Hills (Chicago: The Book House for Children, 1954), pp. 76-89.

despot uncle. Jason's personal attributes contribute to his accomplishment of his mission. Had he had a different personality, he might not have succeeded. Throughout the Western folk tales, the themes of individual bravery and obedience are repeated. The hero's motives are of love, honor, justice, and loyalty. He is usually rewarded in the end, but the material rewards are rarely the original motivating force.

Peach Boy's motives stand in stark contrast to those of Roland and the Jacks of English fairy tales. Peach Boy and his family have not experienced the evils of the ogres; the ogres are a vague menace over the horizon. Peach Boy feels in his heart that he should go and kill the foreign devils and take their property. His family is surprised when he tells them of his plans. Peach Boy's motives are also rather base. He desires to steal the ogres' treasures. His success is due to his ability to persuade various animals to do his work for him and to his sheer audacity. Personality characteristics, such as loyalty, bravery, or obedience, don't enter directly into this story. Peach Boy receives no instructions on how to achieve his goals from his elders. The Western heroes—Jack, Roland, and Jason—on the other hand, are instructed by their elders or superiors on how to accomplish their missions.

A child reading Peach Boy would assume that the story's moral is one of national interests. If national interests are perceived to be at risk, attacking foreigners, killing them, and stealing their goods is perfectly acceptable behavior. In fact, Peach Boy was a basic part of the imperialist education curriculum during the 1930s and 1940s, as the Japanese prepared for war on the foreign devils.[6] China was invaded first, followed by the attack on Pearl Harbor, and the invasion of the other Asian nations. Just as Peach Boy of legend liberated his people from the domination of the ogres and seized their land and wealth, so did the Japanese Greater East Asian Co-Prosperity Sphere intend to rid the Orient of the white imperialists. As Bruce Feiler found during his recent tenure as an English teacher in the Japanese school system, Peach Boy is still a revered and common topic of study in the elementary school system. Peach Boy exemplifies the perfect Japanese youth.[7] Feiler discusses in his book how the Japanese have felt the pressures of external forces throughout their nation's history and perceive their situation as being under the thumb of giants. The Japanese often feel as though their nation is Peach Boy and the ogres or devils are the Americans. Morita said, "America is a giant in many ways and, in many ways, Japan is a dwarf. This obvious contrast has been exploited by the Americans often in the past."[8]

---

[6]Bruce Feiler, *Learning to Bow* (New York: Ticknor and Fields, 1991), pp. 139-141.
[7]Keigo Seki, *Folktales of Japan* (Chicago: University of Chicago Press, 1963), pp. 40-43.
[8]Morita and Ishihara, *The Japan That Can Say No,* p. 58.

CHILDREN OF THE GODS The native religion of Japan is Shintoism. The primary tenet of Shintoism states: "Japan is the country of gods. Our country is founded by a heavenly ancestry; the reign of our country is transmitted forever by the Sun Goddess. Such things have happened to this country of ours that nothing is comparable to them in other countries. That is why this country is called the country of the gods."[9] Unlike the Chinese, who have had a succession of different dynasties, the Japanese believe that the line of emperors in Japan has been unbroken since the Sun Goddess.

Another tenet of Shintoism is the emphasis on what Nakamura, a professor of philosophy at the University of Tokyo and author of the well-respected *Ways of Thinking of Eastern Peoples,* terms the social nexus or social group, in contrast to belief structures based on universal truths and laws. In Japan, behavior is controlled by the group rather than by a system of laws. Consequently, the determination of good versus bad is dependent upon the effects of the action upon the group. If the group benefits, then the action is good. If the group does not benefit, then it is bad.

A characteristic of the Japanese people has been their ability to absorb foreign influences and remain remarkably unchanged. Nakamura attributes this cultural ability to the Japanese focus on social nexus and harmony. The result is a lack of confrontation and criticism within Japanese culture.

These ideas and concepts have an effect on consumer behavior in Japan. The decision to buy Japanese products is seen as good for the group and, therefore, becomes a moral issue. Consumers do not demand better products or sue when a product is found to be unsafe because this would cause confrontation and criticism of something Japanese. Criticizing products from other countries is perfectly fair, because these exist outside the Japanese culture.

JAPANESE BRAINS ARE DIFFERENT The divineness of the Japanese people and their emperor gives rise to a belief in the uniqueness of the Japanese. This uniqueness leads to the inevitable conclusion that foreign products won't be suitable to Japanese needs. American baseball bats couldn't be imported because Japanese baseballs were different. American contractors were denied work on the Osaka airport because Japanese soil is unique and the contractors wouldn't understand its geology.[10] American tanks and warships were unsuitable for Japanese use because they were too big. Lt. General Katsuichi Tsukamoto explained to journalist David Evans that the warship "doesn't suit the size of the people" and the tanks are

---

[9]Hajime Nakamura, *Ways of Thinking of Eastern Peoples: India-China-Tibet-Japan* (Honolulu: East–West Center Press, 1964), p. 393.

[10]Sam Jameson, "In Japan, Unique Is a State of Mind," *Los Angeles Times,* August 2, 1988. Part I, p. 1.

"too big to operate in Japan."[11] I was told by one of Ray's Japanese graduate students that Americans can't remember origami patterns like the Japanese because the Japanese are right-brain dominant and Americans are left-brain dominant.

HIGH-QUALITY HAMBURGERS   My husband Ray came back from a business trip visibly agitated one evening. He had been visiting a former student at his plant, where complex telephone switching systems are made for a lucrative and competitive worldwide market. The products from this plant compete directly with products made by AT&T in the United States and Northern Telecom in Canada. As expected, the student was very polite and, after an interesting tour of the plant and a viewing of the products made there, had set up a lunch meeting with his supervisor in a private lunch room.

The three of them were chatting pleasantly about benign topics. To make conversation, Ray noted to the supervisor that he spoke very good English and wondered where he had learned to speak such good English. Although most Japanese take six years of English in school, very few of them learn conversational English, concentrating instead on learning the grammar and dictionary-type rote learning.

The supervisor said that he had spent six months in Minnesota trying to sell some switching systems in that state. To carry on the conversation, Ray asked him if he was successful in his venture to sell his products there. He said, no, he wasn't successful, and then said that the American market is very hard to break into.

Ray mimicked for me the natural reaction he had to this statement, which was a backward motion of the head as his eyebrows raised. Ray told me that he really did not want to say anything about this statement; after all, his host had been very gracious, but Ray couldn't help himself.

"Oh," Ray said as his head swung backward. "What percentage of the American market in switching systems is controlled by foreign firms?"

"Twenty percent," was the reply.

"How many American telephone switching systems are there in Japan?"

"Seven," was the reply. "All from Northern Telecom."

Well, Northern Telecom is a Canadian company, not American, but 7% wasn't too bad, even if it was a Canadian instead of an American company. Whole markets are closed to foreign products, and it was surprising that telephone switching systems, a market which could easily be controlled by the government, had such a high percentage of foreign products.

---

[11]David Evans, "Japanese Doing a High-Tech Two-Step with Tanks, Ships," *Chicago Tribune*, December 20, 1991. Section 1, p. 13.

"Seven percent is a high percentage of the market for foreign products." Ray said.

"No, not 7%, seven switching systems."

"Seven," Ray said. "Out of how many switching systems in Japan."

"20,000," was the reply.

"There are 20% foreign switching systems in the United States, but only seven out of 20,000 foreign switching systems in Japan, and you refer to the American market as being closed." The incongruity of his earlier statement about a closed American market had not registered. The remark was followed by a shrug which said, "So."

"The thing about American companies is that if they find a product of high quality at a low price, they will buy it," Ray said. "I've noticed that Japanese companies or people will not buy foreign products even if they are better than Japanese products at a lower price." We had just read an article about a high-tech American product that wasn't purchased in Japan, even though this product could have increased the quality of some Japanese products, until a Japanese company had time to copy it.

Obviously, the supervisor was starting to wonder about the nerve of this relatively young American and he replied carefully, trying to appease my husband.

"We think that American companies like McDonald's are very good."

Sometimes we make jokes in the States that the only thing Americans can do right is to cook and sell a hamburger. Did anybody really believe this, though? This person, from a major international company, actually believed that American companies could not make anything of higher quality that was more complicated than a hamburger. How had this attitude been shaped? We learned that if one person had a certain attitude, almost everybody else we talked to in Japan believed the same thing.

As an aside, we later found out that the Northern Telecom switching systems were actually preferred by the operators who used them in Japan because they were so easy to use, unlike the Japanese switching systems which were known for being difficult to use.

TOSSING MORE THAN PIZZAS AT SHAKEY'S   The Japanese are known for their distrust of foreigners. The degree to which this distrust is ingrained is disturbing. My family and I were visiting some American friends in Yokohama one Saturday afternoon. We went to dinner at the Shakey's pizza parlor near the department store where we had been purchasing origami supplies. We were quietly talking and eating when all of a sudden a chair on the far side of the restaurant went flying through the air. Just as quickly, two Japanese men stood up and began pushing each other. Everyone in their party was standing up, and the fight didn't end until one of the women climbed on the back of one of the fighters. The fight ended as quietly and quickly as it had began. The chairs were replaced upright and the party left. Throughout the fight, the only noise was that of furniture moving and the scuffling of feet, no shouting. The restaurant management all came out of the kitchen to watch, but no one made a move to call the police or break up the fight. The rest of the Japanese patrons acted as if nothing was happening. Only my husband and his friend seemed concerned. They were debating the wisdom of breaking up the fight when it ended abruptly. I was really concerned that a John Wayne-type barroom fight might develop where everyone in the restaurant would become involved. I described this fight to Mrs. Tanaka because I found it very disturbing. I may have grown up in a cowboy town in Montana, but I must have led a sheltered life because the fight in Yokohama was the only public brawl I've ever witnessed. Mrs. Tanaka's first response was "Were they Japanese?"

Often when unusual events occur in Japan they are first attributed to foreigners or foreign sources, just as Mrs. Tanaka's first assumption was that the pizza parlor fighters were non-Japanese. The *Japan Times*, October 21, 1990, reported the deaths of two children who drank tainted water at their kindergarten school in Urawa, located in Saitama Prefecture. The other people affected included 113 children and 72 parents from the school, who had been sick as early as October 10 following a sports festival held at the school. The cause was leakage from neighboring septic tanks which was entering the school's well. The school had ignored regulations requiring yearly testing of the water, and they had violated prefectural governmental requirements that all well water must be boiled before drinking.

The problem was initially blamed on foreigners and not on the school. The toxic strain of *E. coli* was thought to be foreign. "Because the Type O-157 colicillus is rare in Japan, it is thought that a student or parent may have acquired it overseas, the [prefectural health] bureau said."[12] The subsequent public debates about the wisdom of using well water were illuminating. After the public health center in Urawa tested 240 wells and found dangerous levels of bacteria in 70 of them, citizens' groups defended the use of well water, claiming that the treated city water contained cancer-causing agents. A housewife defended Japanese tradition: "We use both kinds of water in our house, but it has to be well water to make tea or to drink during summertime. Tap water is only for watering because it smells like bleach."[13]

---

[12] "Fatal Outbreak at School Started Earlier," *Japan Times*, October 22, 1990. p. 2.
[13] "Saitama Child Deaths Spark Debate on Well Water Use," *Japan Times*, November 2, 1990. p. 2.

NIHONJINRON   I ruffled a few feathers at my going-away dinner party at my Japanese neighbor's house. One of my neighbors offered to show me how to prepare sushi rolls, and I watched carefully. My other neighbors told me that Mrs. Okada was very good at rolling sushi and it was very difficult. I've worked with my hands my whole life, including a four-year stint as an amateur potter, so I figured it couldn't be too hard. In classic *gaijin* fashion, I made a liar out of my neighbor by rolling the sushi perfectly the first time. Afterwards, I realized that I should have acted the fool and pretended to be all thumbs, but such behavior does not come easy to me.

Books explaining the differences between Japanese and other nationalities are so popular in Japan that they form an entire literary genre. The name for such books is *nihonjinron*. In his definitive study of *nihonjinron, The Myth of Japanese Uniqueness*,[14] Peter Dale, a British classical scholar, outlines how this genre preserves the ideology of the past for the post-World War II generation. These books play a serious role in how the Japanese perceive themselves and should not be dismissed lightly. On a more alarming note, they also preserve the nationalistic spirit which General Douglas MacArthur strived to suppress in his restructuring of Japanese society. Dale makes the case that the *nihonjinron* replace the old thought police as a method of thought control.[15] If this is true, it would help to explain the vehement Japanese reaction to Western books which break through the illusions of *tatemae* and explain the Japanese to Westerners. Perhaps, because they understand too well the power of popular books, the Japanese consider *Trading Places, More Like Us, Rising Sun, Agents of Influence,* and *The Enigma of Japanese Power* to be Western versions of *nihonjinron*. Ishihara's response to the translation of his book, *The Japan That Can Say No*, takes on new meaning in this light. *Nihonjinron* is for Japanese eyes only, and the exposure of Ishihara's attitudes toward Americans could potentially destroy the illusions so carefully built up by the Japanese. Bear in mind that as long as the Japanese are being told in *nihonjinron* that maple syrup is the only thing worth bringing back from America, American businesses will have little chance of breaking into Japanese markets.

MAKING COOKIES IN A WASH BASIN   The second reason
the Japanese don't buy foreign products is cultural. The Japanese have been submitting to governmental decrees of proper behavior for centuries. Certain foods are presented in certain types of ceramics and particular seasons require wearing particular colored kimonos. There is a right way and a wrong way of doing almost everything

---

[14]Peter Dale, *The Myth of Japanese Uniqueness* (New York: St. Martin's Press, 1986).
[15]Ibid., p. 17·

in daily life. One overriding principle is dedicated use. An item often has one use only, and no creativity should be applied to finding new uses for that item. The teapot is a good example and there are others.

When I started making desserts in Japan for my neighbors, I needed a big mixing bowl. There were some plastic bowls in the apartment, but they had been in the bathroom. I didn't want to use anything plastic without knowing its past history, so I explored the neighborhood shops looking for an alternative bowl. Sometimes there were outdoor peddlers in front of the supermarket, but I could never figure out their schedule. Some peddlers came to our train station stop only once during our stay. Finally, I found a little mom-and-pop hardware store. At least half of their merchandise was outside the shop. It took them hours to open and close their store every day. They had two kinds of serviceable bowls—stainless steel and plastic. The stainless steel bowls were frightfully expensive and too big to lug back to the States, so I selected an appropriate-sized inexpensive plastic bowl. I blissfully made cookies in it. One afternoon, though, I invited my neighbor, Mrs. Matsuoka, to come over to watch me make cherry pie and sample it later with coffee. I spent a lot of afternoons with my neighbors in this fashion. I got out my supplies and began to explain how to cut the flour into the shortening for the pie crust. I hadn't gotten too far into my demonstration before Mrs. Matsuoka exclaimed with a giggle, "That's a washing basin. That's not a mixing bowl."

"Well, it's new and it's clean and I've never used it for a wash basin," I retorted. "The stainless steel bowls are expensive. I don't want to spend too much money on things I can't take home with me." This seemed perfectly logical to me.

Mrs. Matsuoka continued to look amused, but she ate the pie.

Later, I learned to my horror that I had acquired a reputation in the neighborhood as that person who made pies and cookies in a wash basin. I took small comfort in the knowledge that everyone always ate all my pastries and always asked for the recipes.

SALAD DRESSING IN MY COFFEE   The dedicated-use principle of the washing basin was applied erratically, however. The last week we were in Japan, we had dinner with my neighbor, Mrs. Tanaka. She managed to get her husband to come home early that evening, and all eight of us crowded around her dining room table for a combination Japanese-Italian dinner. Mrs. Tanaka had spent six weeks with an Italian-American family in New England as a teenager, and she often spoke fondly of her visit. She was especially wistful about the marvelous blueberry pies and lasagna made by her host mother. As a going-away gesture, I had offered to fix lasagna and blueberry pie for the dinner in her apartment. I began planning a month in advance, and I picked up crucial ingredients wherever I could find them. I had to go to Yokosuka Chuo for the Maine blueberries, which cost $5.00 for a 16-ounce can; the international supermarket Kinokuniya, in Kamakura, had lasagna noodles; and the local supermarket carried tomato paste and meat. Kraft Parmesan cheese was available in Japan, but only in tiny 4-ounce containers which cost 280 yen—which, in 1990, was slightly over $2.00. I never could find ricotta cheese, so I settled for cottage cheese mixed with mozzarella.

Dinner began with a Japanese version of tossed green salad, with white creamy salad dressing in Mrs. Tanaka's glass creamer. I noted that it was a creamer, not a salad dressing cruet, but I said nothing. We munched our way through the sushi and the lasagna. After dinner, coffee was served with the blueberry pie and ice cream. I looked around for the cream and sugar. I hadn't seen Mrs. Tanaka remove the salad dressing creamer, and there it sat on the other side of the table. I debated. Was the white creamy stuff cream or salad dressing? Should I ask? What if it's salad dressing and I put it into my coffee? I already had a big enough reputation for being a crazy *gaijin,* and I really didn't want any new stories circulating. After considerable thought I decided to take a chance. After all, I had eaten steamed gingko nuts and survived; how bad could creamy salad dressing in coffee possibly be? I took the first sip. Instant relief. It was cream. I really wanted to say something about improper use of Western implements, but I refrained.

BAKING CAKES IN A RICE MAKER   Failing to consider the cultural differences between Japanese and Americans can result in disasters in the business world. George Fields, in his book, *From Bonsai to Levi's*, recounts his marketing mistake.[16] In the late 1960s he was working for General Mills trying to stir some life into the Betty Crocker cake mix market. Japanese housewives then didn't have ovens, and many of them still don't. In order to sell cake mixes, Fields needed an alternative baking mechanism. Almost all Japanese households at the time had an electric rice maker. A flash of Yankee brilliance led Fields to suggest to his company that they develop a cake mix which could be baked in a rice maker. They complied and called it Cakeron. It didn't sell despite the growing market for Western-style cakes in Japan. Attempting to ferret out the problem, Fields began conducting focus group sessions with his prospective customers. They liked the taste of the cake just fine. They understood the procedure. What was the hang-up? Finally, he was able to discover the problem. The Japanese housewives were worried about the cakes' flavoring tainting the rice. Japanese rice has a tradition of purity in Japan, and chocolate- or vanilla-flavored rice would be totally unacceptable. The real problem was the constant usage of the rice maker. Women made a big batch of rice in the

---

[16]George Fields, *From Bonsai to Levi's* (New York: Mentor, 1983), p. 43.

evening in their machines and used that rice for meals the next day. They often didn't have time before the next evening to clean out the machine, bake a cake, reclean the machine, and make more rice. So the rice maker stayed a rice maker and the Cakeron stayed on the supermarket shelf.

The story doesn't end there, however. Fields' use of the rice cooker was a precursor for a later Japanese product, the bread maker. This appliance is ubiquitous in Japan today but redundant in America, where all kitchens have at least one oven. It has been marketed to the high-end consumer market in the United States. The bread maker has one fundamental drawback, however: It makes lousy bread. The outside is always burnt and the inside is usually doughy. Worse yet, because many of the appliances resemble rice cookers in both external and internal shape, the bread is often cylindrical, which makes it very hard to slice. Needless to say, even the square bread makers make weird-shaped bread slices. About the only good thing you can say about them is they do make your house smell good while the bread is baking, but that's a lot of money for an odorizer.

The appliance wouldn't be noteworthy except that it is used as an example of Japanese ingenuity. Ikujiro Nonaka discusses the development of the bread maker in a *Harvard Business Review* article.[17] He writes, "New knowledge always begins with the individual. A brilliant researcher has an insight that leads to a new patent." He neglects to acknowledge Fields' important contribution to the bread maker. He goes on to describe the process that Matsushita used in developing the machine. Their principal problem was the burnt outside and the doughy inside. According to Nonaka, that problem was solved "creatively" after a researcher apprenticed with a master baker for a year to learn more about bread making. My experiences with these appliances and the bread I tasted while in Japan stand as silent rebuttal of Nonaka's claims of Japanese prowess in developing new products.

BARBIE IS TOO SEXY   Mattel's attempts to market Barbie dolls in Japan is another good example of the importance of cultural ideals in marketing. Even though American mothers have been complaining about Barbie's oversized bust since the doll was introduced in 1959, American girls have bought countless versions of Barbie plus her various friends and relations. Named for the youngest daughter of her creator, Barbie has represented the glamour and the sophistication of adulthood to young girls. The Takara Company's Japanese fashion doll, Licca, resembles the heroines of Japanese comics: doe-eyed and innocent. She's flat-chested and comes with accessories which range from school-girlish to designer fashions.

---

[17]Ikujiro Nonaka, "The Knowledge-Creating Company," *Harvard Business Review*, Nov.-Dec., 1991, pp. 96-97.

Mattel has tried on at least three occasions since 1959 to market Barbie in Japan. Their failure is attributed to the Japanese preference for flat-chested, naive, and innocent-looking dolls. A recently reported study supports this cultural reason. Sanrio, a Japanese novelty company, conducted a market survey of American and Japanese potential customers. The Japanese females aged five to mid-twenties found Sanrio products attractive, but the American females after the age of seven found the products too cute and childish.[18] Mattel's fourth try at selling Barbie came on the heels of a cultural change in the public's perceptions of sexuality. Over the past thirty years, Japan's young people have become more sophisticated, according to Teresa Watanabe of the *Los Angeles Times*.[19] Changing habits and diets have led to an altered Japanese figure, and popular culture and taste has changed as well. TV shows discuss how to make your bustline bigger with lingerie, and one Japanese fashion magazine admonished: "To be ashamed of a big bust is old thinking. A bust is a woman's individual weapon that needs to be asserted." Perhaps there is something to this analysis.

Since Mattel launched their recent attempt at the Japanese doll market, sales have increased dramatically. The big department stores were targeted, as opposed to the mom-and-pop shops which carry Japanese toys only. The Hakuhinkan store in Tokyo's Ginza reports Barbie sales exceeding Licca sales. Sales figures are strong at other toy stores and departments across Japan. Manabu Yoshida, the Mattel promoter, feels that public acceptance of Barbie's more mature image will contribute to a permanent high market share.[20] His only concern is Mattel's perseverance in opening up the Japanese doll market. He hopes they won't give up as easily as they did the last three times.

IF WE DON'T HAVE IT, YOU DON'T NEED IT!   The third reason Japanese don't buy foreign products is straightforward. You can't purchase what is not on the store shelves. I grew up in a small town in southwestern Montana, and I can remember my mother complaining about the merchants' attitudes toward keeping stock in their stores. She had worked in Chicago's Merchandise Mart in the early 1950s and had an urbane attitude about shopping. She often characterized the Bozeman merchants by imitating them sarcastically: "If we don't have it, you don't need it." The bureaucrats and businessmen in Japan take an amazingly similar approach toward their consumers. They tell them they don't need certain items, they glorify simplicity and poverty to mask the lack of goods

---

[18] Merry White, *The Material Child* (New York: The Free Press, 1993), p. 126.
[19] Teresa Watanabe, "'Doll Wars'" Challenge Female Ideal," *Los Angeles Times*, October 27, 1992, p. H2.
[20] Ibid.

and services, and whenever necessary they cite national interests as reasons for denying their customers.

Japanese consumers are incredibly ignorant of the lifestyles in other industrialized nations. The American households shown on Japanese television consist of the Ingalls' 1870s frontier cabin on *Little House on the Prairie* and the Cartwrights' ranch on *Bonanza*. The other American shows on Japanese TV, such as *Wonder Woman* and *Knightrider*, are completely lacking in realistic clues about how Americans work and play. Think back: Did you ever see a *Wonder Woman* episode in which Lynda Carter bakes a cake or does her laundry? Likewise, the American movies shown in Japan tend to be macho shoot-em-ups. I don't recall Rambo having much of a domestic life. The printed media also neglect to inform their readers about American lifestyles. I used to try and describe my kitchen to my neighbors when they would ask me various questions. I called my mother-in-law before her November trip to Japan and asked her to bring along a copy of *Better Homes and Gardens* so I could show my neighbors what the possibilities are.

REMODELING HEADACHES   One day, Mrs. Tanaka came down from her fifth-floor apartment to mine for some coffee and conversation. We began talking about the kitchens in our apartments. She said the kitchens were too small to have the conveniences of American kitchens. I showed her my magazine from the States with all the fancy cupboards and appliances. She repeated her original statement: "Japanese kitchens are too small to have all those nice things."

I couldn't let Mrs. Tanaka's comment go unchallenged. With my usual enthusiasm, I jumped out of my kitchen chair and started redesigning the kitchen. I explained while gesturing to the different areas of the kitchen.

"This kitchen is no smaller than the kitchen in many American apartments. It just isn't efficient. The doorways are in all the wrong places. If this was a regular doorway instead of a sliding screen, you could lengthen the existing countertop and double your space. Instead of having this buffet here, you could make much better use of the space with traditional cupboards and counters. These cupboards over the sink are way too high. They don't need to be so small, either. If they came down to here you could reach all the lower shelves and save the existing shelves for little-used items. Plus, you need more outlets in the kitchen. Two outlets are not enough. It's dangerous to have this outlet over here because too many people in this apartment complex run the extension cord from this outlet through the doorway over to the counter. The stove should be moved away from this doorway because the wind could blow the curtains into the gas flame which isn't safe."

I was just getting warmed up when Mrs. Tanaka got a stricken look on her face and made some excuse to go home. After that I kept my remodeling ideas to myself.

She had never reacted that way to anything I had said or done, and she never responded to my comments so abruptly again.

BUILD IT AND THEY WILL COME

Mattel's recent marketing campaign for Barbie coincides with the giant Toys 'R' Us invasion of the Japanese toy market. When the American company first bought property to build the first four Toys 'R' Us stores in Japan, their biggest obstacle was the Large-Scale Retail Store Law, which limits the size of retail stores.[21] Other obstacles included high land prices and general cultural feelings against American products. In 1994, there were sixteen Toys 'R' Us superstores in Japan, with projections of thirty-five stores by 1996. An average U.S.-located Toys store makes $10 million per year, but the Japanese stores are averaging $15-$20 million.[22] At first, Japanese toy makers were reluctant to anger their mom-and-pop store owners by supplying products for Japanese Toys 'R' Us stores. The broad-based approach coupled with the success of the stores has altered the position of the Japanese suppliers. The toy stores currently have 4% of the market, with an expected market share of 10% within two years. Japanese commentators attribute the superstores' success to changing Japanese lifestyles, although the popularity may be due to giving Japanese consumers access to the same choices Americans have enjoyed for so many years.

SHARON STONE IN SMILE OF ICE

American movie distributors face many of the same obstacles that other American businesses encounter when trying to market their products in Japan. When Sharon Stone's *Basic Instinct* was shown in Japan, the title was changed to *Smile of Ice* and the film was billed as a movie about an intense, complex woman![23] *Terminator II* made $44 million in Japan and was promoted as a heart-warming woman's movie. This was interesting to me, since I wouldn't consider *Terminator II* a classic "chick flick." American films made the majority of the $312 million foreign film revenues in Japan, yet only 15% of the possible movies are shown to the Japanese audiences. Why? Two Japanese film studios, Toho and Shochiku, control film distribution in Japan. Their Japanese market share is 40%, the highest domestic share in the industrialized world not including the United States. The Japanese have no intentions of losing that share to the Americans, despite the fact that the worldwide average domestic market share is only 20%.

---

[21]"Toys 'R' Us Plans to Open Four Outlets," *Japan Times*, October 26, 199,. p. 14.
[22]Gale Eisenstodt, "Bull in the Japan Shop," *Forbes*, January 31, 1994, pp. 41-42.
[23]Leslie Helm, "Selling Hollywood in Japan," *Los Angeles Times*, September 21, 1992, p. D1.

To control the American film industry, Japanese studios allow only 800 of the 1800 movie theaters to show foreign films. The domestic films are largely pornographic and very poor in quality. Poor movie attendance has not changed the studios' position. After World War II, movie attendance was 1 billion visits per year, but last year it was a paltry 138 million. The Japanese studios could make more money if they would open additional theaters to show American films. Five American movies in 1992 accounted for 60% of the entire box office earnings in Japan. Toho and Shochiku could probably make more money if the customers decided what they wanted to see instead of protecting the Japanese film industry by limiting the number of screens which can show foreign films. True competition and open markets would force the Japanese film industry to upgrade their quality. Instead of acknowledging the reality of the situation, Hilo Iizumi of Nippon Herald Film distributors offers this bit of *tatemae:* "The immediate need . . . is for American studios to do a better job of marketing. Too many studios . . . simply import the entire campaign package used in America to Japan without recognizing the differences in the market."[24]

L. L. BEAN COMES TO TOKYO   A tattered yellow photo shows my aunt Bunny at the age of eight standing in front of a one-room schoolhouse in the tiny logging town of Wellington, Maine. She is frozen in time glaring at the cameraman because she had to wear her L. L. Bean boots with a dress for the school picture. In the 1930s, L. L. Bean was a local business supplying the needs of Maine hunters and fishermen, and yes, little girls. My father and my aunt have nothing pleasant to say about those rubber and leather boots. Ask my aunt now and the years fall away and that same glare comes over her face.

"They were all we had to wear," she sniffs. "In the spring, the melting snows would soak through the leather uppers and the rubber bottoms would guarantee that the water would remain in the boots sloshing around your feet."

Sixty years later, L. L. Bean is still selling to young girls, but now they're in Japan. The catalog business is still in its infancy in Japan, but L. L. Bean has a store in Jiyugaoka, a trendy part of Tokyo. The American firm plans more store openings for the future. Bean is marketing a lifestyle of outdoor living to the Japanese. In addition to selling merchandise, Bean is offering a series of courses on everything from fly-tying to repairing bicycles. By pushing the lifestyle, they have been able to overcome the Japanese myth that American goods are low quality. Hiroshi Kawaguchi, a young manager, says that the "rough and tough" goods don't have to meet the usual high standards the Japanese expect from higher-priced clothing.[25]

---

[24]Ibid.
[25]Teresa Watanabe, "A Bean Grows in Tokyo," *Los Angeles Times,* November 24, 1992, p. H4.

BITTER FRUIT   Japan is the largest market for American agricultural products. Ninety-eight percent of the citrus fruit imported to Japan is supplied by the United States.[26] Opening those markets has not been easy, because consumer attitudes remain as a barrier. In Japan fruit is a gift item, which requires that it be packaged attractively, and that is not how Americans normally buy fruit. Melons can be as much as $80.00 apiece. We skipped strawberries while in Japan because each berry, although beautiful, cost $1.00. Sunkist has 65% of the citrus market share in Japan,[27] and Sunkist solved their marketing problem by conducting an educational campaign. Specialty fruits are very large and are wrapped individually. Sunkist encouraged the grocery stores to carry smaller fruit and to package it in groups of six oranges per plastic bag. The oranges come with instructions on how to cut them decoratively and how to squeeze them to make juice. Juice is not consumed widely in Japan. In order to increase consumption, Sunkist promoted fresh-squeezed juice. Oranges were hand-inspected at the California docks before being shipped to Japan, and only the very best of each crop were included. Orange exports have increased from 1.3 million cartons in 1981 to 5.5 million cartons in 1990. All is not well, however.

Sunkist has been too successful in Japan. National interests are at stake, so Japanese agricultural groups have been spreading rumors that imported American lemons are tainted with Agent Orange. Since the Japanese groups began their campaign, Sunkist sales of lemons have dropped 15%. "We're doing all we can with our embassy and officials, but that's the way they do things, and it's very difficult to combat. They're going to do all they can to keep the fruit out, no matter how safe and good it is, no matter how many lies it takes."[28] These bitter words were spoken by Sunkist spokesman Curt Anderson.

SMILE WHEN YOU SAY THAT, PARDNER!   When Japanese come to visit America, they come on well-controlled tours. Their time is tightly scheduled, and they don't get off the bus and wander around in hardware stores checking out American appliances. In addition, the Japanese rarely take the American and European approach to traveling, which includes bed-and-breakfast lodgings and sojourns with the locals. Japanese stick to hotels owned by Japanese companies wherever possible. They don't come to the States to learn about America or Americans; they come to play at historical sights and national parks. To them, America is just one great big amusement park. As a consequence, they don't really gain much knowledge about our standard of living.

[26]Teresa Watanabe, "Food Fight About to Erupt in Japan," *Los Angeles Times,* March 25, 1991, p. D1.
[27]Teresa Watanabe, "Sunkist Squeezing Out Higher Sales in Japan," *Los Angeles Times,* March 25, 1991, p. D3.
[28]Ibid.

Japanese who work in America don't serve as disseminators of knowledge once they return home. Having spent time in America they are already earmarked as being different, which is the worst fate a Japanese person can suffer. Any remarks about the superior quality of life in America would only further ostracize them from their fellow countrymen. Comparing lifestyles between the United States and Japan in an analytical and critical manner isn't within the realm of possibility. The overseas Japanese try very hard to meld back into the background when they return home. Many returning Japanese are very unhappy to come home, and will intimate as much, but they will never be the cause of a grass-roots consumer rebellion against the Japanese government. Americans who optimistically think that America's trade imbalance will be solved as soon as the Japanese become enlightened are succumbing to the very worst sort of ethnocentrism. They are applying their own culture's mechanisms and ideals to another culture and automatically assuming that the Japanese will react to situations as Americans would. Nothing could be farther from the truth or more racist. Never deny the power and existence of another culture.

The success of L. L. Bean and Toys 'R' Us suggests that the Japanese will buy American goods from American sources when they are exposed to these styles of retailing. The story of the film industry and the Japanese distribution system reveals that when the Japanese tell Americans to try harder, they really mean "We're protecting a domestic industry which can't compete against you, so you'll have to perform the twelve labors of Hercules before we'll give you your prized free trade." The lemon tale suggests that even if you do get the market door open, it can slam back shut in your face at any moment. Jason may have returned home with the golden fleece, but the gods did not smile on him long. He angered Hera and died disgraced and alone. The Japanese can be every bit as fickle as the ancient Greek gods were to Jason. Having market share in Japan or the golden fleece does not ensure long-term success. The moral that Americans should see in these stories about Japan is that American products, even when they are the highest quality in the world, will not be brought home by the Japanese.

When the Japanese say they don't bring anything but maple syrup home from the United States, we should remember a legend from Western literature. *The Virginian*, written in 1902 by Owen Wister, is considered by some folklorists to be the greatest cowboy story ever written.[29] Wister developed all the elements of the Western which later became mainstays in Hollywood movies and Western novels: the taciturn cowboy hero with a slow drawl and no name; the loud, hot-tempered, gunfighting villain; the tenderfoot from back East; and the beautiful, innocent young school teacher. In the classic barroom scene, the gunfighter, Trampas, insults the Vir-

---

[29] John Greenway (ed.), *Folklore of the Great West* (Palo Alto, CA: American West Publishing, 1969), p. 225.

ginian during a poker game. The Virginian's response is quick and smooth. "The Virginian's pistol came out, and his hand lay on the table, holding it unaimed," writes Wister. "And with a voice as gentle as ever, the voice that sounded almost like a caress, but drawling a very little more than usual, so that there was almost a space between each word, he issued his orders to the man Trampas: 'When you call me that, smile!'" Perhaps, the next time a Japanese salaryman tells the maple syrup piece of folklore, we should respond with some of our own: "Smile when you say that, pardner."[30]

---

[30]Owen Wister, *The Virginian* (New York: Grosset and Dunlap, 1945), pp. 28-29.

神話品質

Myth 3:
Japanese Consumers are the
Smartest in the World

As the wife of a salaryman working in a Japanese business, I was the family shopper and the consumer. From what I had learned before coming to Japan, I knew that this role was not taken lightly in Japan. Japanese consumers are touted as the most particular, the most demanding, and the most discerning in the world. Merry White described Japanese teenagers as "tough customers, interested in quality and innovation."[1] Harvard professor Michael Porter describes the Japanese as the toughest and most demanding customers, with the Germans a close second.[2] He attributes their demanding nature to their high educational standards. *Fortune* magazine conducted a survey of marketing consultants, managers of customer-complaint departments, and executives of consumer-goods companies to evaluate the world's pickiest customers.[3] They looked at customer expectations of nine different products—athletic footwear, automobiles, breakfast cereals, cosmetics, dis-

[1]Merry White, *The Material Child* (New York: The Free Press, 1993), p. 104.
[2]Faye Rice, "Selling with Tougher Customers," *Fortune,* December 3, 1990, pp. 39-48.
[3]Ibid.

posable diapers, electric irons, laundry detergents, refrigerators, and VCRs. The Japanese were judged to be the most demanding for automobiles, disposable diapers, electric irons, and refrigerators. Americans were the pickiest for VCRs, breakfast cereals (Japanese don't eat them), and cosmetics. Germans were the toughest to please with athletic shoes. People from the Mediterranean countries were the most particular about laundry detergents.

The toughness of the Japanese consumer is often given as an excuse for why they won't buy foreign goods—foreign goods are inferior in quality. The idea that the Japanese are the smartest customers in the world can be examined from several different vantage points—the ability to make educated choices from among many different possibilities, the ability to spend wisely, the ability to understand and evaluate advertising, and the ability to make socially responsible consumer choices.

GOLD MINES IN JAPANESE STORES
A truly smart consumer would be one who, in the face of many choices, could make an educated decision. Such skill would develop with practice and experience through shopping for many different products. If there are only a few indistinguishable products at comparable prices, the decision of which one to buy is easy because the products are interchangeable. If the products are all of comparable quality, Americans will usually buy the cheapest unless they're motivated by the status achieved by owning high-sticker-price items. Americans are also bargain hunters, frequenting the stores with the best prices. A few of us value service and friendliness over price, but the Mart mentality wins out for most Americans. In 1990 in Japan, an item was sold at a fixed price regardless of where it was being sold, tourist traps excluded. For instance, my youngest son's favorite toy in Japan, Ultra Man, was 500 yen at every toy store all over Japan except for the tourist shops around Kanazawa Garden, where it sold for 700 yen.

A desire to maintain the status quo prevents most Japanese companies from starting price wars with each other for market share. The mom-and-pop shops are protected from the big retailers by this kind of price fixing. Shopping for sales and bargains in Japan is nothing like bargain hunting in America. I remember vividly my initial reaction upon going into a big American drug store after three months in Japan. The physical space and the choice of products seemed dazzling. If one operationally defines the smartest customer as one who makes educated choices when there is a wide selection of possibilities with varying price tags and quality assessments, then the Japanese can't be the toughest customers in the world because their choices are so limited within their own country.

The Japanese have been compared by James Fallows to the hapless American miners who lived in company towns and had to buy from the company store.[4] The

---

[4]James Fallows, "Japan's Consumers: Oppressed Class," *The New York Times,* November 27, 1988, Sec. 4, p. 15.

miners had no options, no rights, and no freedom. In a sense, they had no responsibilities either, because the company took care of them, albeit not very well. Like the
miners, the Japanese are victims of companies' greed. How else can you explain the
price discrepancies between items in Japan and the United States?

One reason often given for these price discrepancies is that the Japanese distribution system is so poor that getting the products through the system is expensive.
However, an examination of the data shows that it is only getting foreign goods
through the distribution system that is expensive. A study performed jointly by the
U.S. Commerce Department and the Japanese Ministry of Trade and Industry, carried out in 1989 and 1990, showed that foreign products cost 65% more in Japan than
they do in the United States.[5] Prices of Japanese-made products were slightly lower
in the United States than in Japan. As an example, Japanese-made cameras and film
were 4 to 7% cheaper in the United States. The poor distribution system in Japan can
account for some of the price difference, but it cannot account for foreign products
being so much more expensive than Japanese products.

One of the things that alerted us to the practice of pricing Japanese products
cheaper in the United States than in Japan was when Japanese students came to Purdue University to study. In talking to them, I found that they used this opportunity
to go to American stores and buy Japanese products. The reason: Japanese products
were less expensive here than in Japan.

As another example, airline tickets for Japan Air Lines are cheaper if they are
bought in foreign countries than if they are bought in Japan. In 1990, a Tokyo District
Court ruled that a travel agent could not sell Japan Air Lines (JAL) tickets in Japan
that had been issued in Hong Kong.[6] What would have been the advantage of doing
this? The same tickets on the same airline were 30 to 40% cheaper if they were purchased in Hong Kong or South Korea than if they were purchased in Japan. The high
prices at home ensure high profitability for the company, and the reduced international prices mean that the companies can compete, albeit unfairly, in the international market.

Even in Tokyo department stores, the prices in catalogs to foreign customers
are lower than the prices charged to in-store customers. One column in the *Japan
Times* reported that department stores often have a "secret" catalog for overseas
sales, in this case for china, in which the prices are generally about 20% lower than
those in the store.[7] Most stores in Japan charge the same set price, so there is little
competition and no incentive to reduce price. Overseas, though, where collusion
like this is illegal, the artificially high prices would be unacceptable. There is no
overseas market for overpriced items, so the companies are forced to charge less.

---

[5]David Friedman and Loren Yager, "Why More U.S. Exports to Japan Won't Amount to a Hill of Beans,"
Los Angeles Times, January 12, 1992, p. M2
[6]Editorial, "Still No Air Ticket Bargains," *Japan Times,* September 30, 1990, p. 20.
[7]Jean Pearce, "Getting Things Done, It's Not What You Do," *Japan Times,* November 25, 1990, p. 18.

We did a little study ourselves of the differences between Japanese and American prices. The bulk of what we brought home from Japan was unquestionably toys—our youngest son filled an entire suitcase with Ultra Man monsters. Table 10.1 lists toys and games available in both Japan and the United States.[8] Lego sets made in Denmark, which range from $22.50 to $90.00 in the United States, cost the Japanese consumer $40.00 to $133.00 for the exact same sets. Games made in America cost, on average, twice as much in Japan. Even Walt Disney videos are marked up considerably in Japan. The *Sword in the Stone* cost $18.00 in the States and $38.40 in Japan. This survey showed that Japanese prices were 58.4% higher than American prices.

Table 10.1 Comparisons of American and Japanese prices for various products.

Origin	Product	Japan Price (yen)	Japan Price (dollars)	U.S. Price
United States	Simon game	5,800	38.60	31.47
Denmark	Lego set 6081	9,000	60.00	45.00
Denmark	Lego set 6285	20,000	133.00	90.00
Denmark	Bucket of Legos 1637	6,000	40.00	22.50
United States	Monopoly game	3,000	20.00	9.00
United States	Monopoly Junior game	2,800	14.90	9.00
United States	Sword in the Stone video	5,768	38.40	18.00
United States	Day for Eeyore video	3,502	23.20	9.00
United States	Treasure Island video	5,768	38.40	15.30
United States	Life game	2,980	19.80	11.54
United States	Twister game	2,980	19.80	11.45
Japan	Nintendo Game Boy	14,659	97.70	71.00
	Totals		543.80	343.26
	Average		45.32	28.61

Bear in mind that American manufacturers are not getting any of this extra money charged to Japanese consumers: The Japanese distributors are receiving it. The extra money extorted from Japanese toy buyers is minor compared to the huge amounts of extra profits made when American automobiles are sold in Japan. When the Japanese bought two Buick Park Avenues to appease President George Bush

[8]The Japanese prices came from an advertising circular from the biggest toy store in Toyko, which was printed around Christmas, 1990. The U.S. prices are from major American retailers such as Service Merchandise and Toys 'R' Us adjusted for inflation, since they are 1993-1994 prices. The conversion rate used for translating yen to dollars was the current one at the time of our visit: 150 yen to the dollar.

after his visit in January 1992, each one cost $46,000; the American sticker price was $30,000.[9] Detroit and the American taxpayers didn't see one penny of that added profit. What did the Japanese do to those Buicks to increase their value? For that matter, what did they do to earn that money? Small wonder we can't sell cars in Japan. Think of the consumer outcry in America if American car dealers increased the prices of Hondas and Toyotas by 100% and pocketed the difference? The company store is exploiting the miners. The first people to benefit from open markets will be the Japanese consumers.

KIRIN BEER REBELLION OF 1994?   Despite the fact that Japanese beer costs 44% more in Japan than in the United States,[10] don't expect the Japanese people to riot as some Americans did in 1794 when the price of whiskey increased. Yasue Kobayashi of the Consumer Information Center says: "They [the consumers] don't have the vision."[11] A politician, Koji Kakizawa, summarized the Japanese mindset: "If we ever get hit with stagflation or a recession, consumers will return their allegiance to the producer side. As long as Japan is affluent and growing, they have room to think as consumers, but they will still put the national interest over their own."[12] Another force keeping markets closed is the small merchants, middlemen, and farmers, who like the economy the way it is and who wouldn't survive in an economy like America's. Mom-and-pop shops account for 60% of retail sales in Japan, compared to 5% in the United States[13] The politicians are reluctant to antagonize such a big voting block.

Any American who thinks the Japanese will rise up and rebel when they learn the truth of how their companies and their government have been exploiting them had better start reading their history books. Japan has no history of rebellion like the Boston Tea Party, the Whiskey Rebellion, or Shay's Rebellion, which were all reactions against taxes and higher prices. The Japanese have had their share of anarchists, but that's another matter.

BORROWING FROM PETER TO PAY PAUL   Another way to evaluate who are the smartest customers is to examine how they spend their money. Smart customers don't buy what they can't afford. From the years 1988 to

---

[9]Jim Mateja, "Bush Japan Trip Cuts Trade Deficit by 2 Buicks; $40,999,908,000 to Go," *Chicago Tribune,* January 27, 1992, p. 4-5.
[10]Barbara Buell, "Japan's Silent Majority Starts to Mumble," *Business Week,* April 23, 1990, pp. 52-54.
[11]Ibid., p. 54.
[12]Ibid.
[13]James Fallows, "Japan's Latest Trade War Is with Its Own Consumers," *Business Month,* December 1998, pp. 21-22.

1990, Japan's loans to consumers tripled, to $150 billion.[14] Per capita, this debt came to $4300, compared to the U.S. per-capita debt of $3100. Japanese consumers have been buying too much and putting it on credit cards. Personal bankruptcies reached 40,000 in 1991, up from about 10,000 in 1989. By 1993 there were 30,000 bankruptcies in a nine-month period.[15] The average debt per bankruptcy case is $42,000, which is several times higher than the U.S. rate.

The use of credit cards is not widespread across businesses and services in Japan. Department stores accept credit cards but they are seldom accepted at traditional inns, restaurants, or mom-and-pop shops. Location also dictates the likelihood of credit card usage. Big cities are more likely to have businesses which have credit card services than rural areas.

Department store credit cards in Japan allow people to borrow as much money as they wish on cash loans carrying interest rates of 39%. Unlike the United States, there are no spending limits or credit checks associated with these credit cards. One young worker owed a total of $236,000 charged on 33 different cards. The Japanese blame the current credit crisis on America because of efforts during trade talks to encourage consumer spending in Japan.[16] "It's America's fault....the average person doesn't have the ability to buy," claims a credit counselor, Shoichi Ebina.[17] It is the responsibility of the Japanese government to enact safeguards such as spending limits and credit checks to prevent their citizens from getting so heavily into debt. The financial departments of big retail stores also have a responsibility to charge reasonable interest rates.

MY LIFE, MY GAS   Consumers in the modern world are bombarded by advertising from every medium. A sophisticated consumer knows how to evaluate the massive amounts of information in commercials and print advertising. In order to judge the credibility of the advertising, the consumer must be able to understand the language and the imagery used. The early Infiniti ads, for instance, which were scenic shots of Western America, made no sense to Americans because they didn't show the product being advertised and it wasn't obvious what mountains had to do with a luxury Japanese sedan. Advertisements with lots of French or German in them probably wouldn't work in America either, since we like to know what is being said. These expectations of clear communication are not the norm in Japanese advertisements.

---

[14]Leslie Helm, "Debts Put Squeeze on Japanese," *Los Angeles Times,* November 21, 1992, p. A1.
[15]"Many Japanese Caught in Debt Trap," *Chicago Tribune,* January 10, 1993. Section 7, p. 14.
[16]Ibid.
[17]Ibid.

Advertising in Japan has long been a source of amusement for visitors to Japan. The common use of English in almost random fashion makes it easy for Americans to poke fun. We vividly remember the black-and-white advertisement in the Kyoto train station proclaiming "Dramatic Wedding," above a picture of a naked woman with her arms crossed demurely across her breasts. What was she advertising? We eventually decided that the ad was for wedding packages sold through hotels.

The incredible aspect of the use of English in Japanese advertising is its failure to communicate to the domestic audience. Harald Haarman analyzed the ability of 800 Japanese college students to comprehend such simple English advertising copy as "My life, my gas," "For beautiful human life," and "Do you know me?". He found that only a minority could decipher the English correctly.[18] Why use copy few can understand? Some have suggested that the Japanese use English for its decorative purposes. Others believe that the English, which seems like gibberish to Americans, means something to the Japanese. Haarman's data indicates that the latter isn't likely, but James Stanlow, who also investigated the problem, was told by a well-meaning Japanese: "It doesn't matter very much that Americans don't know what some of our English words mean. What matters, after all, is that we know, right?"[19]

The critical point remains: How can a smart consumer evaluate the messages in advertising when so much of the message is written in a foreign language? The Japanese may study English in their schools, but very few of them are fluent in English. Never mind that most of the English in the advertising is full of misspellings and poor grammar. I often joked with my husband that only he could rent videos at the local Japanese video shop because it clearly said on our card, "Menbership Card." We rented our movies at the "Movie Lental Shop."

USE IT UP, WEAR IT OUT   The last criterion for determining the smartest consumer in the world is the ability to make decisions based on social responsibility. *Fortune* magazine, in its article about the toughest consumers,[20] used this criterion to discuss the rise of a new breed of American consumers. Interest in environmentally correct products is high among Americans: Four out of five said they would pay more for packaging made of recyclable or biodegradable materials. A major component of the environmental movement in the United States is to encourage people to become less materialistic and to follow the old adage, "use it up, wear it out, make it do, or do without." With all the emphasis in America on being environmentally correct, it seems particularly ironic that the Japanese, who

---

[18]Harald Haarman, *Symbolic Values of Foreign Language Use* (Berlin: Mouton de Gruyter, 1989), p. 8.
[19]James Stanlow, "For Beautiful Human Life: The Use of English in Japan," in Joseph Tobin (ed.), *Re-Made in Japan* (New Haven, CT: Yale University Press, 1992), pp. 58-75.
[20]Rice, "Selling with Tougher Customers."

like to describe themselves as being in touch with nature, are the worst offenders when it comes to product churning, which fills landfills with old goods and unnecessary packaging, resulting in irresponsible depletion of natural resources.

SODAI GOMI   There are no old, rusty cars on the streets of Japan. Unlike my home town of Bozeman, Montana, the capital of rusty Subarus, cars in Japan are usually replaced every four years. In Japan you cannot own a car that is over four years old without having it inspected. The repairs necessary to meet the inspection requirements are so extensive that it is easier and cheaper to buy a new car. In 1989, 260,000 old cars were shipped out of Japan to third-world countries.[21] Old appliances, furniture, and household items appear several times a year on Japanese curbsides. The debris, sometimes referred to as *sodai gomi,* creates mountains of garbage and playgrounds for youngsters bent on destruction. We witnessed such an event shortly before returning to the States. American military personnel stationed in Japan know when and where all these free flea markets occur in the towns around the naval bases. They get great stuff at curbside. I replaced my wretched little vacuum cleaner with a slightly better one which I found on a garbage heap. Best of all, it had been thrown away with a clean dust bag, so I didn't even have to buy one.

The local Japanese come early to these events and remove all the electronic items. Memorable images stay with me of old gentlemen cycling away in the twilight with five or six VCRs strapped on the backs of their bikes. I also recall with great clarity the fiendish look of pure glee on Mrs. Tanaka's son's face as he swung his baseball bat at the furniture in the heap. In less than fifteen minutes, he had rendered a nice-looking cabinet totally useless. One of our neighbors was embarrassed when we caught him carrying an abandoned desk from the pile to his apartment. I should have known better, but I saw him struggling with it outside my kitchen window. It was obvious that his ten-year-old son wasn't strong enough to carry his end of the desk up three flights of stairs, so I told my husband to go help him. Mr. Kuroki looked stricken, but we got the desk up the stairs.

Japanese manufacturers encourage consumers to buy new models even if the old ones work just fine. This product churning is paradoxical since Japanese products have such a reputation for quality and durability. Matsushita estimates that the average TV is replaced every six or seven years.[22] Probably no one in Japan has a 1977 Sony television like ours, which incidentally works just fine and has a marvelous picture. Sony's chairman, Akio Morita, and the Ministry of International Trade and Industry have complained about the rapidity with which product develop-

---

[21]"Sodai's Law," *The Economist,* June 24, 1989, p. 36.
[22]Ibid.

ment is damaging profits and annoying consumers.[23] Does anyone really care if a new VCR comes out every six months? How many VCRs do people need in a lifetime? More important is the question every consumer on the planet should ask themselves: How much longer can we continue to be so irresponsible about our natural resources?

One of the reasons Japanese tourists don't like to shop in locally owned tourist stores abroad is that the American and British shopkeepers just put the purchases in bags and hand them over causally to the Japanese tourists. Japanese are accustomed to their shopping rituals, which can best be described as Christmas every day. When you make a purchase in a Japanese store, especially a department store, the item will be boxed and wrapped very nicely no matter what you say. They don't ask you if you want it gift wrapped; they automatically wrap it. They do a wonderful job, although their wrapping procedure is one which uses more paper than Western-style gift wrapping. It's intoxicating to shop, because everything you buy looks like a Christmas present. The clerks are very formal about handing you back your money and presenting you with your boxed, wrapped, and bagged purchase.

There are two things to remember when shopping in Japan: Present the clerk with your money using two hands, with the front of the money facing the clerk; and never buy four of anything. I received dirty looks from middle-aged department store clerks for buying four cups, four spoons, and four forks. In Japanese, the word for death is the same as the word for four, so it is considered very poor form to buy four of anything. Dishes come in sets of three or five. I found this interesting because almost every family I knew in Japan had four people—two parents and two children. Evidently, the superstition didn't apply to family planning.

The excess packaging in Japan weighed heavily on my environmental conscience. The limit was the night we invited our Shakey's pizza-fight friends over for dessert. We stopped at the corner market for snacks, and everyone was in the mood for ice cream. The only kind available consisted of individually wrapped servings in a plastic container with a cardboard exterior. Trying to remove the perfectly formed egg-shaped portions of ice cream from all the layers of packaging was quite an enterprise. There was precious little ice cream, but lots of packaging.

Traveling on trains meant putting up with excess food packaging as well. The only foods available at the train stops were wooden boxes of rice and sushi. While they may have appealed to the Japanese love of wood, they made me lose my appetite because all I could think about was how many rain forest trees were sacrificed for chopsticks and sushi boxes. Japanese appetites for lovely little box lunches and other needs are consuming 10,000 square miles of Southeast Asian rain forest per year.[24]

---

[23]Michael Schrage, "Drive to Obsolescence Needs a Brake," *Los Angeles Times,* July 2, 1992, p. D1.

The Japanese style of packaging has an impact on America's environment. When Japanese companies introduced compact disks as a replacement for vinyl records, they ushered in a new era of wasteful packaging. A record purchase left the buyer with some plastic wrap to discard, but CDs leave Americans with 16,700 tons of useless packaging per year.

Most of the Japanese foreign aid given to other Asian countries is used to build roads, bridges, dams, power plants, and airports so the Japanese can use the natural resources of their neighbors.[25] Few environmental impact studies are ever done, and most countries have few laws to protect their citizens from environmental pollution. Japan's Asian neighbors are at fault as well, since they are willingly sacrificing their environments. The Japanese paid dearly for their own environmental laxness; the Minamata poisonings are just one example of the results of unregulated industrial waste dumping (see pages 40–41). Interestingly, Shintaro Ishihara, the author of *The Japan That Can Say No*, was one of the chiefs of Japan's Environmental Agency, which refused to compensate the victims of the Minamata disaster. Apparently, Japan can say no to its own people and does so on a regular basis.

Depletion of natural resources to satisfy the needs of Japanese consumers is a common occurrence. Smart Japanese consumers must have real tortoise shell folk art objects, eyeglasses, and cigarette lighters. Imitation just won't satisfy the discerning consumer. Over the past two decades, the Japanese have imported parts of 2 million sea turtles for commercial use. Todd Steiner of the Earth Island Institute's Sea Turtle Restoration Project told Rudy Abramson of the Los Angeles Times: "The purchase of sea turtles by Japan is responsible for the greatest killing of endangered species in the world."[26] Japan's behavior over 14 years was in clear violation of the 1977 international convention banning trade in endangered species. For years, the Japanese use of drift nets to catch fish was contributing to the precipitous decline of mammals, birds, and fish in the world's oceans. Japan's response to calls from the international community to stop the use of the nets was typical. Koji Imura, chairman of the squid drift net association, claimed that the numbers of unwanted life captured in the drift nets was "vastly misrepresented by the American environmentalists who are 'emotional.'"[27] In 1990, 10% of the drift net ships surveyed had killed 1758 whales and dolphins, 30,464 sea birds, 253,288 tuna, 81,956 blue sharks, and 3 million fish.[28] All this wildlife became trash. No wonder the environmentalists were emotional.

---

[24]Merrill Goozner, "Japan Is Greener, But Has Far to Go," *Chicago Tribune*, June 3, 1992. Section 1, p. 4.
[25]Ibid.
[26]Rudy Abramson, "U.S. Formally Accuses Japan of Trading in Imperiled Turtles." *Los Angeles Times*, March 21, 1991. Section A, p. 20.
[27]Larry Stammer and Leslie Helm, "Japan Fishing Industry to Halt Use of Drift Nets," *Los Angeles Times*, November 26, 1991, p. A1.
[28]Ibid.

$500 BOUNTY ON KILLER DOLPHINS

$500 BOUNTY ON KILLER DOLPHINS   The following episode illustrates both Japanese environmental attitudes and how "spin doctors" operate in Japan. In the fall of 1990, an incident on the beaches of Fukuejima Island in Nagasaki Prefecture captured our attention. Initial news reports on November 4 said that local fisherman had driven 600 dolphins onto the beach and slaughtered them with the help of residents, including small children.[29] The *Japan Times* printed a front-page photograph of the massacre. Cranes and tractors were then used to pile the carcasses on the beach. The fishermen claimed that the dolphins beached themselves and the fishermen were just putting them out of their misery.

Three days later, ocean ecology specialist Naoko Kakuta was disputing the fishermen's version, saying that massive beachings were unusual.[30] Four or five dolphins might beach themselves, but not 600. By November 7, the deputy mayor of nearby Miiraku was defending the fishermen's actions: "Dolphins eat a large amount of fish, and damage to the town's fishing industry has been serious."[31] The Nagasaki Prefectural government had since 1987 been offering bounties of 5000 yen or around $500 for each dead "killer" dolphin.

The spin on the story continued. Officials speculated that unknown diseases had caused the dolphins to beach. Reports were denied that bounties would be paid in this case. The next day, the fisherman's unions were describing the killer fishermen as "physically and psychologically exhausted."[32] Disposing of the half-ton bodies had worn the fishermen out.

The verity of the earlier accounts was being questioned. The newspaper *Asahi Shimbun* had reported the fishermen's version, the Tokyo newspaper *Shimbun* quoted the police accounts of mass slaughter, the *Japan Times* relied on police reports and thus echoed the Tokyo paper, and the Kyodo News Service had reporters present at the scene, so they were disputing the fishermen. Four days after the incident, the local police, who had been a source of information for the newspapers, had changed their stories and were now claiming to know only the fishermen's versions.[33]

The *Japan Times* on November 10 ran an article indicating that four of the 600 dolphins had confirmed parasites in their ears and their stomachs were empty, which could account for the beaching. The *Japan Times*, which had carried the original accounts of children killing the dolphins after the fishermen drove them up on

---

[29]"Nearly 600 Dolphins Are Slaughtered After Fishermen Drive Them Ashore," *Japan Times*, November, 4, 1990, p. 1.

[30]"Hundreds of Dead Dolphins Cause Controversy," *Asahi Evening News*, November 6, 1990, p. 2.

[31]"An Offical Defends Killing of Dolphins," *Japan Times*, November 7, 1990, p. 2.

[32]Shinji Ito and Naomi Hirakawa, "Fishermen Called 'Biggest Victims,'" *Japan Times*, November 8, 1990, p. 2.

[33]Ibid.

the beach, altered the strength of its original version in their November 14 issue by saying: "While some reports say fishermen had driven the dolphins onto the beach, the Miiraku Town Fisheries Cooperative Union has denied this."[34]

November 22 found the Fisheries Agency exonerating the fishermen of their role in beaching the dolphins. The agency cautioned against any further description of the unfortunate event as "slaughter" or as a "driving-in" of the dolphins to the beach. Furthermore, the agency asserted that accounts by British and New Zealand news agencies criticizing the fishermen were simply wrong.[35] While some of the fishermen did act improperly, the fishermen did not deliberately kill the dolphins. The article went on to quote the high cost involved in disposing of the dolphins bodies—2 million yen.

Despite the fact that numerous news accounts reported that the villagers hauled away the free dolphin meat, the agency claimed that the stranded dolphins could not be consumed because that would be a violation of traditional dietary custom.

On January 4, 1991, the *Los Angeles Times* reported that Japanese attitudes were changing and Japanese consumers were much greener than they used to be. The author describe the Miiraku incident, but focused not on the needless slaughter, but on the Japan-bashing that followed the reporting of the story in the Western press. The author claimed that Japan is not the same place it was when thousands of dolphins were driven up on the beaches of Iki Kima, Nagasaki Prefecture, in the 1970s.[36] The author failed to realize that the lesser number of dolphins eliminated on Nagasaki beaches in November 1990 had more to do with the reduced numbers of dolphins worldwide than to any improved environmental practices in Japan.

The image is that the smart Japanese consumer considers only quality and not price. Price is not considered because most items cost the same throughout the country. The quality of Japanese products cannot be compared to the quality of foreign products because of the limited number of product choices from other countries. If given a chance, Japanese consumers might become the smartest in the world. But with limited availability of foreign products and comparable prices throughout the country, they are not given the chance. The Japanese consumer could begin to rebel against the unnaturally high prices and demand more choices. More intelligent shopping decisions could be made if the consumer demanded that packaging and products, especially those involving endangered species, correspond more closely to the purported Japanese love of nature.

---

[34]"Scientists, Fisherman Debate Cause of Nagasaki Mass Dolphin Beaching," *Japan Times*, November 14, 1990, p. 2.

[35]"Some Miiraku Fishermen Took Improper Action," *Japan Times*, November 22, 1990, p. 2.

[36]Karl Schoenberger, "Friends for Whales in Japan," *Los Angeles Times*, January 4, 1991, p. A1.

神話品質

Myth 4:
Japanese Companies
Listen to and are
Responsive to Consumers

*T*he television commercial opens with a panoramic view of a prime vacation spot for travelers from all over the world. The camera starts to focus on some of the tourists. A voice-over states how many tourists visit this destination each year. The narrator then makes a startling announcement: None of these visitors are engineers from a Japanese car company. They are all back home in Japan, working hard to make improvements in car design. Japanese engineers are busy beating out other companies while the rest of the world is on vacation.

This ad campaign could have a negative effect. It depicts engineers holed up in some research center with little outside contact. The major problem is that those outside contacts are potential customers. If the Japanese engineers are so busy making design changes but not interacting with customers, how can they understand which design changes correspond to the needs of the customers? Maybe a vacation would be good for these engineers. They could contemplate what customers want or have a chance to observe some customers for themselves. In the United States, many potential car customers take their automobiles on vacation with them. What better place to conduct an informal field study, to observe the cars people are buying and the amount of cargo being stuffed into them? As we saw in Chapter 4, customers ulti-mately decide on the definition of quality.

Japanese companies have a real distrust of customer focus groups or other cus-tomer-based experiments. They have no history of human factors research or cus-tomer surveys. Deming has corroborated this distrust of experiments into Japanese corporate policies. Japanese companies rely instead on intuition. Armchair intuition about customers may work in Japan, but relying on this method causes a problem when products are being exported to satisfy customers in other countries.

PROXIES FOR AMERICAN CONSUMERS I was sitting at a restaurant table with eight employees from a large Japanese electronics company. Many were half-asleep, suffering from the jet lag that was inevitable after traveling halfway around the world. For most of them, conversational English was not a strong point, but I could not complain because my Japanese was not conversational either. They were tired from a busy day at Purdue, identifying technological gardens which could be harvested. I did not know what to say.

I decided to do a quick informal survey.

"What color car do you have?" I asked. Before anyone could answer, I answered for them. "It is probably white or light silver," I stated.

Everyone around the table confirmed my answer. All present had a white or light silver car. Naturally, no one had a black car, since this would signal that he (we were all male) was a member of the *Yakuza*, the Japanese Mafia. They are the only ones in Japan to drive black cars, thus offering a very convenient way for others to identify their choice of occupation.

"How old were you when you got married?" I asked. "You were probably mar-ried at 27. Some of you were married perhaps when you were 28."

The table survey indicated that people were married at 27 or 28. One person was married at 30, and he looked extremely embarrassed when he was forced to admit this.

"How old was your wife when she married you?" Once again I guessed right. "She was probably 24 or 25."

The wives were indeed 24 or 25 when they got married.

This survey helped to break the ice, but only somewhat. I had them at a disad-vantage. A salaryman in a large Japanese corporation must adhere to certain accepted standards for his personal life and the products he buys. I knew a lot about them because I knew these standards; they knew little about me. I did not own a white or light silver car.

In Japan, a quarter of the population lives on the Kanto plain in and around Tokyo. Much of the consumer base for companies is within a short train ride. Japan takes pride in the homogeneity of the country; immigration has been virtually non-existent throughout its long history. Koreans who have been living in Japan for fifty years still do not have the rights of Japanese citizens. Consumers follow fads carefully so as not to stick out. When we were in Japan, all the women were wearing shades of gold and green.

How can these people—the ones responsible for designing products sold in the United States—design products for the diversity of consumers in the American market? American consumers are different from Los Angeles to Philadelphia. The inner cities are different from the suburbs, which are different from rural areas. People in the United States pride themselves on their differences, not on how they are the same. Market analysis is a complex business in the United States. Japanese companies have no experience in this field, because in the past they have had little need to develop these skills.

The Japanese people consider themselves different from any other people in the world. Often they use this attitude to their advantage: They say that foreign companies cannot sell products in Japan because the Japanese are different. Foreign products developed for foreigners will not suit Japanese consumers. They say that Japanese snow is different from European snow, so European skis will not work in Japan. They say they have shorter intestines than Caucasians, so North American food is inappropriate. Japanese roads are too narrow and American cars are too big for the roads. Gasoline costs too much even for low-mpg American cars. They consider themselves different from Westerners, which provides a justification for excluding foreign products.

The paradox is that Japanese companies also consider their Japanese customers as proxies for American consumers. The things a Japanese customer will like will also be favored by American customers. Because the Japanese customers are proxies for Americans, Japanese companies already know their customers. On the one hand, the Japanese consumer is so different from foreigners that foreign products cannot be sold in Japan. On the other hand, Japanese consumers are so similar to American consumers that little market research needs to be done to sell in the United States. This apparent paradox is not bothersome to Japanese companies.

IF YOU CANNOT USE IT, YOU MUST BE STUPID   In the past, when I have done consulting work for American computer companies, the first thing that had to be accomplished was to change the attitude of the computer programmers who write the interactive programs used by customers. The programmers are, of course, extremely familiar with their work and the computers they use. Through this familiarity they are, by definition, completely different from the people who will be using their product. Consequently, they have little understanding of their customers. The attitude of the programmers is that they are computer users, and if they know how to use their program then others should have no trouble with it. If the customers have trouble, then they must be stupid.

In recent years, American computer companies have worked to reverse this attitude and have made remarkable strides in the area of customer-friendly software and hardware products, so that they, more than any other industry, are responsive to their customers. As examples, in 1984, 30-35% of the lines of code in a computer program were devoted to making the program easier for the customer to use.[1] In 1990, this had increased to 47-60% of the code.[2] For these software products, this means that more than half of the costs are associated with fitting the product to the customer. Other American—and Japanese—industries should learn from the American computer companies.

American companies have devoted time and effort to studying their customers. Xerox Corp. was losing market share in its main business of photocopiers, and customers were complaining about the low reliability of their copiers. When the human factors department, responsible for designing products to fit people, responded to these complaints, they found some interesting facts. The source of most service calls were not problems with reliable products. Instead, the customers could not use their copiers and assumed they were broken and needed to be fixed. The copiers were reliable, but the customers considered them low-quality because of usability problems.

The designers and engineers at Xerox did not believe there was a problem. To prove there was a big problem, the human factors people decided to test and videotape the researchers and scientists at Xerox trying to use their own products. I saw this videotape, and the results are often hilarious. The elite researchers at Xerox, the brainpower driving the company into new areas, are shown on the videotape trying to figure out, without many fruitful results, how to use their own products.

From this study, changes to the design came about quickly. Xerox designers and engineers changed the usability of Xerox copiers so that problems such as paper jams were alleviated by displaying the information on how to correct them clearly on the machine. Service calls decreased and customer satisfaction increased. Xerox copiers became the easiest to use in the industry. This occurred because the company was willing to respond to the needs of its customers.[3] The smart people at

---

[1] S. L. Smith and J. N. Mosier, *Design Guidelines for the User Interface for Computer-Based Information Systems* (Bedford, MA: The MITRE Corp., 1984). (Also available from the National Technical Information Service, Springfield, VA.)

[2] F. MacIntyre, K. W. Estep, and J. M. Sieburth, "Cost of User-Friendly Programming," *Journal of Forth Application and Research 1990, 6*(2), pp. 103-115.

[3] John Seely Brown, "Research That Reinvents the Corporation," *Harvard Business Review*, January-February 1991, p. 102.

Xerox could not use the products, so the designers and engineers could not defend the old argument that people who could not use the product were just plain stupid.

Responsiveness to customers is increasing at other American companies as well. Apple Computer has designed its products to be customer-friendly. The Macintosh is an elegant machine which was designed to eliminate mistakes. Customers can manipulate the items on the screen directly. It uses a WYSIWYG design philosophy (What You See Is What You Get) to increase its simplicity. A desktop metaphor makes the machine easier to learn. If people know how to manipulate items on a desktop, then they understand the basic principles of using the Macintosh. Apple has carved out its market niche on customer-friendly products. Part of Apple's design strategy is to bring in customers to test their products before they go to market.

Microsoft Corp. is another company which has concentrated on the customer with exceptionally fine results. Many of the customer-friendly aspects of the Apple Macintosh have been replicated and enhanced by Microsoft. The flexibility of their products is amazing, and the number of features provided in their programs is awesome. Microsoft has designed products that predict the kinds of mistakes people are likely to make, so errors can be eliminated before they happen. They predict what people may want to do with their product so that it can be done. Microsoft has laboratories to test customers on the usability of their software products.

AT&T has long been a leader in designing products that are customer-friendly. For many years, AT&T was hiring more behavioral scientists than any other organization in the world. These scientists were placed in AT&T laboratories to understand the customer and assist in the design of customer-friendly products. The customer innovations in the design of their communication equipment has been exemplary, providing the standards which are copied by other companies around the world. In Indianapolis, where many of the consumer products are tested before they are marketed, the human factors laboratory has contracts with church and civic groups so that people from these groups can be tested on the products before they are put on the market. Any needed design changes are made, based on these customer studies, before the product is marketed.

The list can be extended to other American companies. IBM has extensive laboratories where customers are tested on their products. Around 1980, an IBM vice president decided that IBM products were too difficult to use, and so the company made large investments in hiring behavioral scientists to test the products in customer experiments. They invested in laboratories where these studies take place. Hewlett-Packard performs extensive customer tests on the hardware and software for their computer printers. Other software companies have similar customer laboratories.

American transportation manufacturers are reaching out to customers. For years, aircraft manufacturers have had to design cockpits to fit the physical and cognitive requirements of the pilot. GM and Ford have human factors laboratories where researchers design experiments and customers are brought into the labs to be tested and help determine which design features work and which do not.

FOLLOW THE INSTRUCTIONS   I owned a Japanese-designed and -manufactured hi-fi stereo VCR for over a year, enduring terrible sound quality. Unlike other consumers, I was willing to believe that the problem with the sound might be because I had not pushed the right buttons. The machine had all kinds of buttons, and the simple labels provided few clues to the purposes of the buttons. I tried all kinds of button combinations trying to obtain better sound, but to no avail. I finally started to focus on a button, which could be placed in the on position or the off position, labeled "hi-fi/normal mix." I was not quite sure what constituted a hi-fi/normal mix, but I assumed that mixed must be better than unmixed, so I kept it in the "on" position. I played with other buttons, but the sound quality did not improve.

I was still curious about this mix button. Although I had read the manual many times, I tried again to find an explanation of the function of this button. The instructions told me the obvious: "Place it in the on position to turn on a mix and place it in the off position when the mix was not desired." This explanation did nothing to reduce my uncertainty about the function of the mix. Then I noticed a footnote at the bottom of the page, which I had always ignored because the explanation seemed too obtuse to read. The note at the bottom said this: "When playing back a tape containing the same sound track on both hi-fi and normal audio tracks, a slight time lag is sensed between the two soundtracks, probably with some distortion, in the ON position. Therefore, in such a case, use the OFF position." I found, through experience, that all commercial tapes have the soundtrack on both tracks, and the distortion I was hearing was the poor sound quality I had endured for over a year.

I estimated that I had spent about ten hours trying to fix this problem, and many more hours in frustration over the poor-quality sound. The answer could be found in the instructions, if only they could be interpreted. This should never have been an issue requiring instructions. A button should not have been provided for this feature and, if provided, the ON position should have represented the normal operating mode.

Before going to Japan, I had a difficult time understanding why these Japanese products were so difficult to use when a simple design change could improve the usability immensely. Why rely on instructions—poorly written instructions at that—to enable consumers to obtain high-quality sound. It is widely known in consumer industries that American owners don't read their manuals. From our experiences in Japan, we found an explanation for the reliance upon instruction. Following instructions plays an important role in daily Japanese life. Even the most mundane activities in Japan are accompanied by detailed instructions. While traveling in Japan, we were once surprised to find instructions for how to use the toilet in our hotel room. The point-by-point instructions, along with the color illustration, were quite graphic (i.e., a yellow stream of water) in explaining when males should sit down or stand up.

The noise pollution in Japan can be quite annoying. For a country which values quiet contemplation in a Zen garden, the noise and commotion of the real world is irritating and stressful. Recorded female voices explain how to do everything. Get on an escalator and a female voice explains its proper usage over and over again. The explanation was always polite, preceded by an "excuse me," but we could not understand why people had to be reminded over and over again how to use an escalator. Stand on a street corner, and the female voice tells you how to interpret the traffic signals.

One person told us, "Japanese drivers are the best drivers in the world because we have to read a thick instruction book and pass a lengthy written test on the proper procedures for driving." Another person told us, "Japanese drivers are the best drivers in the world because we had to read a thick instruction book and pass a lengthy written test on the proper procedures for driving." We were always amazed at how people would tell us the same thing using almost the same words. When the second person made this point, we countered that driving skill has very little to do with reading a book and a lot to do with driving experience. Through experience, one learns to predict dangerous situations and how to handle emergency situations. But in Japan, reading a book and following instructions is more important than skill and experience.

One evening we were watching the Japanese news. On this news program, about fifteen minutes were devoted to sports. Often, this time period was difficult to fill. One day a large golf tournament was rained out, nixing the plans for extensive news coverage of the event. Instead of the tournament, the sportscaster spent ten minutes standing in the rain and explaining the intricacies of each hole. In another golf segment, the reporter was talking to a Japanese golf player who had recently changed from amateur to professional status, and they were discussing this procedure. In Japan, one of the requirements for turning pro is to pass a written test. Follow the instructions.

Japanese streets in the cities have virtually no street signs. The numbering on the houses and the buildings is not always posted, and the numbers do not always follow sequentially. To get from one place to another, one usually has to follow detailed instructions written down by someone familiar with the area.

When writing the Chinese characters used in the Japanese language, each character must be drawn following the proper steps. A character not only has to look right, but each stroke has to be done in the right sequence and the right direction. A stroke often involves a change in line width at an exact point in the drawing. Students must learn at least 4000 characters, all with the correct sequence of drawing lines.

Every school child, when doing origami, learns to follow step-by-step instructions. If a step is performed out of order or if the fold is done improperly, then the later folds will not work. Origami may be a good way to teach the importance of tolerances in manufactured products. It also teaches students how to follow instructions.

In Japan, following instructions is very important. There is a right way to do things and the wrong way. This may be fine for regulating and controlling everyday life, but it does not transfer very well to product design. Japanese products place an overreliance on instructions. As an example, I received as a gift from a large Japanese corporation a pen-and-pencil set made in Japan. This set was accompanied by an instruction booklet of four pages. The design of these simple tools was so poor that I found I actually needed to read the instruction book. Opening the pen box was not a simple procedure.

Following this tradition of using instructions, Japanese companies have a tendency to design products based on a design principle characterized as placing knowledge in the head. This is based on the principle that people must learn, through strong reliance on instructions, and then remember how to use products. This makes the design process easier but does not make designs better. Poor designs are often mediated by long, involved instruction books. In Japan, this is an acceptable design philosophy because of the common reliance on instructions in other areas. If one can follow complex instructions, as for the Japanese tea ceremony as one example, then one is a member of an exclusive club. The more complex the design—and the more complex the instructions—the better the design is, because it increases the exclusivity of the club of users.

This is counter to a customer-based design philosophy. This alternative approach is to place the knowledge of how to use the product in the world or, rather, in the product design itself. One should just be able to look at a pen-and-pencil set and know how to use it because the design contains an "affordance" for its use.[4] Like the Apple Macintosh, a design should be error-proof due to "constraints" in

---

[4]Don Norman, *The Psychology of Everyday Things*) (now called *The Design of Everyday Things* (New York: Basic Books, 1988).

how people can use it.[5] Designing for the customer means less reliance on instructions and more reliance on these kinds of design principles.

Observing the reliance on instructions in daily Japanese life, we could better interpret the design principles followed for the Japanese products with which we were familiar. The customer is expected to follow the instructions without deviation. The result is that all over America we have flashing 12:00s on our VCRs because Americans don't like to read instructions and it is not obvious how to set the time on these machines. To be more responsive to customer needs in a foreign market, the Japanese should change their product design strategy from a reliance on instruction books to a reliance on good design principles.

DEMING'S LEGACY   The impact of W. Edwards Deming on the quality of Japanese products has been recounted many times on both sides of the ocean. Americans have credited him with helping to improve the quality of Japanese products through his teachings on statistical quality control. His lectures on the Deming management method have been attended by thousands of people. In Japan, the Deming Prize for Quality preserves his legacy.

If one follows Deming's management points and his writings closely, though, one is left with another Deming legacy: a distrust of information about the customer which could be used in product design. Because an important component of quality products is to design products for the customer (see Chapter 4), this has serious implications for the design of quality Japanese products.

The Fifth Deadly Disease from Deming's management method states that problems occur if one runs a company on visible figures alone. There are many visible figures in a company. In terms of product quality, the visible figures to which Deming refers are product sales. But according to Deming, the visible sales figures do not give the necessary clues about the quality of a product. Deming claims that customer satisfaction is not so easy to measure.

Contrary to Deming's statement, customer satisfaction is easy to measure in several ways. The most objective way is through experimentation. Customers can be tested on different product designs and can be asked directly whether or not they like them. Other objective but indirect measures include the number of errors customers make when using the product, or the time taken to perform a task with the product. Statistical analyses should be performed on the test results to separate the meaningful results from the random results.

Customer satisfaction can also be measured in other ways. One method is to run an informal experiment where customers are brought in and asked to use a product. An informal interview follows in which customers can voice satisfactions

[5]Ibid.

or dissatisfactions with the product. Focus groups are often formed to do this. Videotaping customers using the product, as was done at Xerox, can provide valuable information about usability.

Many products are tried in a test market before they are distributed to the general market. Usually, questionnaires are sent to people who have used the product in the test market to determine their satisfaction. These techniques, although used by many product developers, have been used extensively for testing television shows and movies. Go to a mall or walk along a street in southern California and you have a good chance of being offered free tickets to test market a new movie release. The groups performing these tests have become quite sophisticated in determining the statistical relationship between customer responses on surveys and customer satisfaction for the product when it is released later.

Another approach to customer satisfaction is much more abstract and theoretical. This approach involves applying the psychological theories about the way people think and solve problems to the design of a product. Cognitive psychologists are sometimes hired by product design teams because they have the training to provide insights about the kinds of problems people may have when using a product. Xerox has had some of the most insightful cognitive psychologists, as indicated by their ability to apply cognitive theories to product design. This is how the Xerox Star computer system was developed. Apple used many of these ideas in the design of the Apple Macintosh. Apple has recently hired one of the pre-eminent cognitive psychologists, a university professor from San Diego, Don Norman, to assist in new product design. AT&T has laboratories full of outstanding cognitive psychologists, who understand the application of cognitive theories to product design.

Informal data can be gathered from salespeople. Monitoring the number of calls to the service department can provide a good objective measure of customer satisfaction.

A last approach to measuring customer satisfaction is definitely unacceptable, but it is used too often. Engineers can sit in their chairs and determine intuitively what their customers may need and want. Frequently these intuitions are wrong. As indicated earlier, the engineers or designers working on the product may be exactly the wrong people, because of their familiarity with the mechanics of the product, to be providing this intuition. Their knowledge of how to use the product is contained in their heads. They see no need to design this knowledge into the product, as would occur with a customer-based design. The nightmare for customers is that depicted in the car commercial: engineers working on the product, too busy to take a vacation or to talk with customers, and out of touch with customers' needs and wants.

Deming's legacy to Japanese companies, with regard to the customer, may be an overreliance on intuition to determine customer needs. Reading beyond the

Fourteen Points or the Seven Deadly Diseases in Deming's book, *Out of the Crisis*, could be dangerous to the customer. Deming says, "Satisfaction of the customer that buys today's output can unfortunately only be assessed some time in the future—too late" (p. 170). Later, he says, "A consumer can seldom say today what new product or new service would be desirable and useful to him three years from now, or a decade from now. New product and new types of service are generated, not by asking the consumer, but by knowledge, imagination, innovation, risk, trial and error on the part of the producer, backed by enough capital to develop the product or service and to stay in business during the lean months of introduction" (p. 182). These two quotations indicate that assessing customer satisfaction by asking the customer is a waste of time, according to Deming. One should rely on intuition to determine customers' needs.

What about performing experiments on customers before the product is marketed? Experimentation requires that the researcher analyze the data using tests of significance to look for meaningful differences between products or product features. This should not be done, according to Deming: "Incidentally, chi-square and tests of significance, taught in some statistical courses, have no application here or anywhere" (p. 272). And later: "Empirical evidence is never complete" (p. 351). This is a surprising statement to be made by a statistician. When running experiments, we cannot test everybody. Inferential statistics are used in experiments to infer or predict the effects measured in the experiment when projected from the small number of people tested in the experiment to the larger number of people in the population of potential customers. Empirical evidence is not complete, but statistics allow us to make good predictions to partially complete the empirical evidence. When talking about further books to be read on the subject, Deming suggests that students skip the parts of the books dealing with experiments. "The student should also avoid passages in books that treat…tests of significance, as such calculations have no application in analytic problems in science and industry,"says Deming (p. 369). The implication is that experiments on customers are useless.

To his credit, Deming does indicate that products should be designed for the customer. But by criticizing all the tools which could be used to understand the customer, designing for the customer becomes little more than a slogan. Of course, this violates Point 10 of his Fourteen Points: Eliminate slogans, exhortations, and targets for the workforce. In regard to customers, Deming is statistically out of control.

These writings indicate that Deming has largely rejected a reliance on the visible figures, from formal and informal experiments, which can be used to measure customer satisfaction and determine the needs and wants of customers. Japanese companies seem to follow their guru on this. They do not have the personnel to perform experiments on customers, to analyze the results, and to determine statistically the meaning of the results.

In Japan, cognitive theory is studied some in the universities, but design teams are composed almost entirely of engineers with no behavioral background to understand the customers. Cognitive theories are not applied to product design. The customers are not represented by behavioral scientists.

Without experimentation and statistical tests of significance, without the application of behavioral theories to product design, intuition is the preferred mode in Japanese companies designing products for customers. This is not good news for the customers.

OUT OF THE LOOP   Gary Katzenstein, writing in his book, *Funny Business*,[6] about his experiences working for Sony in Japan, was assigned to a project to develop a marketing strategy for a new computer Sony was trying to market in the United States. The computer was called the Hit Bit, which was short for *hito bito*, meaning "the people" in Japanese. Like a Volkswagen, it was supposed to be the computer for the common person. Because most Americans do not understand Japanese, the name Hit Bit could take on other connotations.

Katzenstein and another American Sony employee criticized the marketing strategy for Hit Bit in a meeting with their Japanese bosses. They said that Americans would not like the name of the computer. They complained that the instruction manual was too simplistic and was not arranged in a logical order. A customer would not be able to follow the instructions. They explained that business executives, one of the target markets for the computer, would not take seriously a computer with a cute puppy on it.

They thought this business meeting had been set up to discuss the marketing strategy. However, like many meetings where consensus is required, the formal meeting was a front (*omote*) to celebrate the consensus which was hammered out in the back room (*ura*) among a select group (*uchi*) of Japanese executives. Although the Americans had a better indication of how to market to Americans, they were not part of this select group and their opinions were not wanted. In fact, proper behavior would have had them corroborating the decisions already made. No changes were made to Hit Bit. The computer was not a hit in the United States—not even a bit of a hit.

In the West, we seem to think that consensus building in Japanese companies occurs when everybody involved in a decision sits around a table and hammers out a decision after hearing from everybody in the room. From the people who have experienced consensus decision making in Japan, this is not at all an accurate picture. One former Japanese manager said: "I don't know where this writing on group

---

[6]Gary Katzenstein, *Funny Business* (New York: Prentice Hall, 1989).

decision making comes from. My boss simply told us what to do and we obeyed."[7] A U.S. employee of a Japanese company stated: "There is less consensus here than in a typical American firm."[8] A Japanese company has a very strong vertical orientation, so everyone knows who the boss is. A consensus in these companies is that the boss makes a decision and everybody agrees with him.

Consensus decision making can more accurately be called slow decision making. To study a problem, work teams will be set up and all the information shared with general managers. In one case,[9] a Japanese company targeted a product in short supply outside of Japan which was experiencing a 2% growth rate. To study the feasibility of introducing a competing product, two work teams were set up. Two more work teams were needed to coordinate the activities between the original work teams and between the managers. Several reports were written. Negotiations took place. This process started in 1980 and ended in 1990. This is not a rapid response to shifting market needs; the market for the product is likely to change drastically in that time.

Decision making is very rigid. Once a decision is made, it is carried out even though conditions may have changed. In the 1980s, Japanese insurance companies decided to invest in U.S. bonds. In the meantime, though, the conditions changed when the dollar declined against the yen. Because the decision had been made, the bonds were bought at a $13 billion loss.[10] The authority and power of the decision makers was preserved by following through with the decision. "This rigidity in service to power often looks like a commitment to the long term in contrast to Americans' short-term focus," says Sullivan, a university professor and consultant to Japanese and American companies. "In reality it is simply intransigence."[11]

Francis McInerney and Sean White are businessmen and consultants to Japanese companies. They wrote a book called *Beating Japan*, in which the major thesis is that Japanese companies have lost touch with their customers. Many of their Japanese clients are crippled by layers of bureaucracy, and the customer is lost somewhere at the bottom of the pyramid. "We have seen Japanese companies with as many as ten layers between frontline employees and the CEO," say McInerney and White. "Sometimes these layers are triplicated, once in the U.S. holding company, again in the Japanese line division, and finally in the Japanese regional marketing organization....Confused? Customers, however, are not confused by all this—they have long since moved on to another supplier."[12] At Toyota Corporation, often con-

---

[7]Jeremiah Sullivan, *Invasion of the Salarymen.* (Westport, CT.: Praeger, 1992). pp. 176-177.
[8]Ibid., p. 177.
[9]Ibid., pp. 180-181.
[10]Ibid., p. 179.
[11]Ibid., p. 179
[12]Francis McInerney and Sean White, *Beating Japan* (New York: Dutton, 1993) p. 86.

sidered the epitome of lean production, ideas had to be approved by seven layers of bureaucracy before they could be implemented.[13]

One of the main problems with Japanese companies marketing to Americans is that American employees of Japanese companies, the ones who may be most likely to know the market and the customers, are given very little decision-making authority. "In one case, we made a presentation to a group of U.S. employees of a Japanese company before visiting their head office in Japan," continue McInerney and White. "These seasoned American managers, with years of experience with their customers, pleaded with us to take their case to Tokyo. They believed we had the ear of the top guy in Japan, while their views were not welcome. And indeed, the decision-makers we met in Tokyo were not the least bit interested in the opinions of their U.S. subordinates, whom they considered next to worthless."[14]

Japanese companies have even made policy decisions to remove Americans from any direct contact with the decisions which are made in Tokyo. Nissan operates an American subsidiary in Carson, California, composed mostly of sales and distribution jobs which are held by American employees. A company memo dictated that the American and Japanese staffs had to be separated by nationality. "In brief, our organization will be realigned so that American staff members, with few exceptions, will report to American managers, and Japanese staff members will report to Japanese managers," wrote Kazutoshi Hagiwara, who is the president of Nissan's U.S. sales operations.[15] This decision increased the authority of the Japanese managers by limiting the Americans' access to Tokyo. American staff members must "consult with Japanese staff member before important (non-routine) telephone conversations or discussions" with the parent company, stated the memo. They also must "invite appropriate Japanese staff members to important meetings, discussions and to off-site trips or conferences." The Americans were removed from making decisions about how to market the products to Americans.

A similar policy existed at Nomura Securities in New York. At Nomura, all confidential personnel records were kept by a Japanese woman and were locked away out of reach of the American personnel manager.[16] The American employees were seen as temporary workers who had no need to learn important company secrets and information. They could not be trusted to use this information wisely.

Almost all decisions are made in Tokyo. The decision makers do not listen to their American employees, who have closer touch with the customers. Sometimes

[13]Ibid., p. 164.

[14]Ibid., p. 68.

[15]James Risen, "Some Japanese Firms Moving to Segregate Staffs," *Los Angeles Times,* May 23, 1990, p. D1, D5.

[16]John E. Fitzgibbon, *Deceitful Practices. Nomura Securities and the Japanese Invasion of Wall Street* (New York: Birch Lane Books, 1991), pp. 132-133.

they do not listen to their Japanese employees in the United States, who may have contact with customers. David Halberstam, in a book called *The Reckoning*, recounted how Nissan first became established in the United States. It was not the meticulously planned operation to take over a market that is often depicted in the media. Before any Japanese cars were ever imported to the American market, Yutaka Katayama, a Nissan advertising manager, was sent to California to see if Nissan could generate any sales. He observed in California that Americans liked pickup trucks because of their versatility and durability. Katayama's communications with Japan repeatedly tried to get corporate headquarters to improve their truck designs to better fit California customers. Katayama said that the customers wanted decent upholstery, better springs, and maybe air conditioning. Because he was in California, he was more familiar with the driving habits of Americans than the Tokyo decision makers. Those in Tokyo thought they knew best. "A truck was a truck, and Americans had no right to use them to drive to work, particularly to offices," related Halberstam in reference to the directions from Tokyo to Katayama. "It was wrong of them [the California consumers]. The trucks should be used for carting heavy goods around….Families had no business riding around in pickup trucks. Japanese families that could afford cars would never be seen in a truck."[17]

RUM RAISIN ICE CREAM, JUST-IN-TIME   Grocery stores
in Japan are still mom-and-pop businesses for the most part. They are very small, with limited numbers of items. The aisles are so narrow that two small-sized shopping carts cannot pass one another. A person bending down to look at an item can back up traffic.

   As could be expected, there were very few brand names with which we were familiar. An exception was Haagen Dazs ice cream. The little store in our neighborhood, which served the needs of the large community centered around our train stop, sold a pint of Haagen Dazs ice cream for around $7.50. This same item would sell for $2.50 to $3.00 at our grocery store in Lafayette. In our first few weeks in Japan, we had quickly bought and eaten all the vanilla and vanilla/chocolate swirl ice cream the little store had to offer. The only kind they had left was rum raisin. We were not so fond of rum raisin that we would spend $7.50 for a pint of it. We figured that a new shipment of vanilla Haagen Dazs would arrive shortly.

   We waited for the new shipment. Because the refrigerator and closet space in our apartment was so small, we usually had to go to the store each day to shop for groceries, but our daily trips produced no new Haagen Daz ice cream. We waited longer. The rum raisin stayed on the shelf. We waited longer. Maybe rum raisin was not so bad after all.

---

[17]David Halberstam, *The Reckoning* (New York: Avon, 1986), p. 434.

We tried other Japanese brands of ice cream, but they did not have the taste or the creaminess of Haagen Dazs, and their prices were high also. One time, I thought I had found a pricing scoop, a real bargain. In the ice cream section had been stocked a large quart-sized package of ice cream, and it was only $6.00. I snatched it up, but was disappointed upon opening the package to find that it contained mostly plastic. In six little cups in the plastic were six little individual scoops of ice cream. The packaging was ten times the size of the ice cream.

At each successive trip to the grocery store, the rum raisin remained on the shelf, with no sign of other flavors. This continued for two-and-a-half months. The rum raisin did not leave the shelf, and the other flavors were not restocked. The grocery store did not check to see what was selling and what was not. Perhaps the two pints of vanilla we purchased the first two weeks were supposed to last for three months, like the rum raisin. The store did not respond to customer demand. The final week of our stay, two more pints of vanilla Haagen Dazs appeared on the store shelves. We made short work of them.

Most groceries in Japan are sold through the small mom-and-pop stores. They appeared to be good at stocking the common items, such as rice, but were not so good at identifying other customer trends. You bought what you could get your hands on.

In the United States, retailing stores are taking more and more responsibility for following consumer trends and making sure that desired items are stocked. Wal-Mart is the best example. Whenever a customer buys something in Wal-Mart, the information is sent electronically to the manufacturer. This information is processed to determine manufacturing quantities and to schedule delivery of the product to stores. This system eliminates the need for costly warehousing and redundant transportation—20 to 30% of the price of an item is due to transportation and warehousing—because the items can go directly to the stores.[18] Items manufactured in the same vicinity as the retail outlet have a cost advantage over items manufactured elsewhere because of the reduction in transportation and warehousing costs and the ability to link the customers with manufacturing.

This is a logical extension of the just-in-time manufacturing system discussed in Chapter 6. Whereas just-in-time has been used to eliminate warehouses for the suppliers-to-manufacturers link, a logical extension is to deliver manufactured items to the customer, through retail outlets, just in time. Unlike supplier-manufacturer just-in-time, where the costs of transportation and warehousing are transferred to the supplier, manufacturer-customer just-in-time does not transfer costs, and savings can occur down the line. More American retail outlets may start to follow the Wal-Mart example.

---

[18]Peter F. Drucker, "The Economy's Power Shift," *The Wall Street Journal*, September 24, 1992, p. A16.

THE CUSTOMER PAYS   What is the origin of the myth that Japanese companies listen to and are responsive to customers? Deming helps to perpetuate the myth. In *Out of the Crisis*, Deming states: "The consumer is the most important part of the production line."[19] Later he says: "Necessity to study the needs of the consumer, and to provide service to product, was one of the main doctrines of quality taught to Japanese management in 1950 and onward."[20] They were taught this, but did they listen? People who are unfamiliar with Japanese companies assume that if Deming makes this kind of point, Japanese companies must be practicing it. This is a myth.

There are some stories from Japanese companies which support the myth. In Japan, people are rotated from job to job and the job rotation provides contact with customers. Since the Japanese auto manufacturers also own most of the distributorships for their cars, many car executives have been rotated through dealerships and have had a chance to interact with customers firsthand. A good percentage of car sales in Japan take place via door-to-door sales. Executives have also performed these job duties. Because Japanese companies do not own dealerships in the United States, this contact does not occur with their American customers.

The Japanese car companies have been able to benefit from some customer trends. They gained their initial toehold in the United States during the first oil crisis, when their small cars with high gas mileage were exactly what American consumers wanted. After that, however, they missed most of the trends. Americans wanted minivans. Chrysler was poised to fulfill that need and now dominates the market. Americans wanted sport utility vehicles. Ford, Chevy, and Jeep dominate that market. Americans wanted pickup trucks. Chevy and Ford dominate that market, and now Dodge has a hot new entrant in the market. Presently, 40% of the American market is for light trucks, minivans, and sport utility vehicles, and none of the Japanese car companies has much of a presence in this important market. In fact, the overall number of vehicles imported from Japan for this important market segment has decreased since 1990.

There are some indications that Japanese car companies are moving away from their most important success of making high-gas-mileage cars. They are building larger and more expensive cars. For sport utility vehicles manufactured by their companies, the gas mileage is very poor. As an example, the Nissan Pathfinder sport utility vehicle has a smaller engine (3.0 liters) than the Ford Explorer (4.0 liters), but it gets worse gas mileage.

Japanese companies are not responsive to American customers. They have very little background or experience in responding to customer needs in a competitive,

---

[19]W. Edwards Deming, *Out of the Crisis* (Cambridge, MA: MIT Press, 1982), p. 5.
[20]Ibid.

heterogeneous society like the United States. They are more familiar with the herd mentality of Japanese consumerism. They have few professionals with the expertise to run experiments on customers. Besides, Deming says that experiments are useless. Their companies are weighted down in bureaucracy. Responding to customer needs requires quick decision making. In Japan, some decisions take years to make and, if the conditions have changed in the meantime, the companies are too inflexible to adapt. The decision makers in Japan are unwilling to listen to their American employees, who are in tune with the American customers. Sometimes they do not listen to their own Japanese employees who are familiar with the customers. The intuition from the Tokyo decision makers prevails.

Japanese companies, if they are not careful, will lose the battle for the consumer in the United States. The American computer and communications companies— AT&T, IBM, Xerox, Apple, and Hewlett-Packard—have developed techniques and laboratories for assessing the needs of the customer. Japanese companies to date have not been able to compete seriously on software and computers where customer-friendly design is essential. If changes are not instituted, Japanese companies will face additional problems as other American companies copy these success stories and develop customer-friendly products.

The trend in American business is for flatter organizations. Businesses have gone through large and painful restructuring periods, shedding middle management. One of the purposes of this restructuring has been to get the decision makers closer to the customers.[21] In some cases, customers are only two or three layers away from the decision makers. Contrast this with up to thirty layers of bureaucracy between American customers and Tokyo decision makers.

As long as Japanese companies believe the myth that they know their customers, the quality of their products will suffer. As they believe that their engineers are proxies for American consumers, important customer trends will be missed. American companies are getting closer to the customers through elimination of middle management and the advent of virtual corporations. Too many employees of Japanese companies in the United States are waiting by the fax machine late at night for the intuitive decision from Tokyo about what the American consumer wants.

---

[21]W.H. Davidow and M.S. Malone, *The Virtual Corporation* (New York: Haper Business, 1992).

Myth 5:
Japanese Companies Practice
Quality Management Methods

"We are making progress on internationalization," said the director of the research labs. My wife and I had been invited to dinner at a traditional Japanese restaurant with two other Japanese families from the research labs along with the director and his wife. We were talking between the courses of steamed gingko nuts and pomegranate sherbet.

If I had been only a temporary visitor for the day on an official tour of the facilities, I probably would not have questioned the statement on the progress on internationalization. But I was not one of the professors just passing through for the day and given a quick tour of the facilities along with a brief lecture about "progress" that I was supposed to echo to my students at my university. I was also not a management professor schooled in the proper images of Japanese business methods. I was there to form my own images. I worked with Japanese colleagues daily, and I was forming my own understanding of how things functioned. If my image was different from what I was told by upper management, I was curious to find out more about the discrepancy. I had been there for two months and I was genuinely curious about where they were hiding these foreign-born workers. "How many foreigners do you have?" I asked cheerfully.

"We have you on the third floor, a Chinese woman researcher on the second floor, and another American researcher on the fourth floor," stated the director. "We have achieved a good deal of internationalization." I was, of course, only a temporary person as a visiting professor. The other two were part of the approximately 4000 employees working in the building.

Internationalization is a current thrust of Japanese businesses under the realization of the emerging global economy and the self-awareness that a homogeneous society such as Japan's, which has shunned contact with the outside world and has never achieved awareness of other cultures, may have to make some changes in response to the new realities. Internationalization was the new reality, and the images had to be reworked to fit the reality.

I probably should have kept quiet, but I have a low tolerance for statements which support an image but not the reality. "Only three people in this huge building as a sign of internationalization?" I said. "When I walk down my hallway at Purdue, I see all kinds of foreign-born people. On my side of the hall, we have one person who was born in Israel and another who was born in England. On the other side of the hall, we have a person born in Greece and another person born in Taiwan. Of nine people, four were born in a foreign country. Among the nine people in my short hallway we have more internationalization than you have in the whole building."

In Japan, as we have emphasized throughout this book, the image is different from the reality. The director was portraying an image of internationalization; I tried to bring him back to the reality but this conversation also indicated that Japanese companies are beginning to realize their own problems as they face global competition in the twenty-first century. They are starting to realize that a homogeneous management style, the clans of Theory Z, may be inadequate for the new realities. However, adapting to face these realities will require more than mere words claiming that internationalization is occurring.

SEARCHING FOR REALITY   The images of Japan are chosen carefully. Just like the cows that were massaged and fed beer only when the reporters visited, the factories and offices visited by outsiders are always chosen carefully and the visits are choreographed to present good impressions. In articles on Japan, I have read of the "lights-out" factory, in which manufacturing occurs by itself, with no human employees. This factory may be the only one of its kind in Japan, but it manufactures a good image of high-tech Japan.

In Japan, each visitor has a host assigned, who carefully controls the images. Ostensibly, the host helps with the language and how to move about in Japan, both of which can be major problems. The host also carefully controls the sights that are seen and interprets the events in acceptable ways.

One of my American acquaintances, who spoke fluent Japanese, wanted to be a host and interpreter on Japanese tourist buses for groups of Japanese tourists visiting the United States. Most Japanese tourists travel in groups, staying at Japanese-owned hotels, riding on Japanese-owned buses, and listening to Japanese hosts and hostesses explain and interpret the American sights. My acquaintance went on some of the tourist buses and was appalled at the information which was being passed to the Japanese tourists. Instead of helping the visitors to understand American culture better, the hosts and hostesses delivered propaganda. The Japanese tourists were told that the United States was too violent for them and they should be careful not to wander away from the tour group. The tours offered attractions complete with vivid descriptions of America's problems, and avoided any areas which would show how typical middle-class Americans lived.

When I was in Japan, I wanted to visit some other research laboratories to see how they operated. Even though my Japanese host was making the contacts at these other places, I was allowed in only one other lab, a small electronic security research laboratory. Sony would not let me visit. Hitachi would not let me visit. They both claimed that their labs contained proprietary information which could not be viewed by outsiders. I wondered if the truth was different. Were these labs so poorly equipped, with outdated equipment, that they would be an embarrassment to the company? I had no way to tell. Our images of Japanese companies are carefully controlled. Americans are allowed only into select sites. The images coming back from Japan are often provided by foreigners who have visited Japan for a few weeks under the strict guidance of Japanese hosts who were provided ostensibly to make their visit easier. Another purpose might be to control the images presented. Reports from these people depict a Japan of Utopian business enterprises which produce quality products efficiently in a corporate atmosphere of trust, loyalty, and family devotion to the company. Are these companies Utopian oases or Orwellian swamps? Do Japanese businesses actually practice the management and manufacturing techniques outsiders often consider the basis for their quality products?

DEMING AND THE SEVEN DWARFS   I had to go to Orlando, Florida, on a business trip last January, and I decided to visit EPCOT Center at Disney World. Having grown up partly in southern California, back when 'E' tickets were prized and saved from one Disneyland trip to another, I had never felt the need previously to visit the park in Florida. Since Anaheim does not have an EPCOT Center, however, this visit to Florida was a good opportunity to see this other Disney attraction. At EPCOT, I was once again struck by the smooth operations of Disney attractions. Nothing is left to chance. Crowd control is as efficient as it can be. The park is spotlessly clean. Everything is miniaturized. At EPCOT, I could walk around the world in an hour by circling the artificial lake. I could see the world without having to worry about the hassles or uncertainties of visiting foreign countries.

At Disney attractions, you expect everything to be controlled in a hassle-free environment. As I was sitting on a bench enjoying the sunshine, my vision of this paradise was interrupted by several birds testing me to see if I was an easy mark for free food. At this moment, I actually caught myself wondering why the Disney management allowed these birds to hassle me for food while I was trying to sit and enjoy myself.

I recalled a conversation that I had in Japan with my host. He told me that Japan has very little more to learn about management from the United States. "There is one exception, though," he said. "We have been impressed with Disneyland. Do you know that when Disneyland opened in Tokyo they had a book this large which explained everybody's job completely?" He gestured with his hand about 12 inches above the table, indicating the size of the book. "The book also explained policies and procedures for the park. Everything ran smoothly when it opened, with no problems and no uncertainty in job assignments. We would like to achieve that in other kinds of businesses."

I had never thought of Disneyland as a model for other kinds of enterprises and thought that my friend was just trying to be courteous to me by finding something nice to say about American management.

I later found out that others also claimed that Disneyland was becoming a model for Japanese businesses. Peter F. Drucker, a management consultant, related a similar conversation he had with a leading industrialist in Japan. "We all knew that it would take Disney three years to work the bugs out of this huge undertaking," the industrialist said. "Instead it ran with zero defects the day it opened. Every single operation had been engineered all the way through and simulated on the computer and trained for, and it suddenly dawned on us that we could do this too. You know, the Americans are now all rushing to install TQM [total quality management, based on Deming's approach]; that'll take ten years before it really works....By that time we'll have zero-defects management and will again be fifteen years ahead of you."[1] A top manufacturing engineer at Toyota also told Drucker a similar story about how they had abandoned TQM for zero-defects management.

What does it mean to run a business similar to Disneyland using zero-defects management? It means that every job has been completely engineered so that every worker knows what to do. This is a return to Frederick Taylor's scientific

---

[1]Peter F. Drucker, *Managing for the Future.* (New York: Truman Talley Books/Dutton, 1992), pp. 182-183.

management method, which was popular in the United States at the turn of the century, when industrial engineers first investigated the best way to perform a job and then specified how that job should be performed, either through instruction or through manuals. One difference from the earlier approach is that the zero-defects approach pursued by Japanese companies relies more on the individual worker, instead of management via industrial engineers, to find the most efficient way to perform a job.

When a Japanese manufacturing plant is started in a foreign country, it is often a replica of an existing Japanese plant, just as Tokyo Disneyland was a replica of the original Disneyland. For these transplants, the jobs are already defined. There is little uncertainty about how it should operate. The Disneyland analogy is very important in this situation. One must remember that Euro-Disney in France was a copy of the three previous Disney attractions. However, smooth operations were not enough to ensure success in that case.

In Japan, Deming has been replaced by Disneyland. Mickey, Goofy, and the Seven Dwarfs are replacing Deming and his beads as the transplanted image of quality from the United States. Disneyland has many useful features which could be applied to improve the efficiency and quality of the production process. Disneyland, with its total emphasis on the comfort of the customer, is a useful model for American companies. We should look in our own backyard to learn from the successes of Disneyland, and the mistakes of Euro-Disney.

PRACTICING THE DEMING MANAGEMENT METHOD IN JAPANESE COMPANIES   Deming never claims outright in his

book, *Out of the Crisis*, that his management method is used by the Japanese companies with which he interacted. Many journalists discussing Deming and Japanese management make the faulty assumption that the Japanese use his methods, but Deming himself relates that some of the worst problems he noticed in management came from Japan.[2] Of course, Deming did not have much nice to say about the American management of companies. In an interview with *The Wall Street Journal*, in which Deming was asked if any large American companies were managed well, Deming says, "Not that I know of."[3]

Upon close inspection, many of his points are not practiced to a great extent in Japan, and if they are, they are used arbitrarily in ways different from the original intent. Deming often criticized management by objective (MBO), rating systems, and pay raises based on merit and review. Instead, Deming advocated that those who had the ability would rise to the top without official reviews. In Deming's view,

---

[2]W. Edwards Deming, *Out of the Crisis* (Cambridge, MA: MIT Press, 1982), p. 491.
[3]"Workplace (A Special Report): Managing Change," *The Wall Street Journal*, June 4, 1990, p. R39.

merit reviews force companies to quantify job performance when it cannot be quantified. Instead, Deming advocates that raises and promotions should be based on the good instincts and intentions of management for equitable treatment of employees. From the viewpoint of employees, however, performance reviews force management to be accountable, because their decisions on pay and promotions cannot be based on arbitrary criteria. If decisions have to be justified, power is removed from the hands of capricious but authoritarian managers.

An example illustrates how performance reviews at Japanese companies can be inequitable or based on capricious criteria when accountability is removed from the process. In a performance review, Fred Coleman, who was in charge of a mutual fund at Japanese-owned Nomura Securities in New York, would have fared very well. The fund he managed performed five and six times better than the Dow Jones average in two successive years. In one quarter, the fund was singled out by a stock analysis service as the number-one performing fund.[4] Instead of being promoted, however, he was fired by Nomura for unsatisfactory performance. His firing seemed to be based on his perceived failure to follow orders. Coleman claims that the orders he refused to follow would have benefited only the company and would have hurt the customer; the company claimed the orders followed company practices.

Coleman's successor as the manager of the fund, Nobuo Katayama, had been trained to follow orders. The same service which had previously ranked the fund number one now ranked the fund number 475 out of the 479 funds it monitored. Under Katayama's guidance, the fund's market value eventually shrank from $31 million to $8 million, and Nomura had to discontinue the fund. Yet management was happy with Katayama's performance. He was promoted to the Tokyo office, where he was put in charge of a $94 million fund.[5] Such capricious and arbitrary performance ratings could occur only under the Deming management method, or some similar system, where pay hikes and promotions do not have to be justified.

Two of the Japanese companies we often associate with the success of the Japanese management style, Sony and Honda, follow the American style of merit raises and promotions more than other Japanese companies do. At Sony and Honda, 50% of promotions and pay hikes are based on merit.[6] At other Japanese companies, merit is considered in promotions and pay hikes only 30% of the time, which is still more often than we are led to believe by reading Deming's writings.

Deming states that MBO can hurt a company, thus implying that the best companies in Japan do not use MBO, other people visiting Japan come back with differ-

---

[4]John E. Fitzgibbon, *Deceitful Practices. Nomura Securities and the Japanese Invasion of Wall Street* (New York: Birch Lane Books, 1991), p. 145.

[5]Ibid., pp. 145–146.

[6]Jan Woronoff, *The Japanese Management Mystique* (Chicago: Probus, 1992), p. 168.

ent views of the use of MBO. "Typically [the best Japanese] companies are replete with the paraphernalia of modern information and accounting systems, formal planning, management by objectives, and all of the other formal, explicit mechanisms of control characterizing [American companies],"[7] states William Ouchi based on his experiences with Japanese companies. Ouchi, a management professor and an adherent of MBO, saw Japanese companies conforming to his preconceptions of management by objective. Deming, decrying the evils of MBO and management theory in general, looked at the same Japanese companies and saw his preconceived opinions—they did not use management by objective. Deming and Ouchi saw what they wanted to see, with very different results. The images fit their perceived reality.

Deming also states that American companies are too concerned with profits and not concerned enough with other important issues such as quality, number of jobs saved, or market share. The implication is that Japanese companies do not place such a large emphasis on profit. This view is not supported by the data. Even back in 1987, the U.S.-Japan Comparative Survey of Corporate Behavior showed that Japanese companies rated profit almost as high as American companies did.[8]

Another important part of Deming's management philosophy is its emphasis on constant improvement or, to use the Japanese term, *kaizen*. This had been welcomed by many workers as a departure from Taylor's scientific management, where the worker is supposed to perform a task in a prespecified fashion and with no deviation from the job description. With *kaizen*, the worker is supposed to be allowed to improve the job whenever necessary. Some people, including Drucker, look at Japanese companies and say that they are practicing the Taylor system of management better than other companies. Others, including Deming, look at the same companies and say that Japanese companies have rejected Taylorism because it is demeaning to the worker.

Several pieces of evidence refute Deming's claim that Taylorism has been rejected by Japanese companies. At Mazda's Flat Rock plant, which probably reflects plant operations in Japan, each task is described in written detail, down to the number of seconds required to perform the task. Specific steps include how a worker should pick up a wrench in his right hand and how many seconds this should take.[9] This is Taylor's scientific management taken to an extreme. Suggestions for constant improvement were solicited by management, but they were not implemented if they ran counter to the rigid work specifications set by management. The unit leader of

---

[7]William Ouchi, *Theory Z* (New York: Avon, 1981), p. 61.
[8]Woronoff, *The Japanese Management Mystique*, p. 170.
[9]Joseph J. Fucini and Suzy Fucini, *Working for the Japanese. Inside Mazda's American Auto Plant* (New York: The Free Press, 1990), p. 151.

the material-handling section at Mazda was asked to name one *kaizen* change which had been implemented in the two years she had been working there. The only one she came up with was changing from string to wire for attaching cards to the carts used to deliver material to the assembly line.[10]

The Mazda plant is not an isolated situation. "They had a suggestion box, but if there was some kind of employee involvement program, they didn't tell us about it," said Barbara Hamilton of her job at Sanyo. "The only time you would sit down with your foreman, you were with your [union] steward and you were in some kind of trouble."[11]

CONSTANTLY DETERIORATING DESIGNS
Constant improvement applies not only to the manufacturing line (the process), but also to product design. Under constant improvement, product designs should be getting better. The opposite seems to be occurring with some of the high-profile Japanese products.

One of the few industries in which Japanese and American companies compete directly is automobiles and light trucks. Half of the total amount of the U.S. trade deficit with Japan is due to automobiles, so Japan has been quite successful in this area. Is this success due to constantly improving designs?

According to experts, Japanese cars have become worse in the last few years, mechanically and design-wise. In a 1993 survey of master mechanics, the mechanics said that the quality of imported cars over the last five years had stayed constant or deteriorated.[12] Design engineers have the expertise to evaluate the engineering designs of different cars. In a survey conducted by *Design News*, a professional magazine for design engineers,[13] American car makers were the only ones to boost their scores on the perceived quality of cars every year for the fifteen years of the survey. Japanese car makes have not shown constant improvement as American cars have.

More objective measures also point to this constant deterioration in the design of Japanese cars. As explained in Chapter 7, Florida's attorney general's office tracked the chronic problems reported for the state's car "lemon law" for each car make in two periods (1989-1991[14] and 1992-1994[15]) separated by three years. The

---

[10]Ibid., p. 152.
[11]James Risen, "Japanese Plants in the U.S.—Is the Honeymoon Over?," *Los Angeles Times,* July 12, 1988, pp. 1, 3, 19.
[12]Cox News Service, "Mechanics Say U.S. Car Quality Rises," *Chicago Tribune,* May 12, 1993, p. 3-4.
[13]Robert N. Boggs, "1994 Design News Auto Survey," *Design News,* October 10, 1994, pp. 104-108.
[14]Robert A. Butterworth, *New Motor Vehicle Make, Model and Manufacturer Study,* 1989-1991 (Tallahassee: State of Florida Office of the Attorney General Lemon Law Arbitration Program, n.d.).
[15]Robert A. Butterworth, *New Motor Vehicle Make, Model and Manufacturer Study,* 1992-1994 (Tallahassee: State of Florida Office of the Attorney General Lemon Law Arbitration Program, n.d.).

Chronic Defect Index, constructed by the state, is a prediction of the number of com-plaints and the severity of the complaints. On this measure, American makes showed improvement by having 19% fewer chronic defects for the newer cars when compared to the older cars. Japanese makes, on the other hand, deteriorated, 18% more chronic defects in the new cars when compared to the cars three years earlier.

Another high-profile product from Japan is VCRs. VCRs are the products most often associated with usability problems. The inability of people to set the clock has become a joke. Any constant improvements in the design of VCRs should be in increasing the usability of these products.

I analyzed the usability of new VCRs from Japan using quantitative modeling techniques and compared the new designs to a ten-year-old VCR made in Japan. All usability measures showed that the new machines had worsened in usability from the machine of ten years ago. As an example, setting a clock is now more than five times as difficult to learn as in the old model. The time needed to set the clock now takes twice as long as it did with the old design. For those who still choose to pro-gram the VCR to record a TV program, this is now three times as difficult to learn as in the old design. Programming the VCR now takes twice as long as it did with the old machine.

As an example of the difficulty and poor usability, setting a clock with a new VCR requires 257 cognitive steps. With the old design the task was still difficult, although not as difficult as with the new design, requiring 111 cognitive steps. That people cannot set the clock on a VCR is not surprising considering these difficult-to-use designs.

The only feature of VCR design which has improved is programming to record a TV program using VCR+. VCR+ is a feature in which the user has only to enter a multiple-digit code, found in television program guides, and the VCR sets the start and stop times and the channel number. When compared to the ten-year-old design, using VCR+ reduced the execution time by 25% and the number of cognitive steps by 41%. One has to remember, however, that VCR+ was developed by an American company, and Japanese manufacturers must license this technology from the Ameri-can company when it is incorporated in the design.

These two high-profile product lines from Japan, cars and VCRs, are actually becoming worse when the most important design aspects are measured. New Japa-nese cars, according to the Chronic Defect Index, have more serious defects than older models. New VCRs are less easy to use than old models. This should not hap-pen if Japanese companies practice constant improvement in their designs.

HOW LOW YOU BOW   Japanese management is known for a team-oriented approach to manufacturing, where even a high-level manager will be seen down on the plant floor interacting with the workers. However, the way in which workers interact with these managers is very status-oriented. Social interactions in Japan are dictated by the position of the people within the hierarchy. How low you bow to people depends on their importance. The language in which you address somebody is dependent on the person's status. Family lineages are studied carefully before marriages are approved. Even businesses consult lineages before hiring someone.

In evaluating Deming's Point 9 (Break down barriers between staff areas), the Japanese adhere to it in one sense and violate it in another. To expect such a hierarchically organized society to break down staff barriers completely is unrealistic.

Japanese companies often convey an image that managers do not get any more perquisites or are treated any differently than line workers. This image is often associated with the factory having one cafeteria where all workers eat together. Gary Katzenstein found out the hard way at Sony that he was expected to eat with his team and no one else. When he attempted to break down staff barriers, he was severely reprimanded by the team members.

Japanese managers require that they be treated with respect. One of the practices which does not contribute to perceived equality of all employees is the requirement that workers must bow and applaud when executives visit the shop floor. Sanyo tried to institute this perquisite for visiting Japanese executives at its American plant. When the workers refused to follow orders by bowing and applauding the executives, the dispute with management evolved into a violent strike in which the police were forced to intervene.[16] "They weren't paying us enough to do it," said Bernice Gardner, one of the workers at the plant who refused to bow and applaud.

DON'T STOP THAT LINE   Quality control at Japanese plants suffers when workers are trying to meet production schedules. A myth often perpetuated is that any worker can pull a cord to stop the assembly line when a defect is noticed. At Mazda's Flat Rock plant, workers who pulled the cord to stop the assembly line because of a defect found themselves in trouble with the team or unit leaders. "Every time some poor bastard pulls the [cord] now, you get a [written report] on it," said Phil Keeling, one of the workers. "He's just asking for trouble."[17] Even though at least 30% of the Mazda cars coming off the assembly line had quality defects, management was not willing to stop production to find the cause of the defects.

---

[16]Risen, "Japanese Plants in the U.S."
[17]Fucini and Fucini, *Working for the Japanese*, p. 152.

Deming's quality management can also be applied to service jobs. In the case of service jobs, employees are trying to manufacture quality service, good customer relations, and quality information on markets and customers. In an analogous way, service companies have suppliers. At the American office of Japan's Nomura Securities Company on Wall Street, employees were dependent on employment agencies to supply them with quality clerical workers. Nomura managed to negotiate fees for the employment services down from the standard 10% to a low 5% to save money. The owner of one employment agency reacted to the lowering of fees by sending his worst candidates. He told the American manager responsible for hiring the workers, "Who do you think I am going to send over to Nomura? If I can place somebody at the higher fee, I am going to do it. All [Nomura] sees from me are people who get turned down all over town."[18] The quality of the people was reduced and the turnover rate skyrocketed. In Deming's terms, the only important supplier to Nomura was the employment agencies. Since price was the overriding factor in decisions about the supplier, quality was reduced and worker turnover was high.

THE DEMING BATTLE PLAN   The ammunition in the trade war between Japan and the United States has been manufactured directly from Deming's Fourteen Points and the Seven Deadly Diseases. Several of the points and diseases are used directly as justification for Japanese practices that many Western businesses and governments consider exclusionary and unfair. One can be sure that Deming did not intend these to become fodder in the trade war, but Deming's points, in the guise of management principles, have become a convenient way to justify these practices. If for no other reason, we must know about the Deming management methods to understand how the trade war is being played out.

Under Point 1 ("Create constancy of purpose"), Deming states that the most important practice of business should be to stay in business and create jobs, not necessarily to make money. Creating jobs means that market share should be increased no matter what the cost. This point can be used to justify two practices which are hurtful to products in other countries: product dumping and predatory business practices.

Other countries are put at a competitive disadvantage when a Japanese company tries to achieve high market share. If the market in this country is truly competitive, then the pricing battleground is moved to this other country. At home, American companies cannot charge high prices for their own products, because they often have had to compete with lower-priced Japanese products. The Japanese can support these lower prices because pricing competition does not occur in their own

---

[18]Fitzgibbon, *Deceitful Practices,* p. 130.

country and company profits can be maintained. This is one of the first battles that Americans have had to fight in their own country, and it is ultimately a losing battle unless the fight is carried to the other shore.

Under Point 2 ("Adopt the new philosophy"), Deming states that American consumers are too tolerant of poor-quality products and will often purchase a product solely on price and with little regard to quality. The implication is that Japanese consumers are more quality conscious, and are willing to pay a high price for a product based on its quality. Even if American or other foreign products were available, Japanese consumers would not purchase them because of their alleged low quality. This myth is examined in more detail in Chapter 9.

Perhaps this point is used to justify the high prices Japanese consumers must pay for their products, as shown in Chapter 10. Japan maintains a built-in competitive advantage over other countries, Western and Asian. When we examined the products in Japanese stores, it was very difficult to find any foreign-made products. There were few American products, few South Korean products, and few Chinese products. Sometimes you could find brand-name items, such as French perfume, as long as the brand name was currently in favor with Japanese consumers. Overall, however, the Japanese consumer pays high prices because of the lack of competition.

What is the practical consequence of these inequities in price and the tactic of increasing market share by charging low prices? By increasing market share through price undercutting, more jobs are created. This strategy works if the prices in the home market are protected. Japanese companies make most of their profits at home, not in foreign markets, which allows them to undercut prices elsewhere. By saying that Japanese consumers are picky, they do not condone poor workmanship, and are willing to pay high prices for high-quality products, the home market can be protected. If Japanese products had to be competitive at home in price and quality, then prices could not be undercut in foreign markets. Most Japanese consumers seem to realize that their prices are unnaturally high, but they put up with it. Deming's points, however, are used to justify closing off the home market to "low-quality" foreign products.

As an example, consider the pricing of a television set. Let's say that a TV which sells for $500 in Japan is being sold for $300 in the United States The low price can be supported because much of the profit is made in Japan. For an American company with no access to the Japanese market (because it makes a low-quality, non-Japanese product), a TV priced at $350 will not sell in the American market because of its noncompetitive price. If the American TV were allowed into the Japanese market, even though that market may be smaller than the American market, it would force Japanese TV prices down, and the prices of Japanese TVs would then have to be raised in America to compensate for the lost revenue.

CARTEL PICKENS   Point 4 of Deming's management method considers the relationships between suppliers and manufacturers ("End the practice of awarding contracts on price alone"). In Japan, the establishment of long-term relationships with suppliers is more important than other considerations such as price and quality. As Japanese companies open transplant manufacturing facilities in foreign countries, the suppliers often follow. Manufacturers and their suppliers are organized into tightly knit cartels, or *keiretsu*, under the direction of a central bank. Most business is conducted within the cartel. In business downturns, the large company will often force the smaller *keiretsu* suppliers to cut their costs or to hire excess personnel. When executives at the large company have to retire at 55, smaller members of the cartel are forced to make room for them. Such relationships violate American antitrust laws, because these practices limit competition.

Deming's Point 4 provides a justification for cartels, monopolies, and trusts. These forms of business were rejected in the United States over a century ago because they favored big business at the expense of consumers, shareholders, and workers. They can be quite profitable, however, for businesses that engage in these practices. American businesses are in a catch-22 with regard to Japanese transplants. American suppliers can never become part of the *keiretsu*, so they cannot develop long-term relationships with the manufacturers. Since they cannot develop long-term relationships, they cannot become suppliers. The Japanese transplants bring over their own suppliers.

T. Boone Pickens, the American investor, got an indication of the Japanese style of business when he and his investment group managed to purchase 26% of Koito Manufacturing, a large Japanese auto-supply company. At the time, he did not realize that Koito was part of the *keiretsu* to which Toyota also belonged. Even though Pickens was the largest single stockholder—Toyota was second at 19%—he was denied a seat on Koito's board of directors even though Toyota, with its smaller share, had three seats. The board of directors was reserved for other members of the *keiretsu*; shareholders, even the largest shareholder, had no rights. After a two-and-a-half-year struggle, Pickens finally gave up.

The *keiretsu* eliminates competition and preserves the status quo. Pickens compared the system to corporate communism, with the centralized decision making more common to the old Soviet Politburo.[19] It limits entrepeneurship and, Pickens states, many American businesses would never have been possible within a *keiretsu*: Federal Express, Apple Computer, Compaq Computer, Nike, Digital Equipment, Genentech, Lotus, Microsoft, Office Depot, Sun Microsystems, Intel, and Cyprus Semiconductors.

---

[19]T. Boone Pickens, "The Dark Side of Japan's Cartels," *Chicago Tribune*, February 29, 1992, p. 1-11

Deming's management method can be used by Japanese companies and bureaucrats to justify a *keiretsu* system in which the status quo is preserved and individual entrepeneurship is stifled. It is a system whereby Japanese companies can buy into American businesses but foreigners can be excluded from any control in Japanese businesses. The Japanese can pick and choose among eligible American businesses after the competitive American marketplace has already established the winners and losers.

Many of the Seven Deadly Diseases can also be interpreted as support for big business at the cost of shareholders or consumers. For Deadly Diseases 1 and 2, Deming complains that American businesses emphasize only short-term profits and have no long-term goals. In the United States, shareholders demand that companies perform well; in Japan, shareholders do not have the right to make these demands. In Japan everybody was happy with this system as long as stock prices were increasing and the economy expanding. In recent years, Japanese shareholders have become bolder in filing lawsuits against companies to protect their interests.[20] One Japanese lawyer, who is also a shareholder in Hazame Corp., sued the board of directors, demanding that they reimburse the shareholders for bribes they allegedly paid local government officials in order to win a construction contract. When the stock market went down in Japan, some favored clients were reimbursed illegally for their losses and the other clients, usually the small clients, were not. This is illegal, and these actions resulted in a flurry of lawsuits. Without shareholder involvement, the companies were free to do what they wanted, because they were not accountable to the shareholders.

LAWYERS' DEADLY DISEASE   Deming's last Deadly Disease states that American businesses have too many lawyers, which drive up costs. This can also be viewed in a different light, however. The threat of litigation provides an incentive to American businesses to manufacture products that are safe, to provide safe working environments, and to protect the rights of the shareholders from illegal and costly business practices by executives or the board of directors. While living and traveling in Japan, we were surprised at the large number of products which we considered unsafe and which, because of the possibility of a lawsuit, would not be on the market in the United States. We would have been reluctant to say this before our trip to Japan, but we came to the conclusion that lawyers can actually work to increase the quality of products and protect consumers.

---

[20]Reuters, "Suing the Management Has Become a Bargain in Japan," *Chicago Tribune*, September 12, 1993, p. 7-9.

Many people forget the reasons for having a strong court system, individual rights, and the practice of law. One purpose is to ensure that any disputes are settled equitably through public discussion in a court of law. Without this system, disputes can get out of hand. A U.S. attorney, who recently spent a year in Japan,[21] found that many disputes involving individuals or small businesses—those not protected by Japanese courts—turned the matter over to the *Yakuza*, the Japanese Mafia, to settle. There was no alternative. A poll performed by Japan's National Police Agency found that of the 2106 firms questioned, 41.2% had paid extortion to shareholder groups which had threatened to disrupt annual stockholders' meetings if they were not paid.[22] Without the threat of lawsuits, shareholders are forced to take such actions, and the companies are also left unprotected.

Deming's management method is not practiced so much to improve the quality of products as to justify business practices which would be illegal or at least questionable in the United States. It can be used to justify the elimination of competition and the proliferation of cartels. High consumer prices in Japan and product dumping in other countries are condoned in the name of maintaining market share and jobs. Shareholders' rights are suppressed. Limited litigation results in the continued manufacture of unsafe products. Japanese companies may be successful due to something only approximating the Deming management method—not because it works to produce high-quality products, but because it eliminates competition at the expense of consumers and shareholders.

LIFETIME EMPLOYMENT   Americans were aware of the lifetime employment practices of Japanese companies when the transplant factories began to open in America. Many jumped at the potential job security offered by these Japanese companies. What the Americans did not know was that even in Japan, lifetime employment is the exception rather than the rule. And in America, lifetime employment applied only to the Japanese.

In 1983, Toshiba decided to remove itself from the personal calculator business in the United States. One American manager at its U.S. offices was retained in order to lay off the complete staff of 41 American workers. All the Japanese managers were returned to Japan to be reassigned elsewhere within Toshiba. As soon as the American manager, James Ristow, who was a 14-year veteran of Toshiba, laid off all the Americans, he himself was let go. "Americans feel that they are a vital part of the company, but when push comes to shove, they will not be figured into the equation," he complained.[23]

---

[21]Richard A. Cole, "Tokyo's Spin on the Law," *International Business*, February 1993, pp. 78-79.
[22]"Third of Firms Polled Bow to Pressure from Extortionists," *Japan Times*, November 21, 1990, p. 3.
[23]Fucini and Fucini, *Working for the Japanese*, p. 130.

Mazda ran into difficult times and almost went out of business when the company had trouble with its Wankel engine, to which the company had made a deep commitment. The company was seen as heroic in both Japan and the rest of the world because it did not lay off a single Japanese worker even though it was almost out of business. With more success and later expansion to the United States, though, the heroism did not apply to American workers. As a cost-cutting measure in 1988, Mazda consolidated its Eastern and Western offices, laying off 70 American employees. In 1993, it laid off 375 American employees.[24] The president of Mazda Motor of America, Yoshinori Taura, was questioned about the policy of letting American workers go as a cost-cutting measure while retaining all the Japanese workers during the worst crisis of Mazda's history. "We feel very, very sorry for them, but we'll give them the best [separation] offer we can."[25]

At Mazda's Flat Rock plant, most of the workers hired were in their early 20s or 30s. Due to the stress of the job—each minute consisted of 57 seconds of physical work—many were worried about what would happen to them when their bodies wore out. "Some of the [workers] out here have asked me, 'Bob, you know I'm able to cut it now, but what happens in three or five years down the road if my body won't take this anymore?'" related Bob Ramp who was a United Auto Workers representative at the plant. "It's an interesting question—and I don't have an answer for them."[26] In Japan, older workers are placed into less demanding jobs such as Mazda's training center, its company dormitories and stores, its national network of car dealerships, or one of the supplier companies in its *keiretsu*. Mazda did not have these jobs to offer in the United States. There are no easy jobs at the Flat Rock plant, because jobs such as driving cars to the loading dock and janitorial services are contracted to outside companies at considerably less pay than the Mazda workers received. There would be no place in the Mazda corporate organization for American workers as they aged.

Other Japanese companies have also pursued layoffs, especially in cases where a business is no longer expanding. After Japan's Bridgestone Tire Company purchased and merged with Firestone, Bridgestone laid off 3,000 ex-Firestone workers.[27] At Firestone, many complained that the best people, in terms of initiative and creativity, were laid off and that some workers—those who were willing to ingratiate themselves with the new bosses—were retained even though they were perceived as having mediocre ability.

---

[24]Michael Williams and John Bussey, "Corporate Focus: Mazda Ponders Its Route Through a Happy Future," *The Wall Street Journal*, Sept. 8, 1993, p. 4.
[25]Fucini and Fucini. *Working for the Japanese*, p. 130.
[26]Ibid., p. 189.
[27]Woronoff, *The Japanese Management Mystique*, p. 174.

Quasar, owned by Japan's giant Matsushita electronics company, had an office in Franklin Park, Illinois. When Quasar started losing business in the United States in 1987, it went from 450 people to 150 people because it lost $20 million in 1985 and did not have the business to sustain higher employment. In 1990, however, Matsushita found enough money to pay $6.13 billion in acquiring MCA Corporation, which included Universal Studios among other treasures. In Quasar's Franklin Park office, 80 of the managers were American and 9 were Japanese. After the job cuts, 14 of the managers were American and 9 were Japanese. Some of the Americans took Matsushita to court, claiming that they were discriminated against when they were fired and their Japanese counterparts were not. Matsushita claimed that the Americans were fired because they could not speak Japanese and were thus incapable of communicating with the home office. The judge ruled that this was not a good excuse. "In the past, many managerial employees of American national origin who did not speak Japanese performed the marketing, financial and managerial duties which Quasar suddenly contended could only be performed by employees of Japanese national origin,"[28] said the judge. The judge told Quasar to pay $2.5 million in penalties, which was less than the $4 million settlement awarded by a jury.

Matsushita appealed the decision of the judge, although not on the basis of discrimination against the Americans—they had pretty much conceded that issue. The appeal dealt with whether or not treaties between the two countries allowed them to discriminate based on citizenship and not national origin. The Circuit Court of Appeals ruled that commercial treaties signed between the two nations allow corporations to put their own citizens in key positions at subsidiary businesses.[29] The judges ruled that the Japanese and American managers were treated differently in the layoffs but that this was acceptable because the bias was based on citizenship and not national origin or race. Maybe this is a distinction which can be understood only by the lawyers. The ruling was overturned and Matsushita paid nothing. To make the Americans feel better, a spokesman said that Matsushita had opened ten manufacturing plants in the United States since the lawsuit and had hired 2000 American workers. This ruling does not bode well for the future for American civil rights as employed by Japanese companies in the United States.

In Japan, the founder of the Matsushita consumer electronics empire has become something of a godlike character. "The man who founded National Panasonic [the popular name of Matsushita in Japan], Konoskuke Matsushita, is known as the god of management in Japan," says Shintaro Ishihara.[30]

---

[28]Merrill Goozner, "Matsushita Guilty of Discriminating Against Americans," *Chicago Tribune*, December 12, 1990, pp. 3-1, 3-5.
[29]William Grady, "Bias Ruling Overturned in Quasar Firings," *Chicago Tribune*, December 5, 1991, pp. 3-1, 3-4.
[30]Playboy Interview: "Shintaro Ishihara," *Playboy*, October 1990, pp. 65–66.

"The reasons for his and for National's success is his allegiance to his people. During a recession, Mr. Matsushita simply would not lay people off. It brings great loyalty to a company when the employees are treated with loyalty and respect. He would not last as a manager of a company in the United States very long." Ishihara apparently missed the news of the Americans laid off by Mr. Matsushita. He is correct in his assessment of Mr. Matsushita's potential as an American CEO. As an American manager, Mr. Matsushita would have been open to lawsuits if hiring and firing decisions were based on national origin.

PIMPING FOR NOMURA   Sometimes top businesspeople in the United States will accept lower salaries at Japanese companies with the implicit or explicit promise of job security. Nomura Securities Company is the largest securities and investment company in Japan. With its success in Japan, it decided to open up branches on Wall Street in the 1970s. Forced into a competitive situation and business opportunities in which it had no experience, the company hired many talented and experienced Americans at lower salaries than they could expect to make at other Wall Street firms but with the implicit or explicit promise of job security. Many were willing to make that trade-off. The salespeople were expected to generate sales by selling foreign securities to investors.

An American salesman, Jules Spohn, was accused by the Japanese management of not making enough sales. According to one of his co-workers, he was supposed to "get his clients drunk and fix them up with girls, the way selling was done in Japan."[31] Spohn said that business was not done this way in the United States, and his clients were not interested in conducting business that way. He was not about to pimp to improve sales. With this being the major complaint against him, he was fired from his job.

WALDEN Z   William Ouchi, in his book, *Theory Z,* describes a business world based on mutual trust, egalitarianism, and primacy of the group. Self-direction of individual employees replaces direction from a hierarchical management structure. A business takes on many of the positive aspects of a clan or family, with few of the negative consequences. The power comes from the employees, in a bottom-up fashion, and not from the authority imposed by a strict hierarchical structure. The employees learn how to be good corporate citizens and, as an extension, good citizens in society. If only this were true. No company—Asian, European, or American—can uphold these kinds of ideals. The book represents a business utopia,

---

[31]Fitzgibbon, *Deceitful Practices,* p. 82.

on the order of B. F. Skinner's *Walden Two* or Thomas More's *Utopia*, with little basis in the real world. It is fine to hold these values as ideals which should be reached in a business Utopia, but to indicate that Japanese businesses and a few enlightened American businesses actually reach this state is wishful thinking.

A more realistic description of a Type Z organization would be Walden Z. The description of Japanese companies by Ouchi could have come straight from B. F. Skinner's book, *Walden Two*.[32] In this book, Skinner describes a Utopian society, following the ideals of Thoreau at Walden Pond, which is predicated on cultural and behavioral engineering of the individuals within the community. In the book, Dr. Burris, a university professor, visits a Utopian society, Walden Two, which has been founded by a former fellow graduate student referred to in the book merely as Frazier. Skinner was a Harvard psychologist who was famous for his research on the psychology of behaviorism and his work on the relationship between reinforcement and behavior. The name Burris is a thinly disguised reference to B. F. Skinner's first name, Burrhus.

Frazier shows Burris around the community and extols its virtues through a wide-ranging discussion of philosophy, government, and culture. Through the education of the children and the nurturing of the group, individualism is stamped out at an early age and the group becomes the focus of everything in the community. Individuals are not given awards for achievements, because the group is also in some sense responsible. "We are opposed to personal competition," Frazier tells Burris. "Our decision to eliminate personal aggrandizement arose quite naturally from the fact that we were thinking about the whole group. We could not see how the group could gain from individual glory."[33] The motivation to succeed and do good work for society comes from the group and not through coercion, authority, or control. "We don't use the motive of domination, because we are always thinking of the whole group," says Frazier. "We could motivate a few geniuses that way—it was certainly my own motivation—but we'd sacrifice some of the happiness of everyone else."[34]

A group orientation like this means that the fate of the individuals rests with the success of the organization. People learn that they all have to work together and cooperate to succeed. "What the plan does is to keep intelligence on the right track, for the good of society rather than of the intelligent individual—or for the eventual rather than the immediate good of the individual," Frazier tells Burris, referring to the plans and goals of the utopia. "It does this by making sure that the individual will not forget his personal stake in the welfare of society."[35] Everyone in the organi-

---

[32] B. F. Skinner, *Walden Two*, 2nd ed. (New York: Macmillan, 1976).
[33] Ibid., p. 156.
[34] Ibid., p. 103.

zation ends up happy because everyone can find his or her place without the personal competition which ruins relationships and ultimately ruins the organization. "We simply arrange a world in which serious conflicts occur as seldom as possible or, with a little luck, not at all,"[36] states Frazier.

Frazier convinces Burris of the ideals inherent in *Walden Two*. At the end of the book, Burris decides to leave his university position and join the commune at *Walden Two*. The book describes a model which other communities and groups can use to achieve the goals of cultural and behavioral engineering.

The parallels between *Walden Two* and the ideal Type Z organization described by Ouchi are overwhelming. Ouchi was also a university professor who made trips to the Utopian business organizations of Japan. Undoubtedly, he was escorted on these visits by earnest individuals, similar to Frazier, who explained the ideals and goals of the organization. In a Type Z organization, the individual becomes of secondary importance to the group. "[T]he nature of things operates so that nothing of consequence occurs as a result of individual effort," Ouchi tells us. "Everything important in life happens as a result of teamwork or collective effort. Therefore, to attempt to assign individual credit or blame to results is unfounded."[37]

In a Type Z organization, a person will naturally gravitate to the jobs best suited to that individual's skills and motivations. A person will do what is best for the society. "[E]ach individual is also effectively told to do just what that person wants," Ouchi explains to the outsider. "In this case, however, the socialization of all to a common goal is so complete…rthat individuals will naturally seek to do that which is in the common good."[38]

The business place is ruled by mutual trust and common goals. "[E]ach person can apply discretion and can work autonomously without close supervision, because they are to be trusted," states Ouchi. "Again, trust underscores the belief that goals correspond, that neither person is out to harm the other."[39] In other words, conflicts do not occur because they would be inconsistent with the common goals understood implicitly by everyone in the organization.

There are other congruences among Deming, Ouchi, and *Walden Two* that are also difficult to ignore. While visiting the dining room, Frazier notes how the tea set has been improved at *Walden Two*. "The main thing is, we encourage our people to view every habit and custom with an eye to possible improvement," says Frazier in defending the premise that a simple improvement in a tea set can be important. "A

[35]Ibid., p. 239.
[36]Ibid., p. 149.
[37]Ouchi, *Theory Z*, p. 42.
[38]Ibid., pp. 71-72.
[39]Ibid., p. 68.

constantly experimental attitude toward everything—that's all we need. Solutions to problems of every sort follow almost miraculously."[40] This is Deming's theory of constant improvement.

At another point, Frazier is discussing the business end of *Walden Two* and the collective sharing of the business. "The profit system is bad even when the worker gets the profits, because the strain of overwork isn't relieved by even a large reward. All we ask is to make expenses, with a slight margin of safety."[41] This sounds like Deming's call for less emphasis on profits and more emphasis on keeping people working.

One of the purposes of Deming's red-and-white-bead demonstration is to show that punishment of workers makes little sense because the individual worker may have little control over the process. The problem lies more with management than with the individual worker. Avoidance of punishment could have come directly from Skinner in Walden Two. "How do you treat a man for a bad case of 'poor work'?" Burris asks Frazier. "With common sense!" replies Frazier. "Take him off the job. If the boy who has charge of collecting eggs breaks too many, give him other work. And the same with a Manager. But why condemn him? Or blame him?" The problem with bad work is that management has not placed the person in the correct job. Firing a person makes no sense.

Deming criticizes individual evaluations of personnel, claiming that the most able people will eventually rise to the top. In Walden Two, the Planners and the Managers are at the top, running the organization for the members. They have achieved these positions not through merit promotions but because they have just been accepted as the ones who should lead. "The Managers aren't honorific personages, but carefully trained and tested specialists," Frazier explains. "How could the members gauge their ability? You work up to be a Manager—through intermediate positions which carry a good deal of responsibility and provide the necessary apprenticeship."[42]

Even the poor relationships between unions and management, criticized by Deming and Ouchi, could have come directly from the Utopian society of Walden Two. "That's the fatal flaw in labor reform. The program calls for a long, dreary campaign in which the [union] leaders not only keep their men dissatisfied but stir up additional and often spurious grounds for dissatisfaction," Frazier tells Burris. "So long as reform remains a battle between labor and capital, the labor leader must 'increase the misery' to heighten the morale of his troops....Here, there's no battle.

---

[40]Skinner, *Walden Two*, p. 25.
[41]Ibid., p. 45.
[42]Ibid., p. 49.

We can freely admit that we like to work."[43] If a union exists in these Utopian societies, it learns that its goals and management's goals are ultimately the same.

SEARCHING FOR THE LOST ISLE OF ATLANTIS The Utopian business worlds envisioned by Deming and Ouchi are similar to the fictional Utopian society of Walden Two and others which have been envisioned down through the centuries. Perhaps we all have had the urge to return to the simplicity and innocence of the Garden of Eden. Explorers and adventurers have sought the lost island of Atlantis based on its description as a Utopian society by Plato. The Spanish explorers Coronado and Pizarro, among many others, spent years trying to find the mythical lost world of El Dorado. Shangri-La only opens itself briefly to the outside world, so the story goes, and many have followed Conway's path in the search for the treasures and ageless wisdom of this mountain city. We all have a desire to search for these lost cities and societies.

The Japanese corporations described by Deming and Ouchi which practice the ideals set forth in other stories of Utopian societies are as elusive to find. Jan Woronoff practiced business in Japan for ten years and could not find the Utopia described by others. "Nearly everyone knows that there is no perfect, or even model, management system in the world," states Woronoff. "[T]his glorification of Japan should have caused more people to wonder whether the "hype" was not greatly overdone."[44] Sullivan went to Japan in the search for Type Z organizations. "[M]ost Japanese, like many Americans, would like to see management guided by it," says Sullivan about Theory Z. "The problem is that Japanese management is not driven by Theory Z, nor is it likely to be."[45] Katzenstein traveled to find the "virtues of Japanese management that had been preached in business school."[46] He soon became convinced that it was not there. "More and more, the adaptations of Japanese corporate approaches and techniques by Western managers seemed like the fruitless pursuit of fad diets."[47] We felt like Coronado or Pizarro when we went to Japan to find our El Dorado of businesses, where everything produced turned to gold. We wished to return to our earlier, more innocent days in the Garden of Eden, where we could retrieve the lost knowledge for producing quality products—lost when our businesses took the bite from the apple of profits.

The literature describing Utopian societies usually follow a discernible pattern. Ideals of the Utopian society are contrasted with the evils of the contemporary social

---

[43]Ibid., p. 148.
[44]Woronoff, *The Japanese Management Mystique*, p. 4.
[45]Jeremiah Sullivan, *Invasion of the Salarymen* (Westport, CT.: Praeger, 1992), p. 100.
[46]Gary Katzenstein, *Funny Business* (Englewood Cliffs, NJ: Prentice Hall, 1989), p. 204.
[47]Ibid., p. 206.

scene, much as Japanese corporations have been compared to the American corporations. According to one description of Utopian books, they "outline vast and revolutionary reforms without the necessity of detailing processes by which the ideal situation may be brought about."[48] The writings of Ouchi and Deming which explain the Utopian ideals should be accepted as part of this tradition. They are useful because they can inspire us to more principled methods of management based on ideals of how to treat each other in a communal business organization. As practical means for achieving these ideals, however, they have little to offer but the inspiration that there may be a better way of doing things. We must remember that the Greek translation of Utopia is "nowhere." The map to the Japanese business Utopia is about as useful as the early maps which pinpointed the location of the Island of Atlantis in the middle of the Atlantic Ocean. This time the maps point to an island in the Pacific.

---

[48]William Bridgewater and Elizabeth Sherwood (eds.), *Columbia Encyclopedia*, 2nd ed. (New York: Columbia University Press, 1956), p. 2049.

Myth 6:
The Japanese Educational System
Is Responsible for Workers
Producing High-Quality Products

When I learned we were going to Japan, as the mother of Wescott, age 6, and Russell, age 3, my first concern was where my two boys would attend school. Russell, who had been attending a local preschool for two years, didn't really need preschooling in Japan for the short time we would be there, but Wescott was scheduled to begin first grade and I wanted him to be ready for second grade when he returned to Indiana schools after our sabbatical year. The Lafayette school corporation assured me that no matter how unusual his learning experiences might be while he was in Japan, Wescott would be permitted to enter second grade if he was able to handle the work. I also talked to the principal of the school my son would be attending when he returned, who told me what academic skills he would need, and I had extended conversations with two of my friends who were elementary school teachers. Fortunately, first-grade skills are pretty basic: manuscript writing, simple addition and subtraction, and learning to read. Since I didn't want the three months in Japan to be too disruptive for my sons, I decided to teach them myself.

THE SQUARISH PINK COUNTRY ON THE MAP   The sojourn in Japan seemed ideal for testing my mettle as a parent/teacher, and I was very excited about the opportunity, viewing it as an experiment or test. If things went well I was prepared to continue home schooling in Indiana, since there are so few private school options in our hometown. Like many Americans, I had been exposed to discussions regarding the sorry state of America's public school system. The National Commission on Excellence in Education published its report, *A Nation At Risk*,[1] in 1983, prompting sweeping discussions throughout American society about our educational crisis. Some of the alarming findings from *A Nation at Risk* included:

- 23 million American adults are functionally illiterate.
- 13% of all 17-year-olds are functionally illiterate.
- SAT scores have declined since 1963 by as much as 50 points on the verbal portion and 40 points on the mathematics portion.
- Between 1975 and 1980, remedial math courses in colleges, designed to bring students up to standards, increased in enrollment by 72%.[2]

Newspaper editorials continued to sound the alarm. A *Chicago Tribune* editorial entitled "Why Johnny Doesn't Like R&D"[3] concluded that unless math and science programs were strengthened, we would lose the technology race. *Time* magazine had an editorial, "Trade: Getting Back into the Game,"[4] which called for bolstering education with a special focus on science and math. Even my home-town paper ran a series of articles on the need for a more qualified workforce and how Lafayette's Jefferson High School was meeting the needs of the next decade.[5] I was teaching statistics to industrial engineers at Purdue during those years and was alarmed enough about these issues to assign readings of these articles and others to my students.

"Don't be complacent," I told them. "Change is coming, and you need to be prepared. You need to be aware of the competitive problems we're facing as a nation in international trade and manufacturing. Education will be the answer to the nation's problems, but the education system is in disarray."

My students from those three years were destined to be the first Purdue industrial engineers in years who would have trouble finding jobs after graduation. To offset this bleak prospect, I reminded them of the importance of humor in maintain-

---

[1]National Commission on Excellence in Education, *A Nation at Risk*, April ,1983.
[2]*Ibid.*, pp. 8-9
[3]Timothy Kelly, "Why Johnny Doesn't Like R&D," *Chicago Tribune*, November 15, 1988, p. 1-17.
[4]Charles Alexander, "Trade: Getting Back into the Game," *Time*, October 17, 1988, pp. 28–29.
[5]Jeff McKinney, "Schools: IIndustry Must Cooperate, Leaders Say," *Lafayette* (Ind.) *Journal and Courier*, June 11, 1989, sec.p. C1.

ing a balanced attitude about life's difficulties, and I read them Dave Barry's reaction to the "dumbing" of America. His solutions to the lack of Americans' geographic knowledge included putting photographs of nude people back into *National Geographic* to entice young boys to learn about far-off places; placing major chain stores in shopping malls in foreign countries, since teenagers can always navigate shopping malls; and making geography simpler by giving countries with exotic names new names, such as "The squarish shaped country colored pink on the map."[6] Little did I realize how much I would need to follow my own advice regarding humor and balance once I arrived in Japan.

Incidentally, the debate started by the 1983 *A Nation At Risk* report led eventually to President Bush's establishment of the America 2000 educational strategy in April 1991. This strategy laid out six goals, ranging from increasing the high school graduation rate to besting the other industrialized nations in math and science achievement scores by the year 2000.[7] American academicians and educational reformists were focusing their attention on the Japanese educational system. Merry White's 1987 book, *The Japanese Educational Challenge*,[8] extolled the virtues of the Japanese school system and the lifestyles of Japanese families. Numerous articles in psychology and educational journals by psychologists Harold Stevenson and James Stigler promoted Japanese schools as exemplary models of how to educate children.[9] Their studies recommended longer school days and longer school years, increased teacher/pupil ratios, national control of curriculum, elimination of student tracking, and increased time spent in recesses. National debate was shifting toward solutions, and educational reforms were being initiated in states around the country. My own children currently attend an Indiana 2000 school with a revised program of instruction. But I'm jumping ahead of myself. In the fall of 1990, as we prepared to go overseas, the condition of America's schools and her industrial future seemed uncertain; pessimism was the overriding public sentiment.

Space and weight in our luggage were big problems, so I was limited to schooling materials which weren't too bulky. The local teachers' supply store had plenty of workbooks for cursive writing and manuscript printing, phonetics, and mathematics for Wescott, and I had a complete set of McGuffey's Readers, from which I selected the first two volumes to be his reading books. For Russell, materials satisfying his intense interest in learning and his competitiveness were a priority. In addition, I needed to keep him occupied while I worked with his brother. Later, after we

---

[6]Dave Barry, "Simplified Geography Is Where It's At," *Chicago Tribune*, October 2, 1988, p. 10-29.
[7]*America 2000: An education strategy* (Washington, D.C.: U.S. Department of Education, 1991).
[8]Merry White, *The Japanese Educational Challenge* (New York: The Free Press, 1987).
[9]See Harold Stevenson and James Stigler, *The Learning Gap* (New York: Touchstone, 1992) for a summary of their articles published before 1990.

arrived in Japan, I discovered that we couldn't have sent our children to Japanese schools even if we had wanted to. Our hosts in Japan were relieved that we had come prepared to do home schooling.

Once we were settled in Japan, my new neighbors evinced an interest in how I was teaching my children. One neighbor, trained as an elementary school teacher, had a professional's curiosity, whereas my other neighbors were interested in the idea of home schooling because of its novelty. Home schooling is not even a remote possibility in Japan, where one's future social status and career are totally dependent on the string of schools one attends. I eagerly showed the wives all the materials I had brought with me, including the cardboard alphabet of animals which we had hung on the walls of our designated school room. I remember earnestly explaining to my neighbor, Mrs. Tanaka, why I preferred McGuffey's readers to contemporary reading texts. In great detail, I expounded on the lack of proper morals and ethical training in modern school books as contrasted with William McGuffey's primers, which reflect the moral philosophy background of that famous educator. Heaven knows what my neighbor thought of all that.

LEARNING TO READ   Teaching my children reminded me of how difficult it is to learn to read. First, I taught Wescott the names of the 26 letters. Then he mastered the sounds of the consonants, the vowels, the blends, and the digraphs. There are approximately 74 different phonemes a first-grader must master. In addition to phonetics, a young reader must also memorize the 100 basic sight words, which are often spelling exceptions to the rules they are concurrently learning. The confusion stems from the apparent mismatch of sounds to writing, or in linguistic terms, the phoneme-grapheme relationship. For instance, the phoneme "sh" can be written as "sh" as in she, "ce" as in ocean, "s" as in sure, "ti" as in nation, and "ss" as in issue. A lot of children, my own included, express a good deal of frustration when initially learning to read and write the English language. Both of my sons required about two years of schooling before they learned to read well. Teaching Wescott his first-grade reading lessons cured me of any illusions about home schooling. I didn't have the patience, and living in Japan made me acutely aware of the necessity of being exposed to other people and to new ideas, which is hard to accomplish within the confines of home instruction.

It made me wonder what it must be like to learn to read and write in Japanese. Imagine learning to read when there are three writing systems (Japanese writing systems technically are not alphabets), each with a different purpose. *Kanji*, borrowed from the Chinese in the fourth century, is used for conceptual words and names. *Kana* syllabaries are phonetic symbols corresponding to syllable sounds. There are two types of *kana* in Japanese—*hiragana*, which is for words not written in *kanji* and for inflectional endings for *kanji* words, and *katakana,* which is used for words which have a foreign origin. Our names, for instance, would always be written in *katakana,* thus providing the Japanese with an unmistakable identification of foreigners. Both *kana* syllabaries have 46 symbols in them.[10] Children learning to read Japanese learn both *hiragana* and *katakana* symbols. The *kanji* characters have to be memorized one at a time. An average Japanese adult knows 3000 *kanji,* a ninth-grader recognizes 1945, and a sixth grader has mastered 996 characters.

By the end of second grade, both of my boys could read the *Chicago Tribune.* They had little interest in anything besides the comics and the sports pages, but if you asked them to read an article aloud, they could do the task with a little help on the big words. Native speakers of both Japanese and Chinese have told me that it is not until the ninth grade that the majority of their children can read a newspaper. Why the difference between reading levels in English and Japanese? The answer lies in the writing systems. To read a paper in Japanese or Chinese, a person must have memorized the 2000 most common *kanji.* In English, novice readers can always sound out the words, and if they don't know the word, they can look it up in a dictionary to discover its meaning. In the worst-case scenario, the English-speaking child spells out the word and a nearby adult tells him or her what it means!

For the Japanese child, the situation is complex. In the *kanji* system of Chinese characters, guessing the meaning is virtually impossible. You either know it or you don't. Sometimes, the character can be broken down into components, but you can't "sound it out" using any system of phonetics. Can you look it up in a dictionary? How do you look up a word you don't know when there is no possibility of alphabetization? In English we organize information by alphabetization, a system which any seven-year-old child can follow; in Japan that is not an option because there is no alphabet. The fifty sounds, written in both forms of *kana,* is the closest thing to an alphabet, and it provides the basic organization for arranging information in Japanese dictionaries and encyclopedias. Mastery of this ordering system is necessary before dictionaries can be used. *Kanji* dictionaries are arranged by the 214 character components called radicals. The resulting arrangement is so complex that indexes are provided according to the radicals, the stroke count of the characters, and the index of readings. A Japanese youngster can't even spell the word out loud, because the syllables have no unique names of their own. Obviously, there are no spelling bees in Japan. To master the skill of reading, a Japanese child must spend hours and hours memorizing three writing systems and the hierarchy of fifty sounds. Small wonder they go to school more days of the year. Small wonder they are taught very young to do repetitive tasks over and over without complaint. The Japanese writing

---

[10]Wolfgang Hadamitzky and Mark Spahn, *Kanji and Kana,* (Rutland, VT: Charles E. Tuttle, 1981). After World War II, two obsolete *hiragana* were dropped from the official listing of syllables.

systems are very inefficient. Learning to read in Japan is just the beginning of a long life of discipline and hard work.

THE YEAR IS SHOWA 63   If the writing systems weren't cumbersome enough, the method of dating in Japan is extremely memory-intensive. Dating on official documents is still done by the era of the emperor's reign and by the duration of his rule. The year 1988 was referred to as Showa 63.[11] Hirohito, the emperor of Japan in 1988, was in the 63rd year of his reign. At the time he was 87 years old and in poor health. His reign, Showa, was called the Era of Enlightened Peace, despite the fact that under his rule Japan launched its brutal aggression against its Asian neighbors and attacked the United States. The reign of the present emperor, Akihito, is referred to as the Heisei era, and his first year as reigning emperor was Heisei 1.

As a test of using this system, try to determine the number of years between Showa 63 and Heisei 4. If a Japanese wants to refer to the year 1578, he has to recall which emperor was in power and how long the emperor had been in power at that time. The age of the emperor gives you some information, but it can't be used for the dating. One lawyer in Japan is refusing to date his legal papers using the old method; he is the only person within the Japanese legal system who is dating with Western years.[12] Consider the implications of such a system. With Western dating, even a small child can figure out that the Norman conquest of Britain occurred before the American Civil War. As soon as a child learns to count, he or she can begin to put historical events into perspective. On the contrary, a Japanese child would have to memorize the emperors and their lengths of reign before building a sense of history. It would be mind-boggling to try and study world history using the Japanese era dating system. Peter Dale, a British scholar, claims the Japanese have no interest in history; their primary concern is tradition, which is a cultural orientation and not a historical one. Thus the dating system reflects and reinforces their attitudes toward learning and knowledge. In Japanese culture, writes Dale, "history is made irrelevant."[13]

The manner in which the Japanese deny their role in World War II reinforces Dale's assessment. Japanese textbooks focus on the Allied bombing of Japan, with particular emphasis on the losses and suffering caused by the atomic bombing of Hiroshima and Nagasaki. There is little or no discussion of the role Japan played in starting the war, beginning with the invasion of Manchuria in the 1930s. No textbooks relate the horrendous brutality of the Japanese army during the 1937 Rape of Nanking, when 120,000 to 300,000 Chinese civilians were raped and killed, mostly

[11]"As Showa Draws to Its Close," *The Economist,* September 24, 1988, p. 37.
[12]"Lawyer Battles Court over Western Dates," *Japan Times,* September 15, 1990, p. 2.
[13]Peter Dale, *The Myth of Japanese Uniqueness* (New York: St. Martin's Press, 1986), p. 20.

by bayonet. Nor do the textbooks inform students about the reasons behind the invasions of other Asian countries. The Japanese born after the war have no knowledge of the Bataan march, the Korean comfort girls, the bridge over the River Kwai, and countless other episodes of atrocities practiced by the Japanese soldiers. Unit 731 and its immoral and reprehensible testing of bacterial warfare agents upon POWs is swept under the *tatami* mat of Japanese collective consciousness. Japanese citizens who try to remind the populace of the role played by Emperor Hirohito in the war are brutally attacked by assassins. The mayor of Nagasaki, one of the few Christians in the political arena, was shot and seriously wounded for his remarks concerning the emperor's responsibility for Japan's hardships caused by the war. Prime Minister Morihiro Hosokawa, who characterized Japan's attacks on its neighbors as "an act of aggression," was also the victim of an attempted assassination. The *nihonjinron* (Japan's popular press) for the public's education is full of denials of the army's activities against civilians. Shintaro Ishihara (author of *The Japan That Can Say No* denies publicly that the Nanking massacre ever occured. The emperor's younger brother, Prince Mikasa, has recently indicated that he told Hirohito of the army's activities in China and showed him movies and photographs of massacred Chinese.[14] The Crown Prince relates that he was horrifed to discover that Japanese military officers were using live Chinese POWs for bayonet practice. The officer told him, "It helps them acquire guts."[15] Against this backdrop of denial, the Japanese are pressing the United States for a formal apology for dropping the Fat Man and the Little Boy—the two atomic bombs—on Japan. They have yet to apologize to the United States for Pearl Harbor and the Baatan March, or to the Koreans, Chinese, Filipinos, New Guineans, Australians, and Sri Lankans for Japanese atrocities.

PLAYING HOOKY FROM SCHOOL

The prevalence of child pornography is a rampant problem in Japan which is not often discussed. The Japanese weekly news magazine, *Friday*, which is a cross between *People* and *Time*, is full of pictures of seminude girls who are often not much older than 13. Most of the photographs looked like amateur photography, raising the possibility that the girls had taken the shots themselves and submitted them to the magazine. A corollary problem is the high percentage of schoolgirl prostitutes. The Tokyo Metropolitan Police Department in 1985 reported an alarming increase of 262% in the number of young girls moonlighting as prostitutes.[16] Tokyo's famous love hotels are being used by

---

[14]Merrill Goozner, "New Hirohito Revelations Startle Japan," *Chicago Tribune*, July 7, 1994, p. 1-1.
[15]Ibid.
[16]"Number of Minors Taken into Custody for Prositution Increases Dramatically," *Japan Times*, January 30, 1986, p. 2.

bored school girls looking for extra money and a little excitement.[17] Even college students visiting in the United States have been practicing the oldest profession. Ron Hasegawa, a reserve officer with the Los Angeles Police Department, was surprised that 16 of the 22 call girls arrested in Los Angeles' Little Tokyo were Japanese nationals attending college in the United States.[18]

Unlike their American counterparts, the sex lives of Japanese school girls do not contribute to the poverty levels. There are virtually no children having children in Japan. Adoption is unheard of and, in a society that values lineages, illegitimate births simply don't happen. Birth control in the form of condoms and abortion is used to prevent unwanted pregnancies. I tried to explain to my neighbor, Mrs. Matsuoka, why abortion was such a volatile issue in America. She couldn't understand the big fuss, since abortion is very common in Japan. An estimated one-fifth of all conceptions end in abortion every year in Japan. For her, the disgrace of an illegitimate birth far outweighed any feelings of guilt surrounding the termination of a fetus. Yet Japanese women who have abortions clearly feel something, since the Hasedera Temple at Kamakura for unborn spirits is visited frequently. There, young women can purchase small statues of Jizobosatsu, the guardian god responsible for unborn souls, to place in the temple accompanied by small mementos for the unborn baby. Once a year the priests take all the statues and burn them as an offering to Jizobosatsu, thus ensuring the babies' salvation. Families who have suffered the pain of miscarriages can make offerings as well.

During our excursions around Japan, I noticed several things which surprised me. The first was that although the children went to school on Saturday mornings, they came home from school right after lunch on Wednesdays. I wondered if, when people count the number of school days in Japan, they count five and one-half or five? Should half-days be counted the same as full ones? I have never seen reference to this in print. The other thing that puzzled me was the large number of high school-age girls in the coffee shops and malls—everywhere I went—during school hours. I only saw them in the afternoons, however, never in the mornings. I knew they were school girls because of their uniforms and book bags. One day I finally questioned Mr. Uchimura about it.

"Why are there so many school girls in the shopping areas during school hours?" I asked.

"Oh," he replied, "it must be exam day. On exam days, the students are dismissed early after the exams and have the afternoon free."

"How many exam days are there?" I asked.

---

[17]Ibid.
[18]George De Lama and Jessica Seigel, "Scared Parents in Japan Buy Security in U.S.," *Chicago Tribune*, March 30, 1994, p. 1-1.

"Usually one a semester."

"Wait a minute," I said doubtfully because, as a former professor of statistics, the odds were starting to bother me. "I see these girls wherever I go—Tokyo, Yokohama, Hiroshima, and stops along my train line."

"Exam day," he insisted.

"Do you mean to tell me that I have managed to be all these different places all over Japan and I just happened to be there on exam days?"

Mr. Uchimura gave up. He looked very mischievous. "Hooky," he said with grin.

Tatemae (image) was gone: For a brief moment, the image was focused. The *honne* (reality) was the serious problem of truancy in the Japanese school system, particularly among teenage girls.

The hooky issue illustrates a dilemma facing many young women in Japan: The social structure is geared toward males. The end goal of the educational system is job placement for men. When the Japanese economy turned down in the early 1990s, job opportunities for women were affected first. In 1992, the Recruit Research Company of Japan reported 2.2 job openings per male looking for employment, in sharp contrast to the less than one opening per female.[19] Many Japanese women have been moving to Hong Kong to pursue better careers, where those with English speaking skills find the job opportunities almost limitless.[20]

The university enrollment reflects the reality for Japanese women. In Japan in 1988, only 26.3% of the bachelors' degrees and 13.3% of the graduate degrees were awarded to women.[21] Contrast this with the United States, where 52.6% of the bachelors' degrees and 48% of the graduate degrees are earned by women. For many young girls in Japan there is little incentive to go to school, hence the hooky problem.

NO ENGLISH SPOKEN HERE   Historically, Japan does not have a tradition of free speech. A major characteristic of the Tokugawa period, which lasted from 1603 to 1868, was the vigorous suppression of individual action and thought. Discussion of politics was illegal.[22] The government carried out an extensive program of censorship. In the Tokugawa schools, diligence and hard work, not creative thinking or brilliance, were recognized as desirable attributes.[23] Students of this era were not taught that knowledge leads to self-discovery or self-awakening. Rather,

---

[19]David Sanger, "Japanese Women in Job Market Find the Door Is Closing Again," *The New York Times,* December 1, 1992, p. A-1.

[20]Career-Minded Japanese Women Find Increased Opportunities in Hong Kong," *Japan Times,* October 17, 1990, p. 3.

[21]*Digest of Education Statistics,* (Washinton, D.C.: U.S. Department of Education, National Center for Educational Statistics), October, 1993, p 421.

[22]Karel van Wolferen, *The Engima of Japanese Power* (New York: Vintage, 1990), p. 255.

[23]Thomas P. Rohlen, *Japan's High Schools* (Berkeley: University of California Press, 1983), p. 50.

they were instructed in the importance of loyalty to the emperor, blind obedience to authority, and the neo-Confucian notion that society is in alignment with nature and therefore one cannot question anything.[24]

Systematic thought suppression continued into the next period of Japanese history. The Meiji period, which lasted from 1868 to 1945, was a paradox. On the one hand, education flourished, with the establishment of elementary and secondary schools for all Japanese citizens and the development of the university system. At the same time, however, the government was taking measures to prevent civil unrest. A series of internal security laws was passed controlling the media and individuals critical of the Meiji regime. These laws were quite severe and effectively cancelled any semblance of freedom of speech. By the 1880s freedom of assembly had been eliminated as well, and by the 1920s movies and other forms of mass entertainment were under government censorship. The Japanese public was intellectually bound and gagged; there was no public involvement in governmental policy. General Douglas MacArthur's plan for Japan following her defeat in 1945 was to implement a free press, an egalitarian educational system, and a democratic government. Despite massive reforms, thought control still exists in Japan, and it becomes evident in a variety of situations. I was quite familiar with the Japanese adage, "A nail that sticks up gets pounded down," but I never realized the implications of such sentiment until the end of my visit.

In three months, I had spent a good deal of time with my neighbor, Mrs. Tanaka. We had discussed many aspects of American and Japanese culture, shared numerous cups of coffee, and eaten one too many desserts together. She had made my stay enjoyable, and I was indebted for her assistance in practical everyday matters such as paying the bills. My American friend in Yokohama lived in a house in a neighborhood of strangers who never spoke to her, and I knew I was very lucky to have lived in an apartment with my husbands' colleagues. They had provided a community for us which eased the shock of living in a foreign land. Many of my neighbors expressed an interest in continuing their English practice after I left. Mrs. Tanaka, who wanted to become a translator for the United Nations, asked me if I knew anyone who would continue to provide her conversational companionship as I had. I didn't. She was visibly disappointed, but I assured her that she could continue her English practice with her neighbors. I explained how my best friend and I had improved our French dramatically by speaking only French to each other every noon hour in junior high school.

I volunteered the following solution. "Why don't you have tea with Mrs. Matsuoka, Mrs. Nagumo, and Mrs. Kimura, and speak only English? That way you'll all stay in practice. That's all that you really need. Lots of practice."

---

[24]Van Wolferen, *The Enigma of Japanese Power*, p. 255.

"Oh no," she replied, looking horrified. "We can't do that."

"Why not? It will be fun."

"The other neighbors wouldn't like it," she answered.

"Why would they have to know? Don't tell them," I countered in typical *gaijin* fashion. "It's your house. Can't you do what you want? It's none of your neighbors' business."

"We can't," she explained.

And that was that.

CAN I VOTE FOR THE BOSTON TEA PARTY? Textbooks must meet Japanese government approval from the Textbook Authorization Research Council. Such monitoring ensures uniformity across the nation but can also compound embarrassing mistakes. We went out to dinner one night with the head of the research laboratory where my husband was working, his wife, and another couple from work. Over dinner we discussed how Americans don't know much about Japan. We concurred with our dinner companions. Our host told us how he had had to study American history to pass the university entrance exams. Something puzzled him, however.

"Could you please explain the Boston Tea Party?" he requested politely.

"The colonists were making a point," I explained. "They wouldn't pay the extra taxes because they felt they were unfair due to insufficient representation in Parliament. They were mad at the British and determined not to let the tea come on shore. So they dressed up like Indians to hide their identity and boarded the ship. They threw all the tea overboard, hence the term Tea Party. It was actually more like a tea riot. It's a pun, a joke."

Our host looked puzzled, so we tried again. Finally, he said to us, "In school we learned the Boston Tea Party was a party like the Japanese Liberal Democratic Party."

"Yes," agreed the other man, "the textbooks said it was a political party."

I was mystified, I couldn't give them an explanation for the misconception.

SACRIFICING FOR EDUCATION   I was surprised one day when Mr. Uchimura told me that he and his family planned to move from the quiet semirural community of our apartment and enter the maelstrom of urban Japan— Tokyo. As a result, he would have to spend four hours a day commuting on the standing-room-only trains from Tokyo to the research lab.

Why would you want to give up all of this," I asked, gesturing around the yards of the apartment buildings, "and move into more expensive and smaller apartments with no place for your girls to play?"

"Because of the schools," he replied. "The schools are better in the bigger cities."

"Oh," I replied, thinking I knew what he meant. "The school systems in the U.S. differ too depending on the location."

"No," he said. "It's not the public schools that are better, it's the private ones."

"I thought that Japan was renowned for its public schools," I countered.

"Maybe so, but I have to send my children to the best cram schools so they can pass the exams."

"Wait," I interrupted. "If Japan's schools are so very good, why do you have to spend so much money for extra education?"

"The children do not learn what they need to know to pass the exams for university in public schools," he explained.

"Well, what are they doing in school then?" I persisted.

"They are learning to be Japanese."

Three years later, none of the families I knew are still living in the apartments. They have all moved to Tokyo or Yokohama so their children can go to quality cram schools and thus have a future. To stay where we were would have condemned their children to reduced opportunities because of the extreme importance in Japanese society of attending the right schools.

JUKU FOR SUCCESS   With all the talk in America about the great school system in Japan and how we should emulate it, I often wonder why these proponents of reform give so little attention to the second school system of Japan, its vast network of *juku* and *yobiko*. *Juku* schools are based on the old Tokugawa system of private academies and specialize in certain topics such as martial arts, flower arranging, music, and other art forms in addition to basic tutoring. The *yobiko* are infamous cram schools which prepare students for college entrance exams. Perhaps if reformers talked about the second school system of Japan, they would be less anxious to reform American schools along Japanese lines. For it is in the network of private schools that the real success of the Japanese, the ability to pass tests, is accomplished. A visiting Japanese minister of education acknowledged the truth of this when he suggested to a rather shocked American Secretary of Education that Americans should adopt Japan's wonderful *juku* system to achieve academic success.[25]

Jukus are big business in Japan. On average, sending one child to *juku* costs about $2500. Japanese families spend an estimated $7 billion per year on the 35,000 *juku* schools in Japan. In Tokyo, about two-thirds of all students attend a *juku*. Nationwide, students are more likely to attend a *juku* as they get older. In grade four about 15% of all students attend *juku*, and this rises to 50% of all students by grade nine.[26]

---

[25]White, *The Japanese Educational Challenge*, p. 180.
[26]National Education Commission on Time and Learning, *Prisoners of Time* (Washington, DC: U.S. Government Printing Office, 1994), p. 25.

To some extent, Americans have the equivalent of *juku* through our private music lessons, craft classes at the YMCA and community centers, and lessons in the arts given at museums and local art centers. What we don't have is the extensive network of private lessons in subjects such as math, language arts, science, and foreign languages. As early as second grade, many Japanese children are beginning to add *juku* classes to their after-school activities. Parents who wish their children to go to top high schools and on to top universities are very systematic and thoughtful in picking a *juku*.

The only way to imagine a cultural equivalent to *juku* or *yobiko* would be to think of requiring your teenager to begin studying for the SAT exams in his or her sophomore year of high school. This is not the best analogy, since the SAT is an aptitude test and the Japanese entrance exam is a proficiency test, but it illustrates the point. In addition to doing high-school work, teenagers would study every night, until one o'clock in the morning, the topics covered on the SAT. They would memorize every vocabulary word ever used on previous SAT tests, and they would master all the math covered. Anything not on the SAT would not be studied. After school, instead of going to a job at McDonald's, your teenager would go to *yobiko*, where the instructor would grill him or her on practice SAT tests. In order to get into college, your child would need scores of 700 or above. If he or she did not make those scores, he or she would spend another year doing nothing but studying the SAT questions. Imagine what Americans' test scores would be if all our college-bound youngsters were going to cram school. Yet this bizarre scenario is precisely what is happening in Japan. The United States has no tradition that comes close to the devotion of the Japanese. We don't have the same approach to education. Instead of cramming endless encyclopedic facts into our students' heads, we have the Renaissance ideal of Leonardo da Vinci. A Renaissance man or woman is a person of letters, an excellent writer, a good speaker, a person of cultural and intellectual depth, not a person who has a head crammed full of disjointed facts. We tend to believe as Plato did, that knowledge acquired under compulsion has no hold upon the mind. We don't value the same characteristics as the Japanese. Thomas Rohlen, in Japan's High Schools, summed up the differences between America and Japan by saying, "Japan has no Renaissance men."[27]

THE MYTH MAKERS Three American academicians have been very successful in propagating myths about the high quality of Japanese education. Merry White, a sociologist at Boston University, painted a complimentary picture of a Japanese society devoted to children and learning in her book, *The Japanese Educational*

---

[27]Rohlen, *Japan's High Schools,* p. 82.

Challenge. Harold Stevenson and James Stigler, both psychologists, have done a series of studies comparing the schools in Chicago and Minneapolis to schools in Sendai, Japan; Beijing, China; and Taipei, Taiwan. The main thrust of Stevenson and Stiglers' findings is that Americans are doing a poor job of educating their children. They recommend that American educators base their school reforms on Japanese practices. Unlike Merry White, who is not afraid to discuss the negative aspects of Japanese culture, Stevenson and Stigler describe a Utopian society which doesn't actually exist. The Japanese schools described in their writings have no truancy, no low student motivation, no bullying, and no teacher-to-student violence.

In many popular writings about the Japanese educational system, White's books are frequently cited with little critical examination of her observations and conclusions. Because of this, her writings contribute to the popular myths about the superiority of Japanese education as compared to the educational systems in other countries. In her first book, *The Japanese Educational Challenge*, she describes the public educational system. Her second book, *The Japanese Overseas: Can They Go Home Again?*[28] deals with the difficulties Japanese families face when they return from stints at Japanese-owned businesses in America. Coming home from America is not an easy transition for these families because of the importance of the social group in Japan. Japanese who have lived overseas have become outsiders to that social group and have to be reabsorbed. The children are labeled *kikokushijo*, which means "returnees," and they are subject to bullying because they behave differently from other Japanese children.[29] Roger Goodman, an anthropoligist who has actually taught at the schools set up to reindoctrinate returnees, found after extensive study that—contrary to popular Japanese belief—the returnees were not behind in their studies. The real reason the Japanese perceive the returnees as different is not because of low academic performance but rather that the returnees, with their "American" sense of internationalism, individualism, and creativity, are a threat to Japan's traditions of harmony and self-sacrifice.[30]

Some Japanese don't wish to expose their families to returnee experiences, so they leave them at home for the two or three years they have to go overseas. People who do take their families take precautions to help their children. My Japanese neighbors in Lafayette work at the Subaru-Isuzu plant, and their son goes down to Indianapolis every Saturday to attend Japanese school so he will be ready for his college entrance exams. His bedroom overlooks our backyard, and every night when my boys play sports with their dad, he sits at his desk in front of the window, study-

---

[28]White, Merry, *The Japanese Overseas: Can They Go Home Again?* (New York: The Free Press, 1988).
[29]Alexander Mackay-Smith, "Returnees Seen as Japan's New Elite," *Japan Times*, November 20, 1990, p.19.
[30]Ibid.

ing. His light is on nightly until after midnight. But if Goodman's analysis of the returnees is right, my neighbor's son is not studying to retain academic standards; he is learning how to study, he is learning how to sacrifice, he is learning how to be Japanese.

CONFOUNDING TEST RESULTS   A major problem with some of the more inflammatory statements in White's books is that they are not justified either by references to other sources of information or by data. An uncritical reader will take these statements as fact; a more critical reader will want to go to the source of the statements. In the absence of references or data, the critical reader cannot simply accept the conclusions of the author. As an example, White writes: "The curriculum—the courses taken and material covered—is so rich that a high school diploma in Japan can be said to be the equivalent of a college degree in the United States."[31] The authors of *Educational Renaissance*[32] parrot this same statement. In neither case is a specific reference cited nor is data provided. What does it mean when White hedges her bets and uses the phrase "can be said"? Anything "can be said," but it is not believable unless facts are provided. An uncritical reader, which could include newspaper and magazine journalists, may assume that this statement was factual, but there is no evidence given to prove it.

An uncritical reader of Stevenson and Stiglers' writings may not realize the methodology problems in their experiments and, in general, the inherent problems in performing any kind of cross-cultural study. Using the scientific method, social scientists try to establish whether the variables manipulated in the experiments caused the differences in test scores. Stevenson and Stigler tried to establish that the Japanese educational system, the variable, caused Japanese children to perform better on math tests. In experimental research, however, results are invalidated when confounds occur. A confound is when something else, besides the variable studied and manipulated in the experiment, is unintentially allowed to have an effect on the results. Researchers in the scientific community systematically evaluate their results and try to determine if any confounds have occurred which would nullify the experimental conclusions.

In the Stevenson and Stigler experiments, several confounds occur, any one of which could invalidate their interpretation of their results. To explain the confounds, the testing procedure of Stevenson and Stigler will be contrasted with that of the Educational Testing Service (ETS), which administers many standardized tests, such as the SAT and GRE tests, taken by students throughout the world. Because the ETS

---

[31]White, *The Japanese Educational Challenge*, p. 73.
[32]Marvin Cetron and Margaret Gayle, *Educational Renaissance* (New York: St. Martin's Press, 1991), p. 7.

tests are used for admission to colleges and graduate schools, ETS, which is internationally the largest developer and administrator of tests, works hard to ensure that their tests are administered fairly.

A specific ETS test is administered to a particular group of students at a scheduled time and location to ensure that the students cannot obtain prior information about the test contents. Stevenson and Stigler administered the tests to students on a one-to-one basis instead of giving all the students at a particular school the test simultaneously. Their test administration technique introduces a confound, called the history confound, into the procedure. The test-taking procedure was very slow in the Stevenson and Stigler experiments, providing plenty of opportunity for the students tested early in the sequence to tell their teachers or other students the content of the test questions.

In an ETS test, all students must read the test questions themselves, and the administrator of the test cannot answer questions from students about the test questions or instructions. This ensures that how the test proctor interacts with the students will not have an effect on the test results. Stevenson and Stigler did not follow this procedure. Tests were administered on a one-experimenter-to-one-student basis, and the experimenter read the instructions and the test questions to the student. In addition, the experimenters were instructed to help students if they became frustrated. This unusual procedure opens up the possibility that different experimenters might interact with the students differently by coaching the students, either consciously or subconsciously, on the correct answers to the problems.

This kind of confound is often referred to as the Clever Hans confound. Clever Hans was a famous German show horse in the late nineteenth century that could perform any mathematical problem as long as the answer was a whole number. If the horse's trainer told him to add four and seven, the horse would stomp his foot eleven times. If instructed to multiply three and four, Hans would stomp his foot twelve times.

Although people were initially amazed by the intelligence of the horse, some doubters wondered how Hans was performing these mathematical feats with his foot. Oskar Pfuengst, a German psychologist, found that when the trainer was placed out of sight of the horse but still within earshot, Clever Hans could no longer perform the trick. Pfuengst determined that Clever Hans was using subtle visual cues, such as a tilt of the head of the trainer, as an indication of when to stop stomping.

Most experimenters try to avoid the Clever Hans confound by having the same experimenter test all students, by having the experimenter be "blind" to the experimental conditions, or by making sure that the interactions between experimenter and subject will be the same for everyone. In ETS tests, the test administrators are not even allowed to look at the test questions, so they cannot unconsciously give away any answers. Stevenson and Stigler did none of these things in order to avoid the Clever Hans confound. They used Japanese experimenters to test the Japanese students and American experimenters to test the American students, raising the possibility that the different experimenters, or even experimenters from different cultures, interacted differently with the students. The experimenters were not "blind" to the conditions and were well aware of the hypothesis of the experimenters that American students should be worse at math than Japanese students. The interactions between experimenter and student were different for each student, because Stevenson and Stigler directed their experimenters to correct motivation problems or to maintain the student's interest in the task through the experimenter's skill in administering the test.[33] A student's score was determined by how far the student got in the sequentially ordered test questions. The questions were ordered from easiest to most difficult, and the experimenter had to decide where to start a student, when to end the testing, when a question was wrong, and whether or not the next question given to a student should be easier or more difficult. Not all students saw the same questions, which meant that the grading of the test was a nightmare . A better way to test the hypothesis would have been to use an ETS-type setup, where the test administrator has little or no interaction with the students, no decisions to make, and thus no effect on the test results. The Stevenson and Stigler experimental results could be invalid due to susceptibility of their research to the Clever Hans confound.

IS THE GLASS HALF-FULL OR HALF-EMPTY? Another difference between the Japanese and American systems is the existence of cram schools in Japan. After the second grade, many Japanese students go to *juku* to learn how to pass the high school examinations. Stevenson and Stigler did not state what percentage of their Japanese and American students went to cram school. Because of the prevalence of cram schools in Japan but not in the United States, this difference should have provided a significant advantage to the Japanese students. This difference results in a logical problem, because the ideal comparison would be between students from public schools in both countries who have never been to cram school. That would be an accurate evaluation of the effectiveness of public schools.

Given these sample-related confounds, conclusions cannot be made about the effectiveness of Japanese versus American school systems. The authors could con-

---

[33]Stevenson and Stigler, *The Learning Gap*, p. 38: "(Children) may misunderstand the instructions, be unable to read the problems, or lose motivation when the problems start to get difficult. A skilled examiner, giving tests one-on-one, can anticipate such possibilities and apply the appropriate correctives by being sure the instructions are clear, reading all of the problems aloud to the child, and attempting to maintain the child's interest in the tasks."

clude, though, that Japanese students from Sendai, who are likely to supplement their education in cram school, perform better on a math test than students in Chicago, the worst school system in the United States, or students in Minneapolis. Generalizing these results to all Japanese schools or all American students is unjustified based on the information given in the reports.

To be fair, almost any test done across cultures would contain some sample-related confounds. The history and Clever Hans confounds could be avoided through better experimental technique. Their presence invalidates the research results. This is not to say that American students would perform better if the confounds did not exist; it means that this experiment did not show scientifically that American school systems should copy the Japanese school systems. American students have many other problems outside of school which might affect their scores. Copying the Japanese school system would not solve these problems, and could introduce worse problems.

In their book, *The Learning Gap,* Stevenson and Stigler speak glowingly of a Japanese classroom where a fifth-grade teacher presents, in the authors' judgment, a dynamite lecture on Piaget's study on the conservation of a quantity of liquid.[34] In the demonstration at the Japanese school, various glasses are taken out and laid out on the teacher's desk. Water is poured into them and the class is asked which glass holds the most water. The students then discuss and graph the results. As trained educational psychologists, Stevenson and Stigler should know that Piaget stated that this conservation-of-liquid phenomenon should be well understood by seven-year-olds, even without any previous instruction about the concept. The Japanese classroom was composed of ten- and eleven-year-olds. The selection of this particular lecture is an example of how researchers' prior ideas can color their perceptions. Stevenson and Stigler, who believed that the Japanese educational system is superior to that of the United States, see an innovative classroom situation in the liquid-in-the-glass lecture. They are affected by the outer appearances, so they see the glass as being half-full. We were wondering why ten- and eleven-year olds had to be taught what seven-year-olds should already understand. We saw the glass as half-empty.

PLAYING TELEPHONE WITH THE MYTH   Merry White
and Stevenson and Stigler have been successful in propagating the myth that the Jap-

---

[34]Piaget was a famous developmental psychologist who studied how children learn about their world. He was especially interested in how children learn about the properties of volume and number. Conservation of a quantity of liquid involves how children learn that a cup of water is the same if it is poured into a tall, thin jar or into a wide, squat jar.

anese educational system is a good model for American educational reformers. This myth is composed of the following components: Americans always score lower than the Japanese on tests of achievement because we have lousy schools; the Japanese have the best school system in the world, they spend more time in school, and they are the most literate society in the world. We decided to try to track down the myths, find the stories behind them, and evaluate how truthful they are.

Our findings from this examination of the education myth reminded us of the children's game of telephone. In this game, the children all stand in a line and the first child in line is given a message. The message is then whispered in the ear of the next child in line. This child, in turn, whispers the message to the next child, and the pattern is continued on down the line. The last child says the message out loud and it is compared to the original message. The fun of the game is showing how the message has been distorted and how outrageous it has become as it is passed from one person to the next. I have often wondered how the messages are distorted. Some people hear things that they want to hear. Others may deliberately distort the message to contribute to the fun of the game.

In tracking down some of the original "messages" about the differences in education systems between Japan and the United States, we felt that we were seeing the children's game of telephone in process. The end messages became distortions of the original messages. They also became more outrageous as they were passed down the line.

AMERICANS ALWAYS SCORE LOWER THAN THE JAPANESE BECAUSE WE HAVE LOUSY SCHOOLS

An AP news article says that American students have to climb up from the lower rungs of international math and science tests and that Japanese classrooms may offer an example for how to do this.[35] An article in *U.S. News & World Report* says that "Half the Japanese performed as well as the top 5 percent of Americans" in calculus tests.[36] *Fortune* magazine asked: "Why are American kids world-class dunces?"[37] Playing telephone with this part of the myth, these were obviously the end-messages from the game. These articles contained very little information about the original message which was passed on down the line.

I tried but failed to find the original message. Two months spent in two libraries with the assistance of six reference librarians and searches through three different

---

[35]Associated Press, "First-Class Teaching Gets First-Class Results in Japan," *Bozeman Daily Chronicle*, April 18, 1994, p. 1.
[36]Thomas Toch, "The Perfect School," *U.S. News & World Report*, January 11, 1993, pp. 60-61.
[37]Allison L. Sprout, "Do U.S. Schools Make the Grade?," *Fortune*, Spring 1990, Special Issue, vol. 121, no 12, p. 50.

databases turned up no actual data concerning the legendary achievement tests. In desperation, I called the education editor of the local newspaper. No luck. Finally, in the *Chicago Tribune* I found an important clue. On May 10, 1994, William Raspberry, a nationally syndicated columnist, published an editorial outlining the findings of the National Education Commission of Time and Learning, which claimed that Americans spend less than half of the time on core courses as their fellow students in Japan, Germany, and France.[38] Hot on the trail, I decided to order the report, but I couldn't learn where to send my request. I asked the director of a research institute which studies U.S. educational policy for help, and he directed his employees to find it. They failed. The librarian at the local library could find the date when Congress had appropriated money for the commisssion, but she found no address. Next, I searched through the listings of important offices in Washington, D.C., and found three probables. I made three long-distance telephone calls and found a government address at which I could place an order. I never did locate the exact title of the report, so I sent a letter describing the topic to the government publications office. Four months later I received the report, entitled *Prisoners of Time,* but was surprised to find that it only had one figure which showed the time differences spent on core courses by high school students. The report did not break down the total time figure into which courses were being studied and which were not. It did not report on the core course time of elementary or junior high students. The lack of hard numbers was surprising, because time can be easily quantified.

During my search I did find some useful information regarding education in the United States. One of the librarians referred me to the *Digest of Educational Statistics,* which is published by the U.S. Department of Education. This compendium contains data on every conceivable aspect of education, including a section entitled "International Comparisons of Education." I thought I was close. There was information on achievement levels for 31 different countries, but unfortunately Japan was conspicuously absent. Americans ranked second in reading literacy for nine-year-olds in a field of 27 countries, but by age fourteen, our students had dropped to ninth out of 31 countries.[39] I know the ranking of students from Trinidad, but I do not know where Japanese students rank.

The popular articles, with the blazing headlines, proved to be of little use also. The *Fortune* article was the most complete—it even had a reference—but it did not say how the science tests were conducted. In chemistry, American high school students were second to the bottom—Canada was at the bottom—and Hong Kong, Britain, and Singapore were at the top, ahead of Japan. In physics, Hong Kong, Brit-

---

[38]William Raspberry, It's About Time: New Study Looks at How Students Learn," *Washington Post,* May 6, 1994, A25.
[39]*Digest of Education Statistics, 1993,* pp. 419-420.

ain, and Hungary scored above Japan, and the United States scored better than Sweden, Canada, and Italy. We could find no journal articles or books about how American school systems should follow the lead of those in Hong Kong, Britain, Singapore, or even Hungary.

From my searches, I discovered that at least six American high school students are the best in the world in math. In the annual International Mathematical Olympiad, these six American high school students had the first perfect score in the history of the competition.[40] The article said that they finished above math powerhouses China, Russia, Bulgaria, and Hungary, but the Japanese students were not mentioned. One of the students, Jacob Lurie, said that his parents never pressured him to study. I wondered how well he would have fared in math if his parents had forced him to study; he might have lost interest in it. In Japan, 18.9% of the students, compared to 10% worldwide, said they studied only because their parents told them to. The same poll found that only 21% of Japanese students said they were interested in their classes, compared to a 78.2% response rate in other countries.[41] In Japanese schools, all students advance at the same rate and there are no special classes for gifted students. Would the Japanese school system and pressure from his parents have caused Jacob Lurie to lose interest in math? Would it have brought him down to the level of a normal student? Are these six students representative of Americans in general? I can't say, but at least six American high school students can do math better than anyone else in the world.

THE JAPANESE HAVE THE BEST SCHOOL SYSTEM IN THE WORLD

Henry Adams, descendent of two American Presidents and writer of the American classic, *The Education of Henry Adams*, once wrote: "Nothing in education is so astonishing as the amount of ignorance it accumulates in the form of inert facts."[42] What would Mr. Adams think of the Japanese school system? According to Rohlen in his book, *Japan's High Schools*, Japanese students are required to memorize the historical facts surrounding different schools of philosophy rather than discussing the basic tenets of those schools. Rohlen points out that the Japanese do not focus on the essence of what we think the Greeks valued—independence of thought and rationality.[43] Instead, they focus on the historical trivia. Rohlen includes a sample of the test in his book and it shows how the students taking this test clearly

---

[40]Esme M. Infante, "Kids from USA Top Winners in World Math Meet," *USA Today*, July 21, 1994, p. D1.

[41]Kyodo News Service, "Motivation Found Lacking Among High School Students," *Japan Times*, November 18, 1990, p. 2.

[42]Henry Adams, *The Education of Henry Adams*, (Norwalk, CT: The Heritage Press, 1970), p. 353. Originally published 1907.

[43]Rohlen, *Japan's High Schools*, p. 97.

had to do a lot of memorization in order to be able to answer the questions. But what do they know about philosophy? Knowing encyclopedic facts about philosophers does not help one to understand philosophy. Facts, as can be tested on an examination, are usually the most superficial aspects about the topics the exams purportedly test. American school systems seem to have taken a different approach, where the concepts, which are not easily tested, are more important than the facts. When I taught statistics at Purdue and USC, I told my students they needed to know the concepts of statistics: how to collect data, how to analyze it, and how to interpret it. The statistical formulas and calculation of those statistics were actually the least important and, therefore, I refused to make my students memorize the formulas or do calculations by hand. Memorizing the facts, by memorizing the formulas, would be of no use to them on the job. Knowing when to use the statistical tests would be crucial.

In some sense it appears that Japanese schools are training students instead of teaching them. The important point appears to be the long hours of studying as opposed to the knowledge gained during the studying. It's an initiation process very simliar to the one I went through in graduate school. I spent a year studying three areas of experimental psychology, knowing that if my professors wanted to, they could write qualifying examination questions which I could never answer. I knew that the important consideration was my willingness to study and my demonstrating dedication to the field. Passing qualifying exams had a very interesting effect on me: I wasn't so timid and unsure of myself as before. The process of entering college in Japan is an evolutionary one: The students are selected in true Darwinian fashion for a life in the Japanese corporations. Like the *samurai,* whose mettle was tested with severe conditions, Japanese students are tested to see if they will be obedient, hard-working, and loyal to the company. They are not taught to be innovative, analytical, or decisive.

The creativity problem among Japanese schooled in a system which emphasizes rote memorization has been recognized within Japan. In 1985, the prime minister of Japan created a council for educational reform to address the issues of producing a workforce which could respond to the changing international manufacturing situation. The council had few problems identifying the weaknesses inherent within the Japanese educational system but, in true Japanese fashion, it could not instigate the recommended solutions.[44]

The finished product should be of paramount importance. Since 61.7% of college-age Americans attend universities, the interesting study would be to compare American college graduates with Japanese college graduates. Japanese universities are notorious for being vacation camps for students. Unike American universities, which often have beautiful campuses, Japanese universities usually look like slums.

---

[44]Van Wolferen, *The Enigma of Japanese Power,* pp. 89-90.

Their buildings are poorly maintained, weeds grow everywhere, hallways are dark, and campuses are surprisingly empty. Our friend, Mr. Uchimura, visited us at Purdue, and remarked on the presence of so many students in the library studying on a weekend. "In Japan, you would never see students in the library on weekends or after 5:00 on weekdays," he told us.

We knew a professor who taught computer science at Keio University in Yokohama, a university usually considered to be among the top five in Japan, and he found the experience very frustrating. Many students didn't come to class, they wouldn't do the reading assignments or homework, they didn't study for exams, and they didn't care about their grades. Plus, in the Japanese university system, nobody flunks, regardless of how poorly they perform. In fact, the corporations which use the universities as employment pools don't care what a student's grades are. The only thing that matters is admission to the university, which is a reflection of how well the students did on college entrance tests. Performing well on these exams means that a student is disciplined, hard working, follows instructions, and has probably attended the correct high schools and cram schools. Success in college does not mean that the student has the academic skills to perform a job, it means that the student has the correct personality or upbringing.

An examination of some figures will illustrate how essential it is to get into the right university or employment pool. Top corporation presidents went to the following universities[45]:

Tokyo	357
Keio	133
Kyoto	125
Waseda	92

About one-third of Sony executives graduated from Tokyo University, over half of Japan Steel section chiefs are Tokyo alumni, and 62.3% of all high national government officials are Tokyo graduates.[46]

Without any reason to study, the Japanese college student shows no interest in learning, despite Deming's idealistic opinions to the contrary. When queried by a *Wall Street Journal* reporter about the role of competition in American schools, Deming declared: "Of course it is bad. People there work for the grade. In school, they studied for the grade; not to learn anything, but for the grade." The reporter then asked, "Is that different in Japan?." Deming replied, "Yes, it is. They work for the knowledge."[47]

---

[45]Rohlen, *Japan's High Schools*, p. 88.
[46]Ibid.

Our experience in Japan was that students in the universities did not work for grades because they had no motivation. A poll conducted by the Japanese Education Ministry confirmed our suspicions. It showed that university students studied an average of eight hours a week, with 42% studying less than five hours per week. Sixty percent of the students said they didn't understand their lectures.[48] More students said they go to universities to find friends (40%) than to learn (25.8%). In the telephone game, Deming has passed along a message to other Americans that has no correspondence to the message in the original data.

JAPANESE SPEND MORE TIME IN SCHOOL   One of the things repeated over and over again is how the Japanese spend more time in school than Americans do. The numbers appear to bear that out: 180 days in American schools versus 240 in Japan. Looking down the list of countries in the *Educational Digest,* this pattern was repeated over and over again for Asian countries. Asian students go to school more days than students in Western countries.

Let's take a closer look at what's happening in the United States versus Japan. My children go to Indiana public schools, so I obtained the 1992 Indiana State Board of Education curriculum requirements and the comparable figures for Japan supplied by the National Institute for Educational Research, 1982.[49] All public schools in Japan are alike, because the curriculum is controlled by national government agencies. Curriculum in the United States is set by the individual states, with local school districts having some flexibility. The curriculum administrator in the Lafayette school corporation indicated that Indiana was typical of U.S. states in its guidelines. I was troubled by the ten-year difference in dates, but there has been very little change in state requirements in the elementary school curriculum, according to the Lafayette curriculum administrator, so she felt the comparison should be valid.

When I charted the time spent on different topics in both school systems, the results were astonishing. Table 13.1 shows the number of yearly school hours by subject, along with the percentage of the time for comparison, since the Japanese go to school more days of the year. What amazed me was that even with the difference in days in school during the year, the Indiana children, with the exception of grade 4, were spending more hours on the core curriculum of language arts, social studies, arithmetic, and science than the Japanese. After six years of primary education, the Indiana children have spent 532 more hours on core curriculum than the Japanese. That is approximately 88 more days over a six-year period, which certainly is

---

[47]"Deming's Demons: The Management Guru Thinks U.S. Corporations Are Crushing Their Workers' Incentive," *The Wall Street Journal,* June 4, 1990, p. 39.
[48]"Higher Education Criticized as Conformist and Complex," *Japan Times,* November 3, 1990, p. 2.
[49]White, *The Japanese Educational Challenge,* p. 69.

Table 13.1 Time (in hours) spent in school on different topics by Japanese and American school children. Percentage of time spent on different topics shown in parentheses.

Topic	Grade 1 Japan	Grade 1 U.S.	Grade 2 Japan	Grade 2 U.S.	Grade 3 Japan	Grade 3 U.S.	Total Grades 1-3 Japan	Total Grades 1-3 U.S.
Language Arts	272 (32%)	450 (47%)	280 (31%)	450 (47%)	280 (29%)	450 (47%)	832	1350
Social Studies	68 (8%)	90 (9%)	70 (8%)	90 (9%)	105 (11%)	90 (9%)	243	270
Arithmetic	136 (16%)	135 (14%)	175 (19%)	135 (14%)	175 (18%)	135 (14%)	486	405
Science	68 (8%)	90 (9%)	70 (8%)	90 (9%)	105 (11%)	90 (9%)	243	270
Music/Art	136 (16%)	72 (8%)	140 (15%)	72 (8%)	140 (14%)	72 (8%)	416	216
Phys. Ed./ Health	102 (12%)	63 (7%)	105 (11%)	63 (7%)	105 (11%)	63 (7%)	312	189
Moral Education	34 (4%)		35 (4%)		35 (3%)		104	0
Other	34 (4%)	54 (6%)	35 (4%)	54 (6%)	35 (3%)	54 (6%)	104	162
Totals	850	954	910	954	980	954	2740	2862
Core Totals	554	765	595	765	665	765	1804	2295

Topic	Grade 4 Japan	Grade 4 U.S.	Grade 5 Japan	Grade 5 U.S.	Grade 6 Japan	Grade 6 U.S.	Total Grades 1-6 Japan	Total Grades 1-6 U.S.
Language Arts	280 (29%)	315 (33%)	210 (21%)	270 (28%)	210 (20%)	240 (22%)	1532	2175
Social Studies	105 (10%)	90 (9%)	105 (10%)	135 (14%)	105 (10%)	120 (11%)	558	615
Arithmetic	175 (17%)	135 (14%)	175 (17%)	135 (14%)	175 (17%)	120 (11%)	1011	795
Science	105 (10%)	108 (11%)	105 (10%)	108 (11%)	105 (10%)	120 (11%)	558	606
Music/Art	140 (14%)	108 (11%)	140 (14%)	108 (11%)	140 (14%)	60 (6%)	836	492
Phys. Ed./ Health	105 (10%)	90 (9%)	105 (10%)	90 (9%)	105 (10%)	120 (11%)	627	489
Moral Education	35 (3%)		35 (3%)		3 (3%)		209	0
Other	70 (7%)	108 (11%)	140 (14%)	108 (11%)	140 (14%)	300 (28%)	454	678
Totals	1,015	954	1015	954	1015	1080	5785	5850
Core Totals	165	648	595	648	595	600	3659	4191

Note: In American schools the category "other" increases in fourth grade due to the time added to accommodate computer training, foreign languages, and the arts. In Japan, after fourth grade, all children take classes in the practical arts which are included in the other category. Percentages do not always add to 100 due to rounding error.

counter to leading conventional thought as expressed by Stevenson and Stigler in their book, where they call for longer school years.

These results indicate that the higher achievement scores (the ones we could not verify) of the Japanese occur because of some reason other than time spent in school. The case for longer school years will have to be made on some other grounds, such as a more structured environment for urban disadvantaged children, etc. A closer look at the numbers may yield some interesting recommendations. In the first three grades, core subjects are emphasized for American students. The achievement scores of early elementary students bear that out. American students decline in standings as they get older. The 1992 reading literacy test scores from selected countries for 9-year-olds have the United States ranked second behind Finland. By age 14 the United States has dropped to ninth while Finland is still ranked number one. U.S. math scores drop from a ranking of ninth to fourteenth while science scores drop from third to twelfth.[50] Indiana first, second, and third graders spend 765 hours per year on core subjects, largely thought to be the crux of schooling. That figure begins to drop off rather radically in the next three grades. By sixth grade, a child in Indiana is spending only 600 hours on core curriculum.

At the same time that the Japanese student is beginning a long period of extra schooling in *juku*, our children are spending less time on core subjects. Also, the Japanese child spends more time on math, and this difference grows as the child progresses in school. In first grade the difference is one hour per year, but by sixth grade the difference has stretched to 55 hours. In six years of schooling the Japanese child has 216 more hours of math. Perhaps, rather than lengthening our school year, we need to spend more time on core curriculum throughout the six years of elementary school and lengthen the school day.

"JAPAN IS THE MOST LITERATE COUNTRY IN THE WORLD"   Less than 0.7% of the Japanese population is illiterate, compared to 20% in the United States," writes Merry White in the introduction to her book.[51] She does not distinguish between the concepts of illiteracy and functional illiteracy, two entirely different concepts. Recent estimations of illiteracy for the United States range from 0.1% to 1.9%, depending on the definition of reading proficiency used.[52] Literacy is defined in the *Digest of Education Statistics* as the ability "to follow brief written directions" and to "understand, combine ideas, and make inferences." Thus literacy rates for Japan and the United States are indistinguishable. What about functional literacy? Literacy rates for Japan always refer to basic literacy; I have never heard nor seen reference to functional literacy in Japan. Functional literacy, or its cousin functional illiteracy, is a concept which has a long and checkered history in the United States. Defining it operationally has been compared to the search for the Holy Grail.[53]

---

[50]*Digest of Education Statistics*, pp. 413, 415, 416, 418, 419–420.
[51]Ibid.
[52]*Digest of Education Statistics*, p. 115.
[53]David Harman, *Illiteracy* (New York: Cambridge Book Company, 1987), p. 8.

The term originated with the Civilian Conservation Corps in the 1930s and was defined to be three or more years of schooling. Over the years, the amount of schooling associated with the definition has increased to completion of high school.

A 1979 report for the Ford Foundation illustrates the difficulties inherent in defining the concept: "The possession of skills perceived as necessary by particular persons and groups to fulfill their own self-determined objectives as family and community members, citizens, consumers, job-holders, and members of social, religious, or other associations of their choosing. This includes the ability to read and write adequately to satisfy the requirements they set for themselves as being important for their own lives, the ability to deal positively with demands made on them by society; and the ability to solve the problems they face in their daily lives."[54] This definition of functional illiteracy is so broad as to be meaningless, which is not to say that there are no educational problems in America. The important point is not to become hysterical and not to confuse literacy with functional literacy. When critics such as Jonathan Kozol cite figures such as "40% of the adult population is illiterate [in Boston]" or "60 million people in America are illiterate,"[55] don't be unduly alarmed. Kozol is referring to functional illiteracy in its loosest definition. Is anybody functionally literate? Is there anybody who always deals positively with society's demands and solves all the problems faced in life?

In statistics, each test which purports to measure something must be analyzed for validity. A test is valid if it does indeed measure the concept it claims to measure. The IQ test is controversial because people question its validity. A possible validity measure for IQ would be how well the IQ test predicts performance in an academic environment. Recently, functional illiteracy was measured by college students' abilities to read bus schedules, among other things. The study found that half the students could not decipher the bus schedule.[56] Based on this research, therefore, one would expect to see half of America's college students milling around bus stops in a state of confusion. Purdue University has 30,000 students, and I have yet to see 15,000 of them wandering around town trying to find their way back home.

When playing telephone with this part of the myth, the Japanese illiteracy rate was sent down the line. Somebody brought in the functional illiteracy rate for Americans, and this was added to the message. These concepts are not equivalent. Nobody has bothered to go back to the original message. The end message is certainly more provocative, but it is inaccurate.

It is time to bring some critical thinking to bear upon the myths of Japanese education. Why do so many Americans fall victim to Japanese *tatemae?* The answers are

---

[54]Ibid.

[55]Jonathan Kozol, *Illiterate America* (Garden City, NY: Anchor Press, 1985), pp. 4–5.

[56]Associated Press, "Report: Students who graduate college often know very little." *The Chicago Tribune,* December 11, 1994, p. 1- 4.

probably complex, but part of the reason is due to a government-sponsored Japanese program to promote *tatemae* in other countries at the expense of the *honne* (reality). At first glance, $2 million a year spent on social studies sounds like a windfall to financially strapped teachers and school systems. The only problem is that the $2 million is spent by the Japanese government to educate American social studies teachers.[57] If the Japanese were presenting the teachers with *honne*, I wouldn't have a complaint. Unfortunately, the teachers are being presented with *tatemae*. The cynics among us would argue that the school teachers should be bright enough to tell fiction from reality, but on the other hand we don't want to be rude and negative—automatically believing the worst—by questioning everything someone tells us. However, the more you know, the less likely someone can mislead or misguide you.

Myths can grow from misinterpretation of facts. As an example, Merry White, in *The Japanese Educational Challenge*, writes: "It has been shown that the lowest math and science test scores in fifth grade classes in Japan are higher than the highest test scores in comparable American schools."[58] She cites Stevenson, Stigler, and Lee's chapter in the book, *Child Development and Education in Japan.* First of all, this particular chapter deals with math achievement scores only. Time spent on language arts, social studies, music, art, and moral education are reported, but no test scores are given for those other topics. Science is not mentioned in this chapter, either in terms of time spent in the classroom or in terms of test scores! Furthermore, and most seriously, her synopsis of the Stevenson et al. report is statistically invalid. He says, "The mean of the American classroom with the highest average level of performance lies below that of the worst performing fifth-grade classroom of Japanese children."[59] White's statement can be read to mean that even the best American student cannot score as high as the worst Japanese student, which is not true.

TIME FOR A RECESS   Rather than comparing ourselves to other countries, perhaps our best strategy would be to use ourselves as as the standard. How does the United States of the 1990s stack up against previous decades? The figures are encouraging. Proficiency scores are rising. In twelve years, nine-year-olds' scores in math have risen from 218.6 to 229.6, scores for thirteen-year-olds have risen from 264.1 to 270.4, and scores for seventeen-year-olds have risen from 300.4 to 304.6. African-Americans have shown large gains in math scores.[60]

[57]Pat Choate, *Agents of Influence* (New York: Knopf, 1990), p. 186.

[58]White, *The Japanese Educational Challenge*, p. 73.

[59]Harold Stevenson, James W. Stigler, and Shin-yin Lee (1986), *Achievements in Mathematics*, in *Child Development and Education in Japan* (Harold Stevenson, Hiroship Azuma, and Kenji Hakuta, eds.), (New York: W.H. Freeman), p.206.

[60]*Digest of Education Statistics*, p. 119.

Science proficiency scores have improved as well among nine- and thirteen-year-olds. Seventeen-year-olds have not shown much improvement, but there are no declines.[61] Reading scores also show some improvement, with the biggest gains coming from African-Americans. These figures indicate that scores are moving in the right direction.[62]

Another set of figures appears at first glance to counter the improvement arguement, however. A statistic which is often mentioned in discussions about America's declining educational state is the SAT scores. The headlines in newspapers often read "SAT Scores Decline Again," leading the populace to believe that Americans are indeed becoming dumber and that we can't compete in the world economy with such declines. A closer examination of the figures reveals a much different story. Since 1966 the math and verbal scores of incoming freshmen have dropped from 466 and 494 to 423 and 476 in 1991. These figures would raise alarm in isolation, but taken within the context of the testing situation and education trends, they tell another story. The test scores for the largest number of students taking the tests have not changed so drastically. Verbal and math scores for whites in 1975 were 431 and 472 compared to 1991 scores of 423 and 476. How much of these changes is due to random fluctuation is difficult to say, but it is worth noting that the big drop in SAT scores noted earlier is not reflected in the majority of the test takers.

So what is going on? It's easy to understand from a statistics point of view. What is happening is that a larger percentage of the population is going to college. In 1960, 45.1% of individuals between the ages of sixteen and twenty-four were enrolled in college. Thirty-two years later that figure had increased to 61.7%. This means that a larger proportion of the population is now taking the SAT tests to get into college. In Figure 13.1 you can see that the entire population of eligible college students is represented by the area under the bell-shaped curve. The second bell-shaped curve represents an estimate of the population in 1960. The third represents an estimate of the population in 1990. As you add more people from the middle to lower ranges of the population, the test score means will drop. This well-known statistical phenomenon, called regression toward the mean, was discovered by Francis Galton, Charles Darwin's first cousin.

In evaluating the SAT scores, one must bear in mind that the score of 500 was the mean of the limited sample of people tested when the tests were first developed; it was not an estimate of the general population mean. The SAT scores in America haven't been dropping due to lousy public schools; they have been dropping

---

[61] *Digest of Education Statistics*, p. 123.
[62] *Digest of Education Statistics*, p. 113.

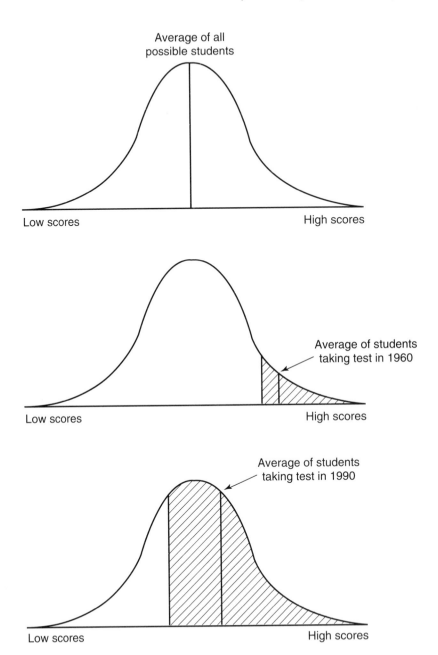

Figure 13–1 *The top curve represents the average of the SAT test if all possible students take the test. The middle figure shows the test average when only a small portion of possible students take the test, such as in 1960. The average score is high. With more people taking the test in 1990, the average will go down.*

because we are sending a larger proportion of our young people to college. The trend in Japan is in the opposite direction. Only wealthy families can afford to send their children to college: "[H]ouseholds with children in college had incomes 40% over the national average in 1980, compared to 20 percent in 1970."[63] Do we really want high SAT scores, or do we want to provide advancement and educational opportunities to a wider segment of our population? If all we really care about is beating the Japanese in the numbers games, we should restrict our college admissions to a level comparable to the Japanese college-bound percentage of 37.4.[64] Then our SAT scores would go up automatically.

The educational problems in the United States are real, and solutions should be sought. But the problems may have less to do with teachers and school systems and more to do with society as a whole. Unwed mothers, a pop culture which glorifies violence, children having children, welfare generations, drugs, and crime all affect test scores and education. Without considering the differences between the cultures, Stevenson and Stigler advise that we should blindly copy the Japanese school system by increasing teacher/student ratios, lengthening the school year, increasing recesses, and adopting a national curriculum. Those solutions have worked for the Japanese as they have attempted to catch up economically with the United States without spending as much money on education as other countries do. The reality in Japan is that schools are substituting rote learning for creativity, a financial burden is placed on parents to pay for private cram schools, students are unmotivated to study on their own when compared to those in other countries, the university system operates at low standards, and the problems with learning the Japanese language mean that students cannot read a newspaper until the ninth grade. Because of this latter fact, book reading must be delayed until the later school years. Japan's national curriculum ensures that students are taught only what the government wants them to know. National education policy in the United States should be based on reality, not on *tatemae*. Tom Peters, writer of the column "On Excellence," recommended that Americans "Forget the Japanese approach. We need to foster imagination, not rote-learning....Kiss the nanny state goodbye. The world does not owe us a living. What happened to the American spirit of self-reliance?"[65] Japanese schools are not the Utopia portrayed by some Americans, nor do they offer a panacea for our own problems. Our answers must come from within.

---

[63]Merrill Goozner, "Heat's on at Japan's Cram Schools," *Chicago Tribune*, January 17, 1991, p. 1-4.
[64]Kobayashi, Victor, "Japan" in *The World Education Encyclopedia*, Vol. II (George T. Kurian, ed.) (New York: Facts on File Publications), pp. 696–715, 707.
[65]Tom Peters, "Brains, Benefits and Biotechnology," *Chicago Tribune*, August 23, 1993, p. 4-4.

Myth 7:
Japanese Workers Produce
Higher-Quality Products
Because their Companies
Treat them Better

Japanese companies, at least the large corporations most people associate with Japan, treat their employees like family. This was our image of the corporations before we went to Japan, and we returned with that image. The only thing which changed was that we had a new definition of a Japanese family. Any comparison of different cultures will usually demonstrate different conceptions of family, so this should not be surprising. What are the differences? Westerners may find "family life" within a Japanese corporation very different from their expectations, just as a person from Japan would find family life in the United States bizarre. Can outsiders really be part of the family of a Japanese company?

Being part of a corporate family can be very enticing, especially during periods of uncertainty. But the Japanese workers will be the first to maintain that their life within the company is not as rosy as it may seem to outsiders. Most of them feel stressed on the job, almost half experience a fear of dying due to overwork, and Japanese employees score the lowest in terms of job satisfaction in cross-national studies.[1]

---

[1]Jeremiah Sullivan, *Invasion of the Salarymen* (Westport, CT: Praeger, 1992), p. 122.

American companies have many problems to work out in the treatment of their workers. Although it appears on the surface that Japanese companies have solved these problems, closer inspection reveals that they still have problems. Examination of the corporate culture also establishes that some Japanese solutions are not exportable.

DIPPING FOR GOLDFISH   Once a year, the research labs where I worked opened the doors on a Saturday to the families of the workers. This was a special time in the life of the corporation, because it demonstrated the company's commitment to the families of the employees. Everyone belonged to the team or the group. Everyone was part of the family. I could show off my workplace to my wife and children.

We were lucky enough to be present for this annual event. Buses left from the apartments in the morning to make the fifteen-minute trip to the lab building. Upon arriving at the building, we were presented with a schedule of activities for the whole family.

We were quickly ushered to the goldfish-dipping activity, in which most of the children were participating. For goldfish dipping, a child is given a sieve which can be dipped into a huge tub containing goldfish. The child chases a goldfish with the sieve until it is caught and can be removed from the bowl.

Our children were anxious to try their hand at this game. Each got in line, received a sieve, and went to it. We were on the side worrying about what to do with the goldfish if they caught one. We could not take it on the plane halfway around the world. We weren't sure what to feed it. We did not know the *kanji* character symbol for fish food. The fish were too little for sushi or sashimi. We were unlucky. Both boys caught goldfish.

"We cannot accept the goldfish," we told our host and colleague. "We do not know what to feed them and we cannot take them with us." We wanted to return the fish to the tub.

"Don't worry about it," was the reply. "You can flush the fish down the toilet if you don't want them." We were handed baggies filled with water and the captured goldfish. We worried that refusing the fish would be some kind of insult. Instead of heading straight for the company restroom, we surreptitiously put the goldfish back in the tub when we thought no one was looking.

The next activity was making paper airplanes. A former employee at the company, as his second career, had become relatively famous for constructing long-distance paper airplanes and had written a book about it. This kind of second career is common in Japan. As is typical at almost all the major corporations, all employees, except the ones in the most important positions, have a mandatory retirement age of fifty-five. About half the companies give the retiring employee a bonus of five or six years' pay in lieu of a pension plan.[2] Many employees find jobs at much less pay at a smaller company within the *keiretsu*, or they pursue some kind of hobby which may have monetary benefits. After a lifetime of devotion to their work and spending minimal time with their families, the husbands are not too welcome around the house or apartment if they have nothing to do. The wives have a term for husbands who retire and are idle: fallen leaves.

Each child went home with a bag full of goodies, and everyone had a good time dipping for goldfish or making paper airplanes. The day reinforced the image of the Japanese company as one happy family.

THE JAPANESE COMPANY AS FAMILY   The Japanese company is like a family. The dream of each parent for his or her children is that the children will grow up to work for a major corporation. Following the path to that goal provides the parents with the security that their children will face few uncertainties and will be taken care of. Parental responsibility is reduced. Society, in the form of the school system, assumes many of the responsibilities. The path to a major corporation is the goal of the parents; other paths are less certain.

Before a child enters school, the mother takes little responsibility for disciplining the child. Discipline will occur later, in elementary school. The elementary schools take responsibility for the young children to teach them how to work within a group and, basically, how to be Japanese. The school takes full responsibility for the children, both inside and outside school, because school rules also apply to how children act after school. The mothers act as extensions of school authority by enforcing the school rules at home. The mother's responsibility to her children is usurped by the authority of the school.

Once a child graduates from elementary school, responsibility is passed on to the junior high school authority. Once again, school rules apply to school hours and after school hours. Teachers will often check on their students at home or at neighborhood locations to determine if they are following the after-school rules. The students are taught discipline, group coercion, and how to acquiesce to authority.

Upon graduation from junior high school, responsibility for the student passes to the high school. High schools have strict rules on how boys and girls interact, if they are allowed to interact much at all. Much of the time after school is spent studying for the university entrance examination or going to cram school, so little social time is available anyway. The teachers continue to check up on the students in school, at home, and in the community.

---

[2]Bill Emmott, *The Sun Also Sets* (New York: Touchstone Books, 1988), p. 84.

Four years of relative and short-term freedom come once the student gets to a university. Never having been given responsibility, becoming responsible for themselves does not come easily. Most students continue to be supported by parents, so financial responsibility is not required. After the rigors of studying for the university entrance examination and the total authority imposed by high school teachers, many college students have not developed the personal responsibility to study much or to go to classes.

After graduation from college, a company hires them and takes on final responsibility. Once he or she is hired, most decisions about an employee will be made by others within the company. A company will usually provide housing for the employee. New employees are often housed in dormitories, and each dormitory has a supervisor to keep an eye on the employees. Each dormitory has a set closing time, and everyone has to be in his or her room by this time. Visitors are limited and controlled. Anyone deviating from acceptable behavior, not only on the job but after hours, risks termination from the company or losing possibilities for advancement. Job assignments are often closely supervised by a mentor. Responsible work is not given to new hires.

While living in the dormitory and working long hours on the job, a man is expected to find a wife from among those available within the family of the company. Company women are acceptable because the company has already done a background check before hiring them. Companies are reluctant to hire women who are not living at home, since their reputations can be questioned.

Marriage is an important event within a company, and the whole group or department will participate in parties before the marriage and provide the bride and groom with gifts. The groom's supervisor or boss will often assume many of the wedding responsibilities of the groom's own father. Once they are married, the couple will move to the company's apartments, which have larger living quarters. The wife will become best friends with the other wives, and the children will grow up with children from the other company families. The family often cannot afford to live elsewhere because of the high housing prices and the relatively low salary of someone starting out in a job. The apartment buildings are heavily subsidized by the companies.

Living in the apartments also allows for better control over the employees. In our apartment complex, similar to practices at other companies, wives were not allowed to have full-time jobs. If a wife had a full-time job, the family would have to leave the subsidized apartments. With the wife at home, the husband can spend longer hours at work, go on business trips with little notice when required, and be available for group entertaining after work and often into the morning hours.

The size of the apartment determines how many children the couple can have and the kinds of things a person can buy. Like all the other apartments, our apartment had two bedrooms, a small kitchen with a table, a living room, and a multipurpose room usually used as a den or TV room. The husband usually had his own room, one of the bedrooms, which was close to the outside door so he could come home late and not disturb the others. The mother usually shared the other bedroom, on the opposite side of the apartment, with the children. Each apartment is given one parking place, so each family is restricted to one car.

Between ages forty and forty-five, a person is given real responsibility on the job. At this time, the family is likely to leave the company apartment for a private home. The children are growing older, and the family needs to relocate to an area with a good cram school. This often involves moving to Tokyo or some other large city. The husband's commuting time to his job can increase dramatically, sometimes to two hours or more each way. The person has finally been given responsibility for living on his own. However, mandatory retirement age is fifty-five, so he has ten to fifteen years of responsibility within the company and at home.

There are very few uncertainties or worries in this kind of system. The man does not have to worry about his children, because his wife and the schools are taking care of them. He does not have to worry about his living quarters. The company will take care of the decisions about where to live. The man does not have to worry about his job because he has lifetime job security if he works at a large company. He can concentrate on the job itself, with little outside distraction.

Within this corporate family, an individual has to assume very little responsibility. Someone or some group is always guiding life's decisions, both at work and at home. At work, supervisors have complete control, and a mentor is a very important person in the employee's life because this person determines salaries and advancements. At home, the dormitory supervisor is in charge, and then the group of corporate families keeps tab on each other. All parts of life are controlled, with little freedom to deviate from accepted patterns of behavior. Life within a company is like living at home with an authoritarian parent. You are locked into your job. This is the family atmosphere of a large Japanese corporation.

We looked at the family atmosphere of the company as a lack of freedom. But in some ways it represents a different level of freedom. It is freedom from making major decisions. It is freedom from responsibility to others, because the schools take major responsibility for the children and the man has little responsibility to his wife. The other women in the apartment will take care of her social needs. It is freedom from being involved with problems at home. It is freedom from uncertainty, which is one of the greatest fears in Japan.

Some people thrive in this system, especially people who have always lived under the power of authority. Someone who fears the uncertainty of individual responsibility and is looking for a secure environment will like working for a Japanese company. There are many downsides to this atmosphere, however. Families are homogeneous and treat outsiders with suspicion. Families have defined roles for wives and children. Responsibility can be gained only after a long period of subordination. If someone tries to leave—betraying the family—then he or she will not be welcomed back.

ALONE IN A GROUP   There was not much room to play baseball at the company's apartment complex. The grounds were too uneven to play on and were laced with concrete drainage ditches that were perfect for twisting ankles or losing balls. The parks were too small to play in. The best place to play was in the driveway in front of the apartment. Here, each apartment had one parking place for one car. In Japan, you cannot buy a car unless you have proof that you have some place to park it. The streets are so narrow that cars cannot be parked on the street. The company provided its employees with one parking spot per family in the apartment complex it had built.

The lack of cars and adequate roads was offset by the extent of the public transportation system. Each small community has a train station as its center of focus. Buses run from the train stations to other locations, and taking the train is a daily routine for almost everyone. In our area everybody knew the train schedule by heart and would arrange their lives around this schedule.

The small car park provided the valuable parking space for the car, but it was also the only place to play baseball with the kids. I never saw any other fathers play ball with the kids; I was the only one. Sometimes a group of boys would organize a baseball game, but no fathers were present. None of the Japanese boys wanted to play baseball with the *gaijin* father and his *gaijin* boys.

There was one exception, though. He was the only boy his age that I ever saw outside by himself. He stood out from the other boys by the virtue of this fact: None of the others played alone. When I first started playing baseball with my boys, he stood off to the side watching, alone. I finally offered him the bat and he took it with little acknowledgment, just a perceptible change in expression.

I pitched the ball to him. His good hits were accompanied by a furtive glance at me. I acknowledged these glances with a very slight nod of my head and a quick suggestion of a smile. After some more good hits, he put down his bat, gave me another small change in expression, and walked silently back to the apartment building. He never said a word to me. I never said a word to him.

I felt a connection to this boy. He was the underdog or the silent loner, but not by his own choice. He was caught in the society. His mother, his younger brother, and himself were slowly being forced out of the family atmosphere of the corporation. His father had died a few months before we arrived. He had literally worked himself to death, dropping dead on the job one day. Since his father no longer worked in the company, his family had to leave the corporate family. The company wives had been like sisters to his mother. The other boys in the apartment had been like cousins. Now this was changing.

This boy's family was slowly making the transition. The boy was no longer included in the group activities of the other boys. The wife could feel her own isolation growing. The uncertainty of the future was causing visible signs of stress in her behavior. The company had agreed to let her live in the apartments until she could make plans for the future, but her options were limited. Women are expected to leave work once they are married, to take on the responsibilities of the family. She had no job skills because she had always seen herself as a wife. The purpose of an early job in the company had been to make her available as marriage material for a company salaryman. Very few companies would be likely to hire a woman in her late thirties. Her existence had been defined by the status of her husband's job, and now she had no status.

Remarrying was a remote possibility. Finding an eligible husband at her age was unlikely. She would not know where to meet somebody or how to play the dating game. A husband candidate would be unlikely to want to assume the burden of someone else's children. Blood ties are very important within Japanese family structure.

Her one option, which she was taking, was to go back and live with her parents. She would probably take care of her parents in their old age, and then her sons would take care of her in her old age. She would have few friends, little support, and her sons would not be able to attend the good private cram schools to get into the good universities. Her late husband was unlikely to have much life insurance, although we did not pry and inquire about this, and the company would not offer a settlement. A lawsuit was out of the question. The comfort of the company family had disappeared.

THE Z CLAN   William Ouchi, in his book, *Theory Z*, describes the Japanese company as a clan which is a natural extension of the traditional clan culture in Japan. A clan is held together by proximity and by the blood ties of the families. A clan-type corporation, which is highly efficient and operates on subtlety and trust, is contrasted to inefficient hierarchies or bureaucracies. Many of the characteristics of a clan corporation, or a corporation operating under Theory Z, are similar to the points in the Deming management method. According to Ouchi, long-term relationships are achieved based on trust and lifetime employment. Contracts are not needed because everyone understands one another based on their similar backgrounds and similar goals. Work and social life are closely connected and are sometimes indistinguishable. Similar to what Deming says, the Type Z corporation places reliance on the coordination of people, not technology, to become more efficient. It has stable employment. For Theory Z to work, management must embrace the new philosophy. Promotions are slow and there are no evaluations. The best people will rise to the top in a slow, controlled fashion without formal evaluations.

There is more to the myth. A Type Z corporation "is one that has no organizational chart, no divisions, no visible structure at all."[3] In this kind of organization, cooperation without rank rules. Decision making can occur from the bottom up, so everyone has a chance to voice an opinion. Once a decision is made, everyone feels ownership of the decision and will do anything to make it work. This is completely counter to the reality of the hierarchical Japanese corporation. In *Beating Japan*, the authors claim that Japanese companies are the most hierarchical and structured in the world.[4] Before any business dealings can occur in Japan, business cards must be passed around because the cards state the ranks of the different people and, therefore, how each person must be treated. A person who is lower in rank has to know his place and treat the higher-ranked person with the proper respect. The organizational chart, manifested in the title of the person on the business card, is of paramount importance in a Japanese business.

A Type Z organization, since it has no hierarchy or organizational chart, relies less on authority, according to Ouchi, and more on cooperation and group decision making. This may be the image, but it is not the reality. Japanese school children are taught at an early age to acquiesce to authority. Discipline through authority is one of the main strengths of the Japanese school system, and the school system teaches this behavior in response to the wishes of the corporations.

A Type Z company is supposed to have managers who are benevolent toward the workers, father figures who accept mistakes. This is not so in many Japanese organizations. Mistakes are unacceptable, so that the normal mode of operation is to avoid risky ventures and uncertainty. An American working in Japan observed, "Theory Z-like theories do not talk about how the system actually works....There is no tolerance for failure. The penalty for failure is out, finished."[5] "Out" does not mean out of a job, necessarily, but it usually means that the employee is given no responsibility and no promotions.

---

[3]William Ouchi, *Theory Z* (New York: Avon, 1982), p. 90.
[4]Francis McInerney and Sean White, *Beating Japan* (New York: Truman Talley Books, 1993), pp. 65–90.
[5]Sullivan, *Invasion of the Salarymen*, p. 102.

An outsider can never be part of the clan. Whereas long-term relationships are valued in a clan, one must be suspicious of people who are not part of the clan, even though they may be part of the organization. Nissan of America, responsible for sales and marketing in the United States, wanted to make sure that the American workers, who are not part of the clan, did not gain access to important corporate information. The Japanese managers of the Americans, even though they held similar job titles, were cautioned to "exercise authority carefully" and to "avoid routine requests for information [from the Americans] without a specific purpose."[6] The Japanese managers, of course, had complete access to any corporate information.

Even Ouchi, however, who lauds Japanese corporations and whose thesis is that American companies should copy the Japanese model, understands the downside of the Japanese clan corporations. "Probably no form of organization is more sexist or racist than the Japanese corporation," says Ouchi.[7] He defends racism and sexism, however, as a natural result of the homogeneity of the clan, through an outrageous hypothetical case where a Type Z corporation has a hiring choice between a white male and a female Mexican-American with equal qualifications on paper. The white male is the good choice because "you are quite certain that you have correctly evaluated this white male engineer as being fully qualified for the job of marketing manager."[8] The female Mexican-American is different, however. "You cannot be sure that what you regard as initiative is truly that; you cannot be sure that the signs you see of ambition, of maturity, or of integrity are what they seem to be. It takes time and experience to learn to read subtleties in one who is culturally different, and because subtleties are everything in the Type Z organization, you cannot be confident that you have correctly appraised this candidate, and she is therefore at a considerable disadvantage, since no one in his right mind will choose an uncertainty over a certainty."[9] With hiring practices which are nonracist or nonsexist, our organizations will become like federal bureaucracies, where "our values of equality of opportunity for all people are crystallized,"[10] The price to pay for these hiring practices based on equality is "inefficiency, inflexibility, indolence, and impersonality."[11] In his next chapter, Ouchi tells us how to institutionalize this discrimination into Type Z corporations.

---

[6]James Risen, "Some Japanese Firms Moving to Segregate Staffs," *Los Angeles Times,* May 23, 1990, D1.
[7]Ouchi, *Theory Z,* p. 78.
[8]Ibid., p. 77
[9]Ibid., p. 78
[10]Ibid.
[11]Ibid., p. 79

RACISM   We were traveling on a train in Japan and I was seated next to a Japanese man who was traveling with his family. He struck up a conversation with me, which was unusual. As with most conversations with Japanese strangers, his first question was, "What do you think of Japan?" Most Japanese we talked with were very interested in our view of their country.

"The people have treated us nicely and we have seen many pretty sights," was my reply.

After some more conversation, he tested his knowledge of the United States against my attitudes. "I understand you have many race problems in the U.S.," he stated.

I acknowledged that we did have problems and we were working hard to address the problems. We had passed laws to outlaw discrimination based on race. Racist remarks were socially unacceptable. I was too polite to ask about race problems in Japan.

Because there are so few races in Japan, there are few acknowledged racial problems. The Japanese have little understanding of other peoples. A major problem in Japan is the treatment of Koreans. During World War II, several hundred thousand Koreans were forcibly removed from their home country to work in Japanese factories as slave labor to support the war effort. After the war, some decided to stay. Almost fifty years have passed, and Korean families have lived and died in Japan; new generations in these families have known no other home. The Koreans are still not allowed full citizenship. In many cases, the third generation of these Japanese-Korean families are still not accepted as Japanese.

The Japanese-Koreans and their descendants are fingerprinted and have identification cards. When this fingerprinting practice was exposed as being racist, Japanese officials responded by considering other means, such as picture identifications, which would still identify them as Korean. They responded to the practice of fingerprinting but did not realize the underlying problem that subjecting any group to a loss of citizenship freedoms, on the basis of race, is a racist policy. Korean students are segregated in their own school system, and Korean high schools are not allowed to compete athletically against Japanese high schools.[12] Korean schools, of which there are twelve in Japan, are not even classified as "schools" under the Japanese School Education Law.[13] Many Koreans have been forced to change their surnames to names which sound more like Japanese names.

Japan is for the Japanese, and no one else. The identity of the country is tied into what it means to be Japanese. Students in elementary schools go through lengthy training about what it means to be Japanese. Children who have been edu-

---

[12]"Korean Schools to Seek Membership," *Japan Times,* November 29, 1990, p. 2.
[13]Editorial, "Let's Start with the Children," *Japan Times,* November 25, 1990, p. 20

cated overseas, due to their fathers' overseas assignments, are not allowed to go back directly into a Japanese school. They must first go to a special school which instructs them on how to be Japanese. The school officials do not want the other students to be tainted by foreign ideas.

Having had minimal contact with other races, the Japanese seem unaware that their practices could be construed as racist. Japanese government officials have a long history of uttering the wrong kinds of remarks. In 1986, Kiichi Miyazawa, who was then the prime minister of Japan, said that blacks and other minorities had lowered U.S. intelligence levels. In 1988, Michio Watanabe, a top party figure and later foreign minister, called U.S. blacks irresponsible spenders. In 1990, Seiroku Kajiyama, the justice minister in Japan, said, "Bad money drives out good money, just like in America where the blacks came in and drove out the whites." Kajiyama indicated that this situation was similar to the one in Japan when foreign prostitutes move into a neighborhood and drive out the good citizens.

Whereas Japanese companies can minimize racial problems when operating in the homogeneous society of Japan, expansions overseas necessitate consideration of racial issues. Problems are often avoided by not hiring minority workers in the United States. Fusao Ishii was the vice president and assistant treasurer who oversaw day-to-day activities at the Wall Street branch of Japan's Nomura Securities Company. An American, John Fitzgibbon, was placed in charge of hiring workers for Nomura. When explaining Fitzgibbon's job assignment, Ishii whispered, "Japanese don't like blacks. They are stupid. Don't hire any."[14] Most employment agencies in New York became aware of the problem and sent over only a handful to interview. Ishii also complained about Jewish employees. "Don't hire any more Jews. They take too many holidays."[15] Japanese management was upset that the three Jewish traders were taking off on Rosh Hashanah and Yom Kippur.

The Japanese transplant auto companies have tried to avoid racial problems by placing the plants in rural areas with mostly white populations: Subaru-Isuzu in Lafayette, Indiana; Toyota in Georgetown, Kentucky; Mitsubishi in Normal, Illinois; Honda in Marysville, Ohio; and Nissan in Smyrna, Tennessee. The exception was Mazda, who at the insistence of Ford, which owns a 20% stake in Mazda, located a plant in Flat Rock, Michigan. At the Honda plant, management required that all job applicants live within a 30-mile radius of Marysville, which effectively excluded the black population in Columbus, 35 miles away.[16] Honda has a 2.8% black worker population, compared to 17.2% for the Big Three manufacturers. Honda has had to

---

[14]John E. Fitzgibbon, *Deceitful Practices. Nomura Securities and the Japanese Invasion of Wall Street* (New York: Birch Lane Books, 1991), p. 128.
[15]Ibid., p. 129.
[16]Joseph J. Fucini and Suzy Fucini, *Working for the Japanese* (New York: The Free Press, 1990), p. 116.

pay $6.5 million to the Equal Employment Opportunity Commission to settle various complaints about its hiring practices.[17] Mazda's Flat Rock plant has the highest percentage of blacks in the workforce, between 14 and 15%, but this is far less than the black percentage of the local population, which is 29%.[18]

LADY KONG   Japan's first newspaper designed for women, Lady Kong, hit the newsstands in 1990. The Japanese themselves understand the low role of women in society because, as the *Japan Times* stated, "the publication is not likely to challenge the subservient role of women in Japanese society."[19] Although three-fifths of the editors and reporters were women, they were assigned only to the entertainment and city guide sections. The men were assigned to run the newspaper and work in the news department because, as the male editor explained, the men will "give the news stories a serious tone."

Lady Kong is a reflection of traditional Japanese attitudes toward women. Women have defined roles in the business world and should not be trusted with "serious" decisions. Clerical women workers are referred to as OLs or "office ladies" in Japan. The huge majority of women working for major corporations hold secretarial or receptionist jobs, and they are hired more for their acceptability as future wives for the men in the company than for their skills. Once they are married, which is the ultimate purpose of working in the company, they are expected to quit their jobs.

As often happens in Japan, the image to be presented to the outside world, that women have equal opportunity to find jobs or move ahead in the job, is codified in an equal-opportunity law. The 1986 law was passed reluctantly by the Japanese Diet before the expiration of the United Nations Decade for Women, which dictated that women should have equal job opportunities. It is only a shadow of a law, because Japan's Federation of Employers Associations worked hard to keep penalty clauses out of the law. The law merely states that Japanese companies should "endeavor" to reach the goal of equal opportunity. A company cannot be penalized for not "endeavoring" enough. The image to the outside world is in the form of the law; the reality is different, as anyone who has worked in a Japanese company can testify.

Of the approximately 100 researchers I came into contact within the company, most of whom were in their twenties or early thirties, three were women. They were all unmarried and had the very lowest salaried jobs. None had any men reporting to

---

[17]Ibid., p. 117.
[18]Ibid.
[19]Mari Yamaguchi, "Feminism Forsaken for Fluff, Fashion, in Male-Run Tabloid Set for Women," *Japan Times*, November 27, 1990, p. 2.

them. These percentages were typical. As a sample of career-track hiring practices for women in Japanese companies, a survey showed that the number of women hired by three of the largest and most prestigious Japanese brokerage firms in 1991 were as follows: Mitsubishi hired 4 women and 213 men; C. Itoh hired 5 women and 198 men; and Nissho Iwai hired 3 women and 127 men.[20] These three companies hired a total of 12 women and 538 men. In the same year, 1991, these companies hired 635 women on noncareer tracks as "office ladies." Fuji Bank is another example of the same trend. Of its 390 recruits in 1992 for career-track positions, only 5 were women. It increased its hiring of OLs the previous year from 65 to 95.[21]

Women are usually put on the clerical track, while men are placed on the career track. In a 1990 study by Japan's Labor Ministry, 97.5% of career-track workers were men and 99% of clerical-track workers were women.[22]

With the equal opportunity "law" and the low number of women hired to career-track jobs, how can the image be so different from the reality? "I think that the equal employment opportunity law has been successful in doing what it set out to do: give women and men equal opportunities," said Hideo Asai, who is the director of personnel management at Japan's Federation of Employers Associations. "It's really up to women now," he continued. "Women still lack the will to work, and they need to have a more professional attitude."[23]

The experience of Chiho Yui, who was a 22-year-old college graduate looking for a job, is probably typical. She applied to twenty companies, without even a slight opening of the door to her. "When I called some of these companies, they said on the phone, before even seeing me, that it would be difficult for any women seeking a career-track position this year because we'd have to compete for those positions with men," related Ms Yui.[24]

A HUMAN TRAGEDY   Unfortunately, the sexual treatment of women, both Japanese and foreign, by Japanese men has had a long and sordid history. These practices, especially for women in a subservient role, have been transferred to the workplace in the form of sexual harassment. To examine attitudes toward women, one must first review a little history. Unfortunately, this history lesson does not appear in the textbooks in Japan.

---

[20]David E. Sanger, "Japanese Women in Job Market Find the Door Is Closing Again," *The New York Times,* December 1, 1992, p. A1.
[21]Merrill Goozner, "In Japan, Women Frozen Out," *Chicago Tribune,* April 2, 1993, p. 1-1.
[22]Teresa Watanabe, "Japan Inc. No Friend to Women," *Los Angeles Times,* August 17, 1992, p. A1.
[23]Sanger, "Japanese Women in Job Market," p. A7.
[24]Ibid., pp. A1, A7.

Probably one of the saddest human stories to come out of the Pacific theater in World War II is that of the "comfort girls." The tragedy of the comfort girls is still continuing today. The story of the comfort girls was not told for many years because of suppression by the Japanese authorities and the shame of the victims to tell their story. One of the first times the story appeared in Japan was in a book entitled *The Pacific War*, by Saburo Ienaga, which was published in Japan in 1968.[25] Ienaga discusses how 370,000 Koreans were forced into war duty by Japan, either as soldiers or as factory laborers. Then he describes the fate of the Korean women. "Korean women were also mobilized by the thousands and shipped off to the battlefronts as 'comfort girls' for Japanese troops," writes Ienaga.[26] "Called Chosenpi (pi was soldiers' slang for 'comfort girl'), they were a sexual outlet for the soldiers. The women were brought right to the front lines for fornication between combat operations, and apparently many were killed in the fighting." Chosen is the Japanese word for Korean.

The Imperial Army seized an estimated 80,00 to 200,000 girls and women to serve as sex slaves.[27] About 80% of those came from Korea, with others coming from China, the Philippines, Taiwan, and Singapore. Some Australian women were also seized from various colonies in the Asian countries overrun by the Imperial Army.[28] A Japanese historian, Soji Takasaki of Tsuda University in Tokyo, indicates that this may be the only time in modern warfare, and perhaps in any warfare at any time in recorded history, in which a government through its military forced women into service as sex slaves for the troops on a large scale.[29]

Although the use of comfort girls, and the Japanese government involvement in it, was suppressed for many years, recently many of the victims and the perpetrators have started to speak out. Kiyoharu Yoshida, 78, a Japanese soldier during the Pacific War, has explained how his divisions kidnapped 950 women over three years beginning in 1942. Of these 950 women, none survived because most were left behind in Korea when the Japanese army retreated. One Korean woman, Kim, explained that she was offered a well paid job by Japanese police when they visited her village. When she reported to the meeting place, she was forced into a military truck and taken away upon threat of death. She was forced into prostitution ten to twenty times a day. The shame was so great that she wanted to die, but through a strong survival instinct, she persevered. She only recently told her story.[30]

---

[25]Saburo Ienaga, *The Pacific War, 1931-1945* (English Translation) (New York: Pantheon Books, 1978).
[26]Ibid., pp. 158-159.
[27]Chieko Kuriki, "Cruel 'Comfort,'" *Chicago Tribune*, March 29, 1992, p. 6-11.
[28]Merrill Goozner, "War Victims Demand Justice," *Chicago Tribune*, April 4, 1993, p. 1-1.
[29]Kuriki, "Cruel 'Comfort.'"
[30]Ibid.

Some of the surviving women have demanded an apology and compensation from the Japanese government. For many years, the government refused to recognize the sex slavery program. When the facts came out, however, and they could not be refuted, the Japanese government apologized to South Korea but would not compensate the victims. Thirty-five former comfort women recently filed a $5.6 million damage suit in Japanese courts, but the compensation issue has not been resolved. The official apology rings hollow to the unfortunate women who had to endure this degradation. As the surviving women eventually die from old age, the issue of compensation becomes moot.

The parallels between comfort girls in the Pacific War and present-day prostitution in Japan are too close for comfort. These parallels can be examined by considering Kim, the Korean comfort girl, who was forced into prostitution for the troops in 1942,[31] and Nioni, a present-day Filipino, who was forced into prostitution in Japan two years ago.[32] Kim was offered a "well paid job" by Japanese police officers. Nioni was noticed by a recruiter outside her high school and was offered a chance for a well paid job as an "entertainer" in Japan. Kim went to the meeting place and was forced into a truck, eventually ending up, after a four-day trip, in a Japanese officer's room where she was forced to strip and have sex. Nioni, after being trained by the recruiter, passed the Philippine government-sponsored audition to obtain an entertainer's work permit and then was driven to a motel where a panel of Japanese entrepreneurs made Nioni and the other girls "open our mouths and [they] examined our teeth and wanted to see the medical certificate which stated none of us was pregnant," according to Nioni. A week later she arrived at Tokyo's airport.

After this first encounter, and upon realizing that she had been misled on the promises of a well paid job, Kim found what she was expected to do. "My life was not human," she said. "I had to 'comfort' ten to twenty Japanese soldiers a day." Upon arriving at a motel outside Tokyo, Nioni was ready to start her work as a dancer. Instead she was guided to a room. "For the next four months," Nioni recalled, "I was locked in that room. A guard was on the floor outside. Each night three, four, sometimes five men would come in and have sex with me. I just let it happen.... There was no one I could protest to." She was never paid for her "entertaining."

The comfort girl system was instituted as a response to the rape and pillage of the citizenry in the Nanking massacre. The Japanese officials wanted some way to relieve the stress of the Japanese soldiers without resorting to violent acts against defenseless citizens. Who knows how many Nankings were averted by this government-sponsored program of sex slavery? Japan now has a thriving sex industry.

---

[31]Ibid.
[32]Uli Schmetzer, "Girls from Manila Awaken to Nightmare in Japan," *Chicago Tribune*, November 20, 1991, p. 1-1.

"Faced with a declining population of eligible women, pressure from long hours at work, experts say Japanese men often seek relief from their stress by flocking to bars and nightclubs after work for business entertainment or private pleasure," according to Uli Schmetzer, who researched the situation. The companies believe that entertainment relieves the stress of their workers, so they routinely pick up all entertainment bills as part of their business expenses. Maybe the companies should sponsor softball leagues instead. At last count, 52 million Americans were playing softball.

As in other business relationships, control is important. Dr. Sussuma Oda, a psychiatrist and professor of mental health at Tsukuba University in Japan, has analyzed the situation and concludes that the sex industry will continue to prosper. "Japanese men are afraid of being refused by Japanese women," says Oda. "However, they feel superior to other Asian women culturally and economically. Paid sex usually satisfies a man's desire to control a woman."[33] Things do not change in Japan very quickly; they just take on another form.

This attitude toward women is reflective of a problem in Japan that spills over into the business arena in how Japanese companies treat women. The bad thing about the whole situation is that there appears to be little public concern about these practices. Instead, the attitudes toward comfort girls are being passed on to new generations of Japanese boys and men. A popular video game for boys in Japan, called Commander's Decision, trains a whole new generation on the comfort girl practices of the Japanese military.[34] In the game, after a long artillery fight in the Gulf of Tonkin, the commander of the Japanese Navy issues the command "Comfort" to his troops. This provides the troops with a three-day break in which they engage the services of the comfort girls. After the break, the Japanese Navy becomes victorious against the United States. The comfort girls are a real part of military strategy for Japanese boys in the fight against the United States. About 300,000 copies of this game have been sold in Japan.

SEXUAL HARASSMENT   Most experts believe that sexual harassment in the workplace is a matter of control and power. Its purpose is to keep women in more subservient roles. Because of the attitudes of Japanese men toward women, the desire for authority and control in the workplace, and the tendency of Japanese victims to accept rather than complain, sexual harassment is a problem in Japanese companies.

A woman's group in Tokyo performed a questionnaire survey on 6500 working women in Japan to determine the incidence and types of sexual harassment on the

---

[33]Ibid.
[34]Associated Press, "Japanese Win WWII—In Fantasy Games and Books," *Bozeman* (Montana) *Daily Chronicle*, June 24, 1994, p. 2.

job.[35] About 70% of the women reported that they had experienced sexual harassment on the job. Thirty percent of the women overall reported having been fondled or hugged by male bosses or colleagues in the office. About 3% reported that they had been forced into sexual relations.

The women reported that many of the tasks they were forced to perform on the job were demeaning. They were often asked to get cigarettes or lunch for the men. They were asked to take shirts to the cleaners. Some reported that they were asked to help their bosses get dressed or to pack the boss's clothes for a trip. When interviewing for a job, women are routinely asked questions about their age, marital status, and whether they plan to continue work after they have children.

These incidents happened within the "family" of the company. Perhaps more disturbing is what happens outside the company. Ninety percent of the women reported that they had been molested by men, such as having their breasts and buttocks fondled, during their commute to work on the crowded trains.

Sexist practices are often imported to other countries along with Japanese transplants. A U.S. House of Representatives subcommittee on employment, chaired by Rep. Tom Lantos of California, was convened to examine some of these practices.[36] In September 1991, Kimberly Carraway, 24, testified to the subcommittee of her experiences at the Japanese-owned Sumitomo Corp. At this office, which employed 60 people, two-thirds were women and all the managers were Japanese. Carraway reported that her Japanese supervisor asked her for pictures of herself in a bathing suit, and she was subjected to sexist remarks. The male managers displayed Sumitomo calendars of nude women. She said that it was clear that women were not placed in management-track positions or given responsibilities other than clerical duties.

After airing her complaints to the subcommittee, she received two anonymous threatening phone calls telling her to stop talking about employment practices at Sumitomo, and she received a letter, on Sumitomo stationary, which said, "I know where you live, I know your routine." Her supervisors reduced her job responsibilities and reprimanded her for minor mistakes. She eventually quit her job, in December 1991, after she became concerned for her safety.

Kenji Miyahara, president and chief executive of Sumitomo Corp. of America, denied Carraway's accusations. "We are not perfect," said Miyahara, "but we do our best to achieve this goal." The company responded to the allegations by releasing a written statement emphasizing the size of its business in the United States and the number of Americans employed by Sumitomo.

---

[35]Chieko Kuriki, "Harassment Mars Workplace in Japan," *Chicago Tribune*, February 2, 1992, p. 6-4
[36]Carol Jouzaitis, "Accuser: Sumitomo Retaliated," *Chicago Tribune*, February 27, 1992, p. 3-1.

LIFETIME EMPLOYMENT   One of the most popularized conceptions of life in a Japanese corporation is lifetime employment. Once hired by a Japanese corporation, a person will have a job for life, a least after a six-month probationary period. Lifetime employment is seen as having many advantages. For the employee, lifetime employment reduces the uncertainty of the future, because the employee knows that the job and a steady income will always be there. The employee can be loyal to the company because of the long-term commitment the company makes to the employee and the reciprocal commitment by the employee to the company. The interests of the employee should become the same as the interests of the company due to this long-term relationship.

Lifetime employment has many benefits for the company, also. The company can invest in training workers because the payoff is a long period of employment of a trained worker. The heavy emphasis on training should result in a workforce which is more efficient and productive. The company also expects a cooperative attitude from its employees, which reduces the need for a confrontational union. Cooperation and understanding replace confrontation and misunderstanding.

Another important side benefit for the company of lifetime employment is that it can operate to keep down salaries, especially for top managers. Since all managers stay in the company and work themselves through the ranks, they have no opportunity to test the market value of their salary. As a result, the salary ratios between the top managers and the lowest managers are much lower than the same ratios in American businesses. In American businesses, top management, if the company is performing well, is rewarded with large salaries. Their market value is high. The huge salaries of the top executives of American companies and the relatively low salaries of the top executives of Japanese companies are often cited as explanations of the greater competitiveness of Japanese companies.

Lifetime employment is not necessarily a long-time tradition in Japan. It grew out of the period immediately preceding and during World War II, in which job-hopping was common. To assist the war effort, the Industrial Patriotic Association passed a series of laws which prohibited unauthorized job changes and issued statements propagandizing about the company as family.[37] The laws were removed after the war, but the tradition of the company as family and the restrictions continue. These restrictions can continue only through the cooperation of all the companies. The companies have implicit understandings with each other that they will not raid workers from other companies. If an employee quits a company, then this employee is unlikely to find lifetime employment work in any other company, because the motivation and loyalty of this person would be suspect.

---

[37]McInerney and White, *Beating Japan,* p. 121.

The most important benefit of the lifetime employment system, as seen by a Japanese company, is that it provides the companies with great power and authority over its employees. With the cooperation of the other companies, an employee has no freedom to move to another company. This means that the employee must do whatever is demanded by the company. The employee accepts the salaries given to him; his market value can never be tested. The employee accepts promotions; talented people get promoted at the same rate as less talented people, especially during the periods of employment before they are given any responsibility on the job. The employee accepts job assignments; these assignments may not utilize the talents of the employee or may involve family hardships due to frequent location changes. The unions work to maintain lifetime employment by sacrificing most other benefits strived for by traditional unions.

Sullivan did a study of eighty-four Japanese firms to determine if the practice of lifetime employment is associated with promoting loyalty and motivation in the workers or if it is associated with exerting power and authority over the employees.[38] By correlating the prevalence of lifetime employment in these companies with the two facts, Sullivan found that lifetime employment was associated with power, control, and authority rather than loyalty or motivation. The practice of lifetime employment fits well with management's need to reduce uncertainty and to exercise power.

American workers look at the image of lifetime employment and the promise of job security with envy, not realizing the sacrifices which must be made and how the system cannot be transferred elsewhere. American employees like to think that they will be rewarded based on their talent, their success, and their hard work. Talented employees, expecting their reward, would find working under a lifetime-employment situation very difficult because less talented people would be promoted at the same rate and given the same pay. American workers would like the option to move to another company if working conditions at one company are poor or if job assignments or location changes are too disruptive. American workers like to test their market value by considering or taking other job opportunities.

Lifetime employment also has many downsides for a company. The practice works best in an environment in which the economy is expanding, companies are expanding, and the labor market is tight with little unemployment. These conditions have been operating in Japan during the postwar expansion, but recent trends indicate that expansion cannot continue indefinitely. This is placing severe strains on the companies. The companies cannot be flexible in periods of downturn or even periods of no growth. This lack of flexibility for the workers on lifetime employment is made up in other employment areas. Workers must retire at fifty-five. Many of the

---

[38]Sullivan, *Invasion of the Salarymen*, p. 123.

women are hired as part-time workers, even though their work hours often exceed forty hours a week, and they are let go in periods of downturn. Excess employees may be foisted upon subsidiaries or affiliated companies, with little input from the workers or the other companies involved.

Rather than be fired, workers covered by lifetime employment are expected to take the hint when it is time to quit. One 51-year-old employee of an audio electronics company was supposed to retire voluntarily.[39] When he refused, he was given an office in the basement of the building, with nothing to do. Week by week the lights were dimmed a little more. He finally decided to quit "voluntarily."

Another problem with lifetime employment is that some workers will have little motivation to perform the job well. With employment guaranteed, salaries predetermined, and promotions performed in lock-step with others, motivation is lacking in many of the employees. Risk taking, with the possibility of a huge success or a large failure, is not pursued. If a risk is taken individually and it results in a success, reward will not be given individually. If the risk fails, then punishment from the authority structure is swift and one can be relegated to lifetime employment in a "window seat," with no authority and little to do except look out the window. Risk is therefore avoided.

From the perspective of a Japanese company operating in the United States, lifetime employment for their American workers makes little sense. The system will work only in an environment of cooperation among all companies to limit the ability of employees to move to other companies. If an American employee could move to another company if the current salary or job assignment was unacceptable, then the lifetime-employment benefits of lower salaries versus market value, and power over the employee would not be part of the system. If employees can move to other companies, then training costs may not pay off. If talented people move to other companies and less talented people stay, then slow and equal promotions for all cannot be achieved.

Lifetime employment in Japan has covered only about 20% of the workforce in recent years,[40] and has fallen from about 35% of the workforce 15 years ago.[41] Americans tend to see lifetime employment as a commitment from the company to the worker which will result in worker loyalty and motivation. Japanese companies are more realistic. They already have worker loyalty due to loyalty to the group, and they have motivation through the power and authority of management. Lifetime employment is used to preserve the power, control, and authority of management.

[39]David E. Sanger, "Layoffs and Factory Closings Shaking the Japanese Psyche," *The New York Times,* March 3, 1993, p. A1
[40]Sullivan, *Invasion of the Salarymen,* p. 119.
[41]Ouchi, *Theory Z,* p. 15.

Some trends indicate that, as growth of Japanese companies slows down or actually declines, lifetime employment is becoming more difficult to maintain. The system now depends on a large force of "temporary" workers, "voluntary" retirements for workers aged forty-five to fifty-five, and foisting unneeded workers on subsidiaries or affiliates.

WORKING AT YOUR DESK CAN BE HAZARDOUS TO YOUR HEALTH
The outcast boy who played baseball with us in Japan was not an isolated case. The problem of white-collar workers dying on the job due to overwork, called *karoshi* in Japan, is an increasingly severe problem. Sitting at your desk can be deadly.

An alarming number of salarymen are dying on the job. A researcher who has been tracking this trend, Dr. Kiyoyasu Arikawa, said that the number of *karoshi* deaths leaped from 10 in 1969 to about 150 in 1987.[42] The number is certainly much higher. Japan's labor ministry received 777 applications in 1989 for compensation because of sudden death at work. In 1986, the number of applications was 500.[43] The labor ministry has applied a very stringent standard for considering someone as a *karoshi* case. The worker must have worked twice the normal number of hours for seven days without rest or must have worked three times the normal number of hours the day before collapsing. *Karoshi* is more likely to be due to long working hours over a long period of time. Under the ministry's standards, very few deaths are *karoshi*. Victim groups estimate 10,000 *karoshi* deaths per year.[44]

Japanese white-collar workers say they are overworked and fear the consequences. Fukoku Life Insurance surveyed 500 salaried workers on their working conditions,[45] and the results were eye-opening for those who may have trouble keeping their eyes open because of overwork. A full 80% of the salaried workers responded that they were overworked, and more than 40% were worried that they might die because of the rigors of their jobs.

A Type Z corporation is supposed to relieve the stress at the office, reduce competition among the employees, create an environment of cooperation and friendship on the job, eliminate authority, increase motivation, and foster creativity. The Fukoku Life Insurance survey indicated that very few of these objectives were being met. About 70% of those surveyed said they felt "stressed" at work. Nearly two-

---

[42]Mari Yamaguchi, "Over 40% of Employees Fear Dying from Overwork, Insurance Poll Finds," *Japan Times,* December 1, 1990, p. 3.
[43]Ibid.
[44]Teresa Watanabe, "When Life on the Job Is Literally Killing You," *Los Angeles Times,* January 14, 1992, p. H6.
[45]Yamaguchi, "Over 40% of Employees Fear Dying."

thirds said they took less than ten days of vacation a year. There were two main reasons for not taking a vacation: 55% said they would be even more overworked from work pile-up during vacation, and 20.4% expressed fears of falling behind their colleagues, and thus their competitors, for advancement within the company.

The fatigue these employees feel at work affects their motivation and creativity on the job. In the survey, 44.4% said they "feel constant fatigue," and 85.3% said that "they just want to sleep more" to alleviate the fatigue. Because of this stress and overwork, 23.3% have "no creativity and motivation," and 23.3% feel "a frequent desire to call in sick."

What about cooperation among colleagues and the paternal management style? When asked about their relationships with their bosses and colleagues, 56.6% said that these relationships were bothersome.

One of the things that struck us when we went to Japan and traveled on the trains was the look on the faces of the salarymen. Most of them had a permanent clench to their jaws. Their bodies appeared to be wound up tight. They would seldom talk to others. When not asleep on the train, most would look straight ahead with no change in expression. Some would read a newspaper or a comic book. The women looked as if they were having more fun and enjoying themselves. Maybe there was some truth to the official's observation that Japanese women were not trying hard enough to get salaried positions.

Toshitsugu Yagi, an advertising executive, was a victim of *karoshi* at age 43. Before he collapsed at home, he wrote of the stress of his job. "Can't it be said that today's armies of corporate workers are in fact slaves in every sense of the word? They are bought for money. Their work is measured in working hours. They are powerless to defy their superiors. And these corporate slaves of today don't even share the simplest pleasures that forced laborers of ages past enjoyed: the right to sit down at the dinner table with their families."[46]

Sullivan claims that Japanese companies do not really operate under the ideals of Theory Z. Instead, Theory Z has become a convenient explanation for Americans to describe how transplanted Japanese companies treat their workers in the United States. It is merely a positive image intended to eliminate the need for more complex explanations which might have negative connotations.

Ouchi explains that Theory Z received its name because it follows from management theories X and Y. The symbol Z also has a larger significance in Japanese history. Before the sneak attack on Pearl Harbor, while the Japanese ambassador was negotiating in Washington, D.C., the commander of the Japanese strike force used the symbol Z to indicate that the Americans at Pearl Harbor were unaware of the impending attack and that it should proceed as planned. As indicated by the writ-

---

[46]Watanabe, "When Life on the Job Is Literally Killing You."

ings of Yagi, some of the workers still feel they are being treated as soldiers in the corporate war. They are dying in the battle as the symbol Z is raised to signify the economic attack.

WHAT CAN WE LEARN?   American companies have many problems and, on the surface, it appears that Japanese companies may have the answers. American companies and the unions often have an adversarial relationship, which impedes the ability to manufacture quality products. In Japan, the companies and the unions cooperate with each other. Insensitivity is indicated when American companies lay off people from their jobs. Japanese employees at the largest Japanese corporations enjoy lifetime employment and do not have to fear job losses. Employees at American companies may feel isolated from the other workers. Japanese companies promote a family atmosphere. Authors of popular books, such as William Ouchi, have claimed that Japanese corporations can be a model for American corporations in solving these problems.

American companies need to confront and solve their problems. Looking to Japan will not provide many answers and could actually cause other kinds of problems. To understand the management of Japanese corporations, one has only to think about how power, authority, and control can be exercised.

The Japanese corporations and unions do cooperate for the very simple reason that they are essentially the same entity. The union has given up any power in exchange for the benefits of lifetime employment and the overall concept of cooperation. My host and colleague was a negotiator for the union before getting his present job. Since he was part of management and not part of an independent union, his performance assessment and future advancement depended on how well he represented management and not the workers he was supposed to represent. In the Flat Rock Mazda plant, the union became part of management. The workers complained that the union ignored health problems of the workers caused by bad working conditions because the union was representing the company instead of the workers. The challenge for American companies is how to maintain separate unions, which will look after the workers, while management and the unions can cooperate on the important issues. Japanese companies have taken one extreme, but this is an unacceptable model for American companies.

The American practice of laying off large number of workers in bad times causes all kinds of hardships, including plummeting morale among the remaining workers. Japanese companies offer lifetime employment. Many Americans, though, may be reluctant to give up the freedom to change jobs in exchange for the security of lifetime employment. Even if this loss of freedom was acceptable to American workers, the system would still not work in the United States because it relies on the cooperation of all companies not to tamper with other workers and not to hire ones who have decided to leave a company. Perhaps the European model would be more acceptable to American businesses. In economic downturns in Europe, many workers reduce the number of hours worked rather than face layoffs.

The Japanese corporation can act like a family. To many people, this atmosphere is very enticing. Japanese workers have few individual responsibilities. This provides a kind of freedom. For Americans, however, this kind of freedom may seem to be actually a lack of freedom. The company provides, but also reduces, the kinds of personal freedoms and liberties that many Americans take for granted. A corporation as family can be insensitive to outsiders, such as members of other races or women who demand better job roles. American corporations must work within a diverse society, providing equal opportunities for workers regardless of race or sex. Diversity is probably one of the greatest strengths of American companies, and this strength should be encouraged. Japanese corporations see diversity as a weakness.

"THEY JUST PASS OUT"   I was in the local gym during a heat wave and I said casually to a fellow weight lifter, "It's too hot to work out."

The person replied, "Yes, we get really hot at work, also."

"Where do you work?" I inquired.

"I work at Subaru-Isuzu." This was the transplanted Japanese auto company in town. "It gets really hot on the line. They don't have air conditioning."

"Is that typical—for manufacturing companies not to have air conditioning?" I asked. The person did not know, because this was the first manufacturing job he had held.

"Do you have people getting heat exhaustion?" I asked.

"Yes," was the reply. "They carry people out all the time. They just pass out on the line."

"Oh, you're kidding," I said incredulously.

"It happened to me last year," he added.

"What did you do?" I asked.

"They carried me down to the clinic and I had to drink liquid with electrolytes in it. It was air conditioned in there. I got to stay there for an hour. I could've gone home, but then I would have lost my bonus and ruined my attendance marks. So, I just went back on the line."

I looked sympathetic.

"It's not as great working out there at Suburu-Isuzu as everybody thought it would be. But I like the money and I need the job. It doesn't do any good to complain. The bosses don't care."

Myth 8:
Japanese Productivity
Is Higher than U.S. Productivity

In Japan every morning as I came to work, I passed by a small conference room on my way to my desk. One morning I noticed a group of about fifteen men in the conference room, all wearing black or gray suits, white shirts, and red ties. Although it was very early and the room was overcrowded, everyone seemed very attentive, and the meeting was in full progress. At 11:30 I passed the room again on my way to lunch. By this time half the participants had wandered off, and the other half had their heads on the table and were fast asleep.

I had heard so much about the productive Japanese worker that I was looking forward to seeing this phenomenon for myself. The reality was different from what I had expected. My personal experiences in Japan indicated that very little work got done during a day, the employees spent much time socializing on the job, parts of the day were spent asleep at the desk, and some work—especially for new employees—can best be described as meaningless busywork. Where did my perceptions of efficient and productive Japanese workers come from? Most of them came from the American media. Some of them came from Japan, where officials complain about lazy American workers. The perceptions did not, however, come from facts and figures, because these indicate that the opposite is true: The overall productivity of Japanese workers lags far behind that of American workers.

ASLEEP AT THE DESK   Before going to Japan I read an interesting book by Michael Lewis called *Liar's Poker*. In the book, Lewis talks about high-pressure jobs at the Wall Street firm of Salomon Brothers. In Salomon Brothers' trainee classrooms, prospective Wall Street traders are put through an intensive program in which performance determines whether an employee gets one of the good jobs or one of the bad jobs. Pressure is high and stress is a problem, but how one handles the classroom instruction is considered to be an indication of how one will handle the stress and pressure of the real job.

One group of trainees was different, however. Of course, the six Japanese trainees did not feel the pressure to perform that the American employees did. Lewis describes their performance like this:

"All six of them sat in the front row and slept. Their heads rocked back and forth and on occasion fell over to one side, so that their cheeks ran parallel to the floor. . . . Their leader was a man named Yoshi. Each morning and afternoon the back-row boys made bets on how many minutes it would take Yoshi to fall asleep. . . . A small cheer would go up in the back row when Yoshi crashed, partly because someone had just won a pile of money. . . ."[1]

Being asleep at one's desk seems to be an acceptable practice in Japan. When I was there, I could usually find someone asleep, especially in the early afternoon. I have never seen anyone asleep at a desk in an American company.

One of the first things that strikes a visitor to Japan is the ease with which people, especially businessmen, can sleep. Riding on the subways in hot cars, with little room to move, businessmen who manage to find seats, close their eyes, and seem to be sleeping. In some public places, such as on the bullet train, it looked as though the entire male population of Japan was tired and trying to get some sleep.

They probably were tired. Indisputably, Japanese workers are at work for longer hours than their American or German counterparts. Japanese workers average 2173 hours work per year compared to Americans' 1890 hours and Germans' 1688 hours. I tried to work a regular 8:30-to-5:30 day, because more hours would be unproductive. Most of the workers in my building stayed until at least 9:00, and some later, on a regular basis.

What were they doing during these 12-hour days? Some of the time was spent sleeping, some of it spent socializing. Socializing with fellow workers is very impor-

---

[1]Michael Lewis, *Liar's Poker* (New York: W. W. Norton, 1989), p. 44.

tant in Japan to cement team cohesiveness and foster cooperation. For advancement in a company, the people you know, especially the person who is your mentor, are more important than what you know. Many companies require their employees to entertain other business associates after work which increases the length of their workday.

The long workdays can be very difficult on family life. For instance, Mr. Tanaka, one of the husbands in our apartment building, made a business trip to the United States. When I am away on business, my wife has a difficult time taking care of the children and the house. So my wife asked Mrs. Tanaka if she needed any help. "No," was her reply. In fact, she said that it was easier with Mr. Tanaka away. With him gone, she did not have to fix a special meal for him every night at 10:00 when he returned home from work. Of course, when he came home the children were already in bed.

Japanese fathers rarely have time to play with their children. Sometimes we would see a father with his children in the toy department of a large department store on a Sunday afternoon, but often he would be very inattentive, almost ready to fall asleep. Play areas at these stores had conveniently placed benches where numerous fathers and grandfathers could always be found nodding off.

One positive side for the economy of the long work hours is the flourishing business in energy drinks and other stimulants which keep people awake on the job. I could go down to the company store and buy "Jolt" cola if I felt I needed a push to stay awake. Hot or iced coffee was an important part of any work area. Mild narcotics were to be found in all kinds of strange energy drinks which are readily available in vending machines throughout Japan. In fact, tonic drinks containing alcohol, caffeine, nicotine, and even cobra extract or essence of seal are now a $1 billion market in Japan.[2] More workers turn to health drinks to battle fatigue—25% of the those polled—than turn to exercise, eating a healthy diet, or taking a sick leave.

The long hours on the job help to contribute to the nonproductivity of the workforce. A well known relationship in psychological research is that as fatigue increases, a person's performance and productivity falls off fairly rapidly. I always felt that I could get more accomplished in an 8-hour day of hard work than my Japanese colleagues could accomplish in their 12-hour days. With a relaxing evening at home, I was refreshed for the next day. I don't know how the Japanese businessmen got anything accomplished at work with their schedules.

However, it appeared that the men preferred this schedule. Their best friends were at work, so they could hang out with them. Their wives expected them to be at work long hours, so the wives could hang out with their friends at the apartment. The men were also free from diaper detail and other household chores.

---

[2]David Lazarus, "That Peppy Potion Packs Quite a Punch," Japan Times, September 30, 1990, p. 18.

WORK FOR WORK'S SAKE   In the Japanese school system, the most successful students are the ones who spend the most time memorizing facts. Students are taught to do school work so they can learn to work hard, rather than learning strategies about how to learn or developing a lifelong curiosity about things. The things they are learning are of little consequence. How hard they are working and the number of hours they work are more important. This attitude is transferred to the workplace. In a Japanese business, the most important thing is to appear to work hard by working long hours. Working hard or working productively is not the issue. "Don't work hard, work smart," is an American corporate saying, not a Japanese one.

An example of work for work's sake in the school system will illustrate this point. In Japan, all students must take at least six years of English instruction. This language instruction consists mostly of vocabulary training or learning grammar rules; conversation is not part of the instruction. Most professionals or businesspeople can read English, but cannot converse in it.

One of the strange experiences for Americans walking in Japan is to be bombarded with cries of "Har-ro" from the school children you pass on the sidewalks. At first, we didn't know what this meant. After a while, though, we figured out that the school children were practicing their English on us and were good-naturedly saying "Hello."

Upon further investigation, we discovered that the Japanese teachers themselves often refer to the kind of English taught in Japan as "Japlish." The official guide on how to pronounce English words provided to Japanese English teachers does not correspond very well with Western pronunciation. Thus, "hello" is taught as "har-ro." Students are expected to learn the official Japanese pronunciation for English, the Japlish, instead of the pronunciation used by native English speakers. When an American English instructor in Japan tried to correct the pronunciation of an English word by a Japanese English instructor, the American was reprimanded that the Japanese way was the official way to pronounce the word and any other possibilities would not be considered.

To a casual Western observer, this kind of attitude might be incorrectly labeled arrogance. More properly, this attitude reflects Japanese values of learning and hard work. To Japanese students and teachers, what is learned is secondary to the amount of work that goes into the learning. Whether the pronunciation of English words is correct to Americans is unimportant compared to the attitude shown by students in learning what they were supposed to learn. For Americans, determining that they had spent hours learning the wrong thing would be considered a waste of time.

Comparing productivity in the workplace between Japan and other countries is difficult because of the different attitudes toward productivity. In Japan, working long hours on what Americans would consider irrelevant work is productive, because it is a reflection of an attitude or devotion which may be important on more relevant tasks. To an American, this would be nonproductive work. There is truth to both of these views.

CONNECTING THE DOTS   Gary Katzenstein was an American who went to Japan to work for Sony Corporation armed with an MBA and a master's degree in computer science. It was not a good fit. In Japan, the kind of university degree you have is meaningless, because the company is more interested in the status of the university you graduated from than any special knowledge you may have acquired in school. Training will be provided by the company, so new employees are expected to come into the job with a willingness to work rather than a willingness to apply what has been learned in school. Katzenstein figured his degrees were credentials so he would be given meaningful jobs; his Japanese employers cared little about his special knowledge and were more worried about his pliability on the job.

Katzenstein was surprised that the kind of work he was given at Sony was meaningless busywork. One of his jobs was to connect the dots from data points. He describes the task like this:

"Day after day I plotted points. As soon as I finished one graph, Ikeda-san produced another nearly indistinguishable set of data.

"I plotted points like a kid connecting dots and delivered the graphs to Ikeda-san and never saw the graphs again. Ten days of plodding point plotting."[3]

Point plotting like this could be done more easily by using a computer and spreadsheet software which is available on most any low-cost computer. A high-tech company like Sony should have had technology to perform this function.

This kind of work system is good for fostering teamwork and loyalty to the company. It is not a good system for achieving productive work. The emphasis on teamwork and loyalty, to the detriment of productivity with meaningful work, is one of the reasons that the productivity of Japanese office workers is so low. Japanese companies are willing to make this trade-off.

Katzenstein did not last very long at Sony. Like many Americans, he was trying to define the importance of his job by the meaningfulness and value of his work. His employers were judging his work according to teamwork and loyalty. He was sent to the company psychologist and given a battery of tests. Following their analyses, he was fired.

---

[3]Gary Katzenstein, *Funny Business* (Englewood Cliffs, NJ: Prentice Hall, 1989), p. 140.

OVERGROWN AND UNDERUTILIZED   The weeds around the apartment buildings were too high. In early September, the weeds were about 3 feet tall and looked as if they had not been mown in several months. Japan has a temperate climate with abundant rainfall to sustain the growth of vegetation. The grounds had no landscaping, no flower beds, and no strategic placement of trees to provide any beauty. If you wanted beauty, you went to one of the famous gardens. That is the picture of landscaping most foreigners take with them from Japan. We were surprised at the lack of landscaping and upkeep of grounds at other locations such as schools, universities, city parks, or apartment buildings.

On this particular day, we were told that all the neighbors were expected to help with the yardwork around the buildings. This event happened three times a year: spring, summer, and fall. Between these three yardwork days, the weeds were allowed to grow because there was no professional staff to take care of the grounds. Everybody in the apartments was expected to pitch in on these three days to take care of the yardwork.

We were anxious to see how this operation would be carried out. In the United States, we can buy Honda lawnmowers. We personally have a Japanese-made engine in our John Deere lawn tractor. We anticipated seeing even more efficient Japanese-made equipment utilized by the people in the apartment building on this clean-up day.

The beauty of the yardwork on this day was not in the equipment which was used, but in the teamwork of the apartment dwellers and the fact that everybody knew his or her assigned role and performed it with gusto. Instead of using lawnmowers or tractors, the men used individual "weed whackers," scythes, or clippers to cut down the overgrowth. The women followed their designated weed whacker to pick up the clippings and place them in plastic bags.

About 40 people were needed to perform the yardwork on about 1 acre of land. It took them around 4 hours to do the work, or 160 labor-hours overall. A lawn tractor with a self-bagging attachment could mow a 1-acre yard in about 45 minutes.

The yardwork was followed by a barbecue for all the workers. Everybody was involved and everybody had a good time. For the Americans, the neighborliness, the cooperation, and the sense of community was certainly enticing. Feeling involved and being part of a group is comforting, and we have missed this sense of belonging since leaving Japan.

The team yardwork was not designed to be efficient; it was designed to foster cooperation, to get to know your neighbors, and to develop a community spirit. It certainly accomplished these goals. This type of activity is similar to other Japanese community cooperation efforts. School children help to clean their own schools by emptying the waste cans, washing the floors, and wiping the chalkboards. One day each spring, the communities along the beach get together to clean the beaches.

Another byproduct of these group activities is that they save money. The company that owns the apartment building did not have to purchase expensive lawn equipment or hire someone to do the yardwork. The schools do not have to hire janitors, although the children have to spend longer days in school so they can perform their cleaning duties. City governments do not have to buy equipment or hire people to clean the beaches.

This emphasis on teamwork and cooperation over productivity translates to businesses also. To save money, businesses do not buy much equipment to support their workers, because they believe that teamwork and loyalty to the company can overcome unsupported working conditions. Computer support is not provided to make people more efficient. Phones are not always provided to all employees who needed them. Work is done by teams working long hours.

Once during a 3-day period at work, the company officials determined that they needed to save money so they decided to lower the temperature in the building to 55 degrees. It saved money, but it was difficult to do any work because the fingers were too cold to move over a keyboard. Everybody was in the same boat, though, and it emphasized to the employees not to waste money.

Sometimes the community spirit of these clean-up days is overinterpreted by outsiders. Westerners sometimes think that because the community is responsible for cleaning up, the community will feel responsible for maintaining it the rest of the time to reduce the amount of work. This is not the case. The Japanese have the same problems Americans have in keeping city streets and city parks clean. The beach closest to our apartment had a 5-foot wide swath of garbage at the tide line. People feel no hesitation in throwing garbage out of car windows. Nobody makes any attempt to clean up the streets, and city crews are not available to do it. Like many things in Japan, things are compartmentalized and everything has its day. People clean up on the clean-up days, and apparently do not think about it at other times.

BATTLEGROUND SUPPORT   The Japanese people have strong beliefs about their strengths and weaknesses. Beliefs about their strengths are taught to them throughout their school days—when they learn what it means to be Japanese—and through corporate cultures. One has only to look at recent and past history to find clues to present corporate behavior. The Japanese are proud of their heritage and their achievements. Their past successes are blueprints for current endeavors. Sometimes, however, their traditions expose weaknesses.

During World War II, some senior Japanese military leaders—such as Admiral Yamamoto, who planned and carried out the attack on Pearl Harbor—knew that Japan had little chance to win the war. The popular opinion, though, was that the particular Japanese characteristics—spirit, discipline, loyalty, hard work, ability to endure hardships, and teamwork—could win any battle against an enemy who did not possess these attributes. With these attributes, little else was needed.

In many cases in the Pacific war, the Japanese soldier was sent into battle with little more support than those personal attributes inherent in being Japanese. Whereas each American soldier in the field had 4 tons of equipment backing him up, each Japanese soldier had only 2 pounds of support equipment.[4] The Japanese soldier in the field also had very little manpower support. This support, which included logistics, transportation, communications, maintenance, and medical support, was essential to keeping the soldiers in fighting condition. Each American soldier in the field had eighteen soldiers behind the lines to supply support services. The other Western armies had an average of about eight to one. The Japanese army had a one-to-one ratio.[5] The Japanese soldier had an incredible ability to endure hardship and an incredible sense of loyalty to his country. The military used this as a crutch. In many battles, though, as many Japanese soldiers died of starvation as died in battle. Many were severely diminished in their fighting ability by malnutrition, because the military did not provide enough support to its soldiers.

Using the Pacific war as an analogy for corporate practices, the soldiers preferred those weapons in which their loyalty and teamwork could be demonstrated. Surprisingly, at least to outside observers, the weapon of choice for the Japanese soldier during World War II was the sword.[6] This sword had a long tradition in Japanese history as the weapon of the samurai warriors. "Lay to heart the saying of an ancient warrior: 'My sword is my soul,'" stated the Japanese Field Service Code. The sword was the manifestation of fighting spirit and loyalty to the country. Teamwork and cooperation among the soldiers were demonstrated in "banzai" charges against the enemy. Swords or bayonets on rifles were little use against machines guns, tanks, and the other firepower of the Allies.

These same characteristics still operate in the Japanese corporate world. Management believes that company spirit, discipline, loyalty to the company, long hours of work, ability to endure hardships, and teamwork will overcome any obstacle. They place reliance on these characteristics instead of providing equipment and other support systems. As examples, the company where I worked provided no centralized maintenance for the computer systems. Each group was supposed to support its own computers. For communications, not everybody had a telephone. People were supposed to share phones. The temperature was kept low to save money. The researchers did not have the equipment support one would find in a typical American research institute.

---

[4]Meirion Harries and Susie Harries, *Soldiers of the Sun* (New York: Random House, 1991), p. 348.
[5]Ibid., p. 369.
[6]Ibid., p. 350.

Just as a modern army requires a modern support system in the field, the modern worker requires a modern support system to be productive. I sometimes wonder how much more productive Japanese workers would be if they were supported better. The prospects would not be good for American competitiveness. But from the perspective of Japanese managers, providing this support would destroy those personal characteristics so important to the perceived success of the company. Demonstrations of loyalty and company spirit could not be displayed if it was too easy to be loyal. The ability to endure hardships could not be demonstrated if the temperature in the building was always at the same comfortable level. Hard work could not be exhibited if the employees used computers to make their work easier. These attributes, and demonstrations of the attributes, are essential in the Japanese corporation to reinforce the personal attributes important to success. In most cases, though, this practice runs counter to producing a highly efficient work place. Such is the paradox of productivity in a Japanese corporation.

(PICTURE) WORD PROCESSING   Performing word processing tasks using the Japanese language is different from typing in English or other Western languages. In English, all words are composed of the 26 letters, which can be represented easily on a keyboard. In Japanese, the main alphabet using the *kanji* system is based on picturelike characters. To learn to read at a very basic level, one must be able to recognize 2000 *kanji* characters; to be highly literate, a person needs to be able to recognize 10,000 characters. Representing this number of characters on a keyboard is not feasible. Because the characters are not composed of basic features, the *kanji* characters cannot be constructed from smaller units. To make the problem worse, the same pronunciation is used for several *kanji* characters.

Performing word processing tasks using the *kanji* characters is problematic. To alleviate this problem and related ones, three other alphabets have been developed for the Japanese language which are based on a single character representation for a syllable. These alphabets are called the *hiragana*, *katakana*, and *romaji* alphabets. The Japanese language contains about 40 syllables, and so words can be constructed from these syllables in these alphabets. The problem is that none of these alphabets has been accepted completely, so written communication still requires the use of the *kanji* alphabet.

Japanese companies have developed word processing equipment to construct *kanji* characters. For this system, the keyboard uses characters from one or more of the alternative alphabets so that all the characters can be represented. The typist enters the syllables of a word using the characters on the keyboard. Since the same syllables can be used in several *kanji* characters, the system searches a database and determines the *kanji* characters that match the sound of the word. These *kanji* characters are then presented on the screen in a menu display. Typically, two to ten *kanji* characters will match the syllable sounds, and these are then presented in the menu from the most frequently used to the least frequently used. The typist must then choose the correct *kanji* character from the menu display. This character is then inserted into the text and the typist must continue this process for all the rest of the words in the text.

Japanese word processing is a very cumbersome process. Many people prefer not to use computers for word processing, writing the characters by hand instead. The archaic Japanese writing system makes information very difficult to access and disseminate. It also is a huge impediment to productivity for any task dealing with information or writing. I have modeled the amount of time it takes to word process using a Japanese system and an English system. By calculating the movement times of the fingers and the cognitive processing time for reading the characters, a Japanese picture word processing system is five to thirteen times slower than English word processing.[7]

WELFARE SYSTEM   While driving to work one morning with my Japanese colleague and friend, we passed a man in the company parking lot who was directing traffic. The man performed this work with gusto, as is usually the case in Japan, although this same function could be performed as easily by a simple stop sign, a stoplight, or better design of the parking lot. The job was superfluous.

Mr. Uchimura looked at the man and commented, "This is Japan's welfare system. The companies hire more people than needed, just to provide people with jobs. We are trying to do the same thing for Americans by building plants there and providing jobs for Americans."

This was a good sentiment and a good justification of Japanese business practices. I pointed out to Mr. Uchimura, however, that Japanese companies are very careful to locate plants precisely where they are not needed to provide a welfare system for Americans. High-labor plants are invariably located in rural areas where there are few unions or ethnic groups, and where employment rates are already high. As an example, a Subaru-Isuzu auto plant was opened in our hometown of Lafayette, a conservative town that has an anti-union atmosphere, few minorities, and an unemployment rate among the lowest in the country. Because they can usually offer better wages in rural areas than local companies, these transplants hire mostly skilled workers who have already been trained and employed by other American companies.

---

[7]R. E. Eberts, *Solutions Manual for User Interface Design* (Englewood Cliffs, NJ: Prentice Hall, 1994), pp. 19–21.

I remember when the plant opened a few years ago, I met an older man and his wife on the Purdue campus. He had come from out of town because he had heard that the auto plant was hiring workers and he needed a job. The dejection on his face will stay with me: He said that the hiring people told him he wasn't smart enough to work there. He told me he was willing to work hard if he only had a job. The vision of this man's face flashed through my mind as my friend was telling me about the Japanese-style welfare system for American workers.

Japanese companies have opened many plants in the United States, providing many Americans with jobs. In 1994, though, we ran over a $60 billion deficit with Japan. Each billion dollars in deficit represents the loss of 20,000 jobs. Thus a $60 billion deficit represents a loss of over 1 million jobs. Unlike a deficit with an undeveloped country, the jobs we are losing to Japan are usually the higher-paying manufacturing jobs or professional jobs. We are losing that battle even with the transplanted companies.

My friend was right about a couple of things. Japanese companies have too many workers. One estimate put the number of excess workers in Japanese companies at 5 to 6 million.[8] In the big companies alone, the ones usually considered to be the world-class competitors, an estimated 1 million redundant workers are being carried.[9] However, if Japanese companies did not provide a welfare system, no one else in Japan would. The government offers very little in terms of a safety net for workers without a job.

FACTS AND FIGURES   When I talk to my industrial engineering class and ask the students which country's workers are the most productive, they usually say Japanese workers. Some say German workers. Very few say American workers. The facts indicate that American workers are much more productive than workers elsewhere in the world.

The facts of productivity are revealing. Overall, American workers are 30% more productive than Japanese workers. Even in manufacturing, Americans are 28% more productive. Most people know that Japanese farmers are notoriously unproductive, 52% less productive than American farmers, but few people realize that other industries and services exhibit an even wider disparity: rubber and plastics, construction, finance, insurance, and real estate.[10]

---

[8]Hori Shintaro, "Fixing Japan's White Collar Economy: A Personal View," *Harvard Business Review*, November-December 1993, pp. 157-172.
[9]Michio Uchido, "Japanese Workers Growing More Independent, Self-Motivated," *Tokyo Business Today*, April 1993, pp. 56-59.
[10]Myron Magnet, "The Truth About the American Worker," *Fortune*, May 4, 1992, p. 50.

The United States excels in high-technology business productivity. In biotechnology, computers, and software, the United States has a significant lead in productivity over Japan and other countries.[11] In retail productivity, the United States excels overall with a 2:1 edge over Japan.

Japan is even with the United States or slightly better in productivity in consumer electronics and automobile manufacturing. When looking at these figures, though, one has to realize the differences between American and Japanese automobile manufacturers. The Japanese auto companies are mostly assembly operations, relying on suppliers for more parts than their American counterparts do. When discussing just-in-time (JIT) techniques in Chapter 6, the auto manufacturers' practice of passing many of the costs to suppliers was discussed. Using a more equitable comparison, comparing Japanese auto companies and their suppliers with American car companies, in terms of the manufacture of the same percentage of the car, Japanese auto companies are actually less efficient than American companies.[12] Harvard economist Dale Jorgenson concludes: "The Japanese work force is very high quality, but not as good as ours, measured in terms of the quality of the worker per standardized hour."[13]

Productivity can also be compared in terms of the amount of goods and services produced in a year. A report by the McKinsey Global Institute, which compared productivity of workers in different countries, showed that the average American worker in 1990 produced $49,600 worth of goods and services.[14] This can be compared to $44,200 of goods and services for the average German worker, $38,200 for the average Japanese worker, and $37,100 for the average British worker. In comparable work, the Japanese worker is closer to the British worker than the American worker.

Similar results were found by the U.S. Department of Labor in an examination of the gross domestic product per employed person for different countries in 1990 and previous years.[15] In 1990, for those countries studied, the order in overall productivity as measured by the amount of goods and services produced were: United States ($45,165), Canada ($41,996), France ($40,405), Belgium ($40,056), Germany ($35,736), Japan ($34,711), Austria ($33,623), Denmark ($30,985), and Korea ($19,550). Overall, Japan was in sixth place in terms of productivity. As a comparison, Japan with its current productivity is at a level to that of the United States in 1963, when each U.S. worker produced $34,656 worth of goods and services.

[11]Tom Peters, "Surprise: America Is Productive," *Incentive,* February 1993, p. 19.
[12]Magnet, "The Truth About the American Worker," p. 50.
[13]Ibid., p. 50
[14]Sylvia Nasar, "U.S. Tops in Productivity Study," *Chicago Tribune,* October 14, 1992, p. 3-2.
[15]Office of Productivity, U.S. Department of Labor, Bureau of Labor Statistics, *Productivity Statistics* (Washington, D.C.: U.S. Government Printing Office, July 1991).

Edward Wolff, an economist at New York University, broke down the figures for different sectors in the economies of the United States, Japan, and Germany.[16] Eight sectors were compared: mining, oil and gas drilling; utilities; transportation and communication; manufacturing; finance, insurance, and real estate; agriculture, forestry, and fisheries; wholesale and retail sales; hotels, and restaurants; and construction. The United States led in productivity in all categories except for finance, insurance, and real estate, for which Germany held the lead. In the important manufacturing area, a U.S. worker produced $66,900 of goods, a Japanese worker produced $52,200, and a German worker produced $38,200. Overall, 94% of Americans work in industries that are more productive than Japan's.[17]

Statistics from Japan also support higher productivity for American workers. Japan's Productivity Center finds similar results to those reported above.[18] This center found that U.S. and British workers produced 24% more than Japanese workers in the manufacturing sector. The gap is even larger when productivity is calculated by work hours. Calculated this way, Japanese workers produced just 61% of the value of goods that American workers do. When broken down into 21 manufacturing sectors, the United States led in 17 of them, including the manufacture of motor vehicles. The American worker led in food, textile, apparel, lumber and wood, furniture, pulp and paper, printing and publishing, petroleum, rubber and plastics, leather, stone and glass, fabricated metal, machinery, transportation equipment, instruments, and miscellaneous including toys. The Japanese worker led in chemicals, iron and steel, nonferrous metals, and electrical machinery.

REASONS FOR HIGHER PRODUCTIVITY   There are many
reasons for the low productivity of Japanese workers compared to American workers. Some have been considered in this chapter: emphasis on nonproductive teamwork, working long hours in a state of fatigue, little support in capital outlays, and consensus decision making—which could more accurately be called slow decision making. Japanese companies put a higher priority on these things than on productivity. In addition, the American workforce is better educated. About 62% of American high school graduates attend college,[19] including 48% of African-Americans and 53% of Hispanic-Americans.[20] This can be compared to the 37.4% of Japanese high

---

[16]Edward Wolff and David Dollar, *Competitiveness, Convergence and International Specialization* (Cambridge, MA: MIT Press, 1990).
[17]Tom Peters, "Brains, Benefits and Biotechnology," *Chicago Tribune*, August 23, 1993, p. 4-4.
[18]Teresa Watanabe, "Americans Lazy? Not So, Says a Japanese Study," *Los Angeles Times*, February 4, 1992, p. A12
[19]U.S. Department of Education, *Digest of Educational Statistics.* (Washington, D.C.: U.S. Government Printing Office, October, 1993), p. 185.

school graduates who attend college.[20] Because of the population differences between the two countries, this means that in sheer numbers more than three times as many Americans attend college as do Japanese.

Another important factor in service industry productivity is that American companies have invested heavily in computer support for their employees. Between 1981 and 1991 American companies invested $862 billion in computer hardware alone and possibly triple that amount if one includes software, cables, and other accessories.[22] As this technology was introduced, however, productivity dipped because the new technology often existed alongside the old technology and workers had to learn how to use the new machines. This short-term dip in productivity can be expected with the introduction of any new technology. This investment has finally started to pay off with increases in productivity and, because Japanese companies were unwilling to make the long-term commitment to computer support, the gap between American and Japanese companies should continue in the foreseeable future.

The McKinsey report cited above concluded that the United States enjoyed higher productivity than other countries because of the government's hands-off attitude toward managing businesses. Since the mid-1970s, airlines, telecommunications, trucking, and some parts of banking have been deregulated. Free trade and openness to foreign investment have also been important considerations in keeping productivity high. In contrast, Japanese government ministries have restricted free trade and limited foreign investment. The government has protected the mom-and-pop stores and restricted the more efficient Western-style retail outlets from operating in Japan. This policy results in low productivity in the retail segment. Free trade has been limited—agricultural products are a good example of this limitation—so Japanese companies do not have to compete with more efficient enterprises and consumers have to pay higher prices because productivity is so low.

American and Japanese workers have different attitudes toward work, according to a Japanese executive who has worked for both American and Japanese companies. Yoshi Noguchi, who grew up in Japan and worked for a Japanese computer company, is currently a director of an executive search and management consulting firm. "In the United States, the emphasis is on results," says Noguchi. "A worker who spends long hours at the office and doesn't accomplish the desired results is inefficient. . . . In Japan, the focus is on the process. Even if a worker cannot produce

[20]Harold W. Stevenson and James W. Stigler, "Elite Schools in US and Japan?," *Christian Science Monitor,* September 22, 1993, p. 12.
[21]Akira Arimoto, *"Japan"* in Walter Wiekremasinghe (ed.), *Handbook of World Education* (Houston, TX: American Collegiate Service, 1992), pp. 443–454.
[22]Myron Magnet, "Good News for the Service Economy," *Fortune,* May 3, 1993, p. 48.

results by putting in long hours, he or she is still respected as a hard worker. How one gets results is as important, if not more important, than achieving the results."[23] In Japan, it does not matter if the person is productive as long as he or she gives the appearance of working hard by working long hours.

Where did the myth of the highly productive Japanese worker and the lazy American worker come from? Sometimes people confuse productivity *gains* with actual productivity. Japanese industry had to start from total destruction after World War II, so there was plenty of room for improvement. For many years, the rate of improvement in productivity has been higher for Japanese workers. This is kind of like a baseball player with a .075 batting average improving 4% each year, compared to a 1% improvement for a batter with a .300 average (this comparison is valid because productivity in American companies was four or five times higher than in Japanese companies after the war[24]). The person with the higher batting average is still the better baseball player. In the 1980s, though, the productivity growth rates in the United States and Japan have been virtually identical.[25]

Japanese bureaucrats are quick to refer to Americans as lazy, which only helps to foster stereotypes unsupported by the facts. In February 1992, Kiichi Miyazawa, Prime Minister of Japan, told the Diet (the Japanese parliament): "I have long felt that [Americans] may have lacked the work ethic." After the remark was reported in the American media, Miyazawa "clarified" the comments by saying; "I had absolutely no intention of criticizing [American workers]." Remarks like this are acceptable if they are unintentional. One of the major Japanese newspapers, the *Asahi Shimbun*, editorialized that Miyazawa had been misinterpreted. "He did not say anything that is very provocative," the newspaper stated.[26]

The statements did not stop. Ten months later, Japanese Labor Minister Masakuni Murakami was quoted as saying that foreigners, other than Germans, do not work. "Foreigners do not work. That is why they are economically being left far behind Japan and Germany," Murakami told reporters.[27] "Sadly, there's been an erosion of the Puritan work ethic in America, a country which taught us so much," said Masao Kunihiro, a member of the Diet's Upper House.[28] A poll performed by *Time* magazine in 1992 revealed that 21% of the Japanese thought Americans were lazy

[23]Yoshi Noguchi, "I Was Not a Hard Worker Because I Didn't Stay Until 9 at Night," *Los Angeles Times,* February 2, 1992, p. 172.
[24]Magnet, *The Truth About the American Worker,* p. 50.
[25]Ibid.
[26]Merrill Goozner, "Japan Chides U.S. Media for Flap," *Chicago Tribune,* February 5, 1992, p. 1-5.
[27]"Foreigners Lazy, Japanese Labor Minister Says." Prodigy interactive personal service, December 14, 1992. Also reported by Associated Press, "Germans, Japanese Work More, Says New Tokyo Official," *Los Andeles Times,* p. A37.
[28]Barry Hillenbrand, "America in the Mind of Japan," *Time Magazine,* February 10, 1992, p. 22.

and only 15% thought Americans were hard working. On the other side of the ocean, only 4% of Americans thought Japanese were lazy and 94% thought they were hard working.[29]

Kabun Muto is a former minister of international trade and industry, who stated that Americans work only three good days a week, not Monday and Friday. "I think Americans should learn to work properly from Monday to Friday", said Muto.[30] Yohio Sakarauchi, the Japanese Speaker of the House, remarked that American workers are lazy. "American workers don't work hard enough. They don't work but demand high pay," said Sakarauchi.[31] "In the West, people avoid work if they could," says Shintaro Ishihara, famous for his diatribes in *The Japan That Can Say No*. "But Japanese people find virtue in working."[32]

The facts do not back up these kinds of statements. If lazy means that Americans do not work productively, then this is false according to the facts. If lazy is defined as too many American workers not working, the facts do not support this either: 66.3% of Americans work for pay, compared to 63% of Japanese.[33] If lazy means that Americans do not work long hours, then this is true only in comparison to Japan, not in comparison to other countries. Japanese workers work more hours than Americans, but Americans work more hours than Germans, yet these government leaders exclude Germans from the class of lazy foreigners.

Theory Z, the book by William Ouchi, may be a primary source for the myth that Japanese workers' productivity is higher than Americans'. On the back cover of the book, the summary exclaims: "At a time when Japanese productivity is the highest in the world, and productivity in the western nations is declining, there is clearly a great deal we can—and should—learn from Japan."[34] This claim of the highest productivity in the world is never mentioned, let alone supported, inside the book.

Inside the book, Ouchi qualifies the claim on the outside cover when he says that "productivity in Japan has increased at 400 percent the rate in the United States over the postwar years."[35] The reader should not confuse the growth rate with actual productivity. Because of the sharing of information and ideas, some convergence of productivity levels should be expected. Mathematical modeling for the years 1950 to 1979 shows that productivity in the United States is expanding faster than the rates at which other countries can catch up.[36] Other countries were actually converging on the productivity rate of Japan's economy slightly faster than Japan's

---

[29]Ibid., p. 20.
[30]Teresa Watanabe, "Japan's Premier Hits U.S. Workers," *Los Angeles Times*, February 4, 1992, p. A1.
[31]Noguchi, "I Was Not a Hard Worker."
[32]"Playboy Interview: Shintaro Ishihara," *Playboy*, October 1990, p. 76.
[33]Magnet, *The Truth About the American Worker*, p. 50.
[34]William Ouchi, *Theory Z* (New York: Avon, 1982).
[35]Ouchi, *Theory Z*, pp. 3-4.

productivity increased. To return to the baseball analogy, the baseball player with the .075 average is improving faster than the one with the .300 average, but this does not mean that this rate of improvement can continue indefinitely, nor does it mean that actual productivity is higher in Japan.

W. Edwards Deming also contributes to the myth. In Chapter 1 of his book, *Out of the Crisis*, Deming postulates many reasons for the poor productivity in American businesses: The poor quality of American products, which actually decreases productivity; emphasis on high-technology manufacturing processes instead of continuous-improvement low-tech solutions as advocated by Deming; poor management practices; and an emphasis on measuring productivity instead of improving it. The last point is important. "Unfortunately, however, figures of productivity in the United States do not help to improve productivity in the United States," proclaims Deming.[37] Measures of productivity are bad because they disprove his point that the United States lags Japan in productivity. Later in the book, Deming simply assumes that Japanese companies are more productive: "[T]he Japanese system is better adapted to greater productivity and to world trade than the American system."[38]

The rates of improvement in productivity were the same for Japan and the United States in the 1980s, which does not bode well for Japan. To expand the batting average example, a batter who started with a .075 batting average in 1945, and who improved at a rate of 4% a year, would be batting .283 in 1980. The .300 batter improving by 1% a year would be batting .398 in 1980. If the rate of improvement since 1980 for both batters was 2% a year, then the batter originally batting .075 would improve his .283 average from 1980 to .395 in 1995. The original .300 batter would be hitting .536, improving from .298 in 1980. The example shows that with the same rate of improvement, the difference between the batting averages expands from 115 points in 1980 to 141 points in 1995. This is the situation in which Japan finds itself for the 1990s and beyond.

In comparing the productivity of workers, the myth needs to be separated from the reality. Ouchi's book helps to support the myth about high productivity in Japan by making an unreferenced, unsubstatiated, and unsupported claim that Japan has the highest productivity in the world. Japan is not a good model to follow in terms of productivity, unless we want to move backwards. In 1990, Japan had only managed to reach an overall productivity level comparable to where the United States was in 1963. Examination of the facts would have nullified Deming's argument that the productivity of American workers is poor.

---

[36]William J. Baumol, Sue Ann Batey Blackman, and Edward N. Wolff, *Productivity and American Leadership* (Cambridge, MA: MIT Press, 1989), p. 102.
[37]W. Edwards Deming, *Out of the Crisis* (Cambridge, MA: MIT Press, 1982), p. 15.
[38]Ibid., p. 100.

Myth 9:
Japan Has Embraced Quality
Principles that Were Rejected
in Other Countries

Several Japanese quality techniques were examined in Chapters 5 and 6. The myth is that Japanese companies practice these techniques even though many were developed by American companies, such as AT&T, which developed statistical quality control (SQC). The premise of the myth is that American companies are not committed to quality because they even rejected quality techniques that were developed in their own country.

THIS BLOB OF BRAINPOWER   "Think of it as a large blob of brainpower," said my friend, Mr. Uchimura, as we were riding on the train to visit some colleagues at Keio University in Yokohama. As a visiting professor from Purdue, I had been asked to give a lecture at Keio. Because I had been standing on my feet in the crowded train for forty-five minutes in hot temperatures, I was thinking of other things. I was trying to determine which of the seated passengers might soon be leaving so that I could stand near them and get their seat as soon as one was vacated. I had missed out on all the other chances. Gathering up packages or glancing behind to the train station were universal signals of someone getting ready to leave, and therefore vacating the precious seat.

"At the end of World War II, the brainpower blob was this big in the U.S.," continued my friend. He pantomimed with his hands indicating a sphere slightly larger than the size of a person's head. "Japan's was smaller." The opposite fingers on his hands were now touching each other.

"Now it is just the opposite. Japan's blob of brainpower has increased in size." His hands indicated a sphere even larger apart than the one representing the brainpower of the United States at the end of the war. "But the brainpower has decreased in the U.S." The fingers on his opposite hands were almost touching each other.

I started thinking about this analogy. The analogy turned into an image of the two blobs of brainpower facing each other across the Pacific Ocean. The blob in Japan was so big that if it rolled across the ocean it would knock our small blob out of its way.

What had happened to our blob? Perhaps our biggest brainpower blob had been amassed at the defense companies as a response to the Cold War threat of the Soviet Union. I now pictured in my own head this huge blob of brainpower—bigger than any of the other blobs—facing a huge blob in the Soviet Union. The Soviet Union blob had fractured and scattered, but we still had our blob pointed in what was now the wrong direction, according to my friend's perspective.

I could picture many other scenes where brainpower was not contributing to the size of our blob, as seen from the perspective of those in Japan: the unemployed; the unmarried teenage mothers who drop out of school and never contribute to the brainpower blob; the Generation Xers who reject the stressful corporate life and personal responsibility for the freedom of working at video stores or fast-food restaurants; the educated pleasure seekers who had drifted into jobs such as ski instructors or white-water rafting guides. "With the storehouse of skills and knowledge contained in its millions of unemployed, and with the even more appalling underuse, misuse, and abuse of skills and knowledge in the army of employed people in all ranks in all industries, the United States may be today the most underdeveloped nation in the world," says W. Edwards Deming in his book, *Out of the Crisis*.[1] Our brainpower is scattered throughout the country, and some of it is just barely together in small masses.

We amassed most of our brainpower to build weapon systems aimed at defeating the blob of brainpower in the Soviet Union. In the meantime, Japan massed its brainpower, not to aim weapons at us, but to aim exportable products at the American markets. We never responded to that blob, and so many of the people we talked to in Japan saw us as a weak nation which had lost its way.

---

[1] W. Edwards Deming, *Out of the Crisis* (Cambridge, MA: MIT Press, 1982), p. 6.

The implication of this little conversation was clear. At one time the United States had much to teach the rest of the world. We taught Japan about quality, through the efforts of Deming and others. But while we were teaching, we forgot some of the lessons we had taught, and our blob of brainpower became smaller. Now we have to increase the size of our blob by relearning what we gave to others. This is the myth.

HANDBOOK EDITIONS AS A MEASURE OF QUALITY

Deming has been a very useful symbol to the quality myth makers. The myth states that Deming, having learned statistical quality control (SQC) from the master, Walter Shewhart, at Bell Labs in the 1930s, was rejected by companies in his own country, went to Japan to receptive audiences, helped Japanese companies make quality products, and returned to the United States to teach American companies what they had developed and then rejected in the years after World War II. It is interesting to note, though, that Deming does not state explicitly that American companies quit using SQC. On the other hand, the main reason for listening to Deming, and a main reason for the large, receptive audiences at his seminars in the United States, was because of the belief in this myth.

Mary Walton, in her book about the Deming management method, is one of the main sources for this myth. Mary Walton is a journalist, based in Philadelphia, who can be credited with rediscovering Deming through her work on a television documentary about quality. As evidence for the myth that SQC was lost in the United States, she uses the example of the statistical handbook developed and published by AT&T which explains SQC, *Statistical Quality Control Handbook.* The first edition came out in 1956, followed by editions in 1958, 1964, 1967, 1970, 1977, and then, according to Walton, "the dates have increased in frequency."[2] Since there were some six- and seven-year periods when no new edition was printed, Walton cites this as evidence that SQC is not used much any more. Although she may not have meant it in this way, her quantifiable measure of quality over time in a company is, therefore, the number of editions of a company's quality handbook. But looking at the dates of the editions, this is not a very convincing argument.

More realistic reasons for slowdowns in the frequency of editions, besides a lack of training in quality techniques, can be found. A better reason for the slowdown in revisions is that the techniques are relatively simple and have not changed much since their development and, thus, no new editions were needed. It makes sense that there would be many revised editions in the early years, when the tech-

[2]Mary Walton, *The Deming Management Method* (New York: Dodd, Mead, 1981), p. 184.

niques were still being developed. Once they were fully developed, and the errors had been hammered out of the editions, no changes were required.

If we are to use AT&T as an example of the lack of use of SQC, as Walton does, then the record has to be examined more closely. At Western Electric (the manufacturing arm of AT&T before divestiture), all manufacturing engineers were required to take at least a four-day course in statistical quality control, following the original techniques of Shewhart and the books and manuals developed for those techniques. This was always a requirement, and continues to be a requirement today. For most, this course supplemented prior courses at universities. As an indication of quality at Western Electric and AT&T, each telephone manufactured by AT&T had to survive a 6-foot drop test before it could be sent to a customer. These phones, from the 1940s until divestiture—just the period in which Walton claims SQC was lost in the United States—were of the very highest quality because of the techniques practiced at AT&T. Quality in a company over a period of years is not measured by the number of editions of a company's handbook on quality.

A MASTER WITHOUT APPRENTICES   Perhaps the anecdotal evidence Deming uses to claim that SQC techniques were not used by American business after the war is based on his views on how SQC should be taught and learned. He advocates that SQC can only be learned at the feet of a master, in a master-apprentice relationship. "No one should teach the theory and use of control charts without knowledge of statistical theory…supplemented by experience under a master,"[3] says Deming in *Out of the Crisis*. Such relationships pervade Japanese society and occupations, from *sushi* chefs to school teachers. He sought out the master, Walter Shewhart, as his mentor, and fully expected others to seek him out for a similar kind of relationship. This may not have happened to the extent Deming expected in the years after World War II, but there are other reasons for this besides the loss of SQC techniques

A master is needed when the information is so new that it has not found its way into textbooks or college courses, as was the case when Deming sought out Shewhart. In the United States, though, this important work soon found its way into textbooks and courses. Consider Purdue as an example. In the 1940s, SQC was taught in the statistics department. When the School of Industrial Engineering was created in the early 1950s, an SQC course was also taught there. The statistics department course emphasized the math and the theory; the engineering course emphasized the management and the applications. Many management students

---

[3]Deming, *Out of the Crisis,* p. 131.

took the industrial engineering course. Students from all areas—mathematics, statistics, engineering, and management—were exposed to these concepts. The SQC course is the longest-running course in the School of Industrial Engineering, because the material has always been considered to be basic for any manufacturing or process application.

Another reason to enter into a master-apprentice relationship is when what has to be learned is of such a nature that it cannot be explained by words in a textbook; it must be learned by watching someone do it. An example of this is learning carpentry from a master carpenter or learning how to make *sushi* from a master chef. The concepts of SQC are simple enough that they can be explained in words and equations in textbooks; a master is not needed.

Deming apparently found himself in the United States as a *sempai* (master) without an apprentice, because his knowledge had been disseminated through textbooks and college courses. People who had learned about SQC in textbooks and through college courses may not have taken Deming seriously because of some of his radical ideas and unorthodox views on how statistics should be taught. "Experience without theory teaches nothing," Deming states.[4] This is good so far; few statistics-literate people would object to this. But the theory underlying statistics is called the central limit theorem. Almost every textbook and every statistics course discusses this theory at the very beginning, to provide a foundation for the course. In Deming's seminars, however, he showed very little respect for the theory behind statistics and, one could argue, actually misrepresented the theory to the audience.

Mary Walton recorded verbatim one of the exchanges in a Deming seminar which showed this misunderstanding of theory. In his seminar, Deming used a bag containing red and white beads, in which 80% of the 4000 beads were white and 20% were red. In statistical terms, a sample is taken when some number of beads, say 50 beads, is removed from the population of all beads, which, in this example is the 4000 beads in the bag. The number of red beads in the sample is called an observation. With many 50-bead samples taken from the bag over a period of time, the central limit theorem states that the distribution of the number of observations of red beads from the samples will be a normal distribution (a bell-shaped curve) with an average, or mean, which approaches the mean of the population. Thus, with a sample size of 50, the observations (the number of red beads) from these samples can bounce around between 0 and 50 but, over time, most of the observations from these samples will cluster around 10, which is 20% of 50. The mean of these observations will approach 10.

Deming asked the audience what would be the mean of the number of red beads from all these samples. Someone in the audience says 10, which is correct.

---

[4]Deming, *Out of the Crisis*, p. 317.

Deming asks why. Someone in the audience says because of the central limit theorem, which again is the correct answer. Deming ridicules this answer. "Central limit theory," he says. "Wish you'd tell me what it is. I've been getting along now for fifty-five years without it. I didn't want to know what it is, but tell me. What the hell do you mean? Central limit theory. Put that away. That's one of the problems that we face in teaching of statistics. Teaching people what's wrong and doing it very well."[5] The person who came up with the answer was right, but Deming ridiculed the answer, complained that the person was taught wrong, and dismissed the most basic aspect of statistical theory. A university professor espousing the need for theory, and then ridiculing those who use theory, would not have a receptive audience at companies with people trained in statistical methods.

In Japan, though, because the Japanese did not have these techniques spelled out in the textbooks, and because the Japanese had a tendency to use the master-apprentice model in all kinds of occupations, Deming finally found the apprentices he was seeking. This did not mean that American companies were unwilling to utilize SQC techniques and Japanese companies were. It meant instead that the Japanese had no other sources to turn to, while the American company personnel were learning these techniques in college. There is no evidence for the myth that American companies ever quit using SQC.

Deming's claim that SQC can only be learned through a master-apprentice program can do more harm than good. Master-apprentice relationships are expensive, and they are dependent on the limited availability of a master (Deming died in February 1994). If companies actually believe in this necessity, then people will be impeded in their attempts to learn SQC techniques. If your company does not practice SQC, do not wait for a master to appear. Go to the local college and pick up the essentials.

A PROFESSION OF MANAGEMENT   "Students in schools of business in America are taught that there is a profession of management; that they are ready to step into top jobs. This is a cruel hoax," says W. Edwards Deming in *Out of the Crisis*.[6] Deming believed that we are teaching our business school students the wrong thing. We should not teach them about the profession of management, we should teach them about the Deming management method. In actuality, there may be little difference between what Deming has taught to his Japanese clients and what the business schools have taught to American students through the years.

Duncan and Van Matre, management professors writing in the journal *Business Horizons*, claim that Deming's Fourteen Points and Seven Deadly Diseases can be

[5]Walton, *The Deming Management Method*, p. 49.
[6]Deming, *Out of the Crisis*, p. 130.

classified under six headings, most of which have been taught as management theory in business schools for a number of years. They are[7]

- The purpose and mission of business organizations
- Philosophy instead of technique
- Instruction and training
- Cooperation-competition-conflict
- Manager-worker relations
- Quantitative goal setting

We will examine each of these points to determine how they relate to Deming's philosophy.

Deming sees long-term survival of the firm as the purpose and mission of business organizations. His Point 1 (Create constancy of purpose toward improvement of product and service) addresses this issue. One of the problems with American companies, says Deming, is the lack of constancy of purpose (Deadly Disease 1) because of a company's emphasis on short-term profits (Deadly Disease 2). Duncan and Van Matre find many of these same ideas in books published in 1938[8] and 1954[9] and taught in business schools for a number of years.

Deming argues that the pursuit of quality must be the philosophy of a company; techniques, such as applying technological gadgets to a problem, will fail unless management is committed to them. Several of Deming's points address this idea: Adopt the new philosophy (Point 2); cease dependence on inspection to achieve quality (Point 3); improve constantly and forever the system of production and service (Point 5); and put everybody in the company to work to accomplish the transformation (Point 14). Duncan and Van Matre relate these ideas to those of Frederick Taylor, who was influential during most of the twentieth century through his ideas and teachings on scientific management. Taylor also advocated that scientific management should be a company philosophy and that merely applying parts of it, without understanding the underlying reasons, would result in failure.

Deming emphasizes instruction and training through two points: Institute training on the job (Point 6); and Institute a vigorous program of education and self-improvement (Point 13). He believed that quality problems were due to faults in management rather than problems with the workers. These ideas are very similar to those of Taylor, Duncan and Van Matre contend, because Taylor indicated that man-

[7]Jack W. Duncan and Joseph G. Van Matre, "The Gospel According to Deming: Is It Really New?," *Business Horizons,* July-August 1990, pp. 3-9.
[8]Chester I. Barnard, *The Functions of the Executive* (Cambridge, MA: Harvard University Press, 1938).
[9]Peter F. Drucker, *The Practice of Management* (New York: Harper, 1954).

agement should be responsible for using scientific management to train and instruct the workers in the proper way to perform a job.

The cooperation-competition-conflict category refers to Deming's Points 4 and 9: End the practice of awarding business on the basis of price tag (Point 4); and Break down barriers between departments (Point 9). Duncan and Van Matre argue that Point 4 does not really represent a radical idea, because any rational manager will look at total cost, including warranty costs and delivery delay costs, when considering a supplier. In Point 9, Deming advocates the breakdown of barriers between departments. This is similar to the ideas of an influential 1931 book by Mooney and Reilly,[10] who stated that goals are needed to integrate and coordinate the diverse staff units within an organization.

Deming states that manager-worker relations should be based on a helping relationship (Institute leadership, Point 7) instead of an authoritarian one (Drive out fear, Point 8). In addition, the secret to motivating workers is to give them meaningful jobs (Remove barriers that rob the hourly worker of his right to pride of workmanship, Point 12). An indication of a problem is the mobility of management (Deadly Disease 4). These ideas have a rich heritage in the United States, according to Duncan and Van Matre, through the teachings and writings of McGregor,[11] Maslow,[12] McClelland,[13] and Herzberg.[14]

The only category of the six which had not been accepted practice in American management before Deming's publications, according to Duncan and Van Matre, is that on quantitative goal setting. Deming devotes several points and deadly diseases to the idea that quantitative goals should be eliminated: Eliminate slogans, exhortations, and targets for the workforce (Point 10); Eliminate work standards and management by objective (Point 11); the deadly disease of evaluation of performance, merit rating, or annual review (Deadly Disease 3); and the deadly disease of management by use only of visible figures (Deadly Disease 5). Deming criticizes the management philosophy of management by objective, in which goals are set for workers and departments, and performance is assessed by how well these goals are met. He rejects the work of Taylor and Lillian Gilbreth, who broke work tasks down into basic units to determine the most efficient way to perform the task. These efficient steps were the standards on which to evaluate a person's work. Deming's criticism of work standards and goal setting is the one area in which Deming has been criticized.[15]

---

[10]J. D. Mooney and A. C. Reiley, *Onward Industry* (New York: Harper, 1931).

[11]Douglas M. McGregor, *The Human Side of Enterprise* (New York: McGraw-Hill, 1960).

[12]Abraham Maslow, *Motivation and Personality* (New York: Harper & Row, 1970).

[13]David C. McClelland, *The Achieving Society* (New York: The Free Press, 1961).

[14]Frederick Herzberg, *The Motivation to Work* (New York: Wiley, 1959).

[15]Marvin Mundel, "Now is the Time to Speak Out in Defense of Time Standards," *Industrial Engineering*, September, 1992, pp. 50–51.

There is some evidence to indicate that Deming has been ignored by Japanese and American companies on the issue of eliminating work standards and goals. The Japanese practice of *kaizen,* or constant improvement, follows closely the recommendations of Taylor and Gilbreth to break down tasks into their most efficient units.[16] The just-in-time production system may reduce inventories, but another purpose is to speed up the production line by eliminating unnecessary motion. In the system used at Mazda's Flat Rock, Michigan, plant, as an example, goals and standards were a major part of the system. In American companies, goal setting and achieving the goal has been an important part of building teamwork and facilitating cooperation.[17] According to Duncan and Van Matre, almost all the data from experiments indicates that setting goals is important to increase workers' motivation and performance. If the data are to be believed—the experimental data and the data from practices in the United States and Japan—then Deming may be wrong on this point. There is no evidence to indicate that goal setting is bad, as Deming states.

DESIGN OF EXPERIMENTS   Around 1985, I started getting questions from students in my class about Taguchi methods. In my statistics class I was teaching design of experiments, and many of the students from industry had heard of Taguchi techniques. They knew that Japanese companies had been practicing these techniques, and that American companies had not yet discovered them. The feeling was that we were falling behind the Japanese in experimental design.

In my statistics classes I had always emphasized that the students should not follow a cookbook approach to experimental design. I emphasized that it was important for them to know statistics, because they were the engineers who would be working to control the manufacturing process through SQC techniques and to improve the process through the design of experiments. Since they were most familiar with manufacturing, unlike statisticians trained only in statistics, they could make the important subjective decisions which were vitally important in designing a proper experiment.

I emphasized how they could come to make these subjective decisions. One experiment often leads to new questions necessitating further experimentation. By being familiar with the manufacturing process, the engineer could understand which potential variables have an effect on the process. As indicated in Chapter 6, an experiment would be too large if all potential variables were included in the design. The size of an experiment can be reduced by eliminating testing for interactions between variables which, from prior experience, are unlikely to have an effect on the process.

---

[16]Joseph J. Fucini and Suzy Fucini, *Working for the Japanese* (New York: The Free Press, 1990).
[17]Henry S. Dennison, *Organization Engineering* (New York: McGraw-Hill, 1931).

I always stressed to the class that the most difficult part of statistics and design of experiments are the subjective decisions which have to be made in the design of the experiments. The statistics calculations are simple and straightforward. Many of these subjective decisions were essential in a kind of technique taught in my class, called fractional replications, where many variables can be tested with a minimum number of observations. The students are taught about the effects of subjective decisions on the interpretation of the results. The interpretation is only as good as the quality of the decisions made earlier.

At the instigation of my students, I started to study Taguchi techniques. Although Taguchi never says so, the techniques are actually one form of fractional replications. Fractional replications preceded Taguchi techniques and were a common skill taught to manufacturing engineers.

One of the main differences between Taguchi techniques and fractional replications is that Taguchi methods are presented using a cookbook approach. A person can determine how many variables will be tested (the particular variable is unimportant), look up a table in a book of Taguchi methods, and determine which experimental design to use. The interpretation of the results is simple, independent of any assumptions. No background or understanding of the manufacturing process is needed in order to use Taguchi techniques. This ran counter to how I had always taught fractional replication, that an understanding of the process is vitally important to making the right kinds of decisions and interpreting the results correctly.

By removing the subjective decisions, Taguchi simplified design of experiments. By removing the tie-in between subjective decisions about choosing the variables in the experiment and the interpretation of the results, however, Taguchi increased the possibility that the results would be interpreted in the wrong way. A person using Taguchi methods may miss important variables which may have an effect on increasing the quality of the product. The results could be interpreted in the wrong way, actually decreasing quality in manufacturing.

Taguchi has removed all theory and the need for critical understanding in the design of experiments. This violates Deming's exhortations that philosophy rather than technique is needed. Deming derides the use of computers as quick technological fixes which do not address the disease but only cure the symptoms. He wants to eliminate rules of thumb and rely on a person's understanding of the system. Yet Taguchi techniques use a simplified, step-by-step approach, which eliminates the need for understanding. Ironically, Genichi Taguchi won the Deming Award in Japan.

I could not understand the use of Taguchi techniques because it seemed to violate what I understood to be Japanese management philosophy, as described by Deming. While I was in Japan, I learned the reason for its widespread use. A main business practice in Japan is to rotate people to different jobs. In this way, employees get a feel for how the whole company works. The negative consequence of this policy is that nobody gains total understanding of all aspects of a job. They are generalists. "Even in specialized positions, there are many amateurs because staff is often allocated with little attention to special training, experience, or inclination," writes Jan Woronoff, who spent ten years in Japan running his own company.[18] In this situation, a cookbook approach and rules of thumb work better than the design-of-experiments approach taught in my course at Purdue and elsewhere. U.S. businesses never lost the ability to design and run experiments to improve the manufacturing process. They are dependent on specialists to design and analyze their experiments. The Japanese companies, with a shortage of statistical specialists, needed a different approach; and when one surfaced, they took it regardless of its theoretical shortcomings.

FOCUSING THE IMAGE ON THIS MYTH   Focusing the image on this myth is difficult because objective indicators are not available. American companies did seem to lapse in quality in the 1960s and 1970s. Focusing on this issue is difficult, though.

University courses have always been available that teach SQC and design of experiments. Did the students apply statistics as they were taught? This is a difficult question to answer. With the wide availability of courses and books on quality in the United States, masters such as Deming were not needed. A master-apprentice program fit in nicely in Japan, where the courses and the textbooks were not available. The Japanese were accustomed to using master-apprentice relationships in other jobs. Focus on Deming, the master, in Japan. He has specialized knowledge craved by Japanese business people. Focus on Deming in the United States. His knowledge is not so specialized. He is sought out in one country and rejected in another. This will color a person's view of the practice of quality in the two countries.

---

[18]Jan Woronoff, *The Japanese Management Mystique* (Chicago: Probus Publishing, 1992), p. 149.

CHAPTER • SEVENTEEN

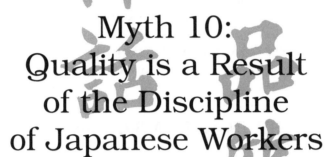

Myth 10: Quality is a Result of the Discipline of Japanese Workers

Discipline, loyalty, and hard work are all stereotypes of the Japanese worker which most Americans would consider virtues. How do the Japanese learn these virtues? What role does the school system play in teaching these virtues? Could this discipline system be transferred to the United States? What price does Japanese society pay for this discipline?

GOLDEN TIMES My wife, our two sons, and I were visiting the beautiful grounds of the Golden Temple in Kyoto. Packs of school children were swarming around the grounds on their annual school holidays. Whenever we went to places like this, our two sons would cause a commotion. Teen-aged schoolgirls would graciously ask us if they could take photos of their friends with our sons. With their curly, golden-blonde hair and the Golden Temple in the background, the images made a symbolic golden bridge between Japan and the United States

On this particular occasion, the picture-taking was causing a traffic jam. Many of the school girls wanted not only to take a picture but also to touch our sons' hair.

288

Small golden-haired boys are a rarity in Japan. I decided to walk on down the path with my Japanese colleague while the picture taking and hair patting continued

At the end of the path, I turned back to see where the rest of the family was. As I started back up the path, I was stopped by an employee of the park, whose sole job was to make sure that everyone walked the paths in the same direction.

There was no one else on the path, so my walking back was not going to cause a traffic problem; that had already been taken care of by the picture taking. I simply wanted to go back to help my wife with the children. This man, however, was not going to let me go the wrong way on the path for any reason. That was his job, and he was doing his job well. In fact, I had to respect this person for the passion with which he performed his assigned job. I had assumed that reason—the need to tell my wife where I was and to help her with the children—was a universal notion and would win out in the end. I was wrong.

DISCIPLINE AT HOME "It is a surprising problem," said the minister. We were visiting with a Christian minister who had spent his whole life in Japan, first as a son of missionary parents and then as a minister at a small Christian church in Tokyo. He was explaining the discipline problems faced at home by the Japanese mothers he knew.

"The mothers have little control over the boys at home," he continued. "They become problems because the mothers make little attempt to discipline them or tell them what is right. Then, all of a sudden, they enter school and the discipline is imposed on them very quickly. They learn discipline—not values—in the school system. Discipline is imposed by forcing the students to learn and adhere to hundreds of rules which may seem arbitrary to us."

The litany of problems he was describing are familiar to Americans: absentee fathers, disrespect for women, and lack of moral values. Our image of the Japanese as hard-working, disciplined workers would not have included these problems if we had not witnessed them for ourselves. Our revised image of Japan was consistent with the impressions of other Americans who have spent considerable time in Japan.

Absentee fathers are a problem in Japan. The demands of work, and the after-hour socializing required in building business relationships, mean that fathers have very little time to spend with their children. Ken Schoolland, an American who spent two years teaching in a Japanese university, became well acquainted with his students. One of his students recalled a time when he was young and he saw a stranger walk into the house. He asked his mother who this person was and his mother responded that it was his father.[1]

---

[1] Ken Schoolland, *Shogun's Ghost: The Dark Side of Japanese Education* (New York: Bergin & Garvey, 1990), p. 22.

It is not unusual for the children to be in bed at 8:00 each night while the father returns home at 10:00. Saturday is a partial or full work day for the father, and Sunday is often spent pursuing hobbies such as golf. A study showed that children feel isolated from their fathers. In this poll, 50% of the college-age sons indicated that they did not communicate any more with their fathers, but 80% still communicated with their mothers.[2]

The mothers are the disciplinarians in the family. A poll performed by the Japanese prime minister's office indicated that mothers are in charge of discipline in the home in more than 84% of the families surveyed; fathers took charge in only 6.3% of the families.[3] The study concluded that fathers are losing their influence within the family. The male respondents said that they believe mothers should take care of the children or that the children did not like their fathers to get involved. In Japan, though, discipline is based on authority rather than ethics. Women traditionally have had little authority in Japan—small boys learn this quickly—so the mothers often use guilt as a method of control. Physical discipline is saved for the school system to administer.

OVER 100% OF THE POPULATION PRACTICES RELIGION
Religious images come readily to mind: the temples in Kyoto; the giant Buddha in Kamakura, which survived the typhoons that destroyed the temple around it; the tea houses that convey the sense of an ascetic lifestyle; the Zen gardens that reflect a people in harmony with nature. A blue haze floats over Mt. Fuji and the cherry blosom are in bloom.

From the outside, Japan appears to be a very religious society: 80% of the people practice some aspects of Buddhism, 80% practice Shintoism, and 1% practice Christianity. Seventy to 80%, however, do not consider themselves believers in any religion.[4] Over 100% of the population practices religion, but a vast majority consider themselves nonreligious. To outsiders, the paradox is disturbing, because we may be inclined to think that a person can practice only one religion.

Shintoism, the native Japanese religion, deifies ancestors and a multitude of nature gods, around 800 of them, including rocks, unusual trees, and waterfalls.Shintoism has been associated with Japanese nationalism, which reached its modern height in the xenophobia of the period just before World War II. Whereas most religions have a myth about the creation of the world, Shintoism has a creation myth just for the Japanese islands. Another basic premise is that the emperor's ancestry can be traced back to the sun god, and before World War II the emperor was treated like a god on earth. The announcement of Japan's defeat in World War II by Emperor Hirohito was a significant event because the god-emperor was not sup-

---

[2]William Bohnaker, *The Hollow Doll* (New York: Ballantine Books, 1990), p. 182.
[3]"Fathers Losing Influence, Survey Says," *Japan Times,* October 24, 1990, p. 3.
[4]Edwin O. Reischauer, *The Japanese Today* (Tokyo: Charles E. Tuttle, 1988), p. 215.

posed to speak to the people. The Japanese islands are seen as the chosen islands, and the Japanese people are seen as the chosen people; some of these ideas parallel those in Judaism and Christianity. The people are very proud that before World War II the Japanese islands had never been invaded by outside forces. Shintoism is practiced nowhere else in the world.

The religious practice of Shintoism involves offerings, prayers, and a clapping of hands to get the attention of the local nature god. Local Shinto festivals are very colorful, but have little to do with any daily religious practice. Happiness and prosperity are important themes in the religion, but obtaining these things has little to do with living one's life in a certain way and more to do with following simple guidelines on how to worship the gods. We were surprised to find that Shintoism has no moral or ethical belief system and no codes or guidelines for how to live one's life or treat other people.

The other major religion, Buddhism, was imported from India via China. Like so many other things brought to Japan, Buddhism was changed significantly to assimilate and adapt to Japanese thought and practices. While Buddhists on the Asian continent attempted to ascertain the absolute or universal truths, Buddhism in Japan emphasized the concrete and how truth is fluid dependent on the situation and fleeting intuition.[5] Whereas Buddhism on the Asian continent emphasized the need to discipline one's mind, this was transformed in Japan to an emphasis on discipline of mind, but only in a social context. There were rules and regulations to follow in a social context, but one could think whatever one felt emotionally.[6] The emphasis was on feeling natural emotions, but suppressing the outward expression of these emotions.

The Buddhists of India and China developed a discipline based on universal and absolute truths. This concept was not carried over to Buddhist practice in Japan, where truth was defined in terms of concrete and observable reality. An example is the drinking of alcohol. The Indian and Chinese Buddhists considered drinking to be a religious sin. In Japan, though, drinking was popular. The people were already drinking, so this observable event must signify its truthfulness. "Is it a sin to drink?" asked one of the influential Japanese Buddhist philosophers. "In truth you ought not to drink, but drinking is after all a custom of this world."[7]

One of the difficult aspects of living in Japan and interacting with the people is the fleeting notion of truth. As Westerners, we assumed that everyone believes in some absolute truth based on a few simple rules such as the Golden Rule or the Ten Commandments. In the West, laws and contracts have been developed to codify these absolute truths. In Japan, though, truth can change according to the context or

---

[5]Hajime Nakamura, *Ways of Thinking of Eastern Peoples: India-China-Tibet-Japan* (Honolulu: East-West Center Press, 1964), p. 350.
[6]Nakamura, *Ways of Thinking*, p. 374.
[7]Ibid., p. 378.

merely according to how one feels. Laws and contracts are not absolutes, but may reflect how one felt at the time, which may be different from how one feels now. Truth is based more on the trust one places in another person, which in turn is based on a long-term personal relationship. This attitude worked well in a small village, and some of the practices may transfer to business relationships in a small country. In an international setting, however, where business is practiced among people with different customs and is not based on personal relationships, misunderstandings can occur.

Moral and ethical behavior is usually associated with religious doctrine and principles; they provide the foundation of the doctrines for how one should live one's life. An authority figure can impose discipline by referring to principles that transcend the limits of his or her own authority. In Japan, this is not so. Authority cannot be transcended by principles, religious or otherwise. Discipline is imposed by authority or by social convention. When the Japanese go outside their group, though, then they are outside their discipline and outside the social conventions of the group. The group in Japan can encompass family, neighborhood, village, small business, large corporation, or Japan itself. The rest of the world is not part of these groups.

People in Japan are usually very honest among themselves when it comes to matters of money or personal property. Theft of personal property is rare. On the other hand, these same values do not apply to group behavior. In Japan, it is rare that one person will steal someone else's property, but groups, including corporations, can live outside these laws. As an example, corporations typically underreport profits so as not to pay taxes to the Japanese government. Tax audits of 4860 corporations by the Japanese government showed that 98% (4765) of the companies concealed income to avoid paying taxes.[8]

People you know will do anything to accommodate you as part of the group, but these same friends will have little empathy for strangers outside the group. We were reminded of this one day when we were exiting a train station down a long flight of steps during rush hour. An older lady tripped and started to fall down the steps. I caught her from falling further, motioned her to sit down, and asked whether she was OK. We were surprised at how the other people walking down the stairs reacted. Not one offered to help or asked her if she was all right. In fact, they appeared to go out of their way to avoid her, and she acted as if she was ashamed that she had inconvenienced others by tripping. Since the others on the stairs were mostly businessmen, nobody knew her; she was not part of the group.

Other people told us of similar instances. One of our American friends, who could speak Japanese fluently, told us his solution to the rude behavior of jostling or cutting in line at the train station. When he was confronted with behavior he consid-

---

[8]Jiji Press, "Taxes on 515 Billion Yen Were Avoided by Top Companies, Authorities Find," *Japan Times,* November 8, 1990, p. 9.

ered rude, he would ask, "Don't I know you from someplace?" in Japanese. Because of the possibility that this *gaijin* might be part of some past group, the behavior would turn into apologies and extreme politeness.

DISCIPLINE IN THE SCHOOLS   It must feel like hitting a brick wall at 60 mph. After the undisciplined freedom in the years before school, the discipline imposed on students in school must be quite a shock.

The teachers in Japan have virtually unlimited power over the students, with the threat and use of corporal punishment the main tool to impose their authority. The extent of corporal punishment is difficult to assess. Schoolland, the American university professor who spent two years teaching in Japan, ran informal polls among his students.[9] The results were shocking. Of 227 students polled, 89% reported having been hit by teachers over the years; 17% reported being hit more than fifty times. Morikatsu Imabashi of Ibaraki University did a similar poll of 272 students in 1986, and all reported physical punishment in the lower grades, with an average of 23.5 physical punishments during their years of education. These students witnessed 27 incidents where the students had to be treated at the school clinic or at the local hospital.[10] These results are surprising because of the high numbers but also because the students polled were the elite of the school system, the ones who thrived in the system, passed the national exam, and attended college. The marginal students who did not attend college probably were treated worse.

A tragic case of corporal punishment occurred while we were in Japan. One of the many rules which cannot be broken is being late for school. A teacher, Toshihiko Hosoi, was in charge of closing the school gate at the start of the school day. A fifteen-year-old student, Ryoko Ishida, who had never been late for school before, tried to enter the school right at the bell. Hosoi would not let her in, and Ishida knew the punishment and shame of being late. She tried to squeeze past, but Hosoi closed the gate on her head. After being transported to the hospital, she died from head injuries.[11] Schoolland, in his book, *Shogun's Ghost,* mentions another case during his stay of a fatal beating resulting in death at the hands of teachers. He mentions two other cases that resulted in brain damage to students.

Physical abuse from teachers can be severe. After finding that so many students had been hit in school, Schoolland tried to ascertain informally how hard his students had been hit. He slammed his hand on the table as hard as he could and asked his students if they had ever been hit that hard. Forty percent said they had. He

---

[9]Schoolland, *Shogun's Ghost,* pp. 50-51.
[10]"Poll: Kids Get Punished 23 Times as Students," *Daily Yomiuri,* January 20, 1986 (reported in Schoolland, *Shogun's Ghost,* p. 50).
[11]Kyodo News Service, "Gate-Closing Teacher Indicted for Professional Negligence," *Japan Times,* September, 15, 1990, p. 2.

ascertained that most of the times the students were hit on the head (34%) or the face (33%). The punishment was often inflicted for small offenses such as a student not being able to answer a math problem or forgetting homework.[12]

Schools in Japan have complicated and exacting rules and regulations, mostly in the range of 200 to 300 rules, for all manner of dress and behaviors both in and out of school. Students have to carry a booklet of the written rules; some of the rules are unwritten. There are rules on the length of skirts and the length of hair. Schools have regulations against girls wearing polka-dot or colored panties. The color of rubber bands on school projects is specified. One boy was punished for having five eyelets in his shoes instead of the required six.

Nonconformity in personal appearance is outlawed. Some girls have naturally red-tinted hair, but in the schools hair is supposed to be black and so they are forced to dye their hair. On the other hand, girls who have naturally black hair are not allowed to dye it. Perms are outlawed, and girls who have a natural curl to their hair must have it straightened. The teachers are allowed to have permed hair and, generally, they are not expected to adhere to the same rules as the students.

Inspections for adherence to the rules are frequent and thorough. When a rule is found to have been broken, sometimes the teachers will not tell the student which rule was broken. The rules can be enforced or changed at will as a means of reinforcing the authority of the teacher. The student has no recourse if accused of a rule violation. The students learn that, by virtue of their authority, and the absence of an underlying value structure, the teachers can make, change, and enforce the rules without question.

The other important source of discipline is group pressure. In many schools, an upper class will be given authority to set and enforce rules for the lower classes. With myriad rules already in place, it may be difficult to think of new ones. These additional rules usually seem even more arbitrary than the official school ones. If someone does not adhere to a rule, or sticks out in any way, then the group will often resort to bullying tactics. Suicide is one outlet for those students who for some reason do not adhere to the conformity of the group.

As could be expected from this authoritarian atmosphere, school can be stressful or painful for many students. In fact, when Japanese students were given a test to determine psychological anxiety, half the students replied that it was psychologically painful or unpleasant to go to school.[13] Japan's health ministry estimates that four out of ten children are developing adult health problems such as ulcers, diabetes, high blood pressure, and obesity. In recent years, sales of wigs to fifth and sixth

---

[12]Schoolland, *Shogun's Ghost,* pp. 52-53.
[13]Ibid., p. 114.

graders has doubled, so they can hide their stress-caused bald spots. Many times the mothers do not allow the children to play. In one survey, two-thirds of the children had to make special appointments to play, and 53% did not play at all after school, citing fatigue, going to cram school, or other appointments as reasons. "In my opinion, this is one type of child abuse," says Urako Kanemori, a family practioner at the Tokyo Psychological Educational Institute.[14]

School children in Japan are controlled by their teachers and by their peer group. Children learn to follow the rules without question. This stifling atmosphere often results in open rebellion from students in the form of violence against teachers. Such undisciplined behavior is dealt with by the imposition of more rules and regulations, and the cycle continues.

If a foreigner were to ask, the Japanese would say that corporal punishment is against the law. But like the Buddhist prohibition against drinking, if a custom is different from the law, then the custom takes precedence over the law.

THIS LAND IS YOUR LAND   One night we saw on Japanese television a concert by the folk group Peter, Paul, and Mary. They sang Woody Guthrie songs from the dust-bowl days, Bob Dylan protest songs from the 1960s, and material they had written themselves. They took the best songs from many periods and made them their own.

We were curious to see how a Japanese audience would respond to these very American songs. Some songs, such as "Autumn to May," have no deep meaning and, if they can be understood at all, are understood in similar ways by any audience. But some of the songs are about freedom, liberty, justice, and individualism—and many speak out against authoritarianism. In "If I Had a Hammer," Pete Seeger's lyrics state the American ideals and struggles: "It's the hammer of justice, it's the bell of freedom, it's the song about love between my brothers and my sisters all over this land." In Bob Dylan's "Blowin' in the Wind," Dylan sings of freedom and responsibility to others: "How many years can some people exist before they're allowed to be free? How many times can a man turn his head pretending he just doesn't see?"

Peter, Paul, and Mary started singing "This Land is Your Land" by Woody Guthrie. We happened to know a lot about Guthrie; the Japanese audience had no reason to know who he was or even that he had written the song. Guthrie traveled around the United States in the 1930s singing and writing about the people who had been uprooted by the Depression. He challenged Big Business for exploiting the workers and the land. He celebrated the individual, and railed against authority. He

---

[14]Teresa Watanabe, "A Lesson for Japan's Kids: Play," *Los Angeles Times,* September 14, 1992, p. 1.

complained that the land owners and business owners were too far removed from the people to see the effects of their policies on the suffering workers.

A man who knew Guthrie personally, Edward Robbin, describes him like this: "Woody was a guy who couldn't stand to see kids with swollen hungry bellies. He wanted his people to have jobs and better pay. He was a passionate union man. He wanted people to have good houses and land to grow things and above all, freedom to sing and speak and grow and drink and gamble and have whatever kind of fun and happiness this place can provide."[15] The compassion in the songs and the celebration of the individual's spirit to endure in bad times are not things that seemingly would translate well to other cultures, including Japan's, out of the context of Guthrie's times. Peter, Paul, and Mary sang the song:

> *This land is your land, this land is my land.*
> *From California to the New York island;*
> *From the redwood forest to the Gulf Stream waters,*
> *This land was made for you and me.*

Peter, Paul, and Mary left out Guthrie's pointed verses, which most Americans are unfamiliar with:

> *Nobody living can ever stop me,*
> *As I go walking that freedom highway;*
> *Nobody living can ever make me turn back,*
> *This land was made for you and me.*
>
> *As I went walking, I saw a sign there,*
> *And the sign it said "No Trespassing,"*
> *But on the other side it didn't say nothing,*
> *That side was made for you and me.*
>
> *In the shadow of the steeple I saw my people;*
> *By the Relief Office I seen my people;*
> *As they stood there hungry, I stood there asking;*
> *Is this land made for you and me?*[16]

---

[15]Edward Robbin, "This Train Is Bound for Glory," in Harold Leventhal and Marjorie Guthrie (eds.), *The Woody Guthrie Songbook* (New York: Grosset and Dunlap, 1976), p. 25.
[16]TRO © Copyright 1956 (Renewed), 1958 (Renewed) and 1970, Ludlow Music, New York, NY. Used with permission.

Then Peter, Paul, and Mary invited the Japanese audience to join in with them on the refrain to the song. The camera panned to the audience as we watched everybody sing the words we knew so well:

> *This land is your land, this land is my land,*
> *From California to the New York island;*
> *From the redwood forest to the Gulf Stream waters,*
> *This land was made for you and me.*

There was some truth to the words they were singing. A Japanese company had recently purchased one of the most beautiful spots on the California coast: Pebble Beach Golf Course. People were not welcome without a membership. Japanese companies owned 80% of downtown Los Angeles. Our timber from the national forests was going to Japan at artificially low government prices to be processed and sold back to us at much higher prices as manufactured boards. A Japanese company had recently purchased Rockefeller Center in downtown Manhattan. Matsushita Corp. had bought MCA, which included Universal Pictures, Universal Studios Theme Parks in Florida and California, and the concessions in Yosemite National Park. In my mind I could see parallel images side by side on a screen: one image from the 1930s and another image from the 1990s. Move them together and they overlapped perfectly. The images were one. We did not want to think about it any more.

Initially we were perturbed at this scene. But upon further reflection, we thought that the Japanese audience could learn from the Woody Guthrie songs, and that Peter, Paul, and Mary's choice to invite audience participation only on "This Land" instead of on something like "Puff, the Magic Dragon" may have had a reason. The money for which the Japanese had worked so hard was now going to buy golf courses in California, while their own homes would be more appropriate in a Third World country. The infrastructure was falling apart in the cities—only 40% of the homes have sewage systems[17]—yet their companies owned the ice rink at Rockefeller Center. Now that the economy in Japan has gone south (and east), the money may no longer be available to fix these problems. They missed a golden opportunity to advance the standard of living of their people.

With hard work and discipline, American workers pulled themselves out of the Depression Woody Guthrie sang about. What kind of hard work and discipline would be needed now? Years later, do our modern workers have the work ethic and the discipline to improve their situation? What could we learn about discipline and hard work from Japan?

---

[17]Kensuke Yanagiya, "Prosperity's Base: ODA," *Japan Times*, October 16, 1990, p. 20.

THE QUESTION OF DISCIPLINE   Few people would question that the Japanese worker is more disciplined than the American worker. Japanese workers are willing to do the exact same thing each time in order to produce a product which adheres to quality standards and has few defects. They will acquiesce to the authority of their superior or the pressure of the group. This is not a myth. The myth is that we could transfer this system to our culture, or that we would want to. A related myth is that discipline is needed to do these kinds of jobs.

The discipline learned in the Japanese educational system transfers well to the workplace. Those students who succeed in the educational system succeed precisely because they have learned to be disciplined in their work habits, because they do as they have been told, and they have learned to accept group pressure.

The surprising thing about the discipline in Japan is that it is not based on a moral or ethical code. Discipline taught in the schools is not based on learning absolute truths about how to live one's life or how to treat other people. The absolute truth taught in schools is the supremacy of authority and the coherence of the group, which are then used to define disciplined behavior, to determine when discipline has been broken, and to establish the kind of punishment warranted. The punishment may be severe, but it must be accepted without question or recourse. Questioning usually results in more punishment.

This kind of system may be good for catching up to competitors. What do you do once you are on the top? Being on the top is different from trying to catch up. Wages in Japan have increased so much that manufacturing is moving abroad, so having a disciplined workforce on the manufacturing shop floor is becoming superfluous. The new attitude in Japan seems to be that blue-collar work, the work where discipline may have the most effect on product quality, can be done in Indonesia or Mexico without affecting productivity or quality.[18] Much of the manufacturing is done automatically, without human hands, by machines and robots. Discipline may be required to catch up to others, but innovation in products and management is needed to stay on top. Innovation is incompatible with the kind of discipline practiced in Japanese schools, in which conformity is valued at all cost, students learn to fear learning, and the heart of the system is authority and not individual responsibility.

In Japan, Americans are seen as being weak and undisciplined. The Japanese do not think that Americans have responded in the correct way to their challenge. They have taken over whole markets in the U.S. economy, and Americans have acquiesced. They have bought our buildings and our land, and Americans do little to protest. They have responded in similar situations by closing off their markets and limiting foreign acquisitions of their land or their buildings.

---

[18]Peter F. Drucker, *Managing for the Future* (New York: Truman Talley Books/Dutton, 1992), p. 178.

On the other hand, not responding to these challenges requires discipline of a different sort. Americans believe that a free market will provide more choices to consumers and allow products to be sold at lower prices. In Japan, the free-market discipline is not adhered to, and consumers pay the price. It takes discipline not to close off markets in angry response to foreign competition.

Americans believe that anybody or any company offering a superior product should be able to sell that product to consumers. If Japanese products are better, then they should be available to American consumers. The Japanese politician Shintaro Ishihara states that Japanese products should be protected from superior American products to protect their market share. It took American discipline not to restrict Japanese competition at a time when U.S. companies were struggling. But competition has brought higher-quality products to the American consumer. We have benefitted from foreign competition.

Americans believe that discipline comes with individual responsibility. A system which cherishes individualism has to tolerate and accept failures of the system for some people. It takes discipline not to impose authoritarianism on everybody, and stamp out innovativeness, because some people abuse a free system. This is the kind of discipline that we believe is needed for America to stay strong and competitive in world markets.

Our university systems are open to people from all over the world. Knowledge progresses through open systems, although the payoff may not be obvious at the time. It takes discipline to keep these doors open and not insulate ourselves from the rest of the world.

It takes discipline not to close off American markets because we may be losing market share to products from other countries. We believe that through competition our companies will become stronger. If we close off markets, then our companies will always remain uncompetitive. Sometimes American companies or workers apply pressure to stave off this foreign competition. It takes discipline not to respond to this pressure.

Japan and the United States are practicing different forms of discipline. In Japan, discipline comes from authority and group pressure, not from underlying values or ethics. This system would not transfer to the United States, with its history of questioning authority and idealizing the individualistic frontier spirit. In the United States, discipline comes from public policies to preserve competition, free market access to any one, and individual freedoms. Discipline comes from working to preserve these aspects of the U.S. market. Japan does not practice this kind of discipline because it is counter to the short-term interests of the corporations and their workers.

The Japanese people we talked to supported their system and understood that discipline derived from authority, with the threat of physical coercion, and the pressure from the group. They accepted that their children may be punished in school as a means of imposing discipline. The belief is that such discipline will make the student become a better person and a more productive Japanese.

At Mazda's Flat Rock, Michigan, plant, the Japanese managers tried to impose discipline on the American workers in the same ways as they used in Japan. One habit they brought with them was that when they became angry with workers, they tapped the workers on their safety helmets with long pointer sticks. "Sometimes, if they wanted to get your attention, they'd tap you with their pointers," said Peter Barrow, one of the workers. "It was a custom for them to do this in Japan, but the Americans got pretty upset by it. I remember a few people got mad and just grabbed the pointers and broke them, and that put a stop to the Japanese tapping people."[19]

[19]Joseph J. Fucini and Suzy Fucini. *Working for the Japanese* (New York: The Free Press, 1990), pp. 109-110.

The Mechanisms of *Tatemae*

At the end of our stay in Japan we had a few free days between when I stopped working at the research labs and our scheduled departure. This gave us some time to see a little more of Japan and to say goodbye to the other residents of our apartment building. The women of the apartment building were kind enough to invite us to lunch in one of their apartments on the day before we left for home.

After finishing our lunch, one of our neighbors said that she had videotaped a recent television show about our home town, Lafayette, Indiana. Would we care to watch it? We had no idea why she would have watched, and taped, a TV show about Lafayette, but we were curious to see it.

LATE-BREAKING NEWS STORY: GERMANS PAINT THE INTERIORS OF THEIR HOMES   We went to our neighbor's apartment to watch the tape. Like other apartments we had visited, this one was not very well maintained. We had discovered that poorly maintained living spaces were the norm rather than the exception in Japan. The discovery came one night while we were watching the translated Japanese news on television. One of the news teams was on assignment in Germany, and they had visited a private home for a tour by the residents. The owners were talking about their home and mentioned in a matter-of-fact manner that they had just finished painting the interior of the house.

On this particular news show we had come to expect very unemotional responses by the newscasters to most of the crises of the day. Another bomb went off in one of the temples to protest the upcoming coronation of the emperor. No problem, everything is taken care of, this has happened several times in the last couple of days as radical groups use bombings as a public display of their disapproval of coupling the government-sanctioned coronation with the Shinto religion.

A full-scale battle between police and some radicals, representing rice farmers around Narita Airport, protesting the expansion of the airport, is shown, with the police using water hoses to knock the radicals out of the three-story structure they had built for the protest. Nothing to get excited about, just another battle at the airport.

Another report shows day laborers in Osaka burning down a train station because they are upset about collusion between the police and organized crime in handing out jobs and then keeping part of the compensation. No problem, this will soon go away also as the police and organized crime regain their accepted and traditional positions.

That people would paint the interior of their homes themselves, this was exciting. The newscasters got very animated about this newspiece, discussing it in some length. This segment elicited more emotional responses than the bombs or the airport battles. The riots in Osaka were of secondary interest. The Germans actually painted the insides of their own houses.

In the apartment we were visiting, we could see the reason for the excitement. No evidence of past maintenance work, or even heavy cleaning, was apparent. The wallpaper was peeling in sections from the wall. The carpeting was tattered in the high-use areas. The brown globs of mildew on the ceiling had gone unwashed for a long time. Electrical extension cords were strewn across the carpet to reach from one side of the kitchen to the other. No improvements or even basic maintenance had ever been done. In Lafayette, as in other parts of the United States, one of the busiest places on a Saturday morning is the local lumberyard or home fix-it store. Everybody seems to be working on some kind of home improvement project. Home improvement was obviously not a weekend hobby in Japan.

We thought that the television show on Lafayette provided a chance to communicate to our neighbors that Americans are not lazy, that we take pride in our homes and in our community. The television show would surely include pictures of the well-maintained homes and green lawns. The pride of the community, the courthouse, had recently been meticulously restored through donations from groups throughout the community. Any picture of Lafayette would surely have to include the courthouse in the panorama, because all the sight lines downtown were carefully maintained to include the historic courthouse.

We had tried to dispel some of the myths our Japanese neighbors had about American lifestyles. We had shown a couple of our neighbors pictures of our home. With all the Japanese tourists visiting the United States, with all the television shows about life in America, and all the movies, they seemed to know very little about how Americans actually live. This television show on Lafayette would be a good way to communicate about American lifestyles.

CHARLES DARWIN VISITS THE HIGH SCHOOL   To

watch the television show we were offered the choice seats on the couch in front of the television, with the other women standing because there were no other seats. They stood off to one side.

The show started off with some special reports on high schools throughout the United States. The first report showed African-American high school students in an inner-city New York school having to pass through metal detectors to ensure that no students were carrying guns. The second report showed a day-care center set up at a Latino high school in East Los Angeles so that junior and senior high school unwed mothers had some place to leave their young children when they returned to school.

Then we got to the main feature of the show, Lafayette's Jefferson High School. A scene of Lafayette introduced this segment. Although we were familiar with Lafayette, we did not immediately recognize where this panorama had been shot. The famous courthouse was not in the scene. No private homes were shown. The place actually looked pretty grubby. The panorama would meet people's expectations if they were looking for the decline of the industrial Midwest.

Next, scenes of students entering Lafayette's high school were shown (no metal detectors in this case). We then saw a teacher in front of his class. The camera froze on the shot. Wait. This was not an information show about American lifestyles or high schools, as we had expected. This was a television game show. In some ways, it was a silly combination of the old "What's My Line" show and a version of "Hard Copy," but without even "Hard Copy's" dubious journalism standards. In the show, the celebrity contestants are divided into three two-person teams, and each team gets a chance to try to guess why, in this instance, the teacher is so unusual. After many silly tries without anyone giving the correct answer, one of the teams finally got it: The teacher dresses up as a historical figure when teaching his history class. The still-shot unfroze and we saw the teacher preparing for class, by putting on make-up and a wig, and coming to class as Charles Darwin. More silly comments by the celebrity contestants followed.

The hostess of the Lafayette segment of the show, a former pop singer, then went into Jefferson High School to talk to some of the students in English, with Japanese translations subtitled on the screen. First, she talked to a group of students about what they wear to school and whether or not they would like to wear the traditional uniforms of Japanese school boys and girls. One of the Americans came into the scene wearing a typical Japanese uniform. Everyone laughed and said they would rather not wear uniforms. What were the American students allowed to wear to school? The students said that they could wear pretty much what they wanted. One of the students offered jokingly that they could even come to school dirty.

As we sat on the couch watching this, we noticed out of the corner of our eye that all the women were watching us closely—not the television screen, but us. At just this time a student entered the scene on the screen from the left, walked in front of the hostess, paused, dropped his pants, and mooned the camera. As he exited stage right, we saw a close-up of the hostess's face as her hand covered her open mouth and she screamed, "Aaaaaaaa."

Next, the scene changed to the school parking lot, where the camera focused on a car entering the lot and swerving around. The car came toward the camera and pulled into a parking space, but suddenly put on its brakes to stop quickly. We heard sounds of breaking glass and scrunching metal. We never saw what the car hit, because cartoon balloons superimposed over the point of impact said, "CRASH!!! BAM!!!."

After being in Japan for three months, our initial reaction to the show was that it was refreshing to see our hometown, with American kids who had the freedom to show their individuality. We were tired of Japanese kids staring at us on the trains, making comments, and giggling because we looked different. Our boys were getting tired of having their hair rubbed every time we went out in public.

Later, though, we came to realize that the show was just another instance of the propagandizing about Americans and the rest of the world which occurs regularly on Japanese television. The show fulfilled its purpose. First, the violence of Americans was emphasized by showing the students passing through the metal detector. Second, the immorality of Americans and the breakdown of the American family was emphasized by showing the in-school day-care center for the children of unwed mothers. Third, the show demonstrated that, given individual freedom, young people will abuse that freedom. We have the freedom to wear what we want to school, but students abuse it by coming to school dirty. Students have the freedom to drive to school, but they do not have the discipline or the responsibility to deal with this freedom. They ram other cars. Students have no sense of decency; they pull down their pants to be funny. Americans are violent, immoral, irresponsible, and undisciplined.

THE BUTT OF THE JOKE   The image presented on the television show is not exactly the one that school officials would want to convey to the rest of the world. We were wondering why the administration at Jefferson High School had let the Japanese film crew into the school to film a television game show which makes the school the butt of all the jokes. Since we were leaving for home the next day, we convinced our hostess to let us have the tape so that we could take it with us. We were curious to find out what had happened in Lafayette.

Jefferson High School is one of the top academic schools in the Midwest. With Purdue University, a leading science and engineering university, just across the river, the community has a good supply of highly motivated students. Some of the largest manufacturing companies in the world have plants in the area: Eli Lilly (pharmaceuticals), Great Lakes Chemical Corp. (chemicals), and Caterpillar (large-vehicle engines). A joint manufacturing plant between Subaru and Isuzu, and scores of Japanese automobile supply companies, have recently moved into the area. Lafayette often finds itself in the lists of best places to live in the country because of the large number of good jobs, the low crime rate, and the affordable housing prices. Lafayette's Jefferson High School is one of the few high schools in the country that has won the distinction of being named a Blue Ribbon school twice. One of the nice things about the high school is the diversity of the students: children of professors, lawyers, physicians, and the working class all attend the same high school.

We were able to find out many interesting things about this show. The television producers did not tell the school officials that they were shooting scenes for a game show. Rather, they told the administration that they were shooting a documentary, were interested in innovative teaching methods, and wanted to publicize some of the teaching innovations used at Jefferson.

When making the initial contacts with the high school officials to gain permission to tape the segment in the show, the hostess was not introduced as a famous pop singer, but was portrayed as an educator who had received degrees from famous North American universities. There was actually an element of truth to this. She had received a degree in education from the University of Toronto, and she attended Stanford University for a short time. It was a misrepresentation of the truth, however, because the producers never mentioned that she would be recognized instantly in Japan not as an educator but as a pop singer.

The principal has a standing policy at Jefferson not to let television crews into the school. In this one case, however, he decided to make an exception so that the Japanese could develop a better understanding of Americans. The usual arguments were used to obtain cooperation from the reluctant Americans. This show would be useful to further mutual understanding between Americans and Japanese. The television show producers travel around the world, promoting world peace and harmony among all people of the world. These are lofty goals which could not be denied. Americans are always suckers when it comes to these kinds of ideals.

The outright lies and misrepresentations used to gain permission to use Jefferson High School as the victim for the jokes of a Japanese game show were minor compared to the manipulations of the camera crew to make an American high school look as bad as possible. The production team went into the situation with a script of bad things they wanted to show and staged the scenes, again through deception, to achieve the desired effects.

The mooning scene was obviously staged. The hostess knew what the student was about to do—she reacted before he started to pull down his pants—whereas the spectators looked genuinely shocked. The school officials did not know that student interviews were taking place in the school cafeteria; no permission had been given. In order to do these interviews, the Japanese television crew missed the scheduled visit to the industrial arts classroom.

For the parking lot scene, we found out that the camera crew members had said they wanted to go outside for a smoke. This was at lunchtime, Jefferson has a closed campus policy, and no cars are allowed to enter or leave the monitored parking lot. We froze the tape and watched the reactions of the people on the sidewalk next to the "accident." We have witnessed several accidents, and the immediate reaction of others in the vicinity is always to look around. This is an automatic response which cannot be avoided. In this scene, though, nobody reacted. The only evidence that an accident had occurred was the loud crashing noises which could be heard on the tape; the actual crash was never shown. No accident report was ever filed with the school about this incident. The school officials accepted the explanation of the camera crew that they were only going outside to smoke; there was no reason to question this because, after all, this was a simple documentary that they were filming and surely nothing bad could be filmed in the parking lot in the middle of the school day.

WHEN A DOCUMENTARY DOES NOT DOCUMENT

Japanese television shows actually have a sordid history of faking shots or distorting the truth in the name of entertainment. The most prestigious network in Japan, NHK, was criticized recently for faking a documentary called the "Unknown Kingdom of the Himalayas."[1] The "documentary," a very popular form of television show in Japan, faked six scenes in its two-hour depiction of life in a small self-governing country, Mustang, high in the Himalayas on the border between Tibet and Nepal. The documentary showed the television crew arriving on foot when they actually arrived by helicopter. A cameraman staged a scene in which he "passed

---

[1]Merrill Goozner, "Japanese Documentary Was Faked," *Chicago Tribune,* February 4, 1993, p. 1-3.

out" due to altitude sickness. The television crew paid a Buddhist monk to pray for rain after a supposed three-month dry spell. It actually rained while the crew was filming the documentary.

In September 1992, the private television network Asahi aired a "documentary" about the sexual activities of Japanese women with foreign men. It hired several African-American men to portray U.S. soldiers who brag about their sexual exploits with Japanese women. The program portrayed these actors as actual soldiers.

Even talk shows can be faked. Also in 1992, Yomiuri Telecasting Corp. aired a talk show about the working conditions of women nurses. Twelve of the twenty nurses were paid to follow the script given to them by the producers.

PATTERN OF PROPAGANDA

What is so bad about distorting the image of a high school in Indiana? Everybody seemed to have fun. The Japanese celebrities had fun performing on the game show; the Japanese audience got a chance to see another installment of one of their favorite television shows. The people in Lafayette really didn't get hurt because they never heard what happened. A description of the show never appeared in the local newspaper or TV newscast.

This kind of propaganda is hurtful because it falls into a pattern of misrepresentations. Isolated instances of misrepresentation are not necessarily hurtful. It is only when many instances form a pattern that problems ensue. Instead of searching for the truth, reality is manipulated until the images start to form the reality. The Japanese audience was left with images that no words of truth could counter: images of the declining industrial base of the Midwest, metal detectors for guns, unwed mothers and their children, lack of discipline in the schools, and of course the car accident in the parking lot. The images become the reality. Americans are dirty, violent, and undisciplined.

The repetition of stereotypes in the media portrayal of foreigners has been observed by others. A visitor to Japan, Basil Hall Chamberlain, observed that "...the travelled Japanese consider our [Western people's] three most prominent characteristics to be dirt, laziness and superstition....Europe and America make a far less favorable impression on the Japanese visitor than seems to be generally expected."[2]

The amazing thing about the above quotation, though, is that Chamberlain made this observation in 1894 in a book called *Things Japanese*. Things Japanese, and attitudes of the Japanese people, have not changed much over the years.

These kinds of images, from Chamberlain's observations down through the television game shows, send two important messages. First, the people portrayed on the television shows, if they represent the best that America has to offer, are still

[2]Richard Tames, *Encounters with Japan* (New York: St. Martin's Press, 1991), p. 12.

lazy, undisciplined, immoral, and dirty. Japan doesn't need any trade barriers; the Japanese consumer has an automatic, built-in trade barrier against buying products made by these kinds of people. Obviously, the products would be poorly made and of poor quality. Why buy something from these Americans and reinforce this kind of behavior?

Second, the message helps to allay any guilt the Japanese may have about their relationships to the rest of the world. Their economic policy toward the rest of the world has often been described as predatory, and some of the evidence for that policy has been detailed in previous chapters. The strategy is simple. Hold prices high in the home market by keeping out foreign products, sell at prices below cost in the target country to gain market share and destroy the competition, and then control the markets and the prices. In the target countries, people lose jobs, and the jobs which remain are often lower paying. In the target country, foreign products flood the market. Japanese companies pay little or no taxes to the government of the target country because they claim they make no profit, and eventually government programs are strapped for money.

THINGS ARE BAD, AND WE DESERVE IT   Some people may say that such a strategy is not right, or that the strategy is unfair. People who use such a strategy may even start to feel guilty. The national media may start to write articles about how these practices are causing problems in the targeted countries. However, if the problems are not recognized, there is nothing to feel guilty about. If the people having problems deserve them, because of their laziness or lack of discipline, then feelings of guilt can be averted. The problems we face are our own doing. The Japanese have said this many times, we echo the words in our own press, and we start to believe it ourselves.

It is true that American companies and American workers have created many of the problems confronting them today. The other side of the coin cannot be ignored, though. Some of the problems our companies face have been caused by the predatory strategies of Japanese companies. We must be able to separate the two to find solutions to the problems. If we simply accept the stereotypes, then the problems cannot be analyzed and solutions cannot be implemented.

EXAGGERATIONS   Throughout this book we have investigated how the Japanese politicians, the media, and business executives have exaggerated their virtues in regard to quality products. Upon closer inspection, many of these virtues have been exaggerations. Japanese workers are not very productive when compared to American workers. Students from their education system score well on math tests, but the emphasis on test taking creates as many problems as it solves, and it leaves severe gaps in the education of these students. Although the Japanese seem to treat their workers better in terms of lifetime employment, they also tend to have sexist and racist hiring practices, and they literally work some of their employees to death. Japanese companies have been successful in high-technology areas, but they are still scrambling to protect those areas from companies in up-and-coming countries, such as South Korea and Taiwan, while the United States has retained its superiority in leading-edge technology. Japanese executives in Tokyo and Osaka pay little attention to customer trends in the United States, claiming that they know more about American customers than those in contact with these customers.

Even the quality of products was found to be more hype than substance. Japanese and American companies are about even in producing high-quality vehicles when various publications and surveys are considered. Japanese electronics companies are producing high-quality consumer electronics, although evidence was presented that consumers may be dissatisfied with these products, as reflected in the high numbers which are returned to the stores. A listing of the top 100 quality products in the United States showed that the impact of Japanese products on American life has been exaggerated. The exaggerations are carefully cultivated, and critics are quickly attacked. Critics of Japanese companies, morals, or culture are usually dismissed in one or more of five ways: they are labeled as Japan-bashers; they are called racist; they are labeled ignorant about Japan because they have not lived there long enough or do not know the language well enough (only Japanese can understand the Japanese); they are fired under pressure from Japanese interests; and, in Japan, they may face violence or assassination attempts.

BASHING THE "RISING SUN"   Michael Crichton, the author of *Rising Sun*,[3] which depicted some of the salvos in the economic war between the United States and Japan in a work of fiction, was attacked in several of these ways. The reviewer for the *Nikkei Weekly* managed to work in two of the attack methods—Japan-bashing and ignorance about Japan—in one sentence: "Crichton seems to have settled for sitting at home reading a pile of Japan-bashing books written by Americans who can't speak Japanese, have never been there for more than 72 hours and don't have any Japanese friends," stated the review.[4] Racism in the depiction of the Japanese in the movie was captured in another review: "This is a kind of renewal of Fu Man Chu or Ming the Merciless—the Oriental villains who plotted to take over the world," said Yumiko Murikami, who wrote a book called *Yellow Face—How Hollywood Has Depicted Asians in Film*.[5]

---

[3]Michael Crichton, *Rising Sun* (New York: Alfred A. Knopf, 1992).
[4]Merrill Goozner, "'Rising Sun' Is on Far Horizon for Japanese," *Chicago Tribune*, August 15, 1993, p. 1-19.

George Packard, the dean of the Paul H. Nitze School of the Johns Hopkins University, is often trotted out to yell Japan-basher at any criticism of Japan. He lumped together four scholars who had written critical books about Japan and labeled them Japan-bashers in an article for the *Wahington Post* called "The Japan-Bashers Are Poisoning Foreign Policy."[6] The writers he attacked were Chalmers Johnson, a University of California at San Diego professor with 40 years of work on Japan studies, who wrote *MITI and the Japanese Miracle*; Clyde V. Prestowitz, a former trade negotiator who had first-hand knowledge of the trade practices of the Japanese and wrote the book *Trading Places*; Karel van Wolferen, who spent 17 years as a journalist in Japan and wrote *The Enigma of Japanese Power*; and James Fallows, a journalist for the *Atlantic Monthly*, who spent three years in Japan and has written newspaper stories, magazine articles, and books on Japan. With the label of Japan-bashers and by comparing their attitudes to that of McCarthyism, Packard tries to stifle any discussion of the important issues considered in these books and articles. These four revisionists, as they are termed as an alternative to using the term Japan-basher, replied to the criticism. "[W]e ask those who disagree with these contentions to acknowledge that, right or wrong, they are arguments about politics and economics—not expressions of visceral antagonism toward Japan," they wrote.[7] "Nothing in the works we have written, or the lives we have lived, can support the idea that we are simply hostile to the people and culture of Japan."

In 1988, Packard wrote a 16-page advertising supplement to *U.S. News & World Report*, paid for by the Japanese Chamber of Commerce, which was entitled "The U.S. and Japan: Partners in Prosperity." This advertisement had such inserts as "Toyota U.S.A.: An American Phenomenon," "Mitsubishi Forges Strong American Ties," "Suzuki: Partners in Prosperity with the American People," and "A Call for Autonomy at Ricoh." His voice becomes one with the Japanese business interests who paid for the advertisement to promote their products. Yelling Japan-basher complements the sale of Japanese products in the United States.

In a speech given by Crichton at the National Press Club on April 6, 1993, he claimed that the term "Japan-basher" was coined by an official at the Japanese Foreign Ministry. This official said that the term was intended to stifle debate and anyone who used it was his intellectual dupe. It has been very successful in stifling debate, as intended. Even supporters of Japan think that it has been taken too far. "The concept of Japan-bashing has been manipulated to invalidate those Americans

---

[5]Ibid.
[6]George N. Packard, "The Japan-Bashers Are Poisoning Foreign Policy", *Washington Post*, October 8, 1989, p. C4.
[7]James Fallows, Chalmers Johnson, Clyde V. Prestowitz, and Karel van Wolferen, "Beyond Japan-Bashing," *U.S. News & World Report*, May 7, 1990, p. 55.

who have run against the politically correct concept of Japan: the view that Japan is America's constant friend, constant ally and that economic issues are secondary to the primacy of the relationship,"[8] said Steven Clemons, who is the executive director of the Japan-America Society of Southern California. The National Association of Japan-America Societies works to "improve the cultural understanding between the people of Japan and the U.S," according to its mission statement.

RACIST FIGURE SKATERS   Many Americans are deathly afraid to be called racists, and this can be used to effectively stifle criticism of Japan. In the recent world championships of women's figure skating, when their woman skater performed poorly, the Japanese press was quick to say that the judging was racist and always had been racist against Asian skaters. This charge of racism was leveled against the judging even though a Japanese-American, Kristi Yamaguchi, had won the gold medal in women's figure skating at the 1992 Winter Olympics.

Perhaps Shintaro Ishihara provides the best example of calling people racist at any perceived criticism of Japanese government policy. His book, *The Japan That Can Say No,* is full of explosive statements and multiple accusations of racist American policies. All criticisms of closed Japanese markets, even though Ishihara admitted that these markets were closed, were dismissed as racist attacks which had the effect—perhaps intended—of stifling any discussion of important bilateral issues. Perhaps the most blatant example of labeling Americans as racist was when he stated that the United States dropped the atomic bombs on Japan and not Germany because Americans were racist against the Japanese. This argument ignored the fact that the atomic bomb had not yet been developed at the time Germany surrendered. To carry this illogical argument to its preposterous conclusion would mean that dropping the bomb on a defeated and defenseless Germany would have been the only way to demonstrate to Ishihara and his ilk that the bombing of Japan was fair and not based on a racist policy.

ROADBLOCKS ON THE FREEDOM HIGHWAY   We have talked about lifetime employment as it applies to Japanese corporations. If one criticizes Japan, however, one runs the risk of being fired. Pat Choate, who wrote the book *Agents of Influence*, about how Japanese government agencies, corporations, and foundations spent $400 million on lobbying and public relations to influence U.S. government policy, had been employed by TRW Corporation while writing the book. TRW, based in Cleveland, makes auto parts and defense-related products and

---

[8]Goozner, "'Rising Sun' Is on Far Horizon."

does $400 million of business a year with Japanese firms. In August 1990, two months before the book was published, Choate was forced to resign from his $200,000-a-year job as vice president at TRW.

In a lawsuit Choate filed against TRW, he claims that Japanese corporate officials began complaining to officials at TRW-Japan about the book even before it was published. His immediate supervisor at TRW, William Lawrence, was quoted in the suit as saying that Choate was fired because "the book would harm TRW with its Japanese customers."[9] Choate claims that he had authority from TRW to write the book and that he kept TRW informed of his progress.

Choate did not win the suit, an appeal did not overturn the original ruling, and the Supreme Court refused to hear the case. We talked to Pat Choate and his lawyer, Dale Cooder, about this case. Cooder indicated that they knew the battle to win this case would be difficult because federal law states only that employees cannot be fired due to discrimination (race, creed, or sex) or breach of contract. Choate said that TRW knew about the book, they had approved it, he wrote the book on his own time, and the company spent no money on the book. Choate and Cooder also felt they presented sufficient evidence that Japanese officials pressured TRW to fire Choate. All this was immaterial, however, because they could not prove that the firing was due to discrimination or breach of contract. If TRW felt that Choate was bad for business—Japanese officials apparently told them this—then this was sufficient legal reason to fire him. No federal law protects a person's job in this case. Choate's firing may not be fair, but was not against the law.

This incident reminded us of the words from the Woody Guthrie song sung by Peter, Paul and Mary to the audience in Japan (see Chapter 17): "Nobody living can ever stop me, As I go walking that freedom highway." When trying to exercise his freedom to speak out on something he thought was wrong, Choate was sent walking. Speaking out may be stopped if a person is forced to choose between the freedom highway or the fast track of a high-paying job. The possibility of losing a job can be a large roadblock in the criticism of Japan, its companies, or its policies.

Many times the threat of closing down Japanese-owned plants, and throwing people out of work, is also used to stifle discussion and criticism. When Japanese-owned Sumitomo Corp. had to respond to Congressional committee charges of sexual harassment against American women employees, it sent out a press release stating how many Americans were employed by the company.[10] The veiled threat was that any more probing or criticism would result in Americans being put out of work.

---

[9]Stuart Auerbach, "Ex-employee Sues TRW, Charges Japanese Pressure," *Washington Post*, June 25, 1991, p. C3.
[10]Carol Jouzaitis, "Accuser: Sumitomo Retaliated," *Chicago Tribune*, February 27, 1992, p. 3-1.

BASH, BASH, YOU'RE DEAD   With little frank discussion of issues in public, speaking out about Japan in Japan can be dangerous. Hitoshi Motoshima, the mayor of Nagasaki, has paid for his public statements. A year after saying that the emperor should accept responsibility for the suffering of the Japanese people in World War II, Motoshima nearly died from a gunshot wound from a right-wing fanatic who took exception to his statements. "At first I thought I was dying," he said. "For one year before the shooting, I thought I might be killed, so I was prepared for it."[11] Unlike others who may be silenced by an assassination attempt, Motoshima is still speaking out. He publicly stated that Japan should apologize and provide aid to North and South Korea, which were victims of Japan's prewar and wartime aggression.

Morihiro Hosokawa was a breath of fresh air for only a very short period of time as Japanese prime minister before his government was forced to resign. He was the first Japanese leader to speak out on Japan's wartime atrocities against its Asian neighbors, calling Japan's actions in Asia a "war of aggression."[12] He also was a victim of an assassination attempt, from a person who did not think Japan had anything for which to apologize. Emperor Akihito's planned visit to China, where he was to apologize formally to the Chinese people for Japan's role in atrocities before and during World War II, was protested through a series of bomb attacks on political headquarters in Japan.

A recent disturbing trend has been attacks on Japanese reporters. One reporter has already been killed and another seriously wounded. The producer of a television show, Yuichi Katsura, has been the victim of threatening phone calls following the airing of controversial issues. "Some people refused to appear on the show because they felt harassment,"[13] says Katsura. When people appear as panelists on the show, they are told to do so at their own risk.

Yasuhiro Okudaira, a professor at a Japanese university, is alarmed that freedom of speech may actually be declining in Japan. "Legally there is no suppression of freedom of speech, unlike the pre-1945 day," says Okudaira. "But, gradually, in social customs, freedom of speech is declining. People don't want to talk about topics they feel would cause problems. A mood of self-restraint is becoming stronger."[14] The Japanese corporations also have a hand in suppressing discussion of reality or unpleasant topics. "Rather than taking up subjects that are controversial, the media just avoid them for the sake of peace at any price," says Keiichi Katsura, a

---

[11]Brian Covert, "Mayor of Nagasaki Finds Way to Resolve Himself to Fate," *Japan Times,* October 16, 1990, p. 4.
[12]Merrill Goozner, "New Hirohito Revelations Startle Japan," *Chicago Tribune,* July 7, 1994, p. 3-1.
[13]Sam Jameson, "Violence Chilling Freedom of Speech in Japan," *Los Angeles Times,* October 13, 1992, p. H-2.
[14]Ibid.

professor at the most prestigious university in Japan—Tokyo University. "If something really different is taken up, newspapers fear their circulations will drop; TV networks fear sponsors will stop advertising," says Katsura. "The bottleneck is commercialism."[15] The companies are afraid to advertise in publications or on television shows which present controversial topics.

Another way that *tatemae* is preserved is that many of the victims are too ashamed or embarrassed to fight against the images they know to be false. The surviving comfort girls from World War II were too ashamed to speak about what had happened to them during the war. It took forty years before anyone would speak out to demand an apology and restitution from the Japanese government. The principal of Lafayette's high school, which was ridiculed in the game show, has never publicly acknowledged what the television audience in Japan saw. He was too embarrassed to speak about it. Except for a few teachers involved in the filming, people in Lafayette do not know how the facts were distorted and how the "documentary" was staged. Physical and intellectual abuse can continue because people refuse to speak out against the falsehoods that would draw attention to how they were victimized.

YAMATO: THE BATTLESHIP, THE NUCLEAR SUBMARINE, AND THE JAPANESE SPIRIT   Before World War II, the Japanese built the biggest battleship the world has ever known. Called the *Yamato*, the Japanese word for national spirit, the ship displaced 72,000 tons and had nine monstrous, 18.1-inch guns. Regardless of its awesome firepower and its maneuverability, it was obsolete the moment it entered the ocean. Ocean battles had changed from battles of firepower to air battles waged by aircraft carriers or submarine battles waged below the surface. The battleship was no match for aircraft launched from carriers or submarines lurking below the surface, so the *Yamato*'s role during the war was reduced to personal yacht for the commanding admiral, carrying him from one battle area to the next. The huge guns fired few shots during the war, because the Japanese were afraid to betray their position. Her position was zealously guarded and protected by a cordon of accompanying ships, because the military leaders feared that if the *Yamato* was lost, then Japan's spirit, or *yamato*, would also be lost.

After losing the battle of Okinawa, Japan had little left with which to defend itself. There were few ships left, the remaining aircraft had been sacrificed to *kamikaze* attacks on Allied ships, it had no fuel to power the military machinery. The *Yamato* remained. The military leaders ordered it out of its hiding place in Japan's Inland Sea with an escort of a light cruiser and eight destroyers. A crew of 2767 men were

---

on the *Yamato,* another 1167 sailors were on the escort ships, and they did not have enough fuel to return home.[16]

Allied submarines, patrolling the outlet of the Inland Sea, quickly discovered the *Yamato* northwest of Okinawa. Nearly 300 carrier planes were ordered to attack. With the planes swarming around the ship, the large guns fired aimlessly and were useless against the modern attack. A hundred minutes of relentless attacking and countless hits and the *Yamato* rolled over, entombing about 2488 fathers, sons, and husbands forever on this last-gasp suicide mission. With the sinking of the *Yamato,* Japan's spirit sank. Although the military leaders had plans to equip the citizenry with sharpened bamboo poles to defend the beaches against the coming Allied attack, both the military and the government realized that the battle could not be won; defeat was inevitable. Admiral Yamamoto, educated in the United States and the person who planned the attack on Pearl Harbor, admitted that the war was actually lost as soon as the first shot was fired. But the spirit of *Yamato* was supposed to carry the citizens to victory against all odds. The atomic bombs ended the last-ditch plan to sacrifice Japanese civilians on the beaches.

Forty years later the *Yamato* was resurrected, this time as a secret nuclear submarine in a popular comic-book series.[17] In the series, Japan has built the supersubmarine to be manned by a Japanese crew as part of the U.S. Navy. On its test cruise, the *Yamato* turns renegade and flees. The United States vows to destroy it so the technology does not fall into the hands of the Soviets. The *Yamato* manages to elude the Americans, but the Americans make a deal with the Soviets to capture the *Yamato* so that Japan does not become a superpower in East Asia. The U.S. president insists that the *Yamato* be destroyed to preserve the current world order and to crush any reviving fascism or militarism in Japan. An ultimatum is given: Surrender the *Yamato* or Japan will be occupied militarily. Nuclear weapons are pointed at Tokyo and Osaka. We left Japan before the conclusion of this epic sea battle, with the *Yamato* poised off the coast of Okinawa.

This story provides a powerful allegory to how the Japanese perceive their relationships with the rest of the world. They are trying to forge a new world order based on their advanced technology, a technology that can build a nuclear submarine. The old world order conspires against them, threatening military occupation or, even worse, nuclear annihilation. It is the story told by Ishihara in *The Japan That Can Say No.* It is the Japanese classic fairy tale of the Peach Boy, where the foreigners must be vanquished before Japan is destroyed.

The choice of *Yamato* as the name of the battleship and then the nuclear submarine is also very appropriate. The foreigners want to destroy the Japanese spirit, man-

---

[16]Dan van der Vat, *The Pacific Campaign* (New York: Simon & Schuster, 1991), pp. 384-385.
[17]Janet Ashby, "Chinmoku-no-kantai," *Japan Times,* September 28, 1990, p. 20.

ifested in the battleship and the submarine, by destroying the home rice market or through the influence of foreign movies or foreign products. The people have to dig in and protect the *yamato,* the spirit which has sustained them through the millenium. Now, instead of one cruiser and eight destroyers providing a cordon of protection, a *tatemae* barrier is erected for the protection of the Japanese nation. Any emphasis on the negatives of Japanese society would work to destroy the carefully cultivated and manufactured Japanese spirit. The images of *tatemae,* even when they do not correspond to the reality, must be maintained to keep the *yamato* from sinking.

Daniel Boorstin is a Pulitzer prize-winning historian and teacher, and author of best-selling such books as *The Discoverers* and *The Creators.* "Totalitarian societies exaggerate their virtues," says Boorstin. "But free societies like ours somehow seize the temptation to exaggerate their vices."[18] *Tatemae* occurs on a two-way street. Just as Japan has exaggerated its virtues in manufacturing quality products, the United States contributes to these same *tatemae* by exaggerating its vices. In the United States, motivation is often achieved by emphasizing and exaggerating weaknesses. People will be motivated to work hard if they perceive that they are falling behind, and they will become dedicated and creative if serious problems need to be solved. In Japan, people are motivated by *yamato* or spirit. Their successes are exaggerated to use as examples for how *yamato* can be used in the future to achieve even greater things.

When examining quality products from both countries, the Japanese people must realize that American products and American society are not as bad as Americans say they are. By complaining, Americans are motivating themselves to do better. On the other hand, when looking at Japanese products, Americans must realize that Japanese products are not as good as the Japanese say they are. The Japanese are using *tatemae* to exaggerate the quality of their products as motivation to achieve greater things by invoking *yamato.*

---

[18]Daniel J. Boorstin, "Why an Eminent Historian Unequivocally States: 'I Am Optimistic,'" *Parade Magazine,* July 10, 1994, p. 4.

Consequences

A beauty pageant may offer the best image of a country's culture. What is beauty? What is the treatment of women? How do you get "world peace" or "stopping hunger" into answers to the questions? What's more important: looking good in a swimsuit; intelligent answers to questions; or talent? Does someone who stands out from the crowd as being different win, or does someone who represents the crowd win?

One night, we had a chance to answer some questions about the culture when we happened to find a Japanese beauty pageant on television. The answers to some of the questions were obvious from watching the first few contestants. A distinctive look—an individual look—was not going to win the contest. The talent was only mediocre. One contestant did an aerobics exercise for her talent. When answering questions, most of the girls giggled behind their hands. Cute and giggly appeared to be the ideal female characteristics.

PERFECT TENS We were not prepared for one of the contestants, though. In the swimsuit competition, out comes contestant number one. There is

317

nothing unusual about her as she moves around the stage. Contestant two, with the numeral "2" across her chest, follows the prescribed route across the stage. The pattern continues through contestant number nine. Then contestant ten enters, wearing a "10" across her chest. Right behind her comes another contestant wearing a "10," followed by another and another and another, all wearing "10s" on their swimsuits. It couldn't be, we say to ourselves. A team entry in a beauty contest? This is the most individualistic of any kind of competition. But it had to be. In the evening-gown competition, contestant number ten, all five of them, wore the same evening gown and appeared all at once. They were all there to answer the one question put to them by the host. In the talent part of the show, they were five members of a rock band, all on the stage at the same time. They all came out on the stage giggling as the host announced that contestant ten had finished in third place, quite a respectable showing.

Which other culture on earth would even consider placing a team entry in a beauty contest? The Japanese had taken a Western institution, the beauty pageant, and twisted it around to fit their culture. How do you judge a team entry? Do you take the best body part from each person and mentally combine them into a single contestant's form which is the best combination of all five? This would help them all in the competition. Or do you average all five of them, resulting in a combined image. This would lessen their chances of winning. They obviously had an advantage answering the question and possibly when performing in the talent portion of the show.

In the West, we had always been taught to see the beauty in the individual. We see the beauty in the skillful individual play in baseball. We see the beauty in the virtuoso pianist or the brilliant researcher. We have a "star" of the show. As evidenced by the beauty pageant, the Japanese see the beauty in the group or in the team. Teamwork in baseball is important for winning games. The pianist should not be too flamboyant and show up the rest of the orchestra. Doing research in a team is important for success. There is no "star" of the show. The attitudes of the people in the two cultures could not be more different.

After the winners had been announced, the host came bounding onto the stage, obviously psyched after having been a part of all this beauty and talent. He invited one of the judges, an American, to be interviewed on camera.

"What did you think of the beauty pageant?" the host asked hurriedly, as if he could hardly wait to hear the answer.

The American judge looked a little bit stunned, and he did not have a ready answer to the question. Perhaps he wanted to say something about the team contestant, but didn't know what to say. Perhaps he was wondering, as we were, if this had really happened. Was the team contestant just an illusion? Was it just an image of what one would expect to occur in Japan? When was this image going to go up in smoke?

All of a sudden the expression on the judge's face changed from one of confusion to one of contentment. He had thought of the answer to the question. "It was very interesting," said the American judge.

The host was obviously pleased by this answer. The outsider had given his blessing to Japan's beauty and talent. It looked as though in his mind the host was saying, in a crescendo of mental sound, "Yes! Yes! Yes!"

METAPHORS, STORIES, AND MYTHS   Throughout this book, we have used metaphors and stories to illustrate some of the myths about the quality of products from Japan. In Chapter 1, we started with the metaphor of the overhead projector. When the overhead projector could not focus images on the screen, because it was a poor-quality Japanese-made product, the solution to the problem was to pull a string to improve the image. Better solutions would have been to find another projector or to fix the broken arm. These would have provided better and more permanent fixes to the problem.

In many areas of Japanese life and Japanese-made products, we found that the image was more important than the reality. Fixing the image is the easy solution; fixing the problem is more difficult. With the malfunctioning projector, fixing the image required only an inexpensive string and someone to pull the string. Fixing the projector, or buying a new one, would have taken some time and resources.

We saw these kinds of quick fixes to problems throughout Japan. In the Nissan minivans that had to be recalled because of engine fires, the correct solution would be to increase the size of the engine compartment, to decrease the size of the engine, or to eliminate the engine add-ons which were causing the overheating. Instead, several recalls were needed to replace small parts ruined by the overheating. These were quick fixes that did not address the problem.

Honda recalled cars in Japan because of a malfunctioning oil switch which could ruin the engine, but these same models of cars were not recalled in the United States until two years later. At that earlier date, the Accord was competing with the Taurus to be the best-selling car in the United States. A recall would have ruined the image of the Accord in the United States and could have affected sales. The image was more important than the fact that these cars had a problem serious enough to require a recall.

Japanese companies dominate the American consumer electronics market. The image is that they have achieved this domination by building quality products. The reality is that consumers are not satisfied with these products, because 5 to 25% of the purchases are returned to the stores. Yet little or no discussion of this appears in newspapers or magazines.

When Japan's Sumitomo Corporation expanded their business to the United States and built offices here, they brought their employment practices with them. When a woman testified before Congress about sexual harassment at Sumitomo, the permanent solution to the harassment would have been to address the problem and realize that practices which are acceptable in Japan may not be acceptable in other cultures. Instead, Sumitomo tried to fix the image. They denied that any problem had occurred. The woman who testified said that Sumitomo employees tried to fix the image, by threatening her, so she would not say anything more in public about her harassment. She later quit, after her job was made too unpleasant for her. The company concentrated on the image instead of the solution.

Japan committed many atrocities during World War II. Instead of taking the difficult approach of confronting these issues, government officials have decided to fix the image instead. Some people in the government deny that the Rape of Nanking ever occurred. The Ministry of Education eliminates discussion of these issues from the school textbooks. They denied the "comfort girl" program until the facts could not be hidden any longer, and then they refused the victims any compensation or apologies. The image is maintained by denying the reality.

PULLING THE STRINGS   For the projector, the image was maintained by pulling on a string. We found other ways that the images of high-quality Japanese products are maintained. When some writers and commentators try to loosen the strings so the image will correspond more closely with reality, people hurl remarks such as "racist" or "Japan-basher." When questioned about why Japan did not have open markets for American products similar to the open markets in the United States for Japanese products, Shintaro Ishihara, rather than respond to the question, characterized the United States as being racist. Akio Morita, the chairman of Sony, participated in this orgy of name calling by being listed as the first author and writing six of the eleven chapters of the book, *The Japan That Can Say No*, which was meant only for a Japanese audience. As soon as he had a chance to say these things to an American audience in an official translation of the book, he pulled back on the strings—he took his name and chapters out of the book—so that the image of Sony would be protected in the eyes of American customers. He did not want to jeopardize sales of Sony products by telling Americans what he really thought of them.

Other criticism is met by cries of "Japan-basher." Clyde Prestowitz, Chalmers Johnson, Pat Choate, James Fallows, and Karel van Wolferen have been writing well-documented critiques of Japanese government policy, business practices, and culture. Perhaps because these books and articles are so well documented, critics cannot argue the points but must instead resort to personal attacks. Because these writers do not parrot the official image of Japan, they are called Japan-bashers. Who is pulling the strings? One of the loudest voices is that of George Packard, of Johns Hopkins University. This is the same person who wrote a 16-page advertising supplement to *U.S. News & World Report* that was paid for by the Japanese Chamber of Commerce. This supplement included sections advertising the virtues of many of the heavyweight Japanese companies: Canon, Toyota, Mitsubishi, Brother, Suzuki, and Ricoh. By writing this advertisement for the Japanese Chamber of Commerce, Packard tied himself to the Japanese companies supporting the Chamber and cried "Japan-basher" when people criticicized Japan and its companies.

The Japanese government tries to pull some strings by giving social studies teachers $2 million for the purpose of furthering better awareness of the Japanese culture. They provide the teachers with a good image of Japan which, they hope, will be passed on to the students. On the other hand, a Japanese television crew comes to Lafayette, Indiana, saying "cultural awareness" to get the principal to allow them to film a "documentary" inside the school. In the version shown in Japan, the television crew pulled some strings and changed the "documentary" into a television game show. The only cultural awareness the Japanese audience was left with was that American students are immoral, undisciplined, and violent. The strings are pulled so that images going to the United States are all positive; negative images are projected from the United States to Japan.

Why can't these important images be discussed without string pulling and name calling? The actions of Akio Morita of Sony seem to characterize the string pulling better than anything else. The proper image of Japan and its companies must be maintained, no matter how hard the strings have to be pulled, so that Americans will continue to buy Japanese products. Strings are pulled so Americans will continue to believe that only Japanese companies can produce high-quality and high-tech products.

THE QUALITY PROPHETS   We used the story of the Cargo Cult

to illustrate how different cultures can misinterpret the actions of others. The natives of New Guinea wondered how the foreigners could seemingly summon the cargo at will by chanting magic words. Sometimes we have a tendency to look at Japanese companies and think that they must be using some kind of magic to be as successful as they are. Just as the Cargo Cult in New Guinea had its prophets, we have our Quality Cult prophets, who claim that they hold the secrets of the Japanese economic magic. Americans are very interested in keeping the cargo coming, so we have been listening to the prophets.

W. Edwards Deming said that he was the true quality prophet and he was responsible for much of the Japanese magic. Indeed, some of his magic words are very important: Top management must be committed to quality; statistical quality control should be practiced; and employees must learn to work better together. Many American companies seem to be following these words. Robert Eaton, the chairman of Chrysler Corporation, recently lashed out at his employees when Chrysler products did not perform as well in the J. D. Power quality indexes as he thought they should.[1] He took several concrete steps to improve performance in the future. Chrysler recently went through a reorganization to make it easier for employees to work in teams and communicate with each other. Chrysler says that this has saved them about $475 million a year and has reduced the vehicle development cycle to three and a half years, which is almost equivalent to Toyota's.[2] Maybe only someone with a strong personality like Deming's could have communicated these messages to top management. The trouble with interpreting the messages from any prophet is that we don't know whether or not the things that were prophesied would have occurred anyway.

Some of Deming's other magic words are just words. The long-range plans advocated by Deming can limit the flexibility and agility of companies. The elimination of goals can have a negative effect on motivation. Without employee assessments, the managers are handed power which can be used capriciously. It is not clear that Japanese companies use these magic words in the way that Deming intended. American companies must evaluate the magic words carefully.

In examining Deming's words in his writings and his interviews, we were surprised at the inconsistencies between his actions and his words. He was famous for his remark, "In God we trust, all others must use data."[3] Yet he ignored the data when it did not fit into his beliefs or his points. Deming said in an interview that Japanese students go to school to find knowledge,[4] yet the data from a survey showed that almost half of them went to college to find friends.[5] He was a statistician, but he dismissed half the field of statistics by saying that data collected in experiments is worthless.[6] His ideas on management are not supported by data, but are supported by anecdotes and stories. In Chapter 5, we cited anecdotes from our own experiences in Japan which ran counter to the Deming management method. In a war of anecdotes, the ammunition will not be effective without the explosive force of data.

---

[1]Jack Keebler, "Quality Woes Anger Eaton," *Automotive News,* June 27, 1994, pp. S1, S6.
[2]David Woodruff, "Chrysler May Actually Be Turning the Corner," *Business Week,* February 10, 1992, p. 32.
[3]Mary Walton, *The Deming Management Method* (New York: Dodd, Mead & Company, 1986), p. 96.
[4]Managing Change: "Deming's Demons: The Management Guru Thinks U.S. Corporations Are Crushing Their Worker Incentive," *The Wall Street Journal,* June 4, 1990, p. R39
[5]"Higher Education Criticized as Conformist and Complex," *Japan Times,* November 3, 1990, p. 2.
[6]W. Edwards Deming, *Out of the Crisis* (Cambridge, MA: MIT Press, 1982), p. 132.

Thomas Murrin, dean of Duquesne University Business School and former Westinghouse executive, remembered his interactions with Deming when he tried to hire him at Westinghouse. "He asked me twenty times if he asked me once, 'Why didn't you listen to me twenty years ago?'" "We had to treat him like God," said Murrin. "I almost had to genuflect."[7]

Magic words from other quality prophets must be evaluated carefully. In general, continuous improvement is good, but it should not be used, as it is by some Japanese companies, to increase the work of production-line employees. This results in stress and health problems. Some American computer companies have been using just-in-time manufacturing successfully to reduce inventories of finished computer products, but JIT will not always work in the United States as it does in Japan. American companies do not have the leverage over supplier companies to force warehouse, labor, and transportation costs onto the suppliers. Taguchi methods contain questionable assumptions which, if not checked, could actually cause product quality to decrease.

Some people think that there is not enough cargo to go around. If the Japanese are getting more cargo than they had in the past, Americans tend to think they are taking cargo which rightly belongs to them. The Japanese tend to think that if they let more outside cargo into their country, Japanese companies will not be able to sell their cargo. Cargo is not like gold, where there is only a very limited amount. There seems to be enough cargo for everybody, so we do not see what the big fuss is about.

Who is taking advantage of whom when it comes to this game of cargo? Americans are receiving cheap cargo from Japan, often paying less for it than the Japanese themselves. Japanese workers have to work long hours making this cargo for the rest of the world. They have more cargo than they had in the past, but because their living spaces are so inefficient and so small, they do not have much space for more cargo. The standard of living of Americans remains high, while the Japanese live in conditions more similar to those in underdeveloped nations.

PLAYING TELEPHONE WITH THE FACTS   After investigating many myths of Japanese culture, we felt that the metaphor of the children's game of telephone adequately described how the facts had become distorted in their retelling down the line. Playing telephone with the facts occurred mostly when discussing education or productivity.

In education, the literacy rates in both countries were whispered down the line. Because the Japanese do not consider functional illiteracy, their illiteracy rate stayed around 1% as it was passed down the line. For Americans, who consider all kinds of

---

[7]John Hillkirk, "World-Famous Quality Expert Dead at 93," *USA Today,* December 21, 1993, p. 1B.

definitions of illiteracy, the actual illiteracy rate started at around 1% but somewhere illiteracy got confused with functional illiteracy and the message became garbled. Illiteracy in America surged to 20% and then climbed to 40%, not because of poor teaching, but because of garbled definitions.

It began to be said that a high school diploma in Japan was equivalent to a college diploma in the United States. We could not even trace this message back to its source. The facts are that Japanese parents have to pay for extra cram schools, because the public schools are inadequate, so their children can pass the college-entrance tests. The children learn many facts, but do not become educated in the Western sense. Along the way, they lose motivation and learn to hate school. When they get to college, away from the coercion of parents and the goal of studying for a test, almost half the students cannot even motivate themselves to study five hours a week. From our experience at Purdue and USC, students with similar study habits would last only one semester at either of these institutions.

Most Americans and Japanese seem to think that Japanese companies are more productive than American companies. We believed this before finding the facts, and most Americans still seem to believe this. For many years, Japanese productivity increased faster than American productivity. After World War II, American productivity was very much higher than the rest of the world's. Over the years, other countries, not just Japan, have converged to the productivity level of the United States, but none has passed this productivity level. Somewhere down the line in the telephone game, this fact of change in productivity became garbled with productivity itself, and people started passing the message that Japanese productivity is higher than American productivity. We have seen this message of the low productivity of American companies change to state that American companies are not competitive.

The facts are much different from this garbled message. In terms of overall productivity, the Japanese have only reached the productivity level of the United States in 1963. In the important area of manufacturing productivity, Japanese companies lag behind American companies. A full 94% of American workers are employed in industries which are more competitive than their counterparts in Japan. American companies have remained competitive because of the hands-off policy of the American government and because consumers have a wide range of products from many countries to choose from. The companies have to remain competitive to stay in business. Government-sanctioned protectionism or a concerted buy-American campaign would work to destroy this competitiveness. The American consumer, through high productivity resulting in lower product prices, benefits from the open-market policy and government-supported competition. Believing the message that Japanese companies are more productive than American companies, the Japanese government has not seen any reason to correct the impediments in their markets.

Competitiveness in the American market, more than the magic words of the quality prophets, has forced American companies to manufacture higher-quality products. Restricting Japanese products from the American market would only reduce the competitiveness of American companies. Although a quality gap may have been present in the 1970s and early 1980s, we could find no current gap between American and Japanese products. As an example of closing the gap, the survey of car mechanics indicated that American cars had been increasing in quality for the last five years, while Japanese cars had not shown any improvement. American car companies were the only ones which improved through the fifteen years of the survey conducted by *Design News*, the professional magazine for design engineers.[8] Using the American experience, opening up the Japanese market to foreign products would be a good way to spur quality improvements in Japanese products. Inaction, by believing the *tatemae* of Japanese quality, hinders Japanese companies.

THE BUSINESS UTOPIA   After seeing Japanese management practices firsthand and after doing research on the experiences of others in Japanese companies, we could not see where these books and magazine articles extolling the virtues of Japanese managers were coming from. In *Theory Z*, William Ouchi describes Japanese management in terms of a business Utopia. The companies are egalitarian. Everybody has lifetime employment. The well-being of the workers takes precedence over anything else. The employees feel like part of a family. Those with ability rise to the top without any performance assessments. The companies are not arranged hierarchically. Everybody participates in decisions. Anybody in the company can talk to anyone else regardless of job title. In most cases, people do not even have to communicate verbally. Instead, employees of Japanese companies just have an intuitive feeling for what others are thinking.

We need a reality check here. One American employee of Sony, Gary Katzenstein, believing the stuff about Theory Z, wanted to talk to Morita about some of the problems he saw in company strategy. Instead of seeing Morita, company officials directed him to the company psychiatrist, who declared that he had psychiatric problems and was stuck in the "pre-nasal stage." He was fired.

Employees of Japanese companies are very status conscious. Before any business can be conducted, business cards must be exchanged so that the status of the participants can be established and the ones with real power can be identified. Consensus decision making is really used to form a consensus with what the boss has already decided. Many of the Japanese business practices can only be understood in terms of how power and authority can be concentrated in the hands of the few. The

---

[8]Robert N. Boggs, "1994 Design News Auto Survey," *Design News*, October 10, 1994, pp. 104-108.

lack of performance reviews puts power in the hands of the bosses. People can be promoted on whim. Usually, loyalty to the company and following orders, no matter how meaningless or costly, are valued more than performance on the job. Lifetime employment, for the few who have it, means that career choices are limited and the company has power to do what it wants. American employees of Japanese companies are fired at will, while Japanese employees are retained through all kinds of business hardships.

In *Theory Z* William Ouchi was exercising a traditional literary writing style in which a Utopian society is contrasted to a real society. Unlike other writers in this genre, he gave his Utopia a real name: Japan. Others have referred to their Utopias by fictional names: the Garden of Eden, Atlantis, Shangri-La, Erewhon, Walden Two. When we compared the characterization of Japanese businesses to that of Skinner's vision of Utopia in *Walden Two*, they were virtually the same. Theory Z corresponds much more closely to a Utopia than to actual Japanese business practices.

Deming saw Japanese management as the Garden of Eden. With a little history, we can appreciate his vision. He first saw Japan after World War II, when the country lay in ruins. The people had nothing. All the major factories had been destroyed. The emerging business leaders were searching for answers and were open to solutions. Deming describes how he would bring food to meetings with business leaders, because the Japanese participants had so little to eat. From nothing, Deming witnessed the genesis of the modern Japanese economy. Although it was not created in six days with a rest on the seventh, the rate of growth of these Japanese companies was almost as miraculous.

Witnessing this phenomenal growth must have colored Deming's perceptions of business practices. He viewed Japanese companies as doing everything right and American companies as doing everything wrong. When asked by a *Wall Street Journal* reporter to name an American company which was doing the right things, he could not come up with a single name. American companies had been thrown out of his Garden of Eden; Japanese companies occupied it.

We could find no evidence that Japanese businesses were doing things much different from American businesses when it came to practicing statistical quality control. We could find no evidence that American management style was the temptation which would lead Japanese business astray. In the Garden of Quality, both American and Japanese businesses were present. Deming could see Adam but not Eve.

RETURN TO THE BEAUTY PAGEANT   When we returned from Japan, people would ask us what we thought of our stay. At first, this question left us stunned and hesitant. We wanted to tell them about the good times we had had and the friends we had met. But we also wanted to tell them about the bad times, the general rudeness of the people when we ventured out on our own, and the antagonism of most of the people to foreigners and outsiders. With our special interest in the quality of products, we wanted to tell them about the poor-quality products we saw in Japan, but we didn't think they would believe us. We wanted to describe the beautiful crafts we had seen in the stores: the lacquer boxes with exquisite finishes and paper products so fragile, yet sensuous. We wanted to capture the sunlight on the crimson-red maple trees in Kyoto, to describe the stillness of the Zen rock gardens, and to relate our feelings at the sight of the thousand-crane garlands left at the foot of the memorial to children at Hiroshima. We wanted to describe the chaotic frenzies of the train stations, the mind-numbing din of a department store's toy section on a Sunday afternoon, and the cacophony of talking escalators. We also wanted to tell them about how the country was run so inefficiently that few of the businesses we encountered would survive if Japanese economy was opened to competition. With these conflicting emotions, we usually had little to say.

"It was very interesting."

And the other person, looking puzzled at our brief answer, would nod and say, "Yes, I bet it was."

Index